Jack the Ripper

Letters From Hell

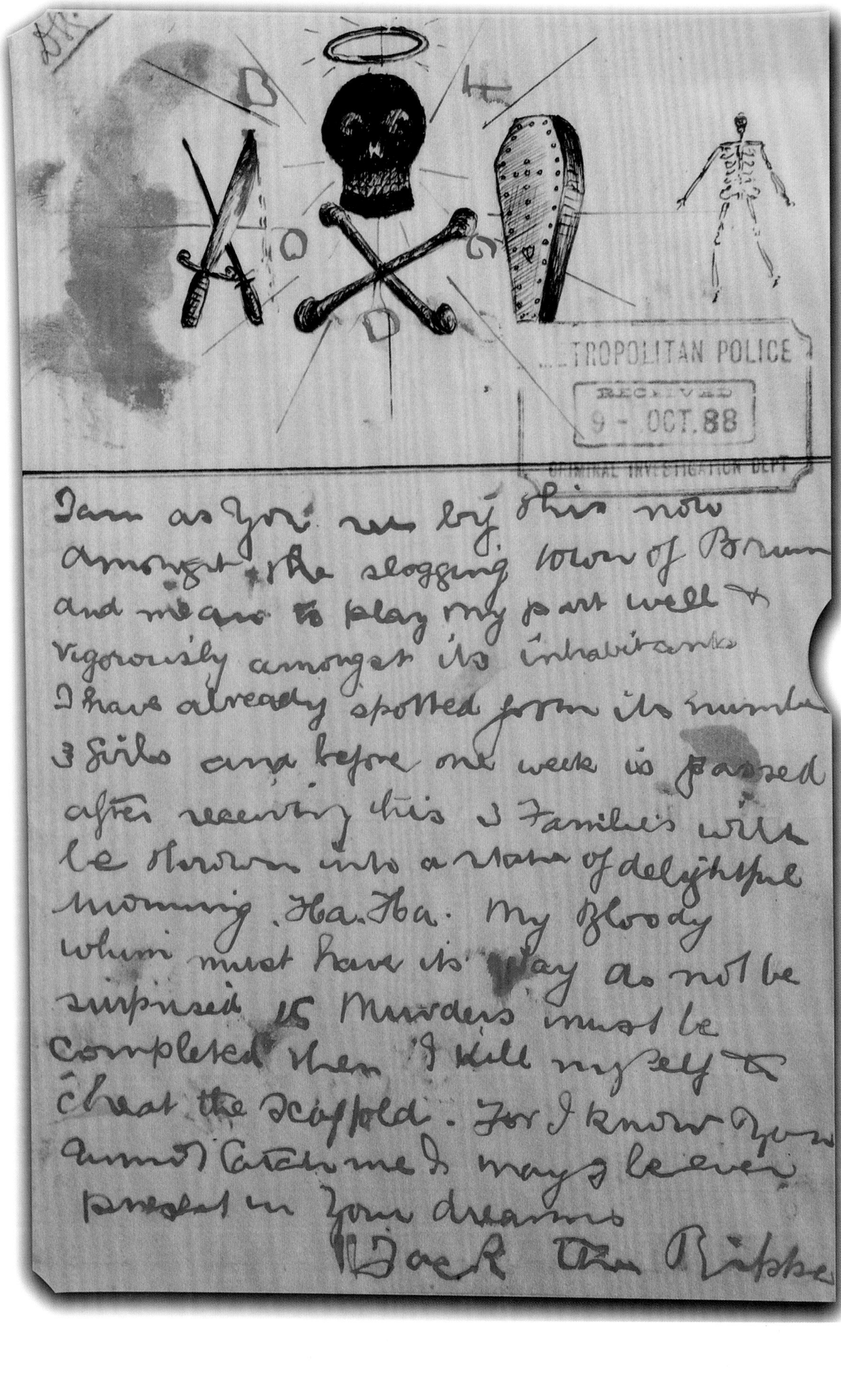

I am as you see by this now
amongst the slogging town of Brum
and means to play my part well &
vigorously amongst its inhabitants
I have already spotted from its number
3 Girls and before one week is passed
after receiving this 3 Families will
be thrown into a state of delightful
mourning Ha Ha. My bloody
whim must have its way so not be
surprised 15 Murders must be
completed then I kill myself to
cheat the scaffold. For I know you
cannot catch me & may be ever
present in your dreams

Jack the Ripper

JACK THE RIPPER

LETTERS FROM HELL

STEWART P. EVANS & KEITH SKINNER

SUTTON PUBLISHING

For Johnny Depp

First published in 2001 by
Sutton Publishing Limited · Phoenix Mill
Thrupp · Stroud · Gloucestershire · GL5 2BU

Reprinted in 2001 (twice)

British Library Cataloguing in Publication Data
A catalogue record for this book is available from the British Library

ISBN 0-7509-2549-3

Frontispiece: One of the most colourful of the 'Ripper' letters. It was posted from Birmingham and is dated 9 October 1888.

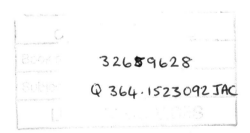

Typeset in 11.5/14pt Photina MT.
Typesetting and origination by
Sutton Publishing Limited.
Printed and bound in England by
J.H. Haynes & Co. Ltd, Sparkford.

Contents

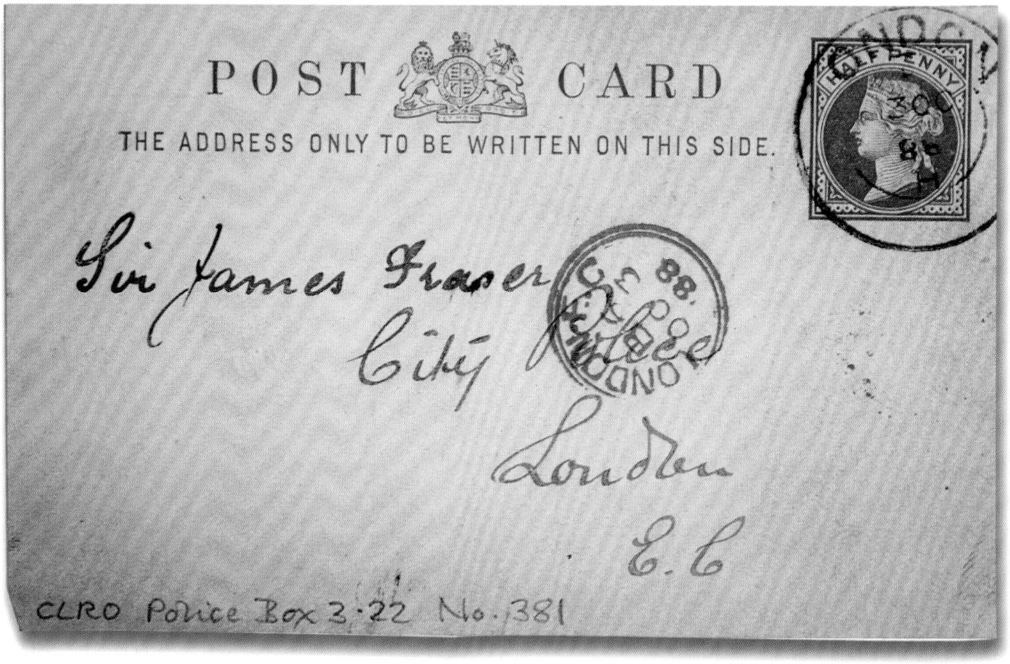
POST CARD

THE ADDRESS ONLY TO BE WRITTEN ON THIS SIDE.

Sir James Fraser
City Police
London
E.C

CLRO Police Box 3.22 No.381

Address side of postcard of 3 October 1888 sent to 'Sir James Fraser, City Police, London, E.C.'

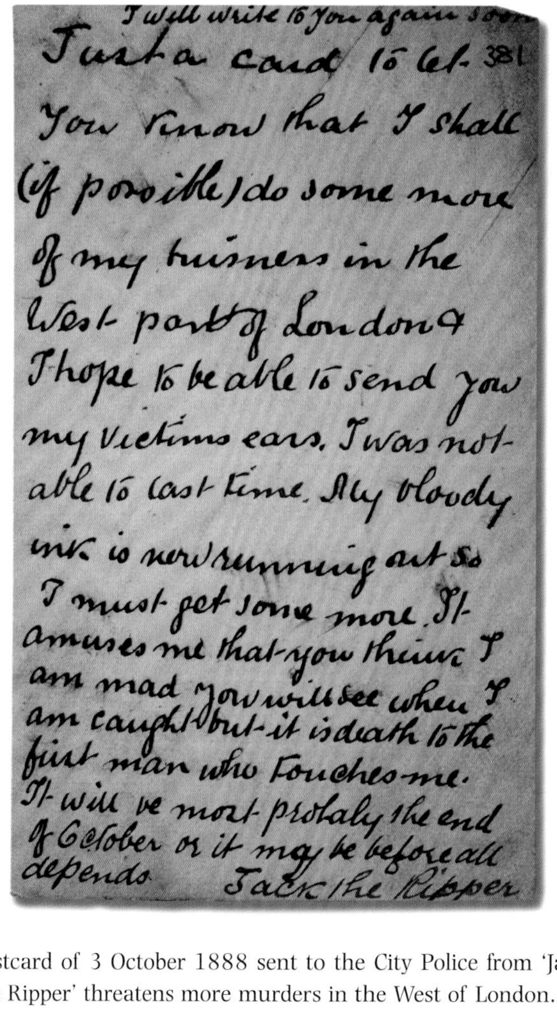
I will write to you again soon
Just a card to let- 381
You know that I shall
(if possible) do some more
of my business in the
West part of London &
I hope to be able to send you
my victims ears. I was not
able to last time. My bloody
ink is now running out so
I must get some more. It
amuses me that you think I
am mad you will see when I
am caught but it is death to the
first man who touches me.
It will be most probaly the end
of October or it may be before all
depends Jack the Ripper

Postcard of 3 October 1888 sent to the City Police from 'Jack the Ripper' threatens more murders in the West of London.

Foreword by Martin Fido

BETWEEN 1958 and 1965 Donald McCormick, Tom Cullen and Robin Odell wrote the three books that determined the popular view of the Whitechapel murders for the next thirty years. They offered different suspects as the real Jack the Ripper: Dr Alexandr Pedachenko, Montague John Druitt, and an unknown Jewish shochet, or ritual butcher. The common reader like myself found each identification quite convincing as he read it, and kept changing his mind about which was the Ripper. And their overall picture of the case was not seriously challenged until Donald Rumbelow's *The Complete Jack the Ripper* appeared in 1975. By accessing the Scotland Yard files denied to McCormick, Cullen and Odell, Rumbelow was able to correct some of their misconceptions.

High among these was the conviction that the Whitechapel murderer himself wrote many of the letters confessing to the crimes that reached Scotland Yard. In particular, he wrote the famous 'Dear Boss' letter and 'Saucy Jacky' postcard addressed to 'the Boss' at the Central News Agency and signed 'Jack the Ripper', which gave the killer a nickname and the world an icon of horror. To this day one is likely to read as 'fact' that Jack the Ripper wrote to the police, taunting them; that he named himself; and that this represents a common practice of multiple murderers.

Actually, despite some high-profile cases like David Berkowitz 'the Son of Sam', the undetected 'Zodiac killer', and the Conn Edison and Una-bombers, it is not especially common for such men to inject themselves into their cases by correspondence. But the historical interest of the cache of Ripper letters held by the Metropolitan and City of London police forces is undiminished. And here, thanks to Stewart Evans and Keith Skinner, who have already given the world of Ripper studies the absolutely indispensable *Ultimate Source Book*, the entire collection is made available to the general reader, with full-colour reproductions of the most important of them, and the best long essay that has ever been written on the Ripper letters.

The general reader will have the opportunity to study facsimiles of the originals, and come to his or her own conclusion as to whether the 'Moab and Midian' letter forwarded by the Central News Agency to Scotland Yard really was (as document examiner Sue Iremonger believed) in the same hand as the 'Dear Boss' letter, and whether the handwriting suggests that Tom Bulling, the journalist who sent the cover letter, could have been the actual author of both. He or she will be able to scrutinise for him- or herself the red ink dots in the 'Dear Boss', and come to whatever conclusions seem appropriate concerning its perfect spelling and adequate grammar, but variously missing or unnecessary punctuation. Stewart Evans' brilliant observation can be confirmed by examination: that the so-called 'Lees' letter, long believed to show some contemporary awareness of the spiritualist medium R.J. Lees' pretended involvement in the case, is actually a 'tecs' letter, making no reference to Lees at all.

The true crime buff may find his attention grabbed by the end of the book, seeing the letter apparently claiming that Mrs Phoebe Hogg was killed by Jack the Ripper, and not by her husband's lover Mary Eleanor Pearcey (who was sometimes herself accused of the Whitechapel murders by those who thought Jack the Ripper might really be Jill). He may be fascinated to see the charge that 'Wainwright's grandson' was one of the Ripper's gang of three, recalling the Whitechapel murderer Henry Wainwright (who cut up and buried his mistress in his warehouse, and then in 1875 had to transport her parcelled-up remains to Southwark by cab when he was evicted for bankruptcy). He will read with fascination the long doggerel poem attacking 'Funk [or 'Flunk'], stupid fool' which seems to be aimed at the self-important lawyer-asylum keeper L. Forbes Winslow for his insistence that the murderer must be a lunatic connected with Finsbury, and that Winslow had taken possession of his boots. And the dedicated Ripper expert will be fascinated by the absent poems. Of all the famous rhymes ascribed to the Ripper, only one has been found on the files:

> O have you seen the devle
> with his mikerscope and scalpul
> a lookin at a Kidney
> With a slide cocked up.

The East End murders featured in periodicals of the day. Here members of the Whitechapel Vigilance Committee are depicted on the lookout for suspicious characters, as published in the *Illustrated London News* of 13 October 1888.

Not even the likeliest (and by far the best written, best rhyming and best scanning) of the others, the rhyme quoted by Chief Constable Sir Melville Macnaghten, is to be found:

> I'm not a butcher, I'm not a Yid,
> Nor yet a foreign skipper,
> But I'm your own light-hearted friend,
> Yours truly, Jack the Ripper.

But then, given Macnaghten's suspected propensity for retaining sensational documents as souvenirs, he might well have absconded permanently with any Ripper letter if it were addressed directly to him or his office.

And all categories of reader should enjoy the coarse forgotten nickname 'Bill the Boweller' that one writer offered as a substitute for Jack the Ripper.

The dedicated Ripper enthusiast who follows debates on the internet will probably regret the courtesy with which Keith Skinner has effaced himself from chapters 15 and 16, while Stewart Evans has carefully refrained from saying anything to which Keith might take exception. For it could have been illuminating to read their apparent disagreement over the vexed question of the late Donald McCormick's sources.

McCormick, the first of the postwar writers on the Ripper, was also the one to give the strongest boost to the Ripper letters. He averred that Dr Thomas Dutton had established by microphotography (and nobody disputes that the intended process must have been what is now called photomicrography: the enlargement rather than the diminution of images by many magnifications) that at least thirty-four of the Ripper letters, including the 'Dear Boss', were in the same hand as the chalk graffiti found on a doorway in Goulston Street over a portion of victim Katherine Eddowes' apron, and long believed to be the work of the murderer. McCormick claimed that many facts he offered were verified by Dr Dutton's handwritten 'Chronicles of Crime', from which Dutton had allowed him to take notes in 1932. And he cited as one of several previously unprinted 'Ripper' rhymes and writings, a piece of doggerel beginning:

> Eight little whores, with no hope of heaven,
> Gladstone may save one, then there'll be seven.

Now it is easy to demonstrate from the successive editions of McCormick's book that he was an utterly unreliable writer, who fudged or fabricated his 'evidence' to fit other people's new discoveries when it suited him. It is not without interest that one of McCormick's own books discussed Gladstone's personal 'mission' to convert streetwalkers. The only living writer to have succeeded in wresting an interview on the Ripper with McCormick came away persuaded that the Dutton 'Chronicles' were at the least misquoted, and may well have been effectively invented by McCormick as a fake source for his own speculations and inventions. He suggested that McCormick might himself have placed the entries in the press which appear to confirm that the 'Chronicles' existed at the time of Dutton's death in 1935. He formed the impression that McCormick had in essence confessed to him that 'Eight little whores' was not a genuine survival from 1888, and he has suggested that it was really written by

McCormick's friend Ian Fleming. But the more he has been pressed for clarification on exactly how much McCormick explicitly admitted, the more it has seemed that a good many of his own conclusions rest on highly subjective deductions from McCormick's evasive replies.

Evidently Stewart and Keith differ as to how completely McCormick has been debunked, or, perhaps more precisely, what degree of credit may be given to ideas supposedly deriving from Dr Dutton's lost 'Chronicles'. One can only regret that the two researchers who know more than anybody else about the letters, both on file and as recorded in books, have put consideration for each other above the relentless pursuit of truth through debate. At the same time, one can only applaud their good manners and delicacy.

This whole question of confessions and sensational information springing up around notorious murders is by no means a matter buried in the past. As the manuscript of *Letters From Hell* reached me, I was in the process of sorting my files following a move, and I had just turned up a forgotten letter that LBC Radio passed on to me a few years ago. It opens:

> In regards to Lee Harvey, Oswald the assassin, I would like to put your friend Martin Fido right on some things that seems to be troubling him. I first met Lee here in London outside the House where he shared a flat With wife, JACK RUBY, and a young chap named RAY, He introduced Jack Ruby as his best buddy in the world, better even than his Brother.

The writer gives his address and signs his name. But the crude insensitivity with which he tries to inflate his own importance by purveying a pack of lies linking Oswald, Oswald's own killer, and Martin Luther King's murderer in a plot to kill Kennedy might just as well have been datelined 'From Hell', and signed, JACK the RIPPER.

Introduction

IN November 1987 a large brown envelope was sent anonymously to New Scotland Yard. It bore a Croydon postmark. Fingerprint tests were carried out but they did not lead to the identification of the sender. The envelope contained old documents relating to the Dr Crippen case and the 'Jack the Ripper' murders. Included was a letter written in red ink, together with its envelope and original police mounting sheet. The letter was creased, a piece was missing from one side, and the ink had bled into the rather poor-quality paper. For many years this infamous document, with its now almost illegible postscript, had been missing from Scotland Yard's files, believed taken as a souvenir by a senior police officer. The public announcement about the return of the documents was not made until August 1988 when it received considerable press coverage and the Deputy Commissioner, John Dellow, gave interviews to reporters. The 'Dear Boss' letter had hit the news again almost a century after its first exposure. A headline in the *Sun* of Friday 19 August 1988 said it all: 'Ripper Taunts Police Again 100 Years On'.

This book includes an examination of that letter and many others. They represent a large body of frequently overlooked primary source material in the official Metropolitan Police files and the City of London Police papers: the correspondence generated by the Whitechapel Murders of 1888–91 and purporting to have been sent by the killer. Other

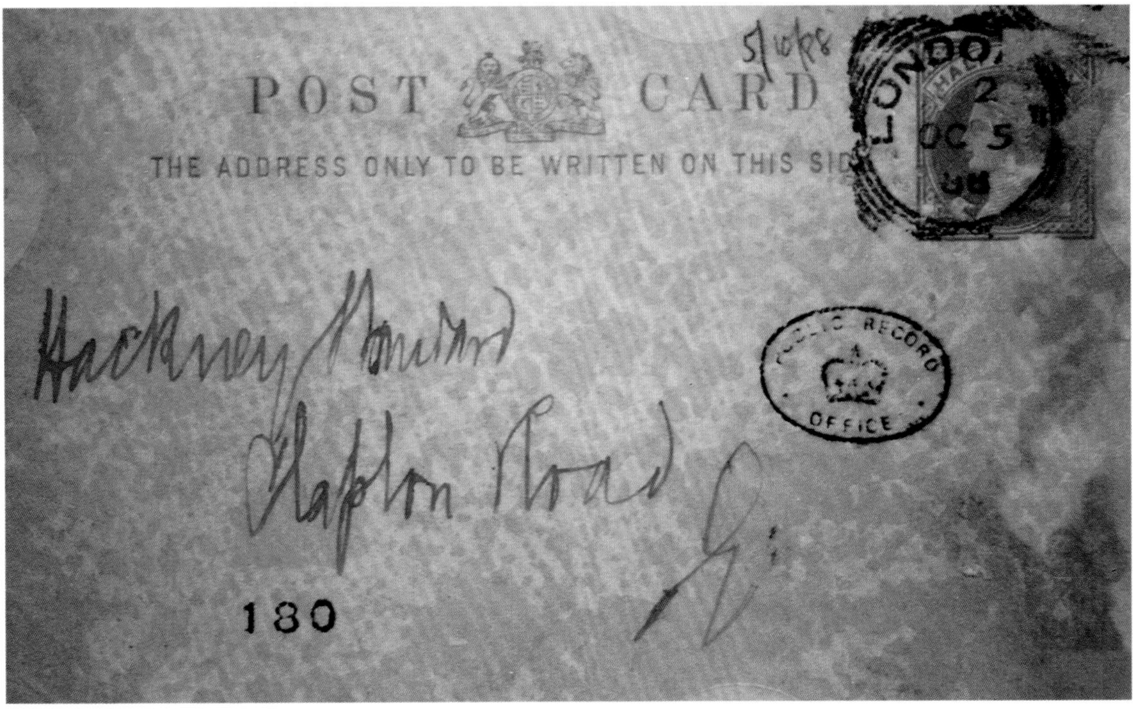

Postcard of 5 October to the *Hackney Standard* (*see* page 95).

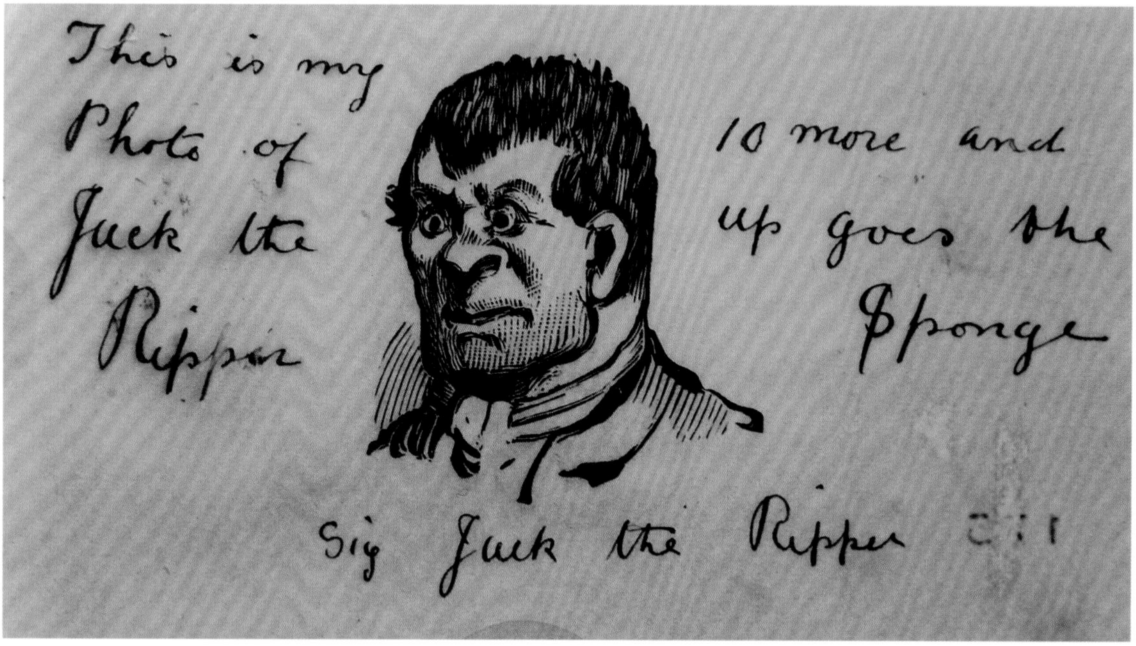

This is my Photo of Jack the Ripper

10 more and up goes the Sponge

Sig Jack the Ripper

Letter dated 12 November 1888 and posted in London WC. It includes a self-portrait of the writer who claims to be 'Jack the Ripper'.

authors have surveyed these documents, of course, but our work has involved examining and transcribing the original letters in the archives. This, we believe, is the only way to fully understand how the correspondence impacted on the case, and to appreciate, almost marvel, at the striking visual impact of some of the letters. Their historical importance lies in their huge social relevance; they reveal not only the thinking of the time, but also the profound effect that the murders had on some individuals and on the Victorian newspapers.

Some of the letters have deteriorated little over the years. Others have fared less well. Much depends on the quality of the paper used. Some are friable, others robust, but at least now they are all properly conserved. The envelopes preserved with some of the letters in the Metropolitan Police files at the Public Record Office (PRO) appear to have suffered the attention of a keen philatelist at some time. Many never bore a postage stamp and are stamped with the Post Office's *2d* charge as a result, but most of those that did have a postage stamp have not survived intact. Presumably prior to their deposit in the PRO someone tore off most of the postage stamps thus damaging these valuable historical documents and removing the information that was carried by their postmarks.

We have not attempted a psychological assessment of these letters, which is beyond the scope of this book and certainly beyond the capability of both authors! But we have been struck by how charged some of them are with emotional energy and personality. A closer study and analysis of them may reveal facets and themes worth exploring or developing. We have merely presented the preserved scripts, thus making them readily available for the first time. What we may be certain of, however, is that the legend of 'Jack the Ripper' resulted from and has endured because of this correspondence. Experts on the case are divided over the status of the documents. We know for certain that some series murderers do write letters to the police, so the possibility can never be excluded that within this material there is an actual letter, or letters, from the real 'Jack the Ripper'.

Part One

Middlesex Street (Petticoat Lane) was at the heart of 'Ripper' territory and was the 'old clothes' district of the East End where the main market commodity was clothing. It was the centre of the Jewish quarter. This photograph, taken in the 1890s, shows the busy Sunday market.

A London street scene from the 1880s – a lost child is spoken to by a police officer. (From the *Illustrated London News*)

— ONE —

'Fifteen more and I give myself up . . .'

THE setting for the so-called Whitechapel murders was the Metropolitan Police-patrolled East End of London and the eastern limits of the City Police area around Aldgate and Bishopsgate. In the late 1880s this was the very poorest area of London and the location of the capital's most squalid and shameful slums. American author Jack London later appropriately called it 'The Abyss'. London was the greatest city in the world in 1888, but the East End was a festering sore on that greatness. A confidential police report to the Home Office of 25 October 1888 stated:

> . . . there has been no return hitherto of the probable numbers of brothels in London, but during the last few months I have been tabulating the observations of Constables on their beats, and have come to the conclusion that there are 62 houses known to be brothels on the H or Whitechapel Divn and probably a great number of other houses which are more or less intermitently [*sic*] used for such purposes.
>
> The number of C.L.Hs. [Common Lodging Houses] is 233, accommodating 8,530 persons, we have no means of ascertaining what women are prostitutes and who are not, but there is an impression that there are about 1200 prostitutes, mostly of a very low condition . . .
>
> The lower class of C.L.Hs. is naturally frequented by prostitutes, thieves & tramps as there is nowhere else for them to go, & no law to prevent their congregating there.
>
> I fear that in driving the Brothel keepers away from certain neighbourhoods much is being done to demoralise London generally, it is impossible to stop the supply while the demand exists . . .
>
> [MEPO 3/141 ff. 158–63]

Our story begins on 3 April 1888, when a gang of three ruffians, one aged only about nineteen, attacked a prostitute named Emma Smith in the street in Whitechapel. She was fearfully injured when a blunt instrument was thrust into her vagina and she died

PC Neil discovering the body of Mary Ann Nichols in Buck's Row, Whitechapel, 31 August 1888.

of peritonitis the morning of the following day at the London Hospital in Whitechapel Road. Robbery was the probable motive and her attackers were never identified. This was later to become known, officially, as the first Whitechapel murder.

On Tuesday 7 August 1888, the body of a second prostitute, Martha Tabram (or Turner), was discovered on the first-floor landing of tenement dwellings called George Yard Buildings in George Yard, Whitechapel. She had been violently stabbed thirty-nine times, one wound penetrating the sternum. Her assailant was never discovered. The press commented on the brutality of this attack, but it was not accorded any great significance. The local CID Inspector, Edmund Reid, carried out a thorough investigation but, again, no offender was identified. No connection was made with the previous murder, and with good reason; undoubtedly the two attacks were unrelated. Tabram had, in all probability, fallen victim to one of her own clients, a risk that all prostitutes take.

When a third prostitute, Mary Ann Nichols, fell to a murderer's knife in Buck's Row, Whitechapel, on Friday 31 August the police, press and public became alarmed. Nichols had been killed in the street, her throat deeply cut, and mutilations inflicted on her abdomen and genital area. Indeed, so deep were her wounds that her viscera protruded from the abdominal cuts. A third unsolved prostitute murder had now occurred in the same geographic area, and was of a similar brutal nature. Past history showed that although this was a violent area of London, murder was not common in the district. The three Whitechapel murders were immediately identified as a 'series' and the press proclaimed that a homicidal maniac was on the loose. The 'fiend', as yet unidentified, had been born, but remained unnamed. 'The Whitechapel Murderer' seemed the most logical title to give him, as no other was known. Even though the name 'Jack the Ripper' had yet to be invented, the legend quickly began to take shape.

Hardly had the excitement over the Nichols' murder subsided when the worst fears seemed to be confirmed. The body of a fourth prostitute, Annie Chapman, was found on the morning of Saturday 8 September in the back yard of 29 Hanbury Street, Spitalfields. The throat had been cut, too, almost to the point of decapitation, and the poor woman had been disembowelled. To heap horror upon horror, the doctor's examination revealed that the killer had removed and taken away her uterus and part of her bladder and vagina. There were two cheap rings missing from one of her fingers. The police could find no clue to the identity of the murderer but as a result of questioning of East End prostitutes the name of a suspect had emerged, 'Leather Apron'. This nickname had been bestowed upon a Jewish slipper-maker called John Pizer who wore the garment that provided his appellation as part of his trade clothing. It was claimed that he extorted money from the prostitutes and bullied them. The nickname was a gift for the sensational press but Pizer's eventual arrest and appearance at Chapman's inquest resulted in his elimination from the police inquiry.

It was in connection with the Chapman murder that there was an early press suggestion of a communication from the murderer. *The Times* of Monday 10 September carried the following report:

An atmospheric illustration from 1888 showing a Victorian pillar-box and street scene. (*Punch*)

> The police, however, have been unable to discover any person who saw the deceased alive after 2 a.m., about which time she left the lodging-house at 35, Dorset-street, because she had not 4d. to pay for her bed. No corroboration of the reported statement that she was served in a public house at Spitalfields Market on it opening at 5 a.m. could be gained, nor of the sensational report that the murderer left a message on the wall in the yard, which was made out to read, "Five; 15 more and then I give myself up." Nevertheless, the police express a strong opinion that more murders of the kind will be committed before the miscreant is apprehended.

The *Daily Telegraph* of the same date carried a similar report, with an additional angle to the story:

> A number of sensational stories are altogether without corroboration, such, for instance, as the tale that writing was seen on the wall of No. 29: "I have now done three, and intend to do nine more and give myself up." One version says some such threat as "Five – Fifteen more and I give myself up," was written upon a piece of paper that was picked up . . .

Although this 'writing on the wall' and 'piece of paper' were totally apocryphal, as far as can be ascertained, the image of the unknown murderer was being developed and the scene set for future alleged communications from the killer, including graffiti.

One of the early theorists spawned by this series of murders wrote to *The Times* and his letter was published on Wednesday 12 September. He was the alienist Dr Lyttleton Stewart Forbes Winslow, who had long experience in dealing with the mentally afflicted:

> TO THE EDITOR OF THE TIMES.
>
> Sir, – My theory having been circulated far and wide with reference to an opinion given to the authorities of the Criminal Investigation Department, I would like to qualify such statements in your columns.
>
> That the murderer of the three victims in Whitechapel is one and the same person I have no doubt.
>
> The whole affair is that of a lunatic, and as there is "a method in madness," so there was method shown in the crime and in the gradual dissection of the body of the latest victim. It is not the work of a responsible person. It is a well-known and accepted fact that homicidal mania is incurable, but difficult of detection, as it frequently lies latent. It is incurable, and those who have been the subject of it should never be let loose on society.
>
> I think that the murderer is not of the class of which 'Leather Apron' belongs, but is of the upper class of society, and I still think that my opinion given to the authorities is the correct one – viz., that the murders have been committed by a lunatic lately discharged from some asylum, or by one who has escaped. If the former, doubtless one who, though suffering from the effects of homicidal mania, is apparently sane on the surface, and consequently has been liberated, and is following out the inclinations of his morbid imaginations by wholesale homicide. I think the advice given by me a sound one – to apply for an immediate return from all asylums who have discharged such individuals, with a view of ascertaining their whereabouts. I am your obedient servant,
>
> L. FORBES WINSLOW, M.B. Camb., D.C.L. Oxon.
>
> 70, Wimpole-street, Cavendish-square, W., Sept. 11.

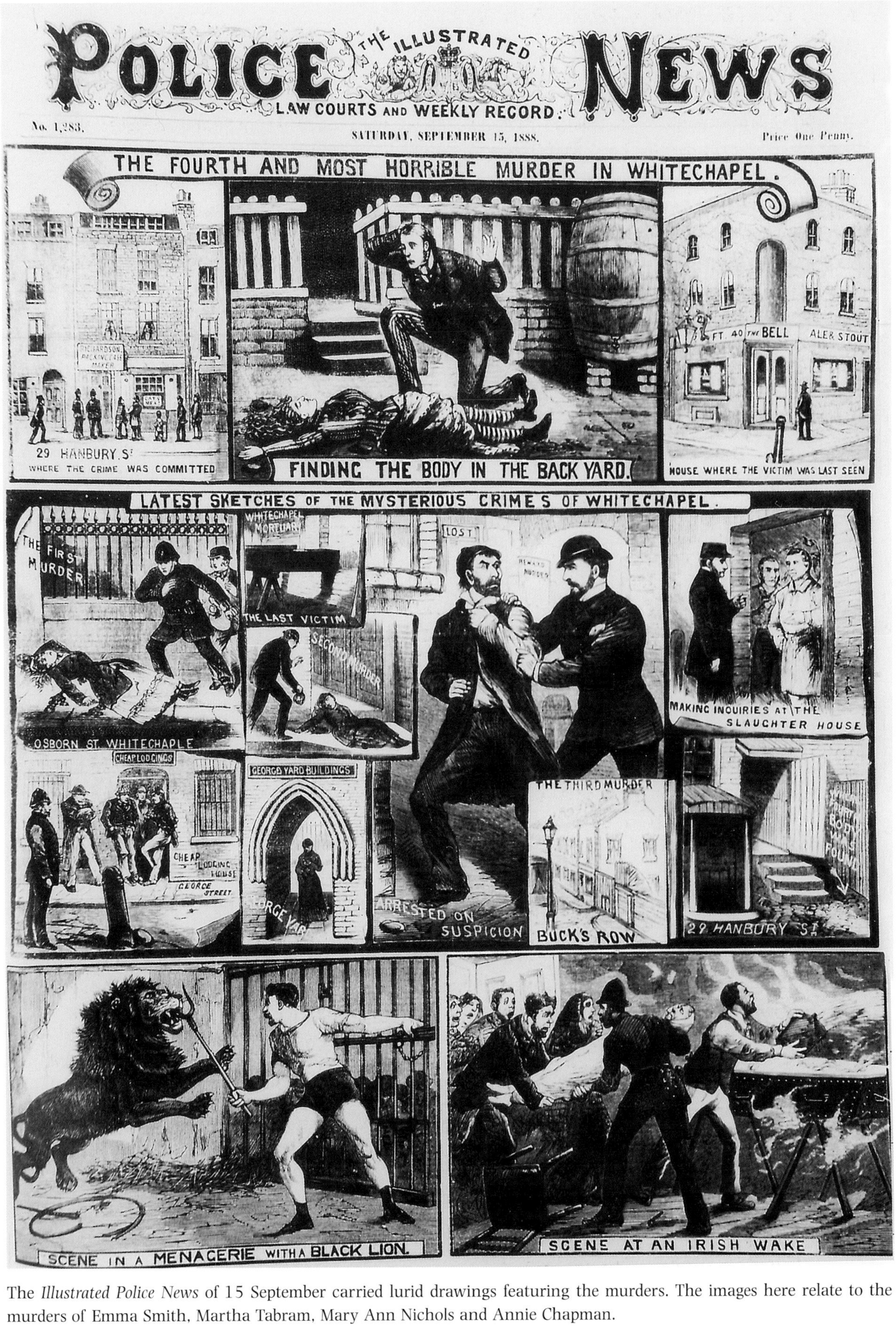

The *Illustrated Police News* of 15 September carried lurid drawings featuring the murders. The images here relate to the murders of Emma Smith, Martha Tabram, Mary Ann Nichols and Annie Chapman.

It was the era of the 'new journalism' and the result of all the high-profile press coverage of the murders, the inquests and the arrest of suspects led to great public excitement, fear and curiosity. The story was selling newspapers on an unprecedented scale. The tabloid press was quick to exploit the tragedies and interest was international. Unknown to the press at the time, a letter was sent, its envelope addressed in a fairly neat hand, to 'Sir Charles Warren, commissioner of police, Scotland Yard'. There was no stamp on the envelope and written across the top was 'on her majesterys service'. The postmark was 'LONDON S.E.' and it was dated 'SP 24 88'; 24 September was the closing day of the Chapman inquest and there was wide coverage in the papers. The letter was received by the Criminal Investigation Department of the Metropolitan Police on 25 September. It read:

> Sep 24 1888
>
> Dear sir
>
> I do wish to give myself up I am in misery with nightmare I am the man who committed all these murders in the last six months my name is so [silhouette of coffin] and so I am a horse slauterer and work at Name [blocked out] address [blocked out] I have found the woman I wanted that is chapman and I done what I called slautered her but if any one comes I will surrender but I am not going to walk to the station by myself so I am yours truly
>
> [second page] keep the Boro road clear or I might take a trip up there
>
> photo [silhouette of a knife] knife
>
> this is the knife that I done these murders with it is a small handle with a large long blade sharpe both sides

The writer of this letter cannot have realised it, but he was to be the forerunner of many who were to plague the police with such communications. In fact, this letter heralded the arrival of its more famous contemporary two days later. The writer also introduced themes that were to recur in later correspondence. He revealed that he was following the press reports by picking up on suspects such as three horse slaughterers (in the Nichols case) and by describing his knife – a description the doctors had ventured at the inquest hearings. Slaughterers, and butchers, were to remain popular as suspects throughout the story of the murders.

This letter did not contain anything that the police could say was known only to the killer, and there is nothing to suggest that they took it seriously. Indeed, the police often received hoax and crank letters in relation to high-profile murder cases that were reported in the newspapers. The motives of the authors of such letters were as diverse as the writers themselves. They included the purely malicious taking the opportunity to ridicule the hated police, the jokers hoping to see their work cause consternation, the grudge-bearers seeking to place false blame for the murders, and those merely hoping to see their misguided writings published.

Such letters may have been easily set aside by the police for what they were, but others seriously misled them and wasted valuable time in the hunt for the murderer. It had been seen before and would be seen again. However, in this case letter-writing was to become a true sensation spawning a deluge of postal communications the like of which had never before been experienced, a deluge that would continue for almost two years before dwindling to a trickle.

on her majestery's service

Sir Charles Warren

commissioner of

police

Scotland Yard

immediately

LONDON·S.E
12
SP24
88

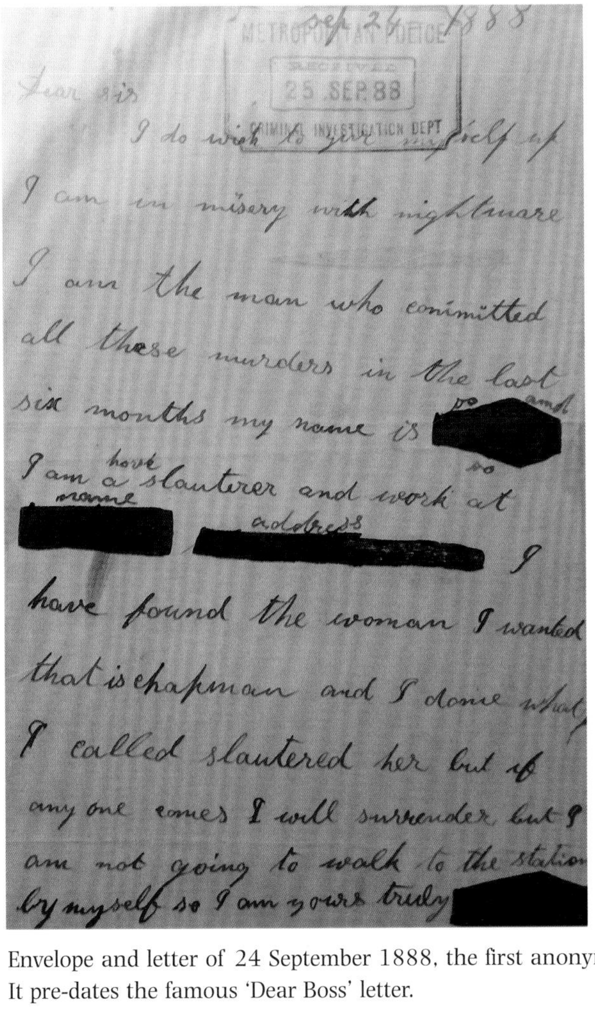

sep 24 1888

METROPOLITAN POLICE
RECEIVED
25 SEP.88
CRIMINAL INVESTIGATION DEPT

Dear Sir

I do wish to give myself up

I am in misery with nightmare

I am the man who committed

all these murders in the last

six months my name is [redacted] so and so

I am a horse slauterer and work at

name [redacted] address [redacted] I

have found the woman I wanted

that is chapman and I done what

I called slautered her but if

any one comes I will surrender but I

am not going to walk to the station

by myself so I am yours truly [redacted]

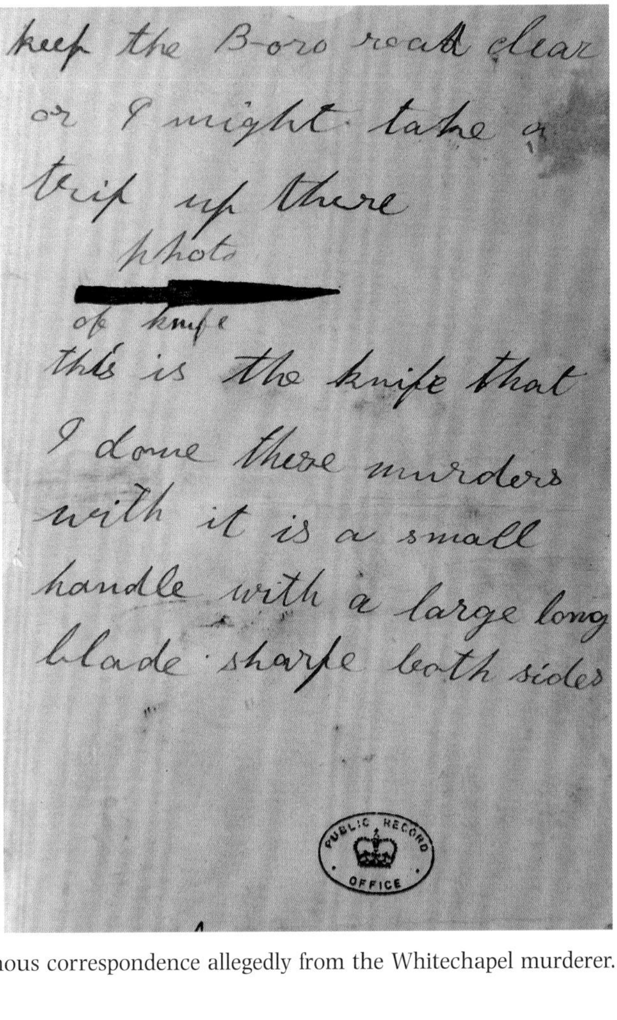

keep the B-oro road clear

or I might take a

trip up there

photo

of knife

this is the knife that

I done these murders

with it is a small

handle with a large long

blade sharpe both sides

PUBLIC RECORD OFFICE

Envelope and letter of 24 September 1888, the first anonymous correspondence allegedly from the Whitechapel murderer. It pre-dates the famous 'Dear Boss' letter.

Left: Stamping letters by hand.
Opposite: The General Post Office's great stone building at St Martin's-le-Grand in the City of London. It was the headquarters of the exceedingly efficient Victorian postal service.

Another worrying aspect of such letter-writers, regardless of the case, is that they are rarely identified, let alone prosecuted. To browse through the dozens of communications preserved in the Metropolitan Police MEPO 3/142 file held at the Public Record Office is a daunting task – there are some 210 of them, not even chronologically arranged. They vary from the barely literate to the respectable and articulate. Among them are some of great interest, and, for all we know, possibly even one or more from the killer himself. It is this possibility that has encouraged past writers and researchers to examine many of the letters carefully in the hope that they may contain some sort of clue or support for a particular theory or suspect.

The General Post Office of 1888 was a well-established government postal service and enjoyed a high reputation for efficiency and security. It was the most popular of the government departments. According to the Postmaster-General, 1,700 million letters and postcards were received per annum, of which nearly a third were delivered in London. The sorting of the letters was quite sophisticated and was done in batches of fifty, the fifty-first stamp being placed in each case on a strip of paper instead of on a letter, so that the number of stamps on the strip gave a tally of the number of fifties that had passed through the operator's hands. In each gallery an officer in charge of a rack changed the stamps with every mail. Each stamper had to get his stamp from the rack and sign for it in a book. The postmark on the letter thus showed not only

the office from which the letter was despatched, but the mail by which it was sent, and the person by whom the impression was made.*

The initials of the London postal districts were added to addresses on letters to guarantee increased security against misdelivery or delay, and ensured increased postal efficiency. Within the EC district there were twelve daily deliveries, and in the other districts eleven. The first commenced about 7 a.m. and, except on Mondays and busy days when there were large arrivals of foreign post, was generally completed throughout London by 9 a.m. In the EC district the second delivery began at about 8.30 a.m. and included the correspondence received by night mail from Ireland and the north mails which arrived at 8 a.m. The third delivery in the EC area corresponded with the second delivery in other districts and began at about 10 a.m. It included the letters collected in London generally at 8.45 a.m. and the correspondence from the 'Scotch mail', which arrived at about 9 a.m. The following nine deliveries were made in every district hourly, and included all letters reaching the General Post Office, or the district post offices, in time for each despatch. The last delivery, extending to all districts, began at 7.45 p.m. Each took about an hour.

* W.J. Gordon, *How London Lives* (The Religious Tract Society, *c.* 1890).

The collection of mail was regular and efficient. The latest times for posting letters at the chief district offices, branch offices, receiving houses and pillar-boxes for the London and suburban despatches, and for the inland, colonial and foreign mails were listed in published tables. In the town districts generally, and in certain suburbs where there was a collection from pillar-boxes at 3 a.m., the receiving office letter-boxes were closed during the night and on Sundays. This was so that letters could not be posted there, but had to be put into pillar-boxes and so had the advantage of the early collection. The main General Post Office was situated at St Martin's-le-Grand. The main district offices were Holborn (WC), Islington (N), Commercial Road East (E), Blackman Street Borough (SE), Buckingham Gate (SW), Vere Street (W), and Eversholt Street (NW). A fine example of a Victorian pillar-box can still be seen in the High Street, Kensington; it is one of the oldest in London.

On Sundays all post offices in the London district were closed, with the exception of those open for the receipt and despatch of telegrams during stated hours. Letters posted on Sundays in pillar-boxes within London's limits, and in some of the nearer suburbs, were collected early on Monday morning in time for the general day mails, and for the first London district delivery.*

Old documents, such as letters, have always held a fascination for historians, researchers and collectors alike. In their yellowing pages many secrets may be found, as well as previously unknown snippets of information; and this is particularly so in connection with an historical murder mystery such as the Ripper case. What is very evident from an examination of the contemporary press and police files, is that the correspondence had an extraordinary and lasting effect on this case. It started a legend that was not to die. It ensured the creation of a 'Ripper'-based industry that thrives today, over 100 years after the event. It also created a super-villain, an enduring bogeyman whose name would figure larger in the annals of crime than any other murderer. And his real name is still unknown.

The famous Victorian journalist, author, playwright and criminologist, George R. Sims (1847–1922), closely followed the murders and provided an informed commentary on the developing story and its great relevance to the press of the day. His regular contributions to the Sunday newspaper the *Referee* appeared under the heading 'Mustard and Cress', and he wrote using the *nom de plume* 'Dagonet' (Dagonet was King Arthur's fool in Malory's *Morte d'Arthur*). Sims was quick to recognise the significance of the crimes. In the *Referee* of 9 September 1888, he wrote:

> The Whitechapel murders, which have come to the relief of newspaper editors in search of a sensation, are not the kind of murders which pay best. The element of romance is altogether lacking, and they are crimes of the coarsest and most vulgar brutality – not the sort of murders that can be discussed in the drawing-room and the nursery with any amount of pleasure. The best element in the cases for newspaper purposes is that they are similar to a murder which was committed near the same spot some time previously, and this enables the talented journalist to start the idea that the four crimes are by the same hand. Given this

* *Dickens's Dictionary of London 1888* (Moretonhampstead, Old House Books, reprint).

George R. Sims, the Victorian journalist, author, playwright and criminologist who was intensely interested in the Ripper murders and wrote extensively on them in the *Referee*.

idea, and "the maniac who lures women into lonely spots and cuts them up" speedily assumes a definite shape. If only the women had belonged to another class, or been in more comfortable circumstances, there might, with skilful manipulation, have been worked up an excitement almost equal to the Marr and Williamson sensation [the so-called Ratcliffe Highway murders of 1811 when two East End families, the Marrs and the Williamsons, were murdered by John Williams].

The murder of the Marrs created such a widespread panic that it led to a great reform in the police administration of the metropolis. The old Charley was voted an anachronism, and he gave way to a corps of civilian guards, who have since developed into our helmeted Roberts. The Whitechapel murder looks like causing the question of inadequate police protection to be trotted out again. As a matter of fact the London police force is utterly inadequate to the growing needs of the rapidly increasing metropolis. The wonder is, not that so many attacks on life and property are made with impunity, but that there are so few. If the criminal classes had anything like organisation, London would be at their mercy.

The police up to the moment of writing are still at sea as to the series of Whitechapel murders – a series with such a strong family likeness as to point conclusively to one assassin or firm of assassins. The detective force is singularly lacking in the smartness and variety of resource which the most ordinary detective displays in the shilling shocker. As a rule, your modern detective waits for "information," instead of making a clue for himself by joining together the links of circumstantial evidence. In the Whitechapel cases the theory is that there is either a maniac at the bottom of them, or that they are the work of a "High Rip" gang. That theory should be followed up until it is proved to be a false one. The decoy system might very well be tried. Decoys could be sent out all over the neighbourhood, and the chances are the bird would be caught by one of them. If a number of old gentlemen had been knocked down and robbed of their gold chains in a certain neighbourhood, the best thing would be to dress up a police agent as an old gentleman, give him a chain, and tell him to expose himself to danger. Directly the thief came he could give the signal, and his confederates in the force would close in, and the thief would be caught. Scotland-yard ought to be able to put temptation in the way of the Whitechapel ruffian (if he is an habitual woman murderer) to make him walk into the trap.

The astute Sims had identified, even at this early stage, its huge potential for the press. His words are at once very colourful and of the greatest importance. Public interest was aroused; the papers were selling as never before. And the missing key to the development of the sensation had been provided. The unknown killer, as we have seen, now had a name – 'Leather Apron'. On 16 September, Sims wrote in the *Referee*:

Room for Leather Apron! . . .

It is only the careful observer, the close student of our insular everyday life, the professional expert, who can thoroughly gauge the extent to which Leather Apron has impressed himself upon the public mind. Up to a few days ago the mere mention of Leather Apron's name was sufficient to cause a panic. All England was murmuring his name with bated breath. In one instance, which is duly recorded in the police reports, a man merely went into a public-house and said that he knew Leather Apron, and the customers, leaving their drinks unfinished, fled en masse, while the landlady, speechless with terror, bolted out of a back door and ran to the police-station, leaving the grim humourist in sole possession of the establishment, till and all. Never since the days of Burke and Hare has a name borne such a fearful significance.

. . . It is astonishing how eagerly the Press seized upon the mere mention of a person with this ordinary nickname, and worked it up into a blood-curdling sensation. The name of Leather Apron has been flashed from pole to pole. It is to-day as much a byword on Greenland's icy mountains and on India's coral strand as it is in Whitechapel and at Scotland-yard. And why? Primarily because there was something in the sound which suggested a big catch-on. It is possible that the harmless individual who was arrested as Leather Apron, and discharged because there wasn't enough evidence against him to convict a bluebottle of buzzing, may not lose his celebrity for a generation. He has been written up with such a vengeance that he will be a famous man to the end of his days.

The booming of Leather Apron in connection with the Whitechapel murders illustrates the bungling way in which the business is being conducted by the police. It is a million to one that when (O that all-important when!) the bona-fide murderer (bona-fide murderer is good!) is arrested he will be found to be someone who never heard of a leather apron in his life. The police may be playing a game of spoof, but the fact remains that in no suggestion made by

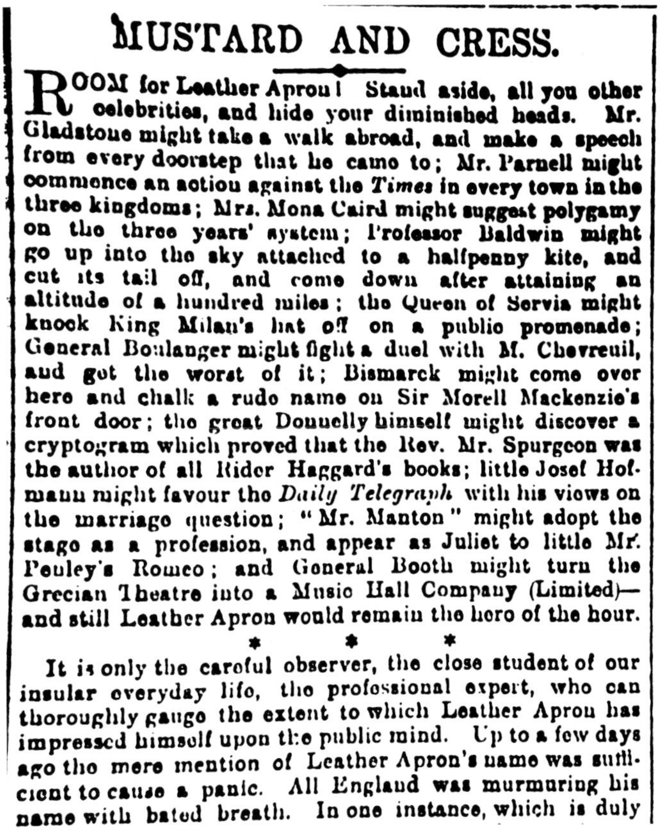

MUSTARD AND CRESS.

ROOM for Leather Apron! Stand aside, all you other celebrities, and hide your diminished heads. Mr. Gladstone might take a walk abroad, and make a speech from every doorstep that he came to; Mr. Parnell might commence an action against the *Times* in every town in the three kingdoms; Mrs. Mona Caird might suggest polygamy on the three years' system; Professor Baldwin might go up into the sky attached to a halfpenny kite, and cut its tail off, and come down after attaining an altitude of a hundred miles; the Queen of Servia might knock King Milan's hat off on a public promenade; General Boulanger might fight a duel with M. Chevreuil, and get the worst of it; Bismarck might come over here and chalk a rude name on Sir Morell Mackenzie's front door; the great Donnelly himself might discover a cryptogram which proved that the Rev. Mr. Spurgeon was the author of all Rider Haggard's books; little Josef Hofmann might favour the *Daily Telegraph* with his views on the marriage question; "Mr. Manton" might adopt the stage as a profession, and appear as Juliet to little Mr. Penley's Romeo; and General Booth might turn the Grecian Theatre into a Music Hall Company (Limited)—and still Leather Apron would remain the hero of the hour.

* * *

It is only the careful observer, the close student of our insular everyday life, the professional expert, who can thoroughly gauge the extent to which Leather Apron has impressed himself upon the public mind. Up to a few days ago the mere mention of Leather Apron's name was sufficient to cause a panic. All England was murmuring his name with bated breath. In one instance, which is duly

Sims' 'Mustard and Cress' column of 16 September made mention of the nickname 'Leather Apron' before the more infamous 'Jack the Ripper' was invented later that month.

> the authorities up to the present is the slightest technical knowledge of the "speciality" of the Whitechapel atrocities shown.

Sims was very critical of the police and their lack of success in the investigation. The police cause was not helped by the fact that the head of the CID, James Monro, had resigned in August 1888 after many clashes with Commissioner Sir Charles Warren. The new head of the detectives, Dr Robert Anderson, took up his duties at Scotland Yard at the beginning of September but almost immediately went on sick leave, departing the country for Switzerland on the day of the Chapman murder and not returning until early October. Some of the criticism may have been unfair, but it was to be found in many of the newspapers of the day. This was a big story and it became bigger and more sensational week by week. It was obviously in the interests of the press to boost reports by whatever means they could. The name 'Leather Apron' had provided a means for doing this, but after the arrest and release of Pizer the nickname was no longer of any use in selling papers and promoting the story of the unsolved murders. Most reports reverted to calling the unknown killer 'the Whitechapel Murderer', but this seemed altogether too mundane and lacked the impact of a catchy sobriquet. Reports on the inquests and the investigation of various suspects kept the topic alive, but there was no telling name to give the story an edge. What was needed was a *nom de guerre* for the unknown and phantom-like stalker of East End prostitutes.

— TWO —

'Yours truly, Jack the Ripper'

THE Central News Agency was founded in 1870 by William Saunders MP, a philanthropist, social reformer and businessman. It opened two years after the Press Association, and was a media service that collected reports by telegraph from correspondents throughout the United Kingdom and abroad. It was turned into a limited liability company ten years after its foundation and swiftly built a reputation for securing scoops, often beating all the other media sources to the big stories. The Central News was twelve hours ahead of everybody else with news of the fall of Khartoum and the death of General Gordon. It telegraphed important events, parliamentary reports, Stock Exchange and market reports, law cases, racing results and other newsworthy items to newspapers, exchanges, clubs and newsrooms. Communications intended for general publication were forwarded to the Central News by messenger or telegraph. In short news was the company's lifeblood and a marketable commodity that would be certain to reach many newspapers.

The Central News Agency enjoyed a good relationship with the London police forces and there is a letter on file in the Corporation of London Record Office from John Moore, manager of the Agency, to Major Smith, Assistant Commissioner of the City of London Police. Dated 19 September 1888, it reads:

> Dear Sir,
>
> Will it be agreeable to you to let us have copies of the Bills which are sent out to the various Police Stations for posting? If you can see your way to doing this you will much oblige.
>
> Yours faithfully,
> John Moore
> Manager

[CLRO, Police Box 3.21, No. 309]

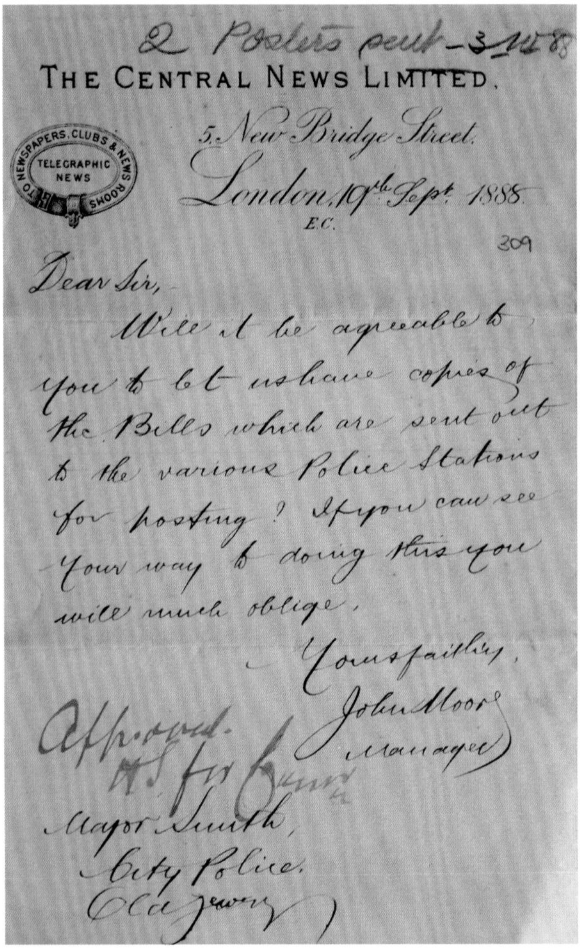

2 Posters sent – 3.11.88

THE CENTRAL NEWS LIMITED.

TO NEWSPAPERS, CLUBS & NEWS ROOMS
TELEGRAPHIC NEWS

5, New Bridge Street,
London, 19th Sept 1888.
E.C.

309

Dear Sir,

Will it be agreeable to you to let us have copies of the Bills which are sent out to the various Police Stations for posting? If you can see your way to doing this you will much oblige,

Yours faithfully,
John Moore
Manager

Approved. H.S. for Comr

Major Smith,
City Police,
Old Jewry

Letter written by John Moore, manager of the Central News Agency, on 19 September 1888 to the City Police asking for bills about the murder. (CLRO Police Box 3.21, No. 309)

New Bridge Street, City of London, looking towards Ludgate Circus and Farringdon Street. The Central News office at 5 New Bridge Street is the lighter-coloured building with a portico, on the left.

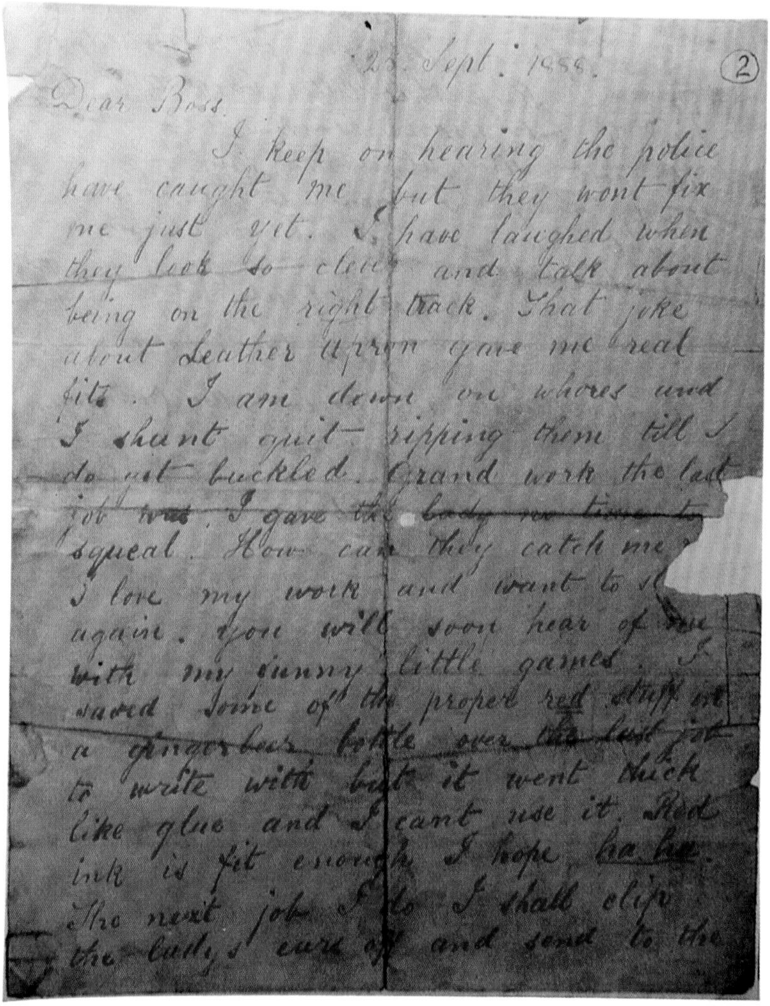

25 Sept. 1888. (2)

Dear Boss.

I keep on hearing the police have caught me but they wont fix me just yet. I have laughed when they look so clever and talk about being on the right track. That joke about Leather Apron gave me real fits. I am down on whores and I shant quit ripping them till I do get buckled. Grand work the last job was. I gave the lady no time to squeal. How can they catch me. I love my work and want to start again. You will soon hear of me with my funny little games. I saved some of the proper red stuff in a ginger beer bottle over the last job to write with but it went thick like glue and I cant use it. Red ink is fit enough I hope ha ha. The next job I do I shall clip the ladys ears off and send to the

The 'Dear Boss' envelope and letter (*right and opposite*) dated 25 September 1888 and sent to the Central News Agency. This letter was the origin of the name 'Jack the Ripper'.

This letter was marked 'Approved. H.S. [Henry Smith, Assistant Commissioner] for Commr.' and '2 Posters sent 3.10.88' was recorded at the top of the letter. It is not clear to which posters this refers, but we can but assume that they must have related to the Whitechapel murders in the Metropolitan Police area for Moore's letter was sent before a murder had occurred in the City police area.

About the time the police received the first letter another anonymous writer was sitting down and composing a communication, his pen charged with red ink. This time it was not to be posted to the police, nor did the writer fail to supply a signature. He dated the letter 25 September 1888, and his message, if it were true, was very clear. The letter was stated to have been received by the Central News Agency at 5 New Bridge Street, Ludgate Circus, on Thursday 27 September 1888 and according to the company, was initially 'treated as a joke'. This letter and its envelope are preserved at the Public Record Office. It bore a penny lilac stamp postmarked 'LONDON E.C. 3 – SP 27 88 – P' and was addressed to 'The Boss Central News Office London City'. The letter ran as follows:

> Dear Boss,
>
> I keep on hearing the police have caught me but they wont fix me just yet. I have laughed when they look so clever and talk about being on the right track. That joke about Leather Apron gave me real fits. I am down on whores and I shant quit ripping them till I do get

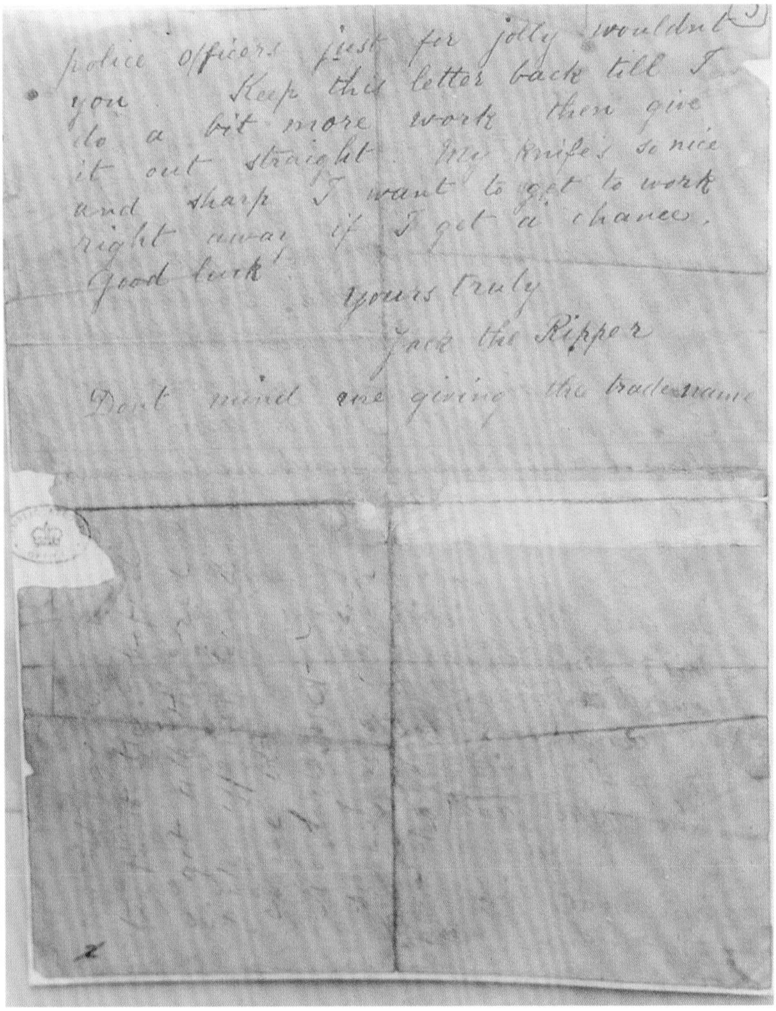

police officers just for jolly wouldnt
you Keep this letter back till I
do a bit more work then give
it out straight My knife's so nice
and sharp I want to get to work
right away if I get a chance.
Good luck.
yours truly
Jack the Ripper
Dont mind me giving the trade name

buckled. Grand work the last job was. I gave the lady no time to squeal. How can they catch me now. I love my work and want to start again. You will soon hear of me with my funny little games. I saved some of the proper <u>red</u> stuff in a ginger beer bottle over the last job to write with but it went thick like glue and I cant use it. Red ink is fit enough I hope <u>ha.ha.</u> The next job I do I shall clip the lady s ears off and send to the
[second page] police officers just for jolly wouldn't you. Keep this letter back till I do a bit more work . then give it out straight. My knife's so nice and sharp I want to get to work right away if I get a chance. Good luck.

yours truly
Jack the Ripper
Dont mind me giving the trade name

Then written at right angles below this:

wasn't good enough to post this before I got all the red ink off my hands curse it.
No luck yet. They say I'm a doctor now
<u>ha ha</u>

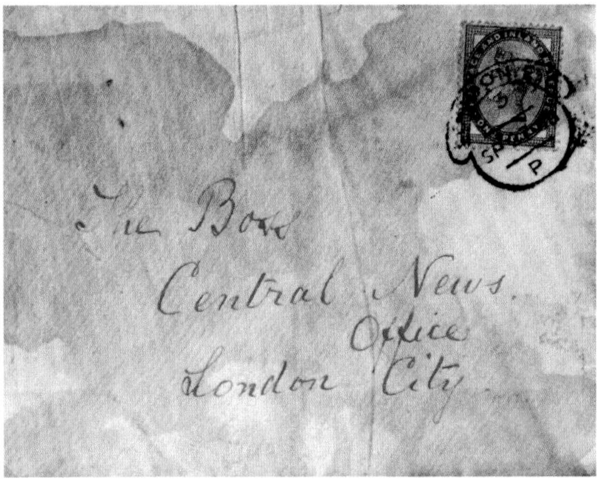

Whatever the provenance of this letter, on Saturday 29 September 1888 it was forwarded to the police by the Central News Agency with the following note:

> THE CENTRAL NEWS LIMITED.
>
> 5, New Bridge Street,
> London, 29 Sep 1888
> E.C.
>
> The Editor presents his compliments to Mr Williamson & begs to inform him the enclosed was sent the Central News two days ago, & was treated as a joke.

This covering note was unsigned but was in the handwriting of Thomas John Bulling, a forty-year-old journalist employed by Central News. What the police thought of this letter upon receipt has not been recorded, but they cannot have known that it was to become the most famous item ever allegedly written by a killer. Nor did they realise that the very appropriate nickname was to become the most infamous and enduring sobriquet ever to be recorded in the annals of murder. The indications are that the police thought the letter to be a hoax, but, as events proved, they had to take it very seriously, and the press was already aware of its existence.

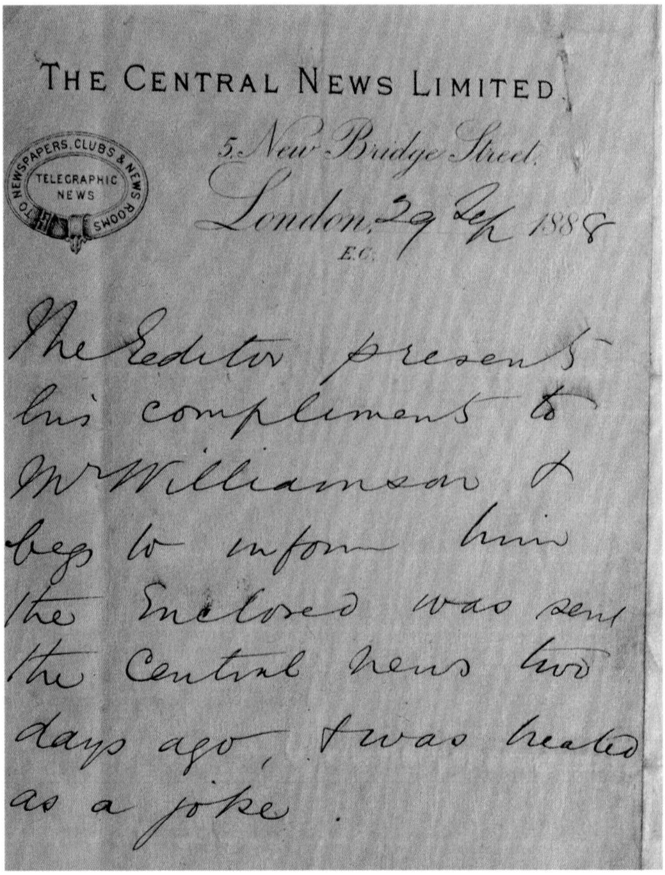

THE CENTRAL NEWS LIMITED.

TO NEWSPAPERS, CLUBS & NEWS ROOMS TELEGRAPHIC NEWS

5, New Bridge Street,
London, 29 Sep 1888
E.C.

The Editor presents his compliments to Mr Williamson & begs to inform him the Enclosed was sent the Central News two days ago, & was treated as a joke.

Note from the Central News Agency in the handwriting of Tom Bulling. It was sent to the police with the 'Dear Boss' letter.

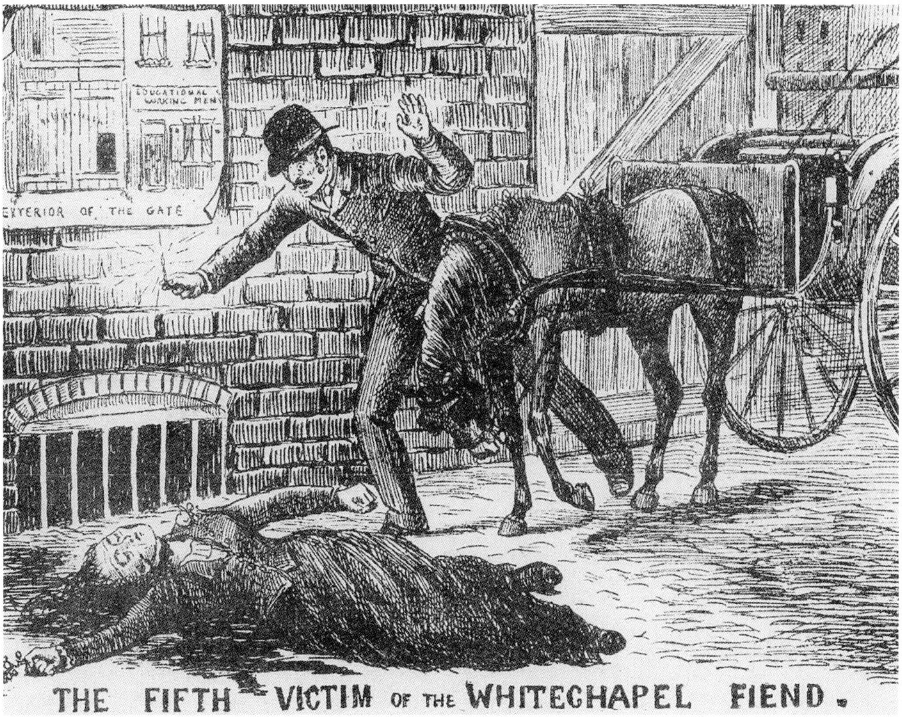

Discovery of the body of Elizabeth Stride at Dutfield's Yard, Berner Street, by Louis Diemschutz, 30 September.

It was noted at the time that the 'Jack the Ripper' epistle contained the obvious Americanisms, 'Boss', 'fix me' and 'quit' and this might be linked to the press reports of Coroner Wynne Baxter's summing up at the Chapman inquest on Wednesday 26 September. Baxter had spoken of a story that had been brought to his notice by 'an officer of one of our great medical schools'. He had attended and had been informed by the sub-curator of the Pathological Museum that an American had called on him and asked him to procure a number of specimens of 'the organ that was missing in the deceased'. Baxter went on, 'He stated his willingness to give £20 apiece for each specimen. He stated that his object was to issue an actual specimen with each copy of a publication on which he was then engaged. He was told that his request was impossible to be complied with, but he still urged his request. He wished them preserved, not in spirits of wine, the usual medium, but glycerine, in order to preserve them in a flaccid condition, and he wished them sent to America direct. It was known that this request was repeated to another institution of a similar character.' Although the 'Dear Boss' letter was dated 25 September, it was not posted until Thursday 27 September, thus allowing the inclusion of ideas that may have been gleaned from the press reports of the inquest.

It arrived on 29 September and the crucial event that was to invest this letter with great importance occurred that very night. In the early hours of Sunday 30 September two murders were committed within an hour of each other and in close proximity. It was the night of the so-called 'double event'. The first of these murders took place in the entrance to Dutfield's Yard, Berner Street, St George's-in-the-east, in the beleaguered Whitechapel (H) Division of the Metropolitan Police. This entrance was on the south side of the International Working Men's Educational Club, a socialist club at 40 Berner Street. The victim was another prostitute, Elizabeth Stride, aged forty-four. She was born in Sweden, but had been a resident of London for twenty-two years and spoke perfect

English. An attack on the woman was witnessed at the entranceway at about 12.45 a.m. by a Hungarian Jew, Israel Schwartz. He saw a man stop and speak to the woman who was standing in the gateway. The man tried to pull the woman into the street, but then turned her round and threw her down on the footpath. The woman screamed three times but not very loudly. Schwartz crossed to the other side of the road where he saw a second man standing lighting his pipe. The attacker called out 'Lipski', apparently to the man with the pipe or Schwartz himself. Schwartz was alarmed and made off in a southerly direction, followed initially by the man with the pipe. Schwartz described the attacker as aged about thirty, 5 feet 5 inches tall, complexion fair, hair dark and with a small brown moustache, full-faced, broad-shouldered; he was wearing a dark jacket and trousers, a black cap with peak and carrying nothing in his hands. About fifteen minutes later the secretary to the socialist club, Louis Diemschutz, returned to the yard in a costermonger's barrow drawn by a pony. As the pony entered the yard it shied and Diemschutz discovered the body of Stride lying just inside the gateway on the right; her throat had been cut. There was no other mutilation of the body and the nature of her injuries and the various attendant circumstances of this murder have resulted in some commentators believing that her attacker was not the person who killed the other victims.

Another witness emerged in the shape of Matthew Packer, a greengrocer and fruiterer of 44 Berner Street, just two doors from the scene of the murder. Packer was interviewed by Detective Sergeant White at about 9.00 a.m. on the day of the murder, but stated he had closed his shop at 12.30 a.m. and had seen nothing suspicious, nor anything of a man and a woman. Packer later told a different story to two private investigators hired by the Whitechapel Vigilance Committee to investigate the murders. He spoke of a suspicious male he had served with grapes at his shop at 11.45 p.m. on the night of the murder. The man had been in the company of the deceased woman Stride. He described the man as '. . . middle-aged, perhaps 35 years, about 5ft. 7in. in height; was stout, square-built; wore a wideawake hat and dark clothes; had the appearance of a clerk; had a rough voice and a quick, sharp way of talking'. This description was published in the *Evening News* of 4 October. Packer was subsequently seen again by the police, furnished another description of the man, and stated that he shut up his shop at 11.30 p.m. His contradictory statements severely damaged his credibility as a reliable witness.

Within forty-five minutes or so of Elizabeth Stride's death, a second murder took place about three-quarters of a mile away and within only approximately ten minutes' walking distance. It was far enough away, however, for this second murder to fall within the boundary of a different police force. The murder of Catherine Eddowes took place in Mitre Square, Aldgate, which was under the aegis of the City of London Police. At 1.35 a.m. three Jews – Joseph Lawende and two friends – left the Imperial Club in Duke Street, Aldgate, which was situated opposite Church Passage, a narrow dimly lit thoroughfare leading into Mitre Square. A man and a woman were standing under the gas lamp at the entrance to Church Passage, and the woman was facing the man. Lawende's companions, Joseph Hyam Levy and Harry Harris, took little notice of the couple but Lawende did pay them more attention, from a stated distance of about 15 feet as he passed towards Aldgate High Street. Lawende was later shown Eddowes' clothing and it was recorded, '. . . but to the best of his belief the clothing of the deceased, which

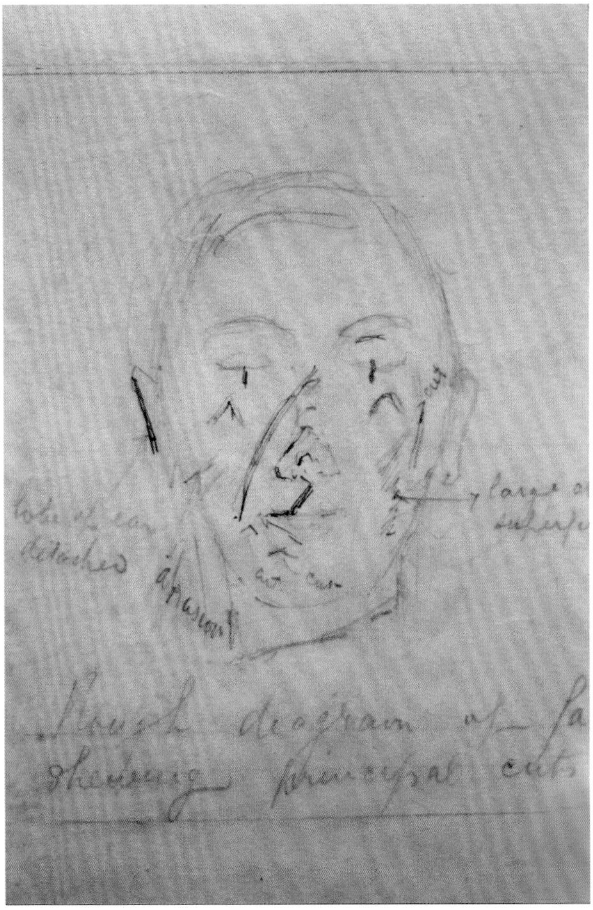

Right: Sketch made for the City Police of the cuts to Eddowes' face. The inverted Vs are clearly visible. *Below*: Sketch of Eddowes' body lying as it was found in Mitre Square on 30 September.

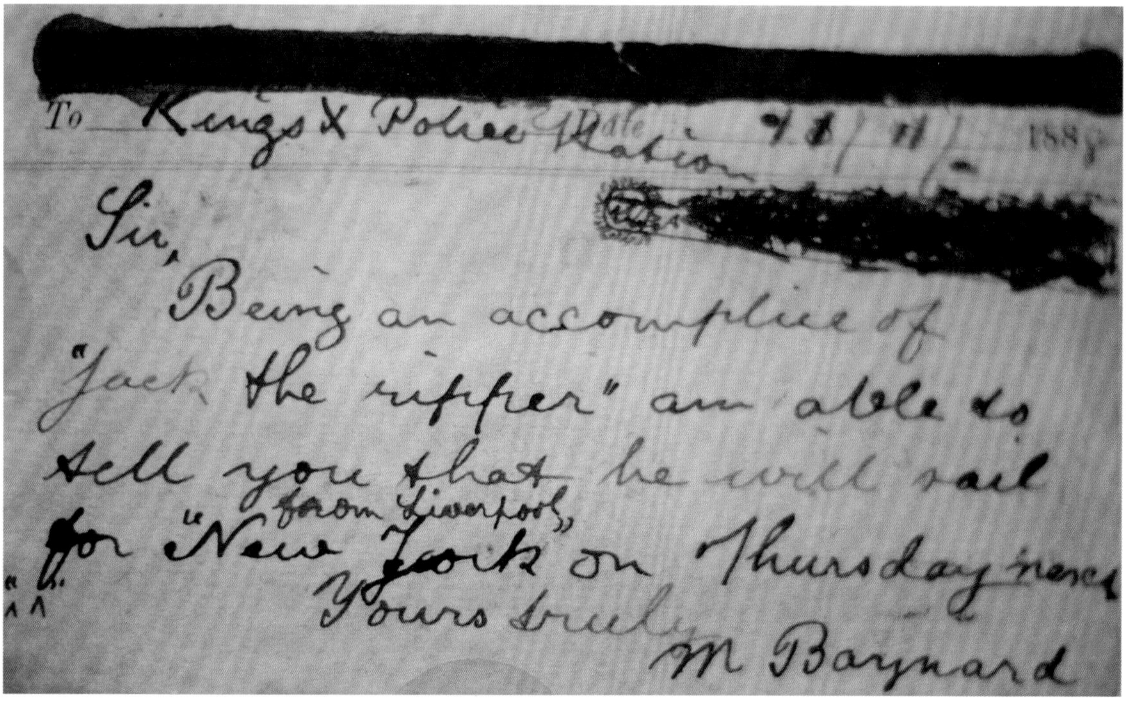
[redacted]

To Kings X Police Station Date ? / ? / 188

[redacted]

Sir,

Being an accomplice of "Jack the ripper" am able to tell you that he will sail "from Liverpool," for "New York" on Thursday next

Yours truly

M Baynard

Postcard of 12 November from an 'accomplice' of 'Jack the Ripper' saying he is about to leave for New York. Inverted Vs drawn at bottom left strangely echo the mutilations on Eddowes' face.

was dark coloured and black was similar to that worn by the woman whom he had seen. And that was the full extent of his identity.' He described the man as aged thirty, 5 feet 7 or 8 inches tall, with fair complexion, fair moustache, medium build, dressed in a pepper-and-salt-coloured loose jacket, grey cloth cap with a peak of same colour, reddish handkerchief tied in a knot around his neck; he had the appearance of a sailor.

At 1.44 a.m. PC 881 Edward Watkins of the City Police entered Mitre Square from Mitre Street, diagonally opposite the Church Passage entrance to the square. On checking the southernmost corner of the square he found the body of Catherine Eddowes lying on the paving stones at the rear of an unoccupied house. She presented an appalling spectacle. She was lying on her back, her head inclined to her left, facing the rear of the house. Her arms were lying by the side of the body as if they had fallen there, palms upward. Her left leg was straight and the right was bent at the knee and thigh. Her clothing was cut open at the front exposing her torso which had been opened with a large jagged cut from the pubis to the sternum. Some viscera had been extracted and lay over her right shoulder, and a detached piece was lying between her left arm and her body. Her throat was cut across and her face mutilated with cuts and slashes. Later examination revealed that her uterus and left kidney were absent, removed by the killer. The lobe and auricle of her right ear had been cut obliquely through and when the body was undressed at the Golden Lane mortuary a piece of her ear dropped from her clothing.

However, what was about to emerge was arguably the only real clue ever left by the Whitechapel murderer – his direction of travel after leaving the scene of a murder.

— THREE —

'The Writing on the Wall'

ALMOST as famous as the early 'Jack the Ripper' correspondence was the apparently anti-Semitic graffiti found just after the Eddowes murder. It was chalked on the entranceway brickwork surround of nos 108–19 Wentworth Model Dwellings, Goulston Street, Whitechapel. The writing was discovered by a patrolling police officer, PC 254A Alfred Long, who was on attachment from the Whitehall Division to supplement his hard-pressed colleagues in the East End. At about 2.55 a.m. Long had discovered a piece of soiled, bloodstained apron lying in this entranceway, and it was proved to have been cut by the murderer from that worn by the Mitre Square victim. Above this piece of apron, written in white chalk on the black brickwork, was the following message:

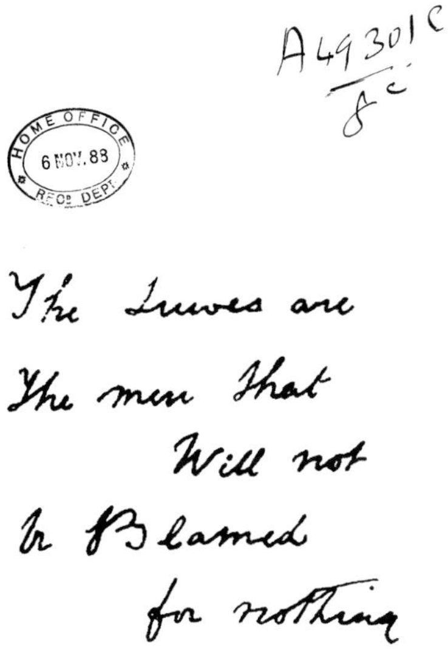

The Juwes are
The men that
Will not
be Blamed
for nothing

Entrance to nos 108—19 Wentworth Model Dwellings, Goulston Street. The 'Juwes' graffiti was chalked on the brick jamb of the doorway. (Photograph courtesy of Richard Whittington-Egan)

This much-discussed and much-analysed phrase may not even have been written by the killer. Had the piece of apron been disposed of in the next entranceway, then a totally different cryptic piece of graffiti might well have been under the microscope. For then, as today, such graffiti were common in the East End of London. This writing was described by Detective Constable Daniel Halse of the City of London Police, who went to the location and examined it, as reading, 'The Juwes are not the men that will be blamed for nothing'. His version involved moving the word 'not' but did not significantly alter any meaning the phrase might have, as it still included a double negative.

Even the exact location of the writing has been the subject of some contention but indications of its true position were clearly given in the contemporary reports. The reason for erasing the message and the height at which it was written on the wall are probably indicated by the following passage in a report written by Superintendent Thomas Arnold:

> . . . my attention was called to some writing on the wall of the entrance to some dwellings No. 108 Goulston Street Whitechapel which consisted of the following words "The Juews are not [the word 'not' has been deleted] the men that will not be blamed for nothing", and knowing that in consequence of a suspicion having fallen upon a Jew named 'John Pizer' alias 'Leather Apron' having committed a murder in Hanbury Street a short time previously a strong feeling ['ag' deleted] existed against the Jews generally, and as the Building upon which the writing was found was situated in the midst of a locality inhabited principally by that Sect. I was apprehensive that if the writing were left it would be the means of causing a riot and therefore considered it desirable that it should be removed having in view the fact that it was in such a position that it would have been rubbed by the shoulders of persons

> passing in & out of the Building. Had only a portion of the writing been removed the context would have remained. An Inspector was present by my directions with a sponge for the purpose of removing the writing when Commissioner arrived on the scene.
> [HO 144/221/A49301C, ff. 197–8]

From this report it seems clear that the chalked message was at shoulder height and, as the Commissioner was to indicate, was on the inner aspect of the entrance surround of the doorway. The inner wall of the entranceway was sufficiently set back from the entrance surround that had the writing been there, it would have been less likely to have been rubbed by the shoulders of people using the doorway. This is supported by both Warren's and Arnold's words about the writing. The location of the graffiti was also written on a map of the area prepared for the inquest by the City surveyor, Frederick William Foster. Rather controversially, for the wording of the message and the spelling of 'Jews' is again different, he wrote:

> 2 doors from Wentworth street & No 3 on the right 4 blocks [from murder site] about 30'0 on right hand side doorway about 20'0 from lamp found inside entrance to Model Dwellings from 108 – 119.
> The Juws are not the men To be blamed for nothing

The Chief Commissioner, Sir Charles Warren, who attended the scene at 5.30 a.m., clearly placed the graffiti:

> The writing was on the jamb of the open archway or doorway visible to anybody in the street and could not be covered up without danger of the covering being torn off at once. –
> [HO 144/221/A49301C, ff. 173–81]

Warren then went on to explain why he had the chalked message sponged away:

> A discussion took place whether the writing could be left covered up or otherwise or whether any portion of it could be left for an hour until it could be photographed, but after taking into consideration the excited state of the population in London generally at the time the strong feeling which had been excited against the Jews, and the fact that in a short time there would be a large concourse of the people in the streets and having before me the Report that if it was left there the house was likely to be wrecked (in which from my own observation I entirely concurred) I considered it desirable to obliterate the writing at once, having taken a copy of which I enclose a duplicate.

A great controversy arose out of this episode. The removal of the message was much to the dismay of the City Police who, quite rightly, wanted it photographed first. Such photography was not a matter of course in those days, and Warren was not prepared to wait at least an hour for it to be done. He did, however, have a copy of the message written out (*see* illustration on page 23). Halse, at the inquest, described the writing as apparently 'recently done' and '. . . about three lines of writing, which was in a good schoolboy hand.' When questioned as to why he thought it was recently done, Halse

Sir Charles Warren, Chief Commissioner of the Metropolitan Police at the time of the murders in 1888. Many of the letters were addressed to him personally.

Major (later Lieutenant-Colonel Sir) Henry Smith, Assistant Commissioner and later Commissioner of the City of London Police.

explained that he 'assumed the writing was recent, because from the number of persons living in the tenement he believed it would have been rubbed out had it been there for any time.' Halse claimed that he objected to the Metropolitan Police erasing the message before it could be photographed. The incident has often been cited as one of the causes of the failure of the City and Metropolitan Police Forces to work together properly on what was now a joint investigation. Any rift was probably more a matter of personalities rather than anything very seriously wrong at an investigative level. Indeed, a letter written by Sir Charles Warren to Sir James Fraser on 9 October 1888 would seem to indicate that there was no great divide:

9.10.88

My dear Fraser

In order prevent our working Doubly over the same ground I have to suggest that our C.I.D. should be in more constant communication with yours about the W. murders.

Could you send an officer to Ch. Insp Swanson here every morning to consult or may I send an officer every morning to consult with your officers.

We are inundated with suggestions & names of suspects.

Truly yours
C.W.

[MEPO 1/48]

However, a critical view was given by Sir Henry Smith, then retired City Police Commissioner, in his 1910 book, *From Constable to Commissioner*, page 161:

> How Sir Charles Warren wiped out – I believe with his own hand, but will not speak positively – the writing on the wall, how he came to my office accompanied by Superintendent Arnold about seven o'clock the same morning to get information as to the murder of Catharine Eddowes, I have already stated on p. 153. The facts are indisputable, yet Sir Robert Anderson studiously avoids all allusion to them. Is it because "it would ill become him to violate the unwritten rule of the service," or is he unwilling to put on record the unpardonable blunder of his superior officer? I leave my readers to decide . . .
>
> The writing on the wall may have been written – and, I think, probably *was* written – to throw the police off the scent, to divert suspicion from the Gentiles and throw it upon the Jews. It may have been written by the murderer, or it may not. To obliterate the words that might have given us a most valuable clue, more especially after I had sent a man to stand over them till they were photographed, was not only indiscreet, but unwarrantable.

The 'Juwes' message written in chalk in the Goulston Street doorway was erased on the order of Sir Charles Warren as he feared an anti-Semitic reaction from the market crowds that would soon be in the street. This photograph of the Sunday morning market in Goulston Street shows just how busy it was.

The *Star* of Saturday 13 October 1888 reported on its front page:

> On the particular point of the obliteration of the handwriting on the wall we are not disposed to blame Sir Charles Warren so heavily as some of our friends in the press. The point is not so important as it at first appeared to be. It is, we believe, quite untrue to say that 'Juwes' is Yiddish for 'Jews.' 'Jews' in Yiddish is Yiddin, the ordinary Hebrew plural, so that the supposition that the writer is a Jew falls to the ground. The only other point that could be proved from the inspection of the handwriting was that the writer was identical with 'Jack the Ripper,' which would no doubt be valuable. Of course, Sir Charles acted with blundering haste and military rashness; but his motive seems to have been just a trifle more creditable than usual. The real gravamen of the charge against him is his general failure to protect the lives and property of the poor. For instance, every one of the murders of which we gave a list the other day were committed on the persons of the poor; and every one of the ransacked neighborhoods mentioned in the *Pall Mall Gazette* were poor districts. That is why we want one united effort to hurl the usurper from his place.

That the graffiti was too good a story to drop is evidenced by the extended press coverage it received. *The Times* of Monday 15 October reported:

> THE EAST-END MURDERS.
>
> In reference to the writing on the wall of a house, in Goulston-street, we are requested by Sir Charles Warren to state that his attention having been called to a paragraph in several daily journals mentioning that in the Yiddish dialect the word "Jews" is spelt "Juwes," he has made inquiries on the subject and finds that this is not a fact. He learns that the equivalent in the Judeo-German (Yiddish) jargon is "Yidden."
>
> It has not been ascertained that there is any dialect or language in which the word "Jews" is spelt "Juwes."

Warren's original intention in erasing the message – to avert anti-Semitic feeling – was well and truly thwarted. Not only had the message appeared in the newspapers, it had also been the subject of protracted public discussion. And a century later researchers and theorists now engage in lively debate about whether the graffiti in Goulston Street had Masonic associations or a cryptic significance.

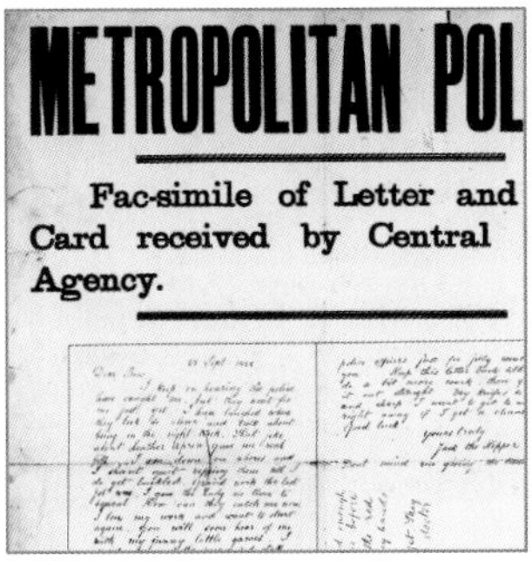

METROPOLITAN POL

Fac-simile of Letter and Card received by Central Agency.

— FOUR —

'Ripperism'

THE remarkable amount of information on the murders carried in the newspapers was a great bonus for the anonymous letter-writers. Sensation was poured upon sensation, and the name 'Jack the Ripper' appeared in many papers on Monday 1 October 1888. The *Star* reported:

> **"Jack the Ripper's" Joke.**
>
> A practical joker, who signed himself "Jack the Ripper," wrote to the Central News last week, intimating with labored flippancy that he was going to commence operations again in Whitechapel shortly. He said he would cut the woman's ears off to send to the police. This morning the same agency received a postcard smeared apparently with dirty blood. It was written with red chalk. It says:–
>
> "I was not codding dear old Boss when I gave you the tip. You'll hear about saucy Jacky's work tomorrow. Double event this time. Number one squealed a bit. Couldn't finish straight off. Had not time to get ears for police. Thanks for keeping back last letter till I got to work again. – JACK THE RIPPER."

Although some press reports indicated that the communications were believed written by a practical joker, there were certain disquieting aspects to them. For a start the 'Dear Boss' letter had been sent just before the two murders of 30 September. It had also contained the threat 'The next job I do I shall clip the ladys ears off and send to the police . . .' and, of course, Eddowes' right ear had been cut obliquely through. The postcard referred to the 'double event' and remarked that 'number one', i.e. Stride, had 'squealed a bit . . . had not time to get ears for police'. According to Schwartz, as we have seen, Stride had 'screamed three times but not very loudly'. Reference was made in the postcard to the previous letter, and although ostensibly in a slightly different hand, appeared to be from the same source. If it was not from the killer then the originator

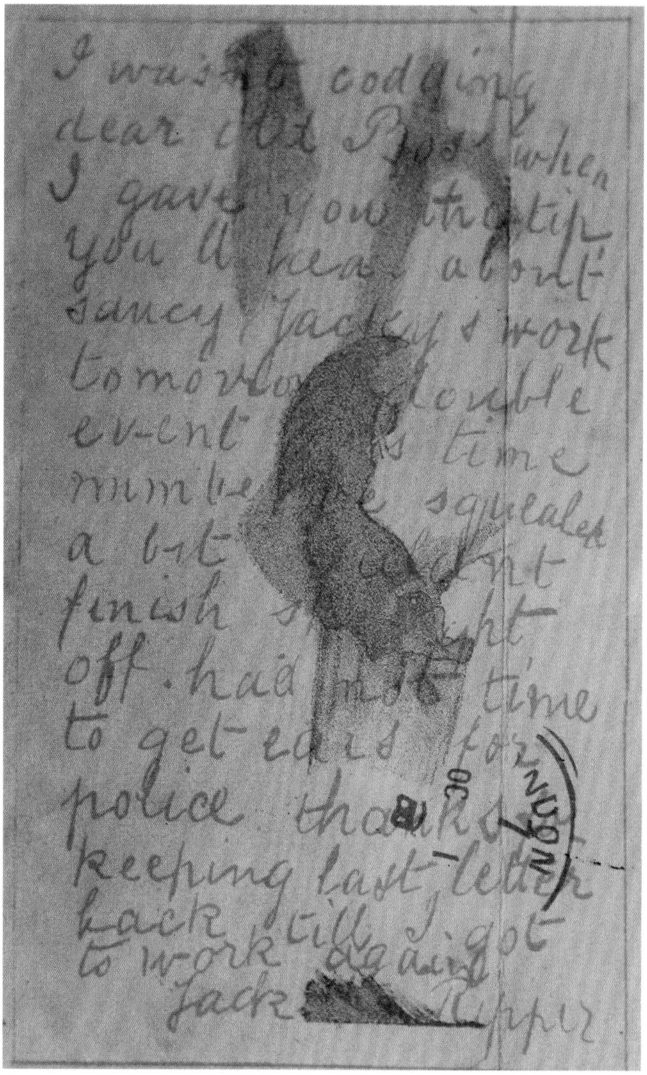
I was not codding
dear old Boss when
I gave you the tip
you'll hear about
saucy Jacky's work
tomorrow double
event this time
number one squealed
a bit couldn't
finish straight
off. had not time
to get ears for
police thanks for
keeping last letter
back till I got
to work again
Jack the Ripper

1888 facsimile of the 'saucy Jacky' postcard dated 1 October and sent to the Central News Agency. The original postcard has been missing for many years.

was apparently informed at an early stage, and the only way to determine whether the letter and postcard really were from the same source was to try to identify the handwriting.

The possibility that the 'Dear Boss' letter and the postcard were from the genuine murderer was not entirely dismissed and many newspapers stated that this was indeed the case. The *East Anglian Daily Times* of Tuesday 2 October reported:

> BLOOD-SMEARED POSTCARD RECEIVED.
>
> The Central News yesterday received a postcard bearing the "London, E.", stamp. The address and subject-matter were written in red, and undoubtedly by the same person from whom the sensational letter already published was received a few days since. Like the previous missive, this also has reference to the horrible tragedies in East London, forming, indeed, a sequel to the first letter . . . The card is smeared on both sides with blood, which has evidently been impressed thereon by the thumb or finger of the writer, the corrugated surface of the skin being plainly shewn . . . It is not necessarily assumed that this has been

the work of the murderer, the idea that naturally occurs being that the whole thing is a practical joke. At the same time the writing of the previous letter immediately before the commission of the latest murders was so singular a coincidence, that it does not seem unreasonable to suppose that the cool calculating villain who is responsible for the crimes has chosen to make the post a medium through which to convey to the Press his grimly diabolical humour.

It was now that hoax letters were to become a problem; they started to plague the police investigation. On Tuesday 2 October, the *Star* reported:

Fourteen More to Come.

The following letter, evidently the work of someone who tried to disguise his style and handwriting, was received this morning. We are not, however, inclined to believe that the actual murderer has favored us with his plan of campaign:–

Oct 1st 1888

MR STAR

as you take greate interest in the Murders i am the one that did it wouldent you like to see me but you shant just yet I mean to do some more yet I have done 6 I am going to do 14 More then go back to america the next time i shall do 3 in one night I dont live a thousand miles from the spot not in a common lodging house

Yours in luck

THE BUTCHER.

A mail van of the 1880s–90s leaving Mount Pleasant. (*Living London*)

The earlier press reports of a message written on a wall at the scene of the Chapman murder and the 'BUTCHER' letter above both indicated a 'target number' of murders to be perpetrated by the killer. 'THE BUTCHER' had possibly borrowed the idea from those earlier press reports. This did not go without notice as the 'target number' of victims was to be repeated many times in later letters. So too was the American theme used by this writer.

The Times of Tuesday 2 October reported:

> Two communications of an extraordinary nature, both signed "Jack the Ripper," have been received by the Central News Agency, the one on Thursday last and the other yesterday morning. The first – the original of which has been seen by Major Smith, the Assistant Commissioner of the City Police – was a letter, bearing the E.C. postmark, in which reference was made to the atrocious murders previously committed in the East-end, which the writer confessed, in a brutally jocular vein, to have committed; stating that in the "next job" he did he would "clip the lady's ears off" and send them to the police, and also asking that the letter might be kept back until he had done "a bit more work". The second communication was a post-card, and, as above stated, it was received yesterday morning. It bore the date, "London, E., October 1," and was as follows . . . [the text of the postcard follows here] . . . The postcard was sent to Scotland-yard. No doubt is entertained that the writer of both communications, whoever he may be, is the same person.

The name and pattern were now established; the stage was set for the flood of letters that was to help ensure the case's enduring notoriety. On 4 October the *Daily Telegraph* published a facsimile of part of the 'Dear Boss' letter which obviously gave the copycat letter-writers valuable raw material. The Central News Agency was the source of many of the syndicated press stories and the letter was widely disseminated. However, even greater importance appeared to be accorded to the communications when the Metropolitan Police produced a large poster bearing facsimiles of the 'Dear Boss' letter and the 'saucy Jacky' postcard (*see* opposite). The poster was issued on 3 October and was put up at many police stations.

The *Star* was not, apparently, in favour of the publication of facsimiles of the 'Jack the Ripper' letters. In a front-page editorial on Thursday 4 October it was critical of the *Daily Telegraph*'s actions, and also shed interesting light on how the Central News Agency was making mileage of its scoop in receiving these communications:

> By the way, why does our friend, the D.T., print facsimiles of the ghastly but very silly letters from "Jack the Ripper?" We were offered them by the "Central News," and declined to print them. They were clearly written in red pencil, not in blood, the obvious reason being that the writer was one of those foolish but bad people who delight in an unholy notoriety. Now, the murderer is not a man of this kind. His own love of publicity is tempered by a very peculiar and remarkable desire for privacy and by a singular ability to secure what he wants. Nor is there any proof of any pre-knowledge of the Mitre-square crimes, beyond the prediction that they were going to happen, which anybody might have made. The reference to ear-clipping may be a curious coincidence, but there is nothing in the posting of the letter on Sunday. Thousands of Londoners had details of the crimes supplied in the Sunday papers.

METROPOLITAN POLICE.

Fac-simile of Letter and Post Card received by Central News Agency.

25. Sept. 1888.

Dear Boss

I keep on hearing the police have caught me but they wont fix me just yet. I have laughed when they look so clever and talk about being on the right track. That joke about Leather Apron gave me real fits. I am down on whores and I shant quit ripping them till I do get buckled. Grand work the last job was. I gave the lady no time to squeal. How can they catch me now. I love my work and want to start again. You will soon hear of me with my funny little games. I saved some of the proper red stuff in a ginger beer bottle over the last job to write with but it went thick like glue and I cant use it. Red ink is fit enough I hope ha. ha. The next job I do I shall clip the ladys ears off and send to the police officers just for jolly wouldnt you. Keep this letter back till I do a bit more work then give it out straight. My knife's so nice and sharp I want to get to work right away if I get a chance. Good luck.

Yours truly

Jack the Ripper

Dont mind me giving the trade name

wasnt good enough to post this before I got all the red ink off my hands curse it No luck yet. They say I'm a doctor now. ha ha

LONDON E.C. SP 27 88

The Boss.
Central News Office
London City.

POST CARD
THE ADDRESS ONLY TO BE WRITTEN ON THIS SIDE

OC 1 88

Central News Office
London City E.C

I wasnt codding dear old Boss when I gave you the tip. you'll hear about saucy Jacky's work tomorrow double event this time number one squealed a bit couldnt finish straight off. had not time to get ears for police thanks for keeping last letter back till I got to work again.
Jack the Ripper

Any person recognising the handwriting is requested to communicate with the nearest Police Station.

Metropolitan Police Office,
3rd October, 1888.

Printed by M'Corquodale & Co. Limited, "The Armoury," Southwark.

Correspondence from a reader published in *The Times* of Thursday 4 October provides another example of how the letter and postcard had fired the public imagination:

TO THE EDITOR OF THE TIMES.

Sir, – Another remarkable letter has been written by some bad fellow who signs himself "Jack the Ripper." The letter is said to be smeared with blood, and there is on it the print in blood of the corrugated surface of a thumb. This may be that of a man or a woman.

It is inconceivable that a woman has written or smeared such a letter, and therefore it may be accepted as a fact that the impression in blood is that of a man's thumb.

The surface of a thumb so printed is as clearly indicated as are the printed letters from any kind of type. Thus there is a possibility of identifying the blood print on the letter with the thumb that made it, because the surface markings on no two thumbs are alike, and this a low power used in a microscope could reveal.

I would suggest – (1) That it be proved if it is human blood, though this may not be material; (2) that the thumbs of every suspected man be compared by an expert with the blood-print of a thumb on the letter; (3) that it be ascertained whether the print of a thumb is that of a man who works hard and has rough, coarse hands, or whether that of one whose hands have not been roughened by labour; (4) whether the thumb was large or small; (5) whether the thumb print shows signs of any shakiness or tremor in the doing of it.

All this the microscope could reveal. The print of a thumb would give us good evidence as that of a boot or shoe.

I am, yours, &c.,

Plymouth.

FRED. W. P. JAGO.

'Jack the Ripper' prototype? The earlier fictional villain 'Spring Heeled Jack' featured in the 'penny dreadfuls' of the first half of the nineteenth century and his influence was immediately recognised by the builders of the 'Ripper'legend.

In light of today's knowledge these are, of course, eminently sensible suggestions by Mr Jago. However, in 1888 there were definite problems with pursuing this idea. The science of fingerprinting was in its embryonic stages, and it would not be until after the turn of the century that the first conviction would be secured by such a method. Indeed, in 1888 the police did not conduct fingerprinting at all. The smear and partial print on the postcard (not a letter as Jago says) were probably not from the killer anyway.

The name 'Jack the Ripper' was brilliant in both its simplicity and conception. 'Jack' was a common enough name and had existing criminal connotations, not least as a result of the exploits of the notorious 'Spring Heeled Jack', a popular early Victorian figure with vague real-life origins who had become endowed with supernatural powers and was the villain in many penny dreadfuls. 'Spring Heeled Jack' was a frightening attacker of women and his identity was unknown. The parallels were obvious. In addition, the Whitechapel murderer's method of mutilating his victims' bodies had often been described as 'ripping' and so the factors behind the invention of the chilling name are fairly clear. The impact and sensation of the name has endured strongly into the twenty-first century, and is as familiar today as it was in 1888.

On Friday 5 October Thomas J. Bulling of the Central News Agency wrote to Chief Constable Williamson as follows:

> Dear Mr Williamson
>
> At 5 minutes to 9 oclock tonight we received the following letter the envelope of which I enclose by which you will see it is in the same handwriting as the previous communications
>
> "5 Oct 1888
>
> Dear Friend
>
> In the name of God hear me I swear I did not kill the female whose body was found at Whitehall . If she was an honest woman I will hunt down and destroy her murderer . If she ['was an honest woman' deleted] was a whore God will bless the hand that slew her , for the women of of [*sic*] Moab and Midian* shall die and their blood shall mingle with the dust . I never harm any others or the Divine power that protects and helps me in my grand work would quit for ever . Do as I do and the light of glory shall shine upon you. I must get to work tomorrow treble event this time yes yes three must be ripped . will send you a bit of face by post I promise this dear old Boss . The police now reckon my work a practical joke well well Jacky's a very practical joker ha ha ha Keep this back till three are wiped out and you can show the cold meat
>
> Yours truly
> Jack the Ripper"
>
> Yours truly
> T. J.Bulling

* Moab was the biblical land situated east of the Dead Sea. The Moabites were severely punished for their treatment of the Israelites. An idolatrous nation, they were made the subject of several prophecies. Midian, was a desert country lying around the eastern branch of the Red Sea. When the Israelites were encamped in the plains of Moab, the Midianites were invited by the Moabites to procure a curse on the children of Israel. For their conduct towards the Israelites they were completely subdued and brutally punished.

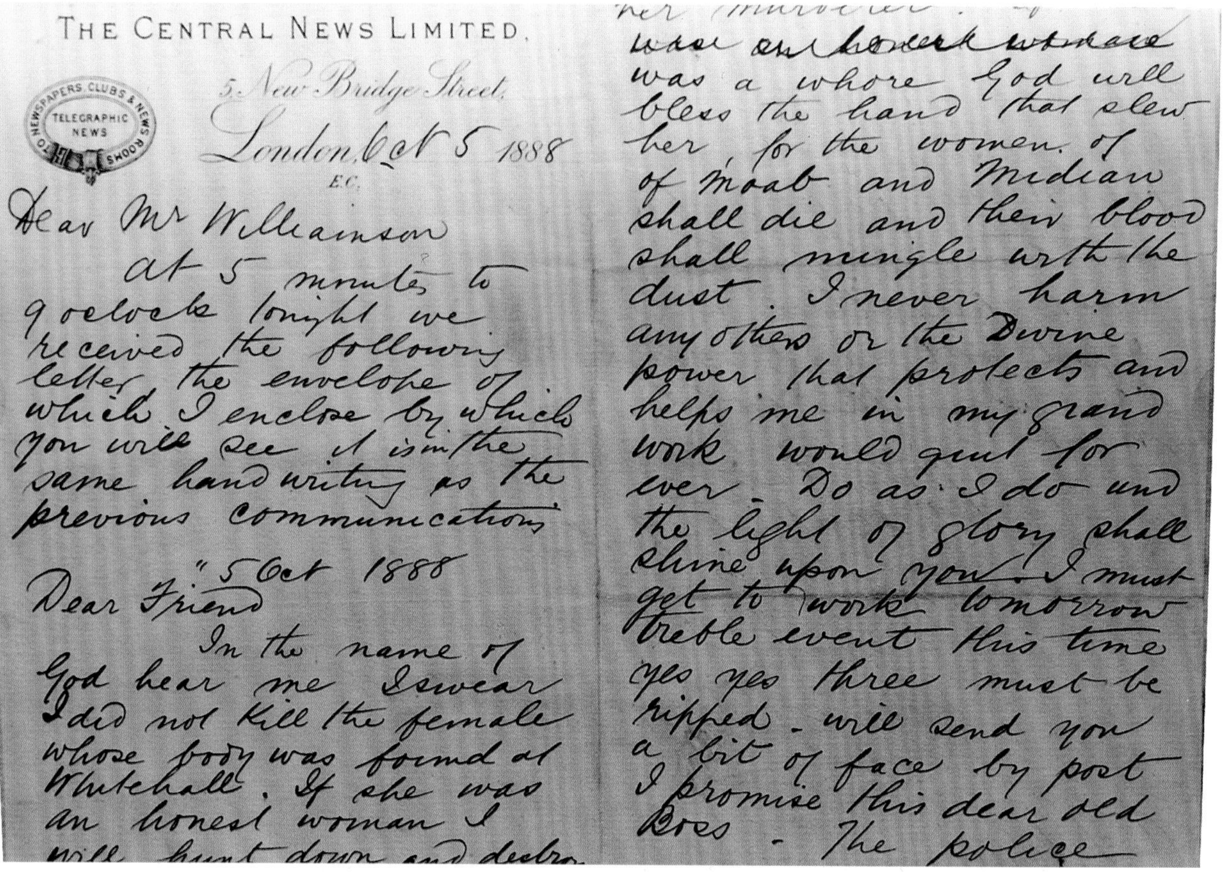

THE CENTRAL NEWS LIMITED,
TO NEWSPAPERS, CLUBS & NEWS ROOMS
TELEGRAPHIC NEWS
5 New Bridge Street,
London, Oct 5 1888
E.C.

Dear Mr Williamson
At 5 minutes to 9 oclock tonight we received the following letter the envelope of which I enclose by which you will see it is in the same handwriting as the previous communications

"5 Oct 1888
Dear Friend
In the name of God hear me I swear I did not kill the female whose body was found at Whitehall. If she was an honest woman I will hunt down and destroy her murderer. If she was ~~an honest woman~~ was a whore God will bless the hand that slew her, for the women of Moab and Midian shall die and their blood shall mingle with the dust. I never harm any others or the Divine power that protects and helps me in my grand work would quit for ever. Do as I do and the light of glory shall shine upon you. I must get to work tomorrow treble event this time yes yes three must be ripped. will send you a bit of face by post I promise this dear old Boss. The police

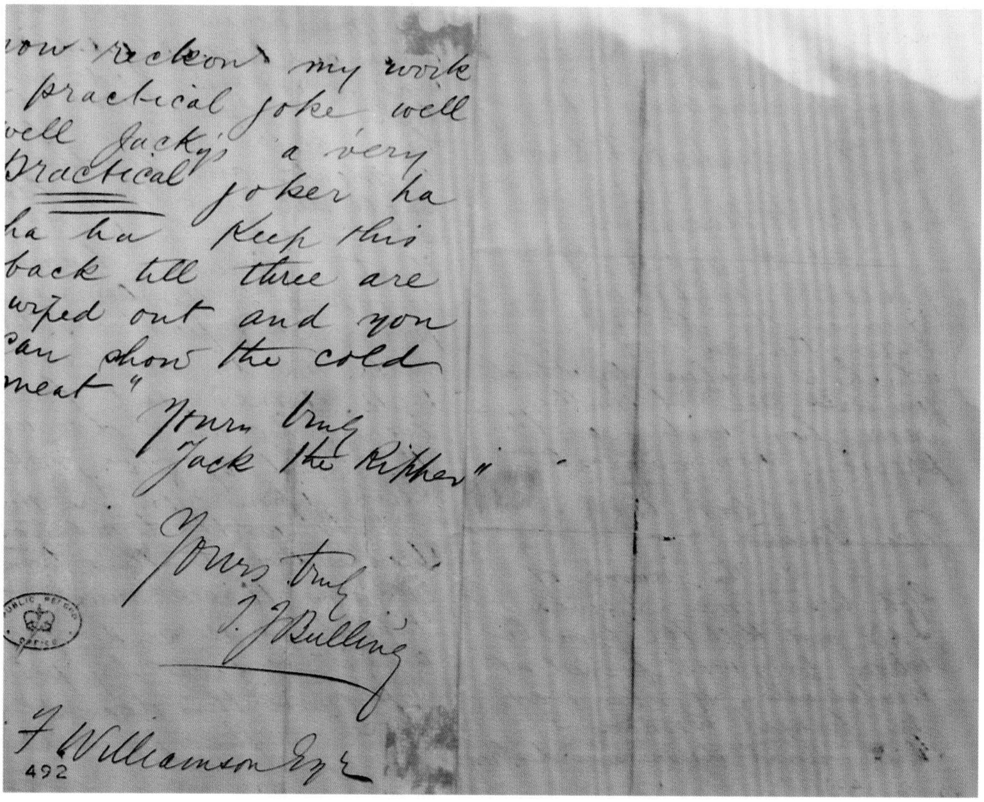

now reckon my work a practical joke well well Jacky's a very practical joker ha ha ha Keep this back till three are wiped out and you can show the cold meat"

Yours truly
"Jack the Ripper"

Yours truly
T. J. Bulling

J. F. Williamson Esq
492

Letter sent from Tom Bulling of the Central News Agency on 5 October to Scotland Yard giving details of another 'Jack the Ripper' letter received.

It seems rather odd that Bulling chose to transcribe this letter instead of sending it and this is possibly very significant in view of the police allegations made regarding the origins of the letters. We see clear echoes of the previous communications and the evident implication that the alleged killer has singled out prostitutes for his attention. There is the denial of culpability for the murder of the woman whose torso had been found in the basement of the Norman Shaw building, New Scotland Yard, which was then under construction on the Thames Embankment. The new idea of a possible motive of religious mania is indicated, together with a good working knowledge of the Old Testament. Then there are the obvious 'echoes' from the previous letter and postcard: 'I must get to work . . .', 'treble event', 'will send you a bit of face', 'dear old Boss', 'The police now reckon . . .', 'ha ha ha', 'Keep this back till three are wiped out . . .' and, of course, 'Yours truly, Jack the Ripper'.

This third 'Dear Boss' communication did not receive the publicity accorded the previous two, and the indications are that the police requested that the Central News Agency did not release the details of it. However, a report in the *Star* of Monday 8 October reveals that it did not go entirely without notice in the popular press:

> Revival of a Discredited Rumor.
>
> The Central News Agency, which first gave publicity to the original 'Jack the Ripper' letter and postcard now resuscitates the rumor, which has already been dismissed as false, that on a wall, within a few yards of the spot where the blood-stained part of an apron was found, were written the words, 'The Jews shall not be blamed for nothing' [*sic*]. The Agency adds that those who saw this writing recognised the same hand in the letter and postcard. The Agency declares that a third communication has been received, which it is deemed prudent to withhold for the present.

This statement by the Central News appears to be all that the police wished the agency to say about the third 'Dear Boss' communication. The *Pall Mall Gazette* of the same date made similar comment to the *Star* but expanded the information somewhat:

> The Central News Agency says: – "A startling fact has just come to light. After killing Katherine [*sic*] Eddowes in Mitre-square, the murderer, it is now known walked to Goulston-street, where he threw away the piece of the deceased, woman's apron upon which he had wiped his hands and knife. Within a few feet of this spot he had written upon the wall, "The Jews shall not be blamed for nothing." Most unfortunately one of the police officers gave orders for this writing to be immediately sponged out, probably with a view of stifling the morbid curiosity which it would certainly have aroused. But in so-doing a very important link was destroyed, for had the writing been photographed a certain clue would have been in the hands of the authorities. The witnesses who saw the writing, however, state that it was similar in character to the letters sent to the Central News and signed 'Jack the Ripper,' and though it would have been far better to have clearly demonstrated this by photography, there is now every reason to believe that the writer of the letter and postcard sent to the Central News (facsimiles of which are now to be seen outside every police station) is the actual murderer. The police, consequently, are very anxious that any citizen who can identify the handwriting should without delay communicate with the authorities.

> Another communication has been received from the writer of the original 'Jack the Ripper' letter, which, acting upon official advice, it has been deemed prudent to withhold for the present. It may be stated, however, that although the miscreant avows his intention of committing further crimes shortly it is only against prostitutes that his threats are directed, his desire being to respect and protect honest women."

Why had Bulling sent only the envelope in which the third letter had been received and why had he written out the alleged letter received in full, yet retained the original? This communication, if correctly attributed to the same source as the others, certainly tends to detract from the apparent veracity of its predecessors. It may also be significant that the official Home Office file HO 144/221/A49301C (ff. 50–1) contains the full extracts from the *Daily Telegraph* of 4 October about the 'Jack the Ripper' 'Dear Boss' letter and 'saucy Jacky' postcard. The material includes the *Telegraph*'s assessment of those missives:

> As we have already announced, the Central News Agency received the above letter on Thursday morning last, and it therefore must have been posted on the Wednesday. The writer uses this threat: "The next job I do I shall clip the lady's ears off, and send to the police-officers." The Central News did not attach importance to this document, and it was regarded in the light of a practical joke, perpetrated for idle amusement; but, curiously enough, the Mitre-square victim did have a portion of the ear cut off. This particular fact escaped observation until it was published in the papers of Monday, and it was, therefore, known to a very few persons on the Sunday. On Monday morning, by the first post, the Central News received a post-card in the same handwriting, and much blood-besmeared. The writer observes "double event this time. Number One squealed a bit; couldn't finish straight off. Had not time to get ears for the police." The letter and the post-card were handed to the Scotland-yard authorities, and, although they do not profess to attach any great importance to them, still they thought it well to have *facsimiles* prepared, and to send them to the Press, in the possibility that the handwriting may be recognised by some one. Some part of the post-card is to a great extent undecipherable, but the reproductions above given, with the opening and concluding sentences of the letter, will give an absolutely correct idea of the whole. The post-card appears to have been scribbled hastily, and the hand is not so firm as that of the letter, but there is very little doubt that both are from the same pen. The writer is probably an American or an Englishman, who has mixed with our cousins on the other side of the Atlantic. "Bos," [*sic*] "Fix me," "Shan't quit," and "Right away" are American forms of expression.

There can be absolutely no doubt that the Central News Agency was wringing every last drop of sensation from the communications and selling good copy as a result. These were lucrative and sensational times for the company and many newspapers were buying the stories. It is crucial to the understanding of the phenomenon of the 'Jack the Ripper' letters that we examine the press development of the coverage of the murders. The newspapers were the vital forum that fuelled the hoaxers and this issue will be explored in later chapters. Certainly during the first week of October 1888 the unknown killer's name was firmly established for all time as 'Jack the Ripper'.

FACSIMILES OF "JACK THE RIPPER'S" LETTER AND POST CARD.

25 Sept. 1888

Dear: Boss

I keep on hearing the police have caught me but they wont fix me just yet I have laughed when they look so clever and talk about being on the right track That joke about Leather Apron gave me real fits------(PART OF LETTER OMITTED)----------

Keep this letter back till I do a bit more work then give it out straight My knife's so nice and sharp I want to get to work right away if I get a chance Good luck

Yours truly
Jack the Ripper

Dont mind me giving the trade name

I was not codding dear old Boss when I gave you the tip you'll hear about saucy Jacky's work tomorrow double event this time number one squealed a bit couldnt finish straight off. had not time to get ears for police thanks for keeping last letter back till I got to work again.
Jack the Ripper

The following is the full text of the letter and post-card. The letter, which had the E.C. post-mark and was directed in red ink, ran:

Sept. 25.

Dear Boss—I keep on hearing the police have caught me, but they won't fix me just yet. I have laughed when they look so clever and talk about being on the *right* track. That joke about Leather Apron gave me real fits. I am down on whores, and I shan't quit ripping them till I do get buckled. Grand work, the last job was. I gave the lady no time to squeal. How can they catch me now? I love my work, and want to start again. You will soon hear of me with my funny little games. I saved some of the proper red stuff in a ginger-beer bottle over the last job, to write with, but it went thick like glue, and I can't use it. Red ink is fit enough, I hope. Ha! ha! The next job I do I shall clip the lady's ears off, and send to the police-officers, just for jolly, wouldn't you? Keep this letter back till I do a bit more work, then give it out straight. My knife's so nice and sharp, I want to get to work right away if I get a chance. Good luck.—Yours truly, JACK THE RIPPER.—Don't mind me giving the trade name.—Wasn't good enough to post this before I got all the red ink off my hands; curse it. No luck yet. They say I'm a doctor now. Ha! ha!"

The post-card bearing the stamp "London, E., Oct. 1," was received on Monday morning. It was as follows: "I was not codding, dear old Boss, when I gave you the tip. You'll hear about Saucy Jacky's work to-morrow. Double event this time. Number One squealed a bit; couldn't finish straight off. Had not time to get ears for police. Thanks for keeping last letter back till I got to work again.—JACK THE RIPPER."

The Coror
Witness:
man myself,
The Coron
not be placed
drink.
Witness:
this city the
Inspector
to the police
Witness:
A Juror:
to the decea
colm, who s
very like the
Did the de
Or by a po
used to cour
she was mar
courted her
having a chi
mother of ni
with her hus
mainder wer
Swedish Ch
with the hus
the truth wh
stood that th
on the Princ
Mr. Edwa
and am assis
day morning
received a c
Dr. Blackwe
panied the c
adjoining N
lying on her
The Coro
There was a
And polic
Was any
Was there
What ligh
the policem
found an in
Was bloo
stopped ble
except the l
Did you
when I cam
Did you
cisely as I f
to the gutt
blood near t
notice at th
with blood.
The right a
Can you
stream of b
Did you l
me, but Dr
and the tim
four minute
three or fo
The outer
Thomas
and work f
after midni
Brady-stree
into White
on the righ
crossed ove
saw a knife
What is
to the fron
step.
The prod
its discovery
a knife such
being flat at
knife would
something
an inch bro
length, and
Witness
round the h
been first f
policeman c
the knife, w
Did the
Leman-stre
Were the
few. I do
Brady-stree
could easily
Did you
where the
Constable
morning at
point duty
when I saw
something
towards hi
"Policema
saw a long-
the knife,
Was it w
blood-stain
with a stri
and he said
something
and he repl
dens." I t
to the poli
chief are th
manner nat
run cold, a
adays." I
before. I
knife was
near the do
The knife
handkerchi
Mr. Geo
square, an
was called
Leman-stre
street, to a
house. I f
tendent W
been seen l
before me.
being turn

Daily Telegraph report of 4 October 1888 reproducing the 'Dear Boss' letter and the 'saucy Jacky' postcard.

The police for their part puzzled over the Goulston Street wall writing and this was reflected in a lengthy report dated 6 November from Chief Inspector Swanson which was forwarded to the Home Office:

> 2.20 a.m. P.C. 254A Long (the P.C. was drafted from A. Division temporarily to assist "H." Division) stated that at the hour mentioned he visited Goldston [*sic*] Street Buildings, and there was nothing there at that time, but at, 2.55 a.m. he found in the bottom of a common stairs leading to No. 108 to 119, Goldston Street Buildings a piece of a bloodstained apron, and above it written in chalk, the words, "The Juwes are the men who will not be blamed for nothing." which he reported, and the City Police were subsequently acquainted at the earliest moment, when it was found that beyond doubt the piece of apron found corresponded exactly with the part missing from the body of the murdered woman.
>
> [HO 144/221/A49301C ff. 184–94]

The underlined wording referred to in the last paragraph attracted a marginal note by the Home Office: 'Differently spelt'. Further on in his report, by way of explanation for the removal of the chalked message, Swanson wrote:

Chief Inspector Donald S. Swanson of Scotland Yard, who was in charge of the Whitechapel investigation. He examined and initialled many of the 'Jack the Ripper' letters.

> Upon the discovery of the blurred chalk writing on the wall, written, – although mis-spelled in the second word. – in an ordinary hand in the midst of a locality principally inhabited by Jews of all nationalities as well as English, and upon the wall of a common stairs leading to a number of tenements occupied almost exclusively by Jews, and the purport of the writing as shewn at page. 3. was to throw blame upon the Jews, the Commr. deemed it adviseable [*sic*] to have them rubbed out. Apart from this was the fact that during police enquiries into the Bucks Row and Hanbury Street murders a certain section of the Press cast a great amount of suspicion upon a Jew, named John Piser, alias, "Leather Apron." as having been the murderer whose movements at the dates and hours of those murders had been satisfactorily enquired into by Met. Police, clearing him of any connection, there was also the fact that on the same morning another murder had been committed in the immediate vicinity of a Socialist Club in Berner Street, frequented by Jews, – considerations which, weighed in the balance, with the evidence of chalk writing on the wall to bring home the guilt to any person, were deemed the weightier of the two. To those police officers who saw the chalk writing, the handwriting of the now notorious letters to a newspaper agency bears no resemblance at all.

This is interesting as it shows that the graffiti was in cursive handwriting, as opposed to block capital letters, and that a comparison was made with the handwriting in the 'Jack the Ripper' epistles.

George R. Sims followed the new and sensational developments of the case closely. Here, contrary to what he had earlier thought, was a story that would easily outstrip the Ratcliff Highway murders of December 1811. The Sunday 7 October issue of the *Referee* saw Sims seizing upon the fresh hysteria:

> JACK THE RIPPER is the hero of the hour. A gruesome wag, a grim practical joker, has succeeded in getting an enormous amount of fun out of a postcard which he sent to the Central News. The fun is all his own, and nobody shares in it, but he must be gloating demoniacally at the present moment at the state of perturbation in which he has flung the public mind. Grave journals have reproduced the sorry jest, and have attempted to seriously argue that the awful Whitechapel fiend is the idle and mischievous idiot who sends blood-stained postcards to the news agency. Of course the whole business is a farce. The postcard is an elaborately-prepared hoax. To imagine a man deliberately murdering and mutilating women, and then confessing the deed on a postcard, is to turn Mr. W. S. Gilbert loose upon the Whitechapel murders at once.
>
> * * *
>
> Everybody has a private theory of his own with regard to these crimes, and naturally I have mine. In all probability mine is as idiotic as the coroner's. But this is such an unpleasant subject – it is becoming such a dangerous subject – that I will spare the public my private views upon the matter, and try and get to something more cheerful as speedily as possible. Bloodshed always has an immense fascination for ordinary mortals. Murders and battles are the things to hurl the circulation of a newspaper sky high, and the Whitechapel lady-killer's essays in lightning surgery have become as a boon and a blessing to men of the Press, who were weary of concocting in their office letters on various subjects of domestic interest, and trying to make them look like genuine outside contributions.

I have said that this series of murders is a dangerous subject, and I honestly think so. The enormous publicity and the sensational turn given to these atrocities are bound to affect the public mind, and give ill-balanced brains an inclination towards bloodshed. There will be for some time an epidemic of savage butchery, and the unfortunate women who have furnished the lightning anatomist with his subjects will be especially liable to murderous attack. Jack the Ripper – now that Leather Apron has retired Jack is the hero of the situation – has already fired the imagination of a vast number of idiots and ruffians. Men with knives in their hands, threatening to 'rip' up a lady, are to be heard of all over the country already . . .

* * *

Not only has Ripperism been put extensively into practice, but vast numbers have yielded to its fascinations in theory. The newspapers, ever ready to take occasion by the hand and make the bounds of fooldom wider yet, have allowed Colney Hatch, Hanwell, and Earlswood to empty the vials of idiocy upon the head of the general reader. Every crackpot in the kingdom who has a whim, a fad, a monomania, a crotchet, or a bee in his bonnet is allowed to inflict it upon the public under the heading of "The East-end Horrors." It is impossible to read the puerile twaddle, the utterly inconsequent nonsense which is served up in a mixed heap for our breakfast every morning in the *D.T.* without feeling that England is indeed in danger . . .

* * *

. . . The Spring-Heeled Jack scare of the good old times had been suddenly revived. However, by Wednesday the scare had somewhat subsided, and the ladies of the East flocked out once more, under the protecting wing of husband, brother, and sweetheart . . .

So the letters, genuine or not, were problematical for the police. Not only did they fire the imagination of public and press alike; they also resulted in more paperwork and investigations for the already hard-pressed detectives. But did the police really believe they were genuine? They *had* issued the posters and sent copies of the 'Dear Boss' letter and postcard to dozens of police stations, but it would be dangerous to assume from this that the police took the missives' authenticity for granted. After all, there was a need to deal with the anonymous letter-writer. To eliminate him from the equation would only assist efforts to find the killer and set an example to others if he could be dealt with in a court of law. There are also examples to show that the police were following up all leads, trivial or not, in their hunt. The letters were an unwanted hindrance. An indication that the police actually believed them to be hoaxes may be found in the Commissioner's letters file, MEPO 1/48, which includes a copy of a letter from Sir Charles Warren to Godfrey Lushington, the Permanent Under Secretary of State at the Home Office:

10.10.88

Dear Mr Lushington

Thanks for memo of Mr Troup. We will look into the matter at once. It is rather a difficult matter. I do not know whether the P.O. can tell in what letter boxes the letter of Jack the ripper is posted.

At present I think the whole thing a hoax but of course we are bound to try & ascertain the writer in any case

If I cannot send you the style of writing on the wall tonight I will send it tomorrow morning.

truly yours
C.W.

The importance of this letter lies in the fact that it indicates that at the highest level the police believed the 'Jack the Ripper' correspondence to be a hoax but it remained incumbent upon them to ascertain the identity of the writer. The fact that the police issued the now famous poster showing the 'Jack the Ripper' letter and postcard cannot be taken to mean that they blindly accepted the documents' authenticity. As good as his word Warren sent a copy of the Goulston Street graffiti to the Home Office the following day:

Dear Mr Lushington , 11. Oct 88

I send you a copy of the writing on the wall at Goulston St. The idiom does not appear to me to be either English French or German but it might possibly be that of an Irishman speaking a foreign language. It seems to be the idiom of Spain or Italy. The spelling of Jews or Jewes is curious.

truly yours
CW.

The Juwes are
The men That
Will not
be Blamed
For nothing

[MEPO 1/48]

Truth of Thursday 11 October passed cryptic comment on the phenomenon of the 'Ripper's' postal communications:

On the doctrine of possibilities, it is long odds against the murderer having written the "Jack the Ripper" letters. He may have, and so may many thousands of others. But there is a coincidence in respect to these letters to which attention has not yet been drawn. The handwriting is remarkably like that of the forgeries which the *Times* published, and which they ascribed to Mr. Parnell and to Mr. Egan. I do not go so far as to suggest that the *Times* forger is the Whitechapel murderer, although this, of course is possible; but it may be that the forger takes pride in his work, and wishes to keep his hand in.

The wide-ranging effects of the correspondence and the publicity it received are shown in the following report which appeared in *The Times* of Tuesday 16 October:

Superintendent Farmer, of the River Tyne Police, has received information which, it is considered, may form a clue to the East-end murders. An Austrian seaman signed articles on

Scenes relating to the Chapman murder at 29 Hanbury Street as shown in the *Pictorial World*, September 1888.

> board a Faversham vessel in the Tyne on Saturday, and sailed for a French port. Afterwards it was found that his signature corresponded with the facsimile letters signed "Jack the Ripper," and that the description of the man also corresponded with that of the Whitechapel murderer circulated by the Metropolitan Police. A man, wearing a slouched hat, carrying a black leather bag, speaking with a slightly American accent, and presenting a travel-stained appearance was arrested at Limavady, near Londonderry, yesterday morning by Constable Walsh, on suspicion of being the man who committed the recent murders in the East-end of London. The arrest was made as a result of the police description of the man wanted. The prisoner refused to give his name or any information whatever about himself. A woman and child who were with him were also taken into custody.

'Jack the Ripper fever' was now at its height, the letter-writers were in the ascendant and the legend was rapidly developing. For the police the correspondence made things worse and hampered their inquiries; for the press it was a sensational boost and increased circulation.

— FIVE —

The 'Enterprising' London Journalists

VIEWED in the context of the great press build-up, the true 'Jack the Ripper' can be seen as a bogeyman created by a sensation-hungry media. Are there reasons for believing that this was the case? Over the years various hints were dropped by senior police officials to the effect that the original 'Jack the Ripper' correspondent was a journalist and that his identity was known. However, it would seem that this belief did not extend to evidential proof; if it had, there is little doubt that the culprit would have been prosecuted.

The first official to indicate that he actually knew the identity of the author of the original 'Jack the Ripper' correspondence was Sir Robert Anderson who was the Assistant Commissioner, CID, at the time of the murders. Anderson retired in 1901 and in early 1910 a serialisation of his reminiscences was published. In *Blackwood's Magazine*, Part VI, March 1910, he stated:

> The subject will come up again, and I will only add here that the 'Jack-the-Ripper' letter which is preserved in the Police Museum at New Scotland Yard is the creation of an enterprising London journalist.

To this is added a footnote which, more than anything else, seems to indicate that the name of the journalist was a theory rather than a proven fact, for if evidence sufficient to prove his identity existed, there would have been no fear of libel:

> Having regard to the interest attaching to this case, I should almost be tempted to disclose the identity of the murderer and of the pressman who wrote the letter above referred to, provided that the publishers would accept all responsibility in view of a possible libel action.

Dr (later Sir) Robert Anderson, Assistant Commissioner (Crime) at Scotland Yard. He claimed to know the identity of the 'enterprising London journalist' who created the 'Dear Boss' letter.

Later that year the reminiscences were published in book form as *The Lighter Side of My Official Life* (Hodder & Stoughton) and the journalist was again mentioned:

> So I will only add here that the "Jack-the-Ripper" letter which is preserved in the Police Museum at New Scotland Yard is the creation of an enterprising London journalist . . .
>
> Having regard to the interest attaching to this case, I am almost tempted to disclose the identity of the murderer and of the pressman who wrote the letter above referred to. But no benefit would result from such a course and the traditions of my old department would suffer . . .

At the time of Anderson's much-publicised theorising, articles about the identity of the 'Ripper' correspondent appeared in many of the newspapers. The following letter was printed in the *East London Observer* of 16 April 1910:

Echoes of the Whitechapel Murders.

To the Editor of the *East London Observer*.

SIR, – In your last issue you amusingly allude to the fact that during the awful period of the Whitechapel murders that the police not only fooled themselves, but were fooled by the reporters. This is quite true, and Sir Robert Anderson, who is just now so much before the public eye, may like to know that the postcards, apparently written with blood, received by the H Division of Police, were the work of an enterprising local penny-a-liner, who used his fore-knowledge to "line" the reports of the receipt of these strange missives. At the time the daily papers seized with avidity any "murder" news, and as the postcards were received by the police the truth of the reports could not be denied. It never occurred to the intelligent C.I.D. that they could have traced the authorship of both postcards and reports. They know better now. The same journalistic operator was probably responsible for the blood-smeared jacket found in the garden of a house in the Mile End-road, once rented by a proprietor of your paper, and now in the possession of the Mile End Guardians as a scattered home. Quite a respectable sum of money was made by the "lining" to the then daily and evening papers of this ghastly "find."

Yours truly,
A WIDE-AWAKE EAST-ENDER.
11th April, 1910.

On 31 May 1913 Sir Melville Macnaghten, Assistant Commissioner, CID, retired from the Metropolitan Police. He had joined the force in June 1889 as Assistant Chief

Sir Melville Macnaghten, Chief Constable and later Assistant Commissioner, believed he could 'discern the stained forefinger of the journalist' in the 'Dear Boss' letter.

Constable, second-in-command to Anderson on the CID (shortly afterwards he became Chief Constable). He had always taken a great interest in the Whitechapel murders and in an interview for the *Daily Mail* of Monday 2 June he stated:

> I have destroyed all my documents and there is now no record of the secret information which came into my possession at one time or another. To-day for the first time since I joined the force on May 24, 1889, I know what it is to be free from official cares, and I shall certainly not write any reminiscences.

Fortunately for us Macnaghten did write his reminiscences and *Days of My Years* was published by Edward Arnold in 1914. In this book Macnaghten recalled the fraught days of the hunt for 'Jack the Ripper'. Chapter IV is entitled 'Laying the Ghost of Jack the Ripper'. Macnaghten begins it with a quotation from a 'Jack the Ripper' communication, and thus highlights the importance of the letters to the case:

> "I'm not a butcher, I'm not a Yid,
> Nor yet a foreign skipper,
> But I'm your own light-hearted friend,
> Yours truly, Jack the Ripper."
>
> ANONYMOUS.

> THE above queer verse was one of the first documents which I perused at Scotland Yard, for at that time the police post-bag bulged large with hundreds of anonymous communications on the subject of the East End tragedies . . .

Macnaghten went on to discuss the murders and the possible identity of the killer (he always favoured the 'drowned doctor in the Thames' theory, i.e. M.J. Druitt, a barrister and teacher, found floating in the Thames on 31 December 1888). He then returned to the subject of the letters and 'Jack the Ripper'. On page 58 of *Days of My Years* he said:

> On 27th September a letter was received at a well-known News Agency, addressed to the "Boss." It was written in red ink, and purported to give the details of the murders which had been committed. It was signed, "Jack the Ripper." This document was sent to Scotland Yard, and (in my opinion most unwisely) was reproduced, and copies of same affixed to various police stations, thus giving it an official imprimatur. In this ghastly production I have always thought I could discern the stained forefinger of the journalist – indeed, a year later [i.e. September 1889], I had shrewd suspicions as to the actual author! But whoever did pen the gruesome stuff, it is certain to my mind that it was not the mad miscreant who had committed the murders. The name "Jack the Ripper," however, had got abroad in the land and had "caught on"; it riveted the attention of the classes as well as the masses.

Although Macnaghten did not state that he *knew* the identity of the originator of the famous letter, as Anderson had done, he did confirm the police belief that it was a journalist and that they had an idea of just which one.

On 23 September 1913 the retired head of Scotland Yard's Special Branch (also known as the Secret Department), ex-Detective Chief Inspector John George Littlechild, wrote a personal letter to George R. Sims. Littlechild had been head of the Special Branch from 1883 to 1893 when he retired. He was therefore at the headquarters of the Metropolitan Police throughout the period of the murders, and was privy to many secrets. The now famous 'Littlechild letter' has been accorded much importance since its discovery in 1993 because it revealed the contemporary and previously unknown suspect Dr Francis Tumblety. However, of crucial importance to Ripper studies were Littlechild's statements regarding the origins of the name 'Jack the Ripper'. He wrote: 'With regard to the term "Jack the Ripper" it was generally believed at the Yard that Tom Bullen [*sic* – Bulling] of the Central News was . . .

the originator but it is probable Moore, who was his chief, was the inventor. It was a smart piece of journalistic work. No journalist of my time got such privileges from Scotland Yard as Bullen. Mr James Munro when Assistant Commissioner, and afterwards Commissioner, relied on his integrity. Poor Bullen occasionally took too much to drink, and I fail to see how he could help it knocking about so many hours and seeking favours from so many people to procure copy. One night when Bullen "had taken a few too many" he got early information of the death of Prince Bismarck and instead of going to the office to report it sent a laconic telegram "Bloody Bismarck is dead" On this I believe Mr Charles Moore fired him out.

It seems probable that Bulling's 'chief', the Moore referred to by Littlechild, was, in fact, the Manager John Moore. This despite the fact that Littlechild refers later in the paragraph to a Charles Moore, who may or may not be the same person. With Littlechild's intimate knowledge of Scotland Yard and its senior officers we at last know the identity of the journalist(s) hinted at by the two top CID officials, Anderson and Macnaghten. Whether or not they were right we may never know for certain. However, we do have good examples of Bulling's handwriting to compare with the original 'Jack the Ripper' correspondence. Another point of interest is the fact that Bulling and Moore, together, visited the Crime Museum ('Black Museum') at New Scotland Yard. Their signatures may still be seen in the visitors' book against the date 26 July 1892. At that time the 'Dear Boss' letter, or a facsimile, was on display.

There are similarities between Bulling's handwriting and that of the 'Dear Boss' letter. If he did write it he would, of course, have had to disguise his normal hand to some degree, such as writing carefully in a deliberate script, instead of his normal flowing style. Indeed, this letter is written in a careful script. And, even if Bulling did not actually produce it himself, might other staff in the office, or maybe Moore, have been willing to put the pen to paper? John Moore had one very large room on the ground floor of the offices at 5 New Bridge Street, and while occupying his editorial chair he could see at a glance all his 'sub' reporters, counting-house and secretarial staffs at work. As the company grew the volume of work necessitated the removal of the 'business' members of the staff to other rooms in the building. John Moore, manager for many years, later became a chairman of the company. He retired in 1907 and took up farming and pig breeding, having originally come from West of England yeoman stock.

R. Thurston Hopkins (1884–1958) is perhaps best known as one of Britain's leading ghost hunters and ghost book authors. He is also remembered for many topographical books. In the early 1900s he worked in London as a journalist; he was with the *Evening News* before the First World War and had many contacts in the journalistic world. It is interesting to note that Hopkins describes a journalist very similar to the picture of Bulling drawn by Littlechild in his writings on 'Jack the Ripper'. Greatly interested in crime and criminals, Hopkins wrote an excellent study, *Life and Death at the Old Bailey*, which was published by Herbert Jenkins in 1935. He devoted the whole of Chapter VIII of the book to the Ripper story and called it 'Shadowing the Shadow of a Murderer' (*Life and Death at the Old Bailey*, pp. 201–20). In it he turned to the vexed question of the 'Jack the Ripper' correspondence:

> But first of all, who christened the phantom killer with the terrible sobriquet of Jack the Ripper? That is a small mystery in itself. Possibly Scotland Yard gave the name to the press and public. At that time the police post-bag bulged large with hundreds of anonymous letters from all kinds of cranks and half-witted persons, who sought to criticise or hoax the officers engaged in following up the murders. The queer verse ["I'm not a butcher, I'm not a Yid, . . ."] at the head of this chapter was one of the many queer documents received by the police. But it was in a letter, received by a well-known News Agency and forwarded to the Yard, that the name first appeared. The Criminal Investigation Department looked upon this letter as a "clue" and possibly a message from the actual murderer. It was written in red ink, and purported to give the details of the murders which had been committed. It was signed "Jack the Ripper." The letter was reproduced, and copies of it were fixed on the notice boards of every police station in the country, in the hope that someone would recognise the handwriting. The name, thus broadcast, "caught on" at once.
>
> It was perhaps a fortunate thing that the handwriting of this famous letter was not identified, for it would have led to the arrest of a harmless Fleet Street journalist. This poor fellow had a breakdown and became a whimsical figure in Fleet Street, only befriended by the staffs of newspapers and printing works. He would creep about the dark courts waving his hands furiously in the air, would utter stentorian "Ha, ha, ha's," and then, meeting some pal, would button-hole him and pour into his ear all the "inner story" of the East End murders. Many old Fleet Streeters had very shrewd suspicions that this irresponsible fellow wrote the famous Jack the Ripper letter, and even Sir Melville L. Macnaghten, Chief of the Criminal Investigation Department, had his eye on him . . .

Early morning despatch of the newspapers in London.

The similarities between Littlechild's description of Bulling and that given by Hopkins (i.e. the breakdown, a Fleet Street journalist) are strong and almost certainly relate to the same man. Thomas John Bulling died of natural causes in 1934 aged eighty-seven years, at St Thomas's Hospital, Lambeth. Whatever the facts may have been, there is no doubt that Tom Bulling was a key player in the story of 'Jack the Ripper'.

Less well documented is a journalist known only as Best. He appears in a third-hand story told in a journalistic fashion in a publication of August 1966. The account appeared in *Crime and Detection* and was inspired by an article published by Professor Francis E. Camps in the *London Hospital Gazette* of April 1966. In 'More on Jack the Ripper' Camps had included a piece on the infamous letters. The article in *Crime and Detection* said:

> Even more interesting is the addition of *The Letters of Jack the Ripper*, about which many surmises have been offered. A personal experience may be the answer.
>
> In 1931, working on an outline for a life of William Palmer, the Rugeley poisoner, a friend mentioned an ex-jockey who was living not far from my home (then, Henley-on-Thames). Through several introductions, to reach this character, I finally arrived at a man named Best, an ex-journalist. He was spry and very clear-minded, though well past 70. He knew the jockey, and arranged a meeting at the house of a friend in a small place called Culham, on the Oxon–Berks border.

> I met the ex-jockey, a vigorous old gentleman of, he claimed, 95. Known as Jack, or John, Faulkener, he had ridden a number of races for William Palmer, and his fund of reminiscences was large.
>
> Returning homewards with me, Best discussed murders, the Whitechapel murders in particular. With much amplifying detail he talked of his days as a penny-a-liner on the *Star* newspaper. As a freelance he had covered the Whitechapel murders from the discovery of the woman, Tabram. He claimed that he, and a provincial colleague, were responsible for all the 'Ripper' letters, to 'keep the business alive . . . in those days it was far easier to get details, and facts from the police, than today.' Best did not mind me having these facts so many years later, and said a close reading of the *Star* of the time might be informative, and that an experienced graphologist with an open mind would be able to find in the original letters 'numerous earmarks' of an experienced journalist at work; the pen used was called a 'Waverley Nib' and was deliberately battered to achieve an impression of semi-literacy and 'National School' training! Best scoffed at the notion that the 'Ripper' had written a single word about his crimes.
>
> Some years before this the late Edgar Wallace mentioned that in his reporting days the better informed Fleet Street men were satisfied that a newspaperman was 'behind' the letters.

One of the 'better informed Fleet Street men' may well have been George R. Sims who wrote in the *Referee* of 7 October 1888, just a few days after the letter and postcard had been received at the Central News:

> The fact that the self-postcard-proclaimed assassin sent his imitation blood-besmeared communication to the Central News people opens up a wide field for theory. How many among you, my dear readers, would have hit upon the idea of "the Central News" as a receptacle for your confidence? You might have sent your joke to the *Telegraph*, the *Times*, any morning or any evening paper, but I will lay long odds that it would never have occurred to you to communicate with a Press agency. Curious, is it not, that this maniac makes his communication to an agency which serves the entire Press? It is an idea which might occur to a Press man perhaps; and even then it would probably only occur to someone connected with the editorial department of a newspaper, someone who knew what the Central News was, and the place it filled in the business of news supply. This proceeding on Jack's part betrays an inner knowledge of the newspaper world which is certainly surprising. Everything therefore points to the fact that the jokist is professionally connected with the Press. And if he is telling the truth and not fooling us, then we are brought face to face with the fact that the Whitechapel murders have been committed by a practical journalist – perhaps by a real live editor! Which is absurd, and at that I think I will leave it.

It is here that Sims strikes at the heart of the mystery of 'Jack the letter-writer', the true begetter of 'Jack the Ripper'. He does so with extraordinary prescience, born of his deep knowledge of the working press and the mentality of the newspaperman.

Until the more plausible candidacy of Bulling emerged, the Best story was the only known indication of any named author of the original letters. Yet it lacks any first-hand

Cartoon of a press man from *Punch*.

credibility and contains telling errors. First, Best is claimed to have stated that '. . . he and a provincial colleague, were responsible for *all* the 'Ripper' letters . . .', a claim that is patently incorrect. He further claimed that '. . . the pen used was called a "Waverley Nib" and was deliberately battered to achieve an impression of semi-literacy and "National School" training!' Again this rings false as the original 'Dear Boss' letter and the 'saucy Jacky' postcard are notable for the neatness of the handwriting and the impeccable spelling. If there is any truth in this journalist's tale it would seem to be that Best and his 'provincial colleague' might have written some 'Jack the Ripper' letters, but most certainly not the original correspondence carrying that infamous name, nor, indeed, many of the other 'Jack the Ripper' letters that are preserved in the official files. Here, again, we find another of the minor mysteries that surround and befog this case. This, of course, is what makes it all the more appealing. But many of these minor mysteries are capable of solution. Each one solved will make the true facts more apparent and help clear the way to a better understanding, if not a solution, of the greater mystery.

— SIX —

A Letter 'From hell'

OCTOBER 1888 witnessed great activity among the letter-writers and the 'Jack the Ripper' hoaxers. Among the reasons for this was the great attention afforded by the press to the 'double event' of 30 September 1888, the wide publicity given to the initial 'Jack the Ripper' correspondence, the graffiti found in Goulston Street, and the general excitement generated with the public. There was no murder committed in the district during October, but the press coverage continued to gather momentum. There were two inquests, many suspects arrested, police house-to-house inquiries, many letters and much else for the eager press to report.

The idea of sending a body part of a victim to the police had already been suggested in the original 'Dear Boss' letter. This had not gone unnoticed as was soon evidenced in a letter received at Scotland Yard on 6 October. Writing in black ink the correspondent jeered:

> Dear Sir
> I don't think I do enough murders so shall not only do them in Whitechapel but in Brixton, Battersea & Clapham. If I can't get enough women to do I shall cut up men, boys & girls, just to keep my hand in practice. Ha! ha! You will never find me in Whitechapel. By the discription in the papers 5ft 7inches is all wrong. Ha! Ha. I expect to rip up a woman or to [*sic*] on the Common at Clapham Junction one day turn
> [second page] next week. Ha.ha.ha. I will send you the heart by parcels post.
> Ha! Ha!
> By, By,
> Dear Sir
> Yours when Caught
> The Whore Killer

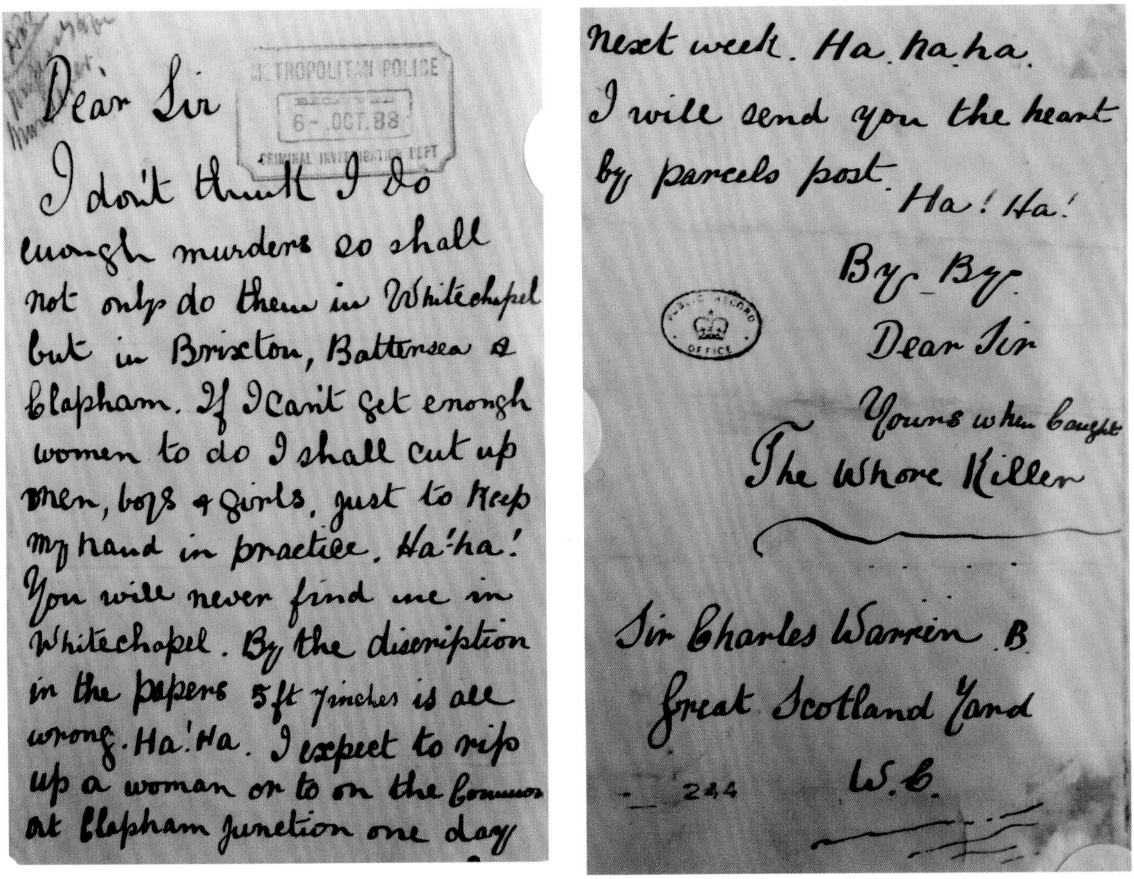
METROPOLITAN POLICE
RECEIVED
6 - OCT. 88
CRIMINAL INVESTIGATION DEPT

Dear Sir

I don't think I do enough murders so shall not only do them in Whitechapel but in Brixton, Battersea & Clapham. If I can't get enough women to do I shall cut up men, boys & girls, just to keep my hand in practice. Ha-ha! You will never find me in Whitechapel. By the discription in the papers 5ft 7inches is all wrong. Ha! Ha. I expect to rip up a woman or to on the Commons at Clapham Junction one day next week. Ha. ha ha. I will send you the heart by parcels post. Ha! Ha!

By-By.
Dear Sir
Yours when caught
The Whore Killer

PUBLIC RECORD OFFICE

Sir Charles Warren B
Great Scotland Yard
W.C.

244

'The Whore Killer' letter of 6 October which, significantly, speaks of sending a heart by parcel post.

Perhaps the most sensational development of the month came when the threat to send a body part was actually carried out. Another letter was posted, this time contained in a small parcel of unknown origin. At the centre of this sensation was Mr George Akin Lusk, a now somewhat legendary figure in the annals of Ripper lore. Lusk had been steadily gaining prominence in the press as the leading light, president and chairman of the 'Whitechapel Vigilance Committee'. This was a group of concerned businessmen and traders who formed together on 10 September 1888 as a result of the fears generated by the murders of Tabram, Nichols and Chapman. Lusk, forty-nine years old at the time, was a builder and contractor, a freemason, a member of the Metropolitan Board of Works, and a vestryman of the parish of Mile End Old Town. His address was 1, 2 and 3 Alderney Road, off Globe Road, Mile End. At first, it would appear, Lusk was not shy of the press attention he received.

Lusk's profile was greatly raised when he penned a petition addressed to Queen Victoria on Thursday 27 September 1888. In it he related concerns over the government's refusal to offer a reward for the detection of the murderer, the lack of police success, and his request for the queen's intervention in the matter. The government would not budge on the question of a reward as in past cases it had proved

George Akin Lusk, chairman of the Whitechapel Vigilance Committee, recipient of the 'From hell' letter and a piece of human kidney.

to produce more harm than good. This issue, or a pardon for any accomplices, was the subject of a continued exchange between Lusk and the Home Office in October 1888.

The Times of Monday 8 October, page 6e, carried the following report:

> In answer to the petition to Her Majesty, presented by Mr. George Lusk on behalf of his Vigilance Committee and the inhabitants of Whitechapel generally, the following letter was received late on Saturday night :–
>
> "Whitehall, Oct. 6, 1888.
>
> "Sir, – The Secretary of State for the Home Department has had the honour to lay before the Queen the petition signed by you praying that a reward may be offered by the Government for the discovery of the perpetrator of the recent murders in Whitechapel, and he desires me to inform you that though he has given directions that no effort or expense should be spared in endeavouring to discover the person guilty of the murders, he has not

been able to advise Her Majesty that in his belief the ends of justice would be promoted by any departure from the decision already announced with regard to the proposal that a reward should be offered by Government.

"I am, Sir, your obedient servant,

"E. LEIGH PEMBERTON.

"George Lusk, Esq., 1, 2, and 3, Alderney-road, Mile-end-road, E."

In reference to the great interest taken by Mr. Lusk in the welfare of the inhabitants of the district, there seems to be no doubt that he has been marked down, for on Saturday evening it became necessary to call in the police for the purpose of keeping a look-out for a mysterious stranger who has been prowling round his premises and his son's house with the object, it is believed, of striking through Mr. Lusk at the Vigilance Committee. After an interview with a constable and a detective-sergeant, the matter was deemed of sufficient importance to warrant the attendance of an inspector from Bethnal-green, and at 10 30 waited on Mr. Lusk and heard his statement of the matter. The description given of this man is as follows:– Height 5ft. 9in., aged 38 to 40, full beard and moustache, matted and untrimmed, dent on the bridge of the nose, florid complexion, wide nostrils, eyes sunken, dressed in a rusty frock coat, white turn-down collar, black tie, no watchchain, deerstalker hat, and the left boot broken out at the left side; carried a brown stick with round top.

This was obviously the kind of attention that Lusk did not want to attract, and all the publicity was not helping matters. In *The Times* of Monday 15 October 1888 there was further mention of Lusk. This included the copy of a letter he had received from Godfrey Lushington at the Home Office, regarding the question of a pardon to accomplices of the murderer, and again refusing to allow the offer of a reward. The article concluded:

Last Friday Mr. George Lusk, who is a member of the Whitechapel Vigilance Committee, received the following letter :–

"I write you a letter in black ink, as I have no more of the right stuff. I think you are all asleep in Scotland-yard with your bloodhounds, as I will show you to-morrow night (Saturday). I am going to do a double event, but not in Whitechapel. Got rather too warm there. Had to shift. No more till you hear me again. "JACK THE RIPPER."

This letter was shown to the police. It bears a Kilburn postmark, and the handwriting is very similar to that of the post-card sent to a news agency, which has been copied and posted on the hoardings throughout the East-end by the police.

Mr Lusk was now a celebrity, his place well established in the continuing saga of the crimes. For him there was worse to come. The big story concerning Lusk broke on Friday 19 October and was widely reported. *The Times* of that day said:

THE MURDERS IN LONDON.

Mr. George Lusk, builder, of Alderney-road, Globe-road, Mile-end, has received several letters purporting to be from the perpetrator of the Whitechapel murders, but believing them

LETTERS from HELL. 14th Thousand. From the Danish. With an Introduction by DR. GEORGE MAC-DONALD. In one vol., crown 8vo., 6s. "Should be read by every thinking mind."—Morning Advertiser.

This advertisement appeared in *The Times* of 7 September 1888. It was echoed in a letter sent to Mr Lusk of the Whitechapel Vigilance Committee the following month.

> to have been the production of some practical joker, he had regarded them as of no consequence. It is stated that a letter delivered shortly after 5 o'clock on Tuesday evening was accompanied by a cardboard box, containing what appeared to be a portion of a kidney. The letter was in the following terms:– "From Hell. Mr. Lusk. Sir, – I send you half the kidne I took from one woman, prasarved it for you, tother piece I fried and ate it ; was very nice. I may send you the bloody knif that took it out if you only wate while longer. (Signed) 'Catch me when you can.' Mr. Lusk." The receiver was at first disposed to think that another hoax had been perpetrated, but eventually decided to take the opinion of the Vigilance Committee. They could, of course, give no opinion as to whether the kidney was human or not, but they decided to take the contents of the cardboard box to a medical man whose surgery is near. The substance was declared by the assistant to be the half of a human kidney, which had been divided longitudinally; but in order to remove any reason for doubt, he conveyed it to Dr. Openshaw, who is pathological curator of the London Hospital Museum. The doctor examined it, and pronounced it to be a portion of a human kidney – a "ginny" kidney, that is to say, one that had belonged to a person who had drunk heavily. He was further of opinion that it was the organ of a woman of about 45 years of age, and that it had been taken from the body within the last three weeks. It will be within public recollection that the left kidney was missing from the woman Eddowes, who was murdered and mutilated in Mitre-square . . .

It is amazing to think that so much information was conveyed so quickly to the public, thus providing yet more material for the hoaxers and heaping sensation upon sensation. Surgeon and Ripper historian Nick Warren challenges the idea that a mere piece of kidney could have provided as much information about its origins as was allegedly given by Dr Openshaw (*The Criminologist*, spring 1989). But it did allow the press to indicate that there seemed little doubt that the piece of organ originated from the Mitre Square victim. Indeed, it is very likely that this story was gilded by the press. The *Star* of 19 October reported:

> . . . he thought it best, however, to submit the kidney to Dr. Openshaw, the pathological curator at the London Hospital, and this was at once done. By the use of the microscope Dr. Openshaw was able to determine that the kidney had been taken from a full-grown human being, and that the portion before him was
>
> PART OF THE LEFT KIDNEY.
>
> It at once occurred to the Vigilance Committee that at the inquest on the body of the woman Eddowes who was murdered at Mitre-square, Aldgate, it was stated that the left

The London Hospital, Whitechapel Road, as it looked in 1888. It was here that Dr Openshaw first examined the 'Lusk kidney' and declared it to be human.

kidney was missing, and in view of this circumstance it was deemed advisable to at once communicate with the police. Accordingly the parcel and the accompanying letter and postcard were at once taken to Leman-street Police-station, and the matter placed in the hands of Inspector Abberline. Subsequently the City Police were communicated with, as the discovery relates to a crime occurring within their jurisdiction. The cardboard box which Mr. Lusk received is about 3½in. square, and was wrapped in paper. The cover bears a London post-mark, but the stamping is not sufficiently clear to enable it to be stated from what postal district of the metropolis the article was sent. On this point it is expected that the assistance of the Post Office officials will be invoked. The portion of the kidney which it enclosed has, according to the medical experts, been preserved for some time in spirits of wine. The person from whom it was taken was probably

ALIVE THREE WEEKS SINCE,

a circumstance which fits in with the suggestion that the organ may have been taken from the body of the deceased woman Eddowes, murdered in Mitre-square. Another fact is that the kidney is evidently that of a person who had been a considerable drinker, as there were distinct marks of disease. The handwriting of the letter differs altogether from that of 'Jack the Ripper' specimens of whose calligraphy were recently published. The writing is of an inferior character, evidently disguised, while the spelling, as will be seen, is indifferent. A few days before he received the parcel Mr. Lusk received a postcard supposed to come from the same source. It reads:–

Dr Thomas Openshaw, curator of the pathological museum at the London Hospital who examined the 'Lusk kidney' and stated it was human. He later received a letter from 'Jack the Ripper'.

Say Boss –
You seem rare frightened, guess I'd like to give you fits, but can't stop time enough to let you box of toys* play copper games with me, but hope to see you when I don't hurry too much.

Bye-bye, Boss.

There seems to be no room for doubt that what has been sent to Mr. Lusk is part of a human kidney, but nevertheless it may be doubted whether it has any serious bearing on the Mitre-Square murder. The whole thing may possibly turn out to be a medical student's gruesome joke.

A further article included an interview with Dr Openshaw, which casts more light on what he had actually deduced about the piece of kidney:

It Had Been Preserved in Spirits.

Dr. Openshaw told a *Star* reporter to-day that after having examined the piece of kidney under the microscope he was of opinion that it was half of a left human kidney. He couldn't say, however, whether it was that of a woman, nor how long ago it had been removed from the body, as it had been preserved in spirits.

It is believed that the 'revolting parcel' is not from the murderer, but is merely a medical student's practical joke.

The Metropolitan Police last night handed the piece of kidney over to the City Police on the assumption that if the whole thing is not, as is most likely, the disgusting trick of some practical joker, it relates to the Mitre-square crime.

So Openshaw was reported to have said that he could only pronounce it to be half of a left human kidney, but could not say that it was that of a woman, nor how long ago it had been removed as it had been preserved in spirits.

Joseph Aarons, the treasurer of the Whitechapel Vigilance Committee, made a statement on the evening of Thursday 18 October about the episode. This account, which adds interesting detail, was printed in the *Daily Telegraph* of 19 October:

Mr. Lusk, our chairman, came over to me last (Wednesday) night in a state of considerable excitement. I asked him what was the matter, when he replied, 'I suppose you will laugh at what I am going to tell you, but you must know that I had a little parcel come to me on Tuesday evening, and to my surprise it contains half a kidney and a letter from "Jack the

* 'Box of toys' is Cockney rhyming slang for boys.

> Ripper.'" To tell you the truth, I did not believe in it, and I laughed and said I thought that somebody had been trying to frighten him. Mr. Lusk, however, said it was no laughing matter to him. I then suggested that, as it was late, we should leave the matter over till the morning, when I and other members of the committee would come round. This morning, at about half-past nine, Mr. Harris, our secretary, Mr. Reeves, Mr. Lawton, and myself went across to see Mr. Lusk, who opened his desk and pulled out a small square card-board box, wrapped in brown paper. Mr. Lusk said, 'Throw it away; I hate the sight of it.' I examined the box and its contents, and being sure that it was not a sheep's kidney, I advised that, instead of throwing it away, we should see Dr. Wills, of 56, Mile-end-road. We did not, however, find him in, but Mr. Reed, his assistant, was. He gave an opinion that it was a portion of a human kidney which had been preserved in spirits of wine; but, to make sure, he would go over to the London Hospital, where it could be microscopically examined. On his return Mr. Reed said that Dr. Openshaw, at the Pathological Museum, stated that the kidney belonged to a female, that it was part of the left kidney, and that the woman had been in the habit of drinking. He should think that the person had died about the same time the Mitre-square murder was committed. It was then agreed that we should take the parcel and the letter to Leman-street Police-station, where we saw Inspector Abberline. Afterwards some of us went to Scotland-yard, where we were told that we had done quite right in putting the matter into Mr. Abberline's hands. Our committee will meet again to-night, but Mr. Lusk, our chairman, has naturally been much upset.

It is important to examine the 'From hell' letter and the accompanying kidney story. This communication is now generally regarded by students of the case as the most likely to be genuine. Unfortunately the City of London Police records were lost in the Second World War Blitz. The only detailed City of London Police report on the case to have survived was written by Inspector James McWilliam, head of the City Detective Department, on 27 October 1888. This eight-page account was sent to the Home Office and is preserved in file HO 144/221/A49301C, ff. 163–70. Fortunately this valuable report contains a reference to the City Police's thoughts on the 'Lusk letter'. McWilliam writes:

> On the 16th Inst. Mr. Lusk No. 1 Alderney Road, Mile End, Chairman of the East End Vigilance Committee received by post a packet containing half of a kidney and a letter photograph copy of which I attach hereto. He did not attach any importance to it at the time, but on mentioning the matter to other members of the Committee on the 18th Inst. they advised him to shew the piece of kidney to a medical man. He accordingly took it to Mr. Reed, 56 Mile End Road, & subsequently to Dr. Openshaw of the London Hospital, both of whom expressed the opinion that it was a portion of the kidney of a human being. Mr. Lusk then took the kidney & letter to Leman Street Station. The kidney was forwarded to this office & the letter to Scotland Yard. Chief Inspector Swanson having lent me the letter on the 20th Inst. I had it photographed & returned it to him on the 24th. The kidney has been examined by Dr. Gordon-Brown who is of opinion that it is human. Every effort is being made to trace the sender, but it is not desirable that publicity should be given to the Doctor's opinion, or the steps that are being taken in consequence.
>
> It might turn out after all, to be the act of a Medical Student who would have no difficulty in obtaining the organ in question.

There are Home Office minutes annexed to this report as folio 171, along with references to the graffiti, the Lusk communication and 'Jack the Ripper'. These are reproduced below in full:

> Mr. Murdoch
> This report tells very little.
> i The City Police are wholly at fault as regards the detection of the murderer.
> ii The word on the wall was "Jewes", not "Juwes". This is important; unless it is a mere clerical error. [Marginal note 'Not so I believe GL.']†
> iii The ½ kidney sent to Mr Lusk is human.
> The printed report of the Inquest contains much more information than this. They evidently want to tell us nothing. [Marginal note 'I don't think so GL.']
> ? Shall we ask them
> A. Did the writing on the wall resemble "Jack the Ripper's": or the enclosed?
> B. Could the ½ kidney possibly be part of the victim's kidney?
> W.P.B.†† Mr Lushington Have you any private information from
> 30.10.88 the Met: Police on the above points, or a facsimile of Jack the Rippers Letters.
> CM* Oct 30.
> It is I think unadvisable to ask these questions officially, but when Mr. Matthews comes to town I would advise that he should ask Sir J. Fraser to come to the H.O. He will then have full particulars. GL 30 Oct 1888.
> H.M.**
> 31Oct./88

This reveals that concern over the letters and the Lusk package was extending to the highest levels in the land. Sir Charles Warren, Chief Commissioner of the Metropolitan Police, was obliged to submit a lengthy report to the Home Office on 6 November 1888 giving his reasons for sponging out the graffiti in Goulston Street (HO 144/221/A49301C, ff. 174–81). He fully explained that he wished to avoid anti-Semitic reaction to the writing, which might have resulted in serious public disorder.

On 6 November, 1888, Chief Inspector Swanson submitted his overall report on the Mitre Square murder and the Metropolitan Police's knowledge of this City of London Police murder case. The report is preserved as HO 144/221/A49301C, ff. 184–94. Swanson wrote (*inter alia*):

> Rewards were offered by the City Police and by Mr. Montagu and a Vigilance Committee formed presided over by Mr. Lusk of Alderney Road, Mile End, and it is to be regretted that the combined result has been that no information leading to the murderer has been forthcoming. On the 18th Oct. Mr. Lusk brought a parcel which had been addressed to him to

† GL was Godfrey Lushington, Permanent Under Secretary.
†† W.P.B. was William Patrick Byrne, Home Office clerk.
* CM was Charles Murdoch, Home Office clerk.
** HM was Henry Matthews, Home Secretary.

Leman Street. The parcel contained what appeared to be a portion of a kidney. He received it on 15th Oct. [*sic*] and submitted it for examination eventually to Dr. Openshaw, curator of London Hospital Museum, who pronounced it to be a human kidney. The kidney was at once handed over to the City Police, and the result of the combined medical opinion they have taken upon it is that it is the kidney of a human adult; not charged with a fluid, as it would have been in the case of a body handed over for purposes of dissection to an hospital, but rather as it would be in a case where it was taken from the body not so destined. In other words similar kidneys might & could be obtained from any dead person upon whom a post mortem had been made from any cause by students or dissecting room porter. [Here there is a marginal note – 'Was there any such p. mort. Made within a week in the E. or E.C. districts?'] The kidney, or rather portion of the kidney was accompanied by a letter couched as follows. –

From hell.

Mr Lusk

Sir

I send you half the Kidne I took from one woman prasarved it for you. tother piece I fried and ate it was very nise. I may send you the bloody knif that took it out if you only wate a whil longer

signed Catch me when you can Mishter Lusk.

The postmarks upon the parcel are so indistinct that it cannot be said whether the parcel was posted in the E. or E.'.C. districts, and there is no envelope to the letter, and the City Police are therefore unable to prosecute any enquiries upon it.

An obvious element of the 'Lusk letter' is that it contains words that appear to be spelled in a way designed to convey an Irish accent, words such as 'Sor' (which an examination of the actual letter reveals as the spelling of 'Sir') and 'Mishter'. This point may be arguable, but there is evidence that in popular literature of the day such devices were used to denote an Irish accent. An example appeared in *Punch* on 16 June 1888:

SHORT AND SHARP.

(*Latest Style.*)

SCENE – *Scotland Yard. Prominent Member of the Clan-na-Gael Conspiracy gang discovered interviewing Chief of Detective Department.*

Prominent Member. The top o' the mornin' to ye, Misther Inspector. Shure now ye didn't expect to see me at all?

Chief of Department. On the contrary, Mr. O'BLAZER, I was advised of your visit.

Prominent Member. Ah! there now! Shure, ye know everything! Maybe, now, ye've got hold of my little programme?

Chief of Department. Yes, I think I can give it you. (*Takes paper from pigeon hole.*) You were to blow up the Mansion House yesterday, the Clock Tower to-day, Buckingham Palace to-morrow, and the Bank the day after. That is correct, I think?

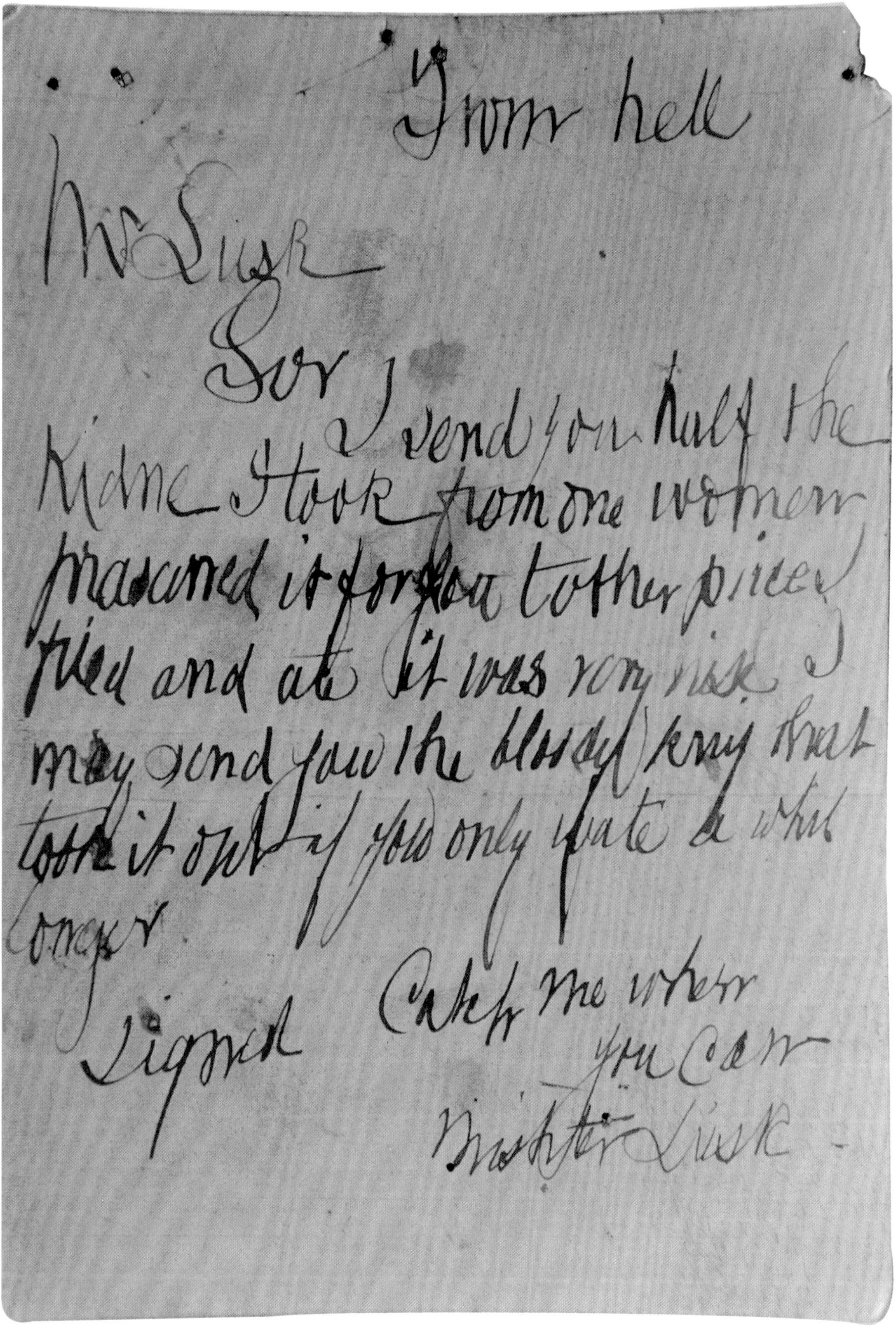

From hell

Mr Lusk

Sor

I send you half the Kidne I took from one women prasarved it for you tother piece I fried and ate it was very nise I may send you the bloody knif that took it out if you only wate a whil longer

signed Catch me when you can Mishter Lusk

The 'From hell' letter of 16 October to George Lusk of the Whitechapel Vigilance Committee. The letter is now missing.

Prominent Member. Bedad, Sorr, it is. But with your fellows a stickin' to me like leeches wherever I go, it's divil a bit of it I can carry out, anyway. Ah! well, ye won't be knowing, I guess, what I've got in this little bag here (*producing a black hand-bag*), and what I'm meaning to do with it?

Chief of Department. Yes, that bag contains three pounds and a half of dynamite, and you have brought it here with the intention of blowing up these premises. I think perhaps, under the circumstances, it will be safer in my keeping. (*Takes it.*)

Prominent Member. Well, there now! Shure ye baffle me entoirely. There seems just nothing for me to do but to be getting home again.

Chief of Department. I think, perhaps, that is about the best thing you can do. We'll undertake to see you safe on board.

Prominent Member. Ah! well, there, now, I'm very much obleeged to ye. Good mornin', Sorr!

[Takes his leave, and is seen safe on board for New York where he arrives in due course, to "report progress".]

The Irish problem and the threat of possible Fenian activity in London loomed large at the time of the Whitechapel murders as the greatest challenge to the security of the capital. It is little wonder, then, that an Irish theme, as well as an American one, should find its way into the story of the Whitechapel murders.

A suggestion as to the possible origin of the 'Lusk letter and kidney' appeared in the *Daily Telegraph* of Saturday 20 October:

A statement which apparently gives a clue to the sender of the strange package received by Mr. Lusk was made last night by Miss Emily Marsh, whose father carries on business in the leather trade at 218, Jubilee-street, Mile-end-road. In Mr. Marsh's absence Miss Marsh was in the front shop, shortly after one o'clock on Monday last, when a stranger, dressed in clerical costume, entered, and, referring to the reward bill in the window, asked for the address of Mr. Lusk, described therein as the president of the Vigilance Committee. Miss Marsh at once referred the man to Mr. J. Aarons, the treasurer of the committee, who resides at the corner of Jubilee-street and Mile-end-road, a distance of about thirty yards. The man, however, said he did not wish to go there, and Miss Marsh thereupon produced a newspaper in which Mr. Lusk's address was given as Alderney-road, Globe-road, no number being mentioned. She requested the stranger to read the address, but he declined, saying, "Read it out," and proceeded to write something in his pocket-book, keeping his head down meanwhile. He subsequently left the shop, after thanking the young lady for the information, but not before Miss Marsh, alarmed by the man's appearance, had sent the shop-boy, John Cormack, to see that all was right. This lad, as well as Miss Marsh, give a full description of the man, while Mr. Marsh, who happened to come along at the time, also encountered him on the pavement outside. The stranger is described as a man of some forty-five years of age, fully six feet in height, and slimly built. He wore a soft felt black hat, drawn over his forehead, a stand-up collar, and a very long black single-breasted overcoat, with a Prussian or clerical collar partly turned up. His face was of a sallow type, and he had a dark beard and moustache. The man spoke with what was taken to be an Irish accent. No importance was attached to the incident until Miss Marsh read of the receipt by Mr. Lusk of a strange parcel, and then it occurred to her that the stranger might be the person who had despatched it. His inquiry was made at one o'clock on Monday afternoon, and Mr. Lusk received the package at eight p.m. the next day. The address on the package curiously enough gives no number in Alderney-road, a piece of information which Miss Marsh could not supply. It appears that on leaving the shop the man went right by Mr. Aarons' house, but did not call. Mr. Lusk has been informed of the circumstances, and states that no person answering the description has called on him, nor does he know any one at all like the man in question.

The Times of the same day reported:

THE MURDERS IN LONDON.

No person is under detention at either of the police stations. The house-to-house search is completed, and has led to no discovery of any value. The householders have offered the fullest assistance to the police throughout the work of inspection. Intelligence was received by the detectives that yesterday afternoon in Islington a strange man was observed to write on a wall the words "I am Jack the Ripper." He was pursued for some distance, but got clear away. The horrible incident of the box containing a portion of a kidney sent to Mr. Lusk, of the Whitechapel Vigilance Committee, is not generally regarded as a practical joke in view of the opinion given by two medical gentlemen, Dr. Openshaw and Mr. Reed. The box and its contents were taken from Leman-street to the City Police Office in Old Jewry, and Dr. Gordon Browne [*sic*], police-surgeon, will examine and make a report in due course. The extra police precautions are still in force.

As Saturday and Sunday – the days which the Whitechapel murderer has hitherto chosen for his work – come round week by week, special precautions are taken by the police as well as by the self-constituted vigilance committee. Last night, when the policemen on night duty were drawn up in their respective station-yards, preparatory to going on their beats, the last letter sent by "Jack the Ripper" was read over to them. It was pointed out that the writer intimated his intention of committing further murders last night, and the necessity for special vigilance was impressed on the police.

Dr Openshaw himself did not escape the attention of the letter-writers, no doubt as a result of the publicity he had received in the newspapers. Thomas Horrocks Openshaw had been appointed curator of the pathology museum at the London Hospital in 1887 and was thirty-two years old in 1888. He had a distinguished career and was a member of the Clinical Society of London. The following letter was sent to him on 29 October:

Old boss you was rite it was the left kidny i was goin to hopperate agin close to your ospitle just as i was goin to dror mi nife along of er bloomin throte them cusses of coppers spoilt the game but i guess i wil be on the job soon and will send you another bit of innerds
Jack the ripper
O have you seen the devle with his mikerscope and scalpul a lookin at a Kidney with a slide cocked up

The envelope containing the letter was postmarked 'LONDON E. OC29 88' and addressed to Dr Openshaw, Pathological curator, London Hospital, Whitechapel.

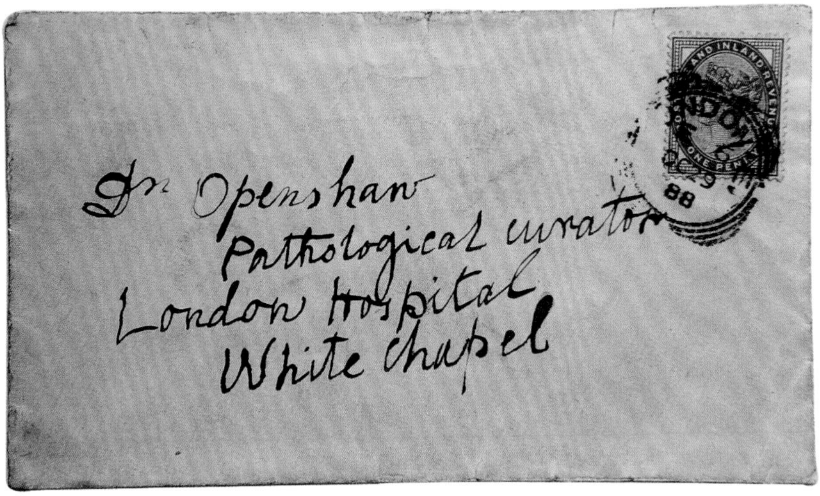

Dr Openshaw
Pathological curator
London Hospital
White chapel

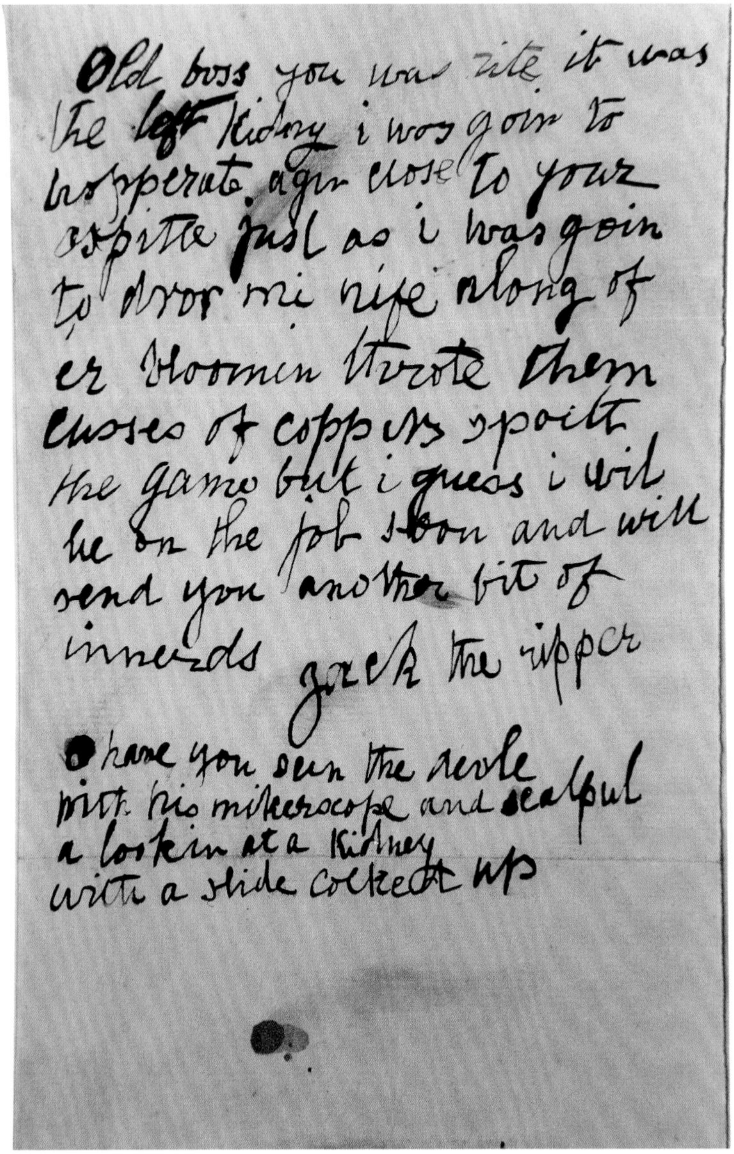

Old boss you was rite it was
the left kidny i was goin to
hoperate agin close to your
ospitle just as i was goin
to dror mi nife along of
er bloomin throte them
cusses of coppers spoilt
the game but i guess i wil
be on the job soon and will
send you another bit of
innerds
jack the ripper

O have you seen the devle
with his mikerscope and scalpul
a lookin at a kidney
with a slide cocked up

The 'Openshaw letter' signed by 'Jack the Ripper' and sent to Dr Openshaw at the London Hospital on 29 October.

A Cornish folktale, published in 1871, contains striking similarities to the postscript of the Openshaw letter:

> Here's to the devil,
> With his wooden pick and shovel,
> Digging tin by the bushel,
> With his tail cock'd up!*

It has been stated (most notably by Derek Davies in his article 'Jack the Ripper – The Handwriting Analysis', *The Criminologist*, Vol. 9, No. 33, 1974) that the 'Lusk letter' and the 'Openshaw letter' were written by the same hand. This must remain a matter of opinion but both letters are reproduced here for the reader to draw his own conclusions. The common subject of the two letters is, of course, the kidney sent to Lusk, and the story it generated.

Catching up with the kidney episode in the *Referee* of 21 October, George R. Sims wrote:

> The papers are lively reading again. What with the Bye-bye Boss gentleman who is giving the Vigilance Committee beans – kidney beans – and the doctors who are dissecting the Emperor Frederick over and over again on our breakfast-tables, there is a rare healthy atmosphere around Press literature. A good, thorough, go-ahead, non-compromising Dare-Devil Dick or Sixteen-String Jack or Sweeney Todd feuilleton is alone wanting to complete the picture.

The medical examination of the half kidney was inconclusive, and the only positive point to emerge from it was a consensus that the remains were human. *The Sunday Times* of 21 October published an interview with Dr Frederick Gordon Brown, the City Police Surgeon, after a resourceful journalist had called on the good doctor at his home:

> THE WHITECHAPEL TRAGEDIES.
>
> Notwithstanding the sensational rumours which were current yesterday afternoon, there is little to chronicle from the scene of the Whitechapel tragedies. The police have now turned their attention to the Thames and Victoria Embankments, and, to quote the words of an inspector, it would be "impossible" for them to bestow more zeal or devotion to the task on which they are engaged. Sensational sheets teem with reports of arrests, but up to the present no arrests have been made. Mr. George Lusk, Alderney Road, Mile End, E., as chairman of the Whitechapel Vigilance Committee, was the recipient of the kidney of which so much has been heard lately.
>
> Calling on Dr. Gordon Brown, of the City Police, last night, our reporter found that he had not quite completed his examination of the kidney which had been submitted to him. He said: "So far as I can form an opinion, I do not see any substantial reason why this portion of kidney should not be the portion of the one taken from the murdered woman. I cannot say

* 'Duffy and the Devil' in *Popular Romances of the West of England* (London, John Camden Hotten, 1871).

> that it is the left kidney. It must have been cut previously to its being immersed in the spirit which exercised a hardening process. It certainly had not been in spirit for more than a week. As has been stated, there is no portion of the renal artery adhering to it, it having been trimmed up, so, consequently, there could be no correspondence established between the portion of the body from which it was cut. As it exhibits no trace of decomposition, when we consider the length of time that has elapsed since the commission of the murder, we come to the conclusion that the probability is slight of its being a portion of the murdered woman of Mitre Square."

Put simply, Dr Brown was saying that, in his opinion, although there was no positive reason to discount the piece of kidney as originating from Eddowes' body, it was, given the facts, an unlikely proposition.

The *Star* of Saturday 20 October 1888 (page 3) carried an update on the 'kidney story':

> WHITECHAPEL.
>
> **Easy to Hoax the Police–The Kidney Story.**
>
> As a motive for the disgusting hoax of the kidney, it is suggested that the person who sent it to its recipient desired to keep up the excitement about the crimes. We are now informed that the information of the receipt of the parcel was sold at a high figure, so that the hoax does not appear so stupid as it seemed at first.

Lieutenant-Colonel Sir Henry Smith of the City of London Police in his 1910 book *From Constable to Commissioner* (Chatto & Windus), devotes a chapter to the 'Ripper and his Deeds' (pages 147–62). As with many retired police officers writing their memoirs, Smith's account contains demonstrable errors. However, the fault seems to be exacerbated by the fact that many of the 'errors' appear to have been made in order to increase Smith's own importance or involvement with the case. This does not alter the fact that Smith's account is both interesting and important. On pages 154–5 he wrote:

> When the body [Eddowes'] was examined by the police surgeon, Mr. Gordon Brown, one kidney was found to be missing, and some days after the murder what purported to be that kidney was posted to the office of the Central News [*sic*], together with a short note of rather a jocular character unfit for publication. Both kidney and note the manager at once forwarded to me [*sic*]. Unfortunately, as always happens, some clerk or assistant in the office was got at, and the whole affair was public property next morning. Right royally did the Solons of the metropolis enjoy themselves at the expense of my humble self and the City Police Force. "The kidney was the kidney of a dog, anyone could see that," wrote one. "Evidently from the dissecting-room," wrote another. "Taken out of a corpse after a post-mortem," wrote a third. "A transparent hoax," wrote a fourth. My readers shall judge between myself and the Solons in question.
>
> I made over the kidney to the police surgeon, instructing him to consult with the most eminent men in the profession, and send me a report without delay. I give the substance of

it. The renal artery is about three inches long. Two inches remained in the corpse, one inch was attached to the kidney. The kidney left in the corpse was in an advanced stage of Bright's Disease; the kidney sent me was in an exactly similar state. But what was of far more importance, Mr. Sutton, one of the senior surgeons of the London Hospital, whom Gordon Brown asked to meet him and another practitioner in consultation, and who was one of the greatest authorities living on the kidney and its diseases, said he would pledge his reputation that the kidney submitted to them had been put in spirits within a few hours of its removal from the body – thus effectually disposing of all hoaxes in connection with it. The body of anyone done to death by violence is not taken direct to the dissecting room, but must await an inquest, never held before the following day at the soonest.

From this we can see that Smith appeared to be a lone voice from the official side who unequivocally accepted the kidney as being that of Eddowes, thus making the 'Lusk letter' genuine in his view. Unfortunately for Smith there is no official evidence whatsoever to confirm the presence of the renal artery, and its correspondence with that remaining in the body, nor to confirm Bright's disease. In fact, the interview with Dr Brown reported in *The Sunday Times* of 21 October indicates quite the opposite: he stated that the renal artery had been trimmed off the piece of kidney and in his opinion it was unlikely that it came from Eddowes. Nor does Inspector McWilliam's report of October 1888 support his chief's 1910 opinions. No report of Mr Sutton, or anyone identifiable as 'one of the greatest authorities living on the kidney and its diseases', has ever been found. Indeed, even if the kidney portion were shown to be diseased in such a way, it would prove nothing as such disease was fairly common in those days.

And what of Lusk himself? What were his final feelings about the gruesome package? Fortunately, his grandson, the late Mr Leonard Archer, wrote a letter to the editor of the *London Hospital Gazette* in April 1966, after that journal had published the article by Professor Francis Camps, the famous pathologist, entitled 'More About Jack the Ripper'. This article reproduced drawings prepared for the Eddowes inquest and examined some of the letters allegedly sent by the murderer. These included the 'Lusk letter'. Mr Archer wrote as follows:

93, St. Ronans Crescent,
WOODFORD GREEN, Essex.
16th April, 1966.

Dear Sir,

I have read the Press reports of the article in your Gazette about the "Ripper" case and would be glad if you would send me a copy of the reprint if it is ready. Perhaps you will be good enough to let me know the cost so that I can send you a postal order.

I am particularly interested in your article because George Lusk was my grandfather. At the time of the murders he was a builder and well-known in the Whitechapel district, hence his Chairmanship of the Vigilance Committee. He lived at the time in Alderney Road which is not far from the London Hospital; I believe he either did some work in the hospital or for some of the staff and in his later years he believed that the kidney was sent to him as a practical joke by someone in the London Hospital! This theory of his may of course have been a way of consoling himself for the fright he had when the parcel containing the kidney came to him through the post, he sought police protection for some days after.

Yours faithfully,
(L.T.ARCHER)

The Editor,
London Hospital Gazette,
The London Hospital,

Thus the mysterious episode of the 'Lusk letter and kidney' was consigned to the pages of history and there it remains unresolved, as do so many of the mysteries of this case. For some the 'From hell' letter accompanied by a section of human kidney plus the views of Henry Smith of the City Police indicate the killer himself sent it. For others the opinions of Dr Brown, the police, and the belief of George Lusk himself tend to tilt the balance in favour of a macabre practical joke.

— SEVEN —

'Most unwomanly . . .'

IT is surprising that despite the large number of 'Jack the Ripper' letters sent, very few culprits appear to have been detected and brought to court by the police. The two most prominent cases both belonged to the fairer sex. The first salutary warning as to the risks of indulging in letter hoaxing appeared in the national press on Monday 22 October when *The Times* reported:

> At the Bradford Borough Court on Saturday, a respectable looking young woman, named Maria Coroner, 21 years of age, employed in mantlemaker's establishment, was brought up on the charge of having "written certain letters tending to cause a breach of the peace." These letters, as stated by the chief constable, purported to be written by "Jack the Ripper," whose object in visiting Bradford, as was stated, was to do a little business before starting for some other place on the same errand. She had written two letters of this character, as she admitted when apprehended, one being addressed to the chief constable and the other to a local newspaper. On searching the girl's lodging the police found copies of the letters. The prisoner excused her foolish conduct on the ground that "she had done it in a joke." She was stated to be a very respectable young woman. The prisoner was remanded until to-morrow, the Bench declining to accept bail.

The case was covered in greater detail in the local press: a lengthy report is to be found in the *Bradford Daily Telegraph* of Monday 22 October:

> THE BRADFORD "JACK THE RIPPER"
>
> APPREHENSION OF THE WRITER OF THE LETTER.
>
> A GIRL'S FOOLISH FREAK.
>
> This morning, as briefly stated in our first edition, the Bradford police succeeded in laying hands upon the writer of the letter signed "Jack the Ripper" which was published in this

paper on the 15th inst., and the writer of various other letters under the same signature which have been addressed to this office and to the police. Prisoner is a young woman apparently about twenty-one years of age, named Maria Coroner, a mantle hand, who has for some time past been employed at Messrs Illingworth and Newbolt's, Westgate. She is said to be a native of Oldham, but has been for the last two years in Bradford and has latterly been lodging at 77, Westgrove Street. The Chief Constable this morning obtained a clue to the writer of the letters in the shape of a sheet of paper and envelope of the same character as those used on one of the letters, and acting on a hint received at the same time sent Detective-Inspector Dobson and Sergeant Abbey up to the address named. On searching the room of the girl the copy of the letter which had been sent to the Chief Constable was found, the handwriting being identical. An officer was sent to the girl's employers, and she was brought down to her lodgings and a more careful search made in her presence. She produced a copy of a second letter from her pocket, and ultimately made a clean breast of the matter, saying that she had written the letter as a "joke." The police have no reason to disbelieve the truth of the girl's story, and at the most she can hardly be accused of anything worse than a very foolish action, but it was considered advisable to take steps which would act as a deterrent to any others inclined to play upon the fears of the public in the same way, and consequently prisoner was taken into custody and brought down to the Town Hall. Nothing is known as to her antecedents. She is a pleasant looking girl, of good figure, and was neatly dressed in black when taken into custody. She appeared very unconcerned when before the magistrates, and appeared to treat the matter more lightly than she will probably be disposed to do after the expiry of the interval between now and next Tuesday, to which day she has been remanded. Her mother is said to be in America, and from letters in her possession it was found she had correspondents in various parts of England, and as far away as Vienna.

THE WRITER BEFORE THE POLICE COURT.

Prisoner was brought up at the Bradford Borough Police Court this morning, before Mr. Arthur Briggs, and Ald. John Hill. – The Chief Constable (Mr. J. Withers) said: The prisoner before you this morning is certainly, to say the least of it, a very foolish young woman. She has been writing letters – first one to myself, which I received on the 15th of October, and which was dated the 14th of October. Seeing that letter was not answered or taken any notice of by the police she wrote one afterwards to the "Bradford Telegraph." That letter was printed by them, but the letter sent to me was not taken any notice of in the slightest way whatever. The letter I received was as follows:–

"Dear Sir, – If the Bradford Police would like to make another gallant capture now is the time. I have arrived in town for the purpose of doing a little business. Bradford is the field that requires my labour. Of course knowing as I do that your men are so (clevah) clever it is not necessary to give my address nor yet describe myself minutely. I will simply state that I am here and alone quite near to the Town Hall.

"I am, my dear sir, yours in the fight against wickedness. "J. RIPPER."

"P.S. – Perhaps you would like my portrait, but you see I am in deep mourning for those ladies that I put to sleep, and do not wish to have one taken."

When I received the letter I thought it was a bit of foolishness on the part of some person and took no notice of it. The following day I noticed a letter printed in the "Telegraph." That letter was to this effect:–

BRADFORD, Oct. 15th 1888.

Sir, – Would you permit me through the medium of your valueable paper to announce my arrival in Bradford. I would have wired you but you see the people would have gone to trouble and expence in order to receive me kindly, particularly the gaurdians of the peace; however, I shall start work as soon as possible as I have other engagements immediately that I finish here. Of course I have informed the Chief Constable by Letter of my presence in town but I forgot to send my card with name and address so that He might know where to call when having a desire to see me, poor dear old Bobbies how very (clevar) they are not so clever as my humble self, hoping that you will give this publication I am

Dear Sir yours Etc. J. RIPPER.

That having appeared in the newspaper it caused a good deal of fear amongst the females in the town, and numerous complaints came to us from persons who were afraid to go out at night. Some people were very frightened indeed, and complaints were brought about people being stopped by men. From certain information which came to my knowledge this morning I directed Inspector Dobson and Detective Sergeant Abbey to go to a certain address at Westgrove Street, and make inquiries for a person of the name of Maria. They went according to orders, and found that the prisoner was not in at the time. They found letters there, however, which were exact copies of the ones to the "Telegraph" and the one he had received. Under the circumstances a warrant was taken out charging this woman that she had written certain letters tending to cause a breach of the peace. On this charge I ask you to remand the woman until Tuesday, so that inquiries can be made.

The Town Clerk (Mr. McGowen), who was present, suggested that the remand had better be for a week, and said there might be something wrong with her mind. If she went about the streets and people knew who she had stated herself to be, she might be in danger.

Mr. Withers said that no doubt that would be so. Mr. Withers proceeded to inform the Bench that the prisoner had admitted that the letters were in her handwriting.

Detective-Sergeant Abbey stated that this morning he and Inspector Dobson went to No. 77, Westgrove Street, and searched the prisoner's room, where they found certain papers. They were satisfied from what they had seen that the letters mentioned had been written from the house, as they found an envelope and a piece of paper similar to that which had been used for the letters produced. He then went to Messrs Illingworth & Newboult's, where the prisoner was employed, and apprehended her. He told her he wanted her to go with him to 77, Westgrove Street, said that he might search her boxes, for they were convinced that she had been writing letters to the Chief Constable. He charged her with doing that, and she denied it, but finally admitted having done so, and said "I did it in a joke." At the house they searched the prisoner's belongings and found copies of the two letters in her box.

Detective Inspector Dobson: She is a very respectable girl, I understand.

The Chief Constable then put in the letter posted to the "Telegraph;" and Mr. Bateson, the cashier at the "Telegraph" office, gave evidence of having received the letter.

The Chairman then addressed the prisoner, stating that whether this was a piece of folly or not they could not tell. She would be remanded until Tuesday.

> The prisoner: Can you accept bail for me?
> The Chairman: No, we cannot. You have acted very foolishly.

The refusal to accept the bail application must have been quite a shock for young Maria, for she found that she was being incarcerated until her next court appearance. Her activities amounted to serious mischief-making and there seems little doubt that the authorities were using her case as an example to others who might have been tempted to write 'Jack the Ripper' letters. The fact that the case appeared in the national press reinforces this view. It is a valuable insight into the machinations of the law in a case where a hoaxer was actually brought to justice.

On Saturday 27 October the *Bradford Citizen* reported on the case. It repeated the details, reproduced the wording of the letter to the police, and then continued:

> It was written on a sheet of black-bordered notepaper, which was ribbed in a peculiar pattern. The handwriting was obviously that of a woman. The Chief Constable did not make public the fact that he had received any such communication, as it was plain at first sight that the letter was simply a hoax, but on the following day a somewhat similar letter was published in a Bradford paper, and this occasioned a good deal of nervousness, and in some cases actual fright, amongst the public in Bradford, which the Chief Constable had desired to avoid. The police have from that time been making diligent efforts to find the writer of these silly but disturbing epistles, and, after spending some time in "shadowing" several innocent people, came upon a clue on Saturday. Detective-Inspector Dobson and Detective-Sergeant Abbey went on that morning to Coroner's lodgings, and came across some letter-paper of the kind upon which the letter was written. Abbey went to Messrs. Illingworth, Newboult and Co.'s shop, and whilst he brought the girl home Dobson searched her boxes. There he found a copy of the letter which had been sent to the Chief Constable in the same handwriting, along with a batch of newspapers containing reports of the Whitechapel murders, one of the visiting cards of Berry, the executioner, bearing the words, "James Berry, public executioner"; an envelope addressed to Major Preston, the Governor of Strangeways Gaol, and part of a letter relating to the recent murder of a warder at that gaol. When the girl arrived at her lodgings she was charged with having committed the offence, and, after first denying her guilt, finally admitted it, and produced from her pocket some more literature of the same kind. She seemed greatly surprised at her detection, and at first at a loss to give any reason for her foolish freak. She afterwards gave the two explanations that it was a joke, and that she had done it to make a sensation, and pleaded that she did not know she was doing anything wrong. Her landlady stated that the girl had read reports of the Whitechapel murders, and had become so excited about them that she (the landlady) was afraid to go to bed at night. The prisoner is a smart-looking woman, apparently of greater intelligence than is usual amongst women of her class. She is supposed to be a native of Oldham, but has lived for the past two years in lodgings in Bradford, and has borne a thoroughly good character . . .

The above report provides some extra information about Maria Coroner, and reveals that she must have possessed a rather morbid turn of mind. Her letter showing interest in the Strangeways' murder and the public executioner's visiting card are, indeed, most singular items for a young Victorian lady to possess. James Berry was the public

Executioner James Berry whose business card was found in the possession of 'Jack the Ripper' letter-writer Maria Coroner. They both lived in Bradford and Berry took an interest in the 'Ripper' murders.

The visiting card of executioner James Berry which was found in the possession of Maria Coroner of Bradford. She was arrested for sending 'Jack the Ripper' letters.

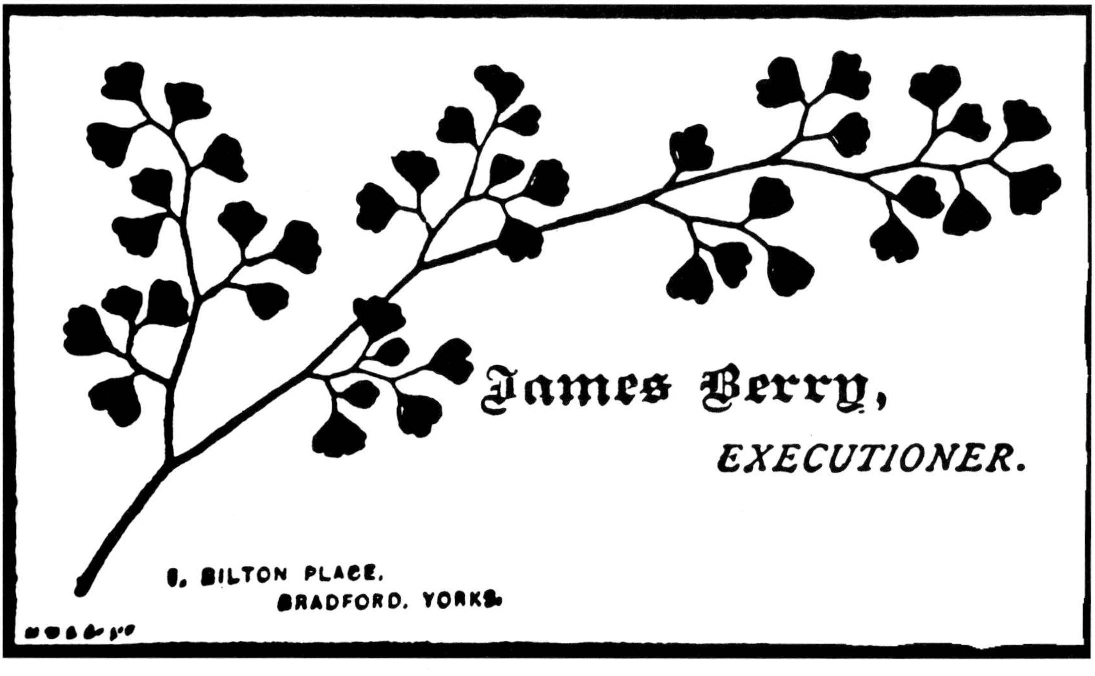

executioner from 1884 to 1891 and he lived in Bradford at 1 Bilton Place, City Road. It is interesting to speculate whether this remarkable young lady had met Berry and asked him for one of his cards. Berry himself was an amateur criminologist who gathered details of the crimes of those he executed. He took a great interest in the Whitechapel murders and executed a speculative Ripper suspect in William Henry Bury, whom he despatched at Dundee in April 1889. It is also interesting to note a report in the *Bradford Citizen* of a youth discovered by the police in Glasgow for writing a 'Jack the Ripper' letter mentioned in this account. He escaped rather more lightly than his female counterparts:

> A lad who is in a respectable position in Glasgow has narrowly escaped prosecution for an offence which is too common at present. He wrote and posted a letter signed "Jack the Ripper," and the Glasgow police, to his utter astonishment, found him out. He confessed his guilt. Owing to his youth and the state of trepidation he exhibited, he has been dismissed with an admonition.

More detail on this youth was carried in the *Weekly Herald* of 26 October. Apparently a letter had been sent to the Glasgow police, in an unstamped envelope, which read: 'Dear ol Boss, – I am known as 'Jack the Ripper', and I am going to pay Glasgow a trip. I hear there are fine women in Saltmarket, Glasgow, so I am going to pay you a visit. – Yours truly, JACK THE RIPPER.' The letter was written in red ink and had been given to Sub Inspector Carmichael. The boy, from a respectable Glasgow family, was identified. He was questioned in the presence of Superintendent Orr at the Central Police Office where he was reprimanded. The boy claimed that the letter had been written 'for a lark' and that he had not posted it. His claim was that he had lost it and someone else must have posted it.

The final disposal of Maria Coroner's case was reported in the *Bradford Daily Telegraph* of Wednesday 24 October:

> THE FEMALE "JACK THE RIPPER" IN BRADFORD.
>
> PRISONER BEFORE THE MAGISTRATES.
>
> The Bradford Borough Police Court was crowded to excess this morning by a number of persons, a great many of whom were females, anxious to see and hear the trial of the prisoner charged with writing letters under the title of "Jack the Ripper." On the charge sheet the prisoner was described as Maria Coroner, aged 22, a mantle-maker, of Westgrove Street, Bradford, and the charge against her was "that she had misbehaved herself by writing certain letters to one James Withers and others, tending to cause a breach of the peace." Mr. Atkinson, in the absence of Mr. Freeman, appeared for the accused, and asked what she was charged with, and on being told it was a breach of the peace under the common law, said "I should like to see the common law, it is so common I have not seen it."
>
> – Mr. Withers proceeded to state the case, the details of which are familiar to the public, as to the accused having written a letter to him and another to the "Daily Telegraph" signed "J. Ripper," which caused considerable fear amongst the females of the town. Having received complaints he felt it to be his duty to make inquiries into the matter, and with the assistance of the police he obtained possession of certain information, and the prisoner was arrested.
>
> – Mr. Atkinson said he admitted that his client had written the letters the subject of the complaint, but did not admit having committed a breach of the peace.

– Mr. Withers said the sending of the letters had been a very foolish freak on the part of the prisoner, and he thought their worships in the letters admitted would find sufficient cause to bind her over.
– Inspector Dobson then gave evidence as to his visit to the prisoner's house and the discovery of the letters.
– Cross-examined by Mr. Atkinson he admitted he considered the letters to be a "lark," and never thought that "Jack the Ripper" was in town. On being arrested the girl said she had written the letters in order to create a sensation and make the newspapers sell. He knew there was nothing in the letters. – Mr. Atkinson said that according to Mr. Dobson there was no breach of the peace, as he considered the letters to be a lark, and thought nothing about them. The prisoner's intention had been to increase the sale of the "Telegraph" and the "Observer," but she had done nothing to commit a breach of the peace. She had made foolish statements only, and for no reason whatever she had been locked up since Saturday. He thought their worships would say that a respectable woman ought not to have been locked up, because she had been foolish, if they did where could they fix the limit?
Mr. Ambler: What did she send the letter to the "Telegraph" for?
– Mr. Atkinson said they had no right to ask her that. There were lots of letters sent to the "Telegraph."
– The Chairman (Mr. A. Briggs) giving sentence said the prisoner had been excessively foolish in her conduct in this matter. They believed, however, she had been more foolish than anything else, or they would have had a different verdict to give. Under the circumstances she would be bound over in her own recognizance of £20 to be of good behaviour for six months. If she was not of good behaviour she would have to go to prison. Throughout the proceedings the prisoner never appeared to regard them with any gravity, but frequently smiled as her acts were enumerated. Besides Mr. A. Briggs the other magistrates on the bench were Mr. John Ambler and Mr. Tom Mitchell.

The second woman to be apprehended for sending 'Jack the Ripper' letters was of an entirely different character to Maria Coroner, and the letters were of an even more thoughtless nature. Miriam Howells, a Welsh housewife, also claimed that she was only having a 'lark'. The case was reported in the *Cardiff Times* of Saturday 24 November:

"JACK THE RIPPER" AT
ABERDARE.

A Piece of Stupid Folly.

At Aberdare police-court on Tuesday, Miriam Howells, the wife of James Howells, labourer, Penrhiwceiber, was charged that she on the 16th inst. feloniously and maliciously sent letters threatening to kill Elizabeth Magor and Margaret Smith. P.S. Luther Rees (Penrhiwceiber) stated that he received the letters produced from the persons to whom they were addressed. – The clerk of the court read the letter received by Mrs. Magor as follows:–

Dear Mrs Boss, – I mean to have your life before Christmas. I will play a —– of a trick with you, old woman. I played a good one on the last, but this will be better. Aint I clever? – Believe me to remain yours for ever,
JACK THE RIPPER. Beware.

He also read the letter sent to Mrs. Smith:–

Dear Miss Boss. Before Sunday night I mean to have your life. I shall be upon you without your thinking. I will play a better trick with you than I did with the last one, and that was clever. –
Yours truly, JACK THE RIPPER. Beware.

The officer said he saw prisoner on Friday night last, and told her about these two letters. He said, "What in the world did you write those two letters for?" and she replied that she meant no harm, and only did it for a lark, and hoped nothing would come of it. She admitted writing the letters, saying Polly Peak posted one, and David Davies posted the other, and that they were all together, and had the *Echo* on the table before them. Prisoner now hoped the magistrates would look over it. If she had thought it was coming to that, she never would have done it. – Mr. Rhys said it was most unwomanly. He did not know how to speak too strongly of such conduct – At the request of Supt. Thomas, prisoner was remanded for a week. She was admitted to bail in her own surety of £50.

The case was further reported in the *Cardiff Times* of Saturday 1 December, after Miriam Howells' next court appearance:

"JACK THE RIPPER" IN ABERDARE VALLEY.

At Aberdare police-court, on Tuesday – before Mr. W. M. North, Mr. R. H. Rhys, and Mr. D. P. Davies – Miriam Howells, married woman, Penrhiwceiber, was charged on remand with sending threatening letters (signed "Jack the Ripper") to Elizabeth Magor and Margaret Smith, on Nov. 16. Mr. T. Phillips appeared for the defence. – Dd. Davies, hairdresser, Penrhiwceiber, said he recollected being in defendant's house on the 16th November. He saw her write some letters, but he did know what was in them. She gave him a letter to post – that produced was the one. He did know what the purport of the letter was. It was only done for a lark. She told him she had written another letter to Margaret Smith, and that Polly Peek posted it. She asked him if he could keep a secret. He said "Yes", and then she told him – Cross-examined: They all met the next morning. Miss Smith had a laugh about it. – By the Magistrates' Clerk: She (Smith) was very frightened until she knew it was done for a lark.

Mrs. Elizabeth Magor, 83, Leigh-terrace, Penrhiwceiber, stated that when she first received the letter produced she was alarmed, and gave the letter to P.C. Luther Rees.

Cross-examined: Mrs. Howell was a neighbour. There was never anything between them. They all met together. Witness's husband was annoyed, and asked defendant for an apology. Defendant gave a written apology, and paid one guinea.

Polly Peek said she had lived with defendant since last Wednesday week. On the 15th instant she saw defendant write the letter produced to Miss Smith, and witness posted it at the Miakin Post Office.

Cross-examined: Witness suggested that the letter should be written to Miss Smith for a lark. Next morning she went to Miss Smith's, and saw Miss Smith open the letter. She explained it, and they had a laugh over it. The letter was handed to P.C. Rees, who said he would take it down the street for a joke. Afterwards there was some annoyance, through the matter getting into the public press.

Miss Smith, confectioner, said she received the letter produced by the second delivery on the 16th inst. She was rather frightened at the time, but she afterwards thought it was a joke. Polly Peek was present when she received the letter, but she did not explain anything then. P.C. Rees happened to go by, and she handed the letter to him. Afterwards Polly Peek explained, and she quite forgave defendant. The letters got into the press in a day or two, and that caused her as much annoyance as the receipt of it. It was generally known in the village who the writer was. It was looked upon as a stupid joke.

Police-constable Rees said on the Saturday morning he saw Mrs. Howell and Miss Peek in Miss Smith's shop. Mrs. Howell said, "Do you think anything will come of it, Mr. Rees?" and she cried. She said the same thing on Sunday morning. On the following Tuesday he arrested her, and when she was in the police-station she said she wrote the letters, and that Davies and Polly Peek were with her and assisted her. They had a copy of the *Echo* on the table, with "Jack the Ripper's" letter in it. She copied it off that. David Davies posted one letter to Mrs. Magor, and Polly Peek posted the other. She added that she had since apologised to Mr. And Mrs. Magor, and had given one guinea towards the Public Institute.

The Stipendiary Magistrate said it was a curious case, and the magistrates wished to adjourn it for consideration. The case was then adjourned for a week, and the accused was admitted to bail in her own recognizance of £28 and one surety of £26.

The verdict of the court was reported in the *Cardiff Times* of Saturday 8 December, and it reflects the true seriousness of the thoughtless actions of Miriam Howells and the two who most certainly aided and abetted her. Although she escaped lightly, the stipendiary magistrate, Mr North, explained the real implications of their actions, reflecting on the truly horrendous crimes in London that had supplied the material for the 'lark':

He said it had been a matter of very grave deliberation with the bench respecting the course they should take with regard to the defendant, because she must know that although she thought she was doing something very funny, she was committing a very serious crime. She sent to two women letters threatening to murder them. She said she only meant it in fun, but it was not a question whether the letters were sent in fun or with the deliberate intention of carrying out the threat conveyed – that was not what they had to consider. What they had to consider was, did she send these letters to these women threatening to murder them. The matter with them was whether they should send her for trial to the assizes, and if she had been so dealt with, she would have been liable to be sent to penal servitude for life. She never thought of that. (Defendant: No, sir.) No; nor did she think of the effect it would have upon these two unfortunate women. He thought it was an equally unfortunate thing for her to have made a joke of the crimes in London of a ruffian, who so far had not been found. She had made a joke of crimes of a revolting character. He hoped she was thoroughly ashamed of it, and that it would be a lesson to her, and to everyone else who had thought well to make these matters a subject of joke, and that they would hear nothing more of this. – Mr. Rhys: Anonymous letters of every kind are bad enough. – The defendant was then dismissed, the magistrates disallowing the expenses of the two witnesses who were with the defendant when she wrote the letters, as they were as guilty as she was. The expenses of Mrs. Magor and Miss Smith were allowed.

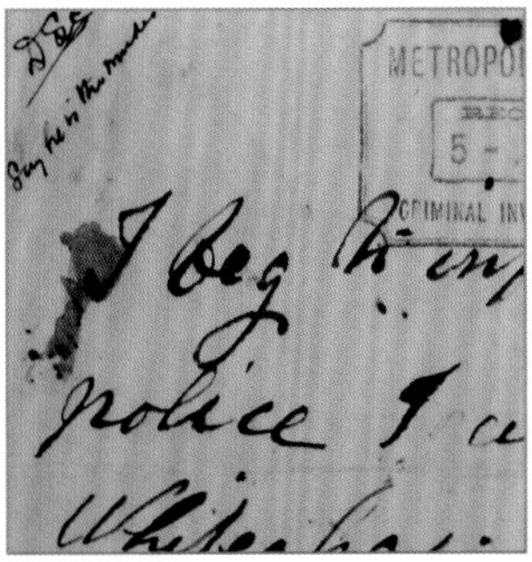

— **EIGHT** —

'I will rip a few more'

AS we have noted, October 1888 was a month when no further killing was added to the East End tally, but it was a month of great excitement for the press and public alike. In addition to the episodes described thus far, the police's file of letters from the alleged murderer continued to expand. The autumnal fog enshrouding the streets of London was supplemented, for the police, by the vexing fog raised by the correspondence. The *Star* of Wednesday 3 October, commented:

> LETTERS OF ADVICE.
>
> The numbers of letters received by the police offering advice or suggestions as to the best way of catching the murderer is something enormous. They come from all over the world. America sends quite as many as all other countries outside of England, and even Australia has been heard from. Practical jokers of the same school as "Jack the Ripper" try to crack their nuts on the police as well as through the Press, but the detectives have yet to learn that they are in possession of a specimen of the way the genuine expert knife handler can use a pen.

An American theme was established in the press and was added to when the London murders were compared to an unsolved series of killings that had been committed earlier in Texas. The *Star of the East* of Wednesday 3 October stated:

> AFTER TEXAS – WHITECHAPEL.
>
> Not a great many months ago, as already briefly reported, a series of remarkably brutal murders of women occurred in Texas. The matter caused great local excitement . . . The crimes were characterised by the same brutal methods as those of the Whitechapel murders. The theory has been suggested that the perpetrator of the latter may be the Texas criminal, who was never discovered. The Atlanta *Constitution*, a leading southern newspaper, thus

puts the argument: "In our recent annals of crime there has been no other man capable of committing such deeds. The mysterious crimes in Texas have ceased. They have just commenced in London. Is the man from Texas at the bottom of them all? If he is the monster or lunatic he may be expected to appear anywhere. The fact that he is no longer at work in Texas argues his presence somewhere else. His peculiar line of work was executed in precisely the same manner as is now going on in London. Why should he not be there? The more one thinks of it the more irresistible becomes the conviction that it is the man from Texas." The Superintendent [*sic*] of the New York Police admits the possibility of this theory being correct, but he does not think it probable. "There is," he says, "the same brutality and mutilation, the same suspicion that the criminal is a monster or lunatic who has declared war literally to the knife against all womankind, but I hardly believe it is the same individual."

On Friday 5 October the *Daily Telegraph* published a letter from an anonymous reader who had been giving some thought to the matter:

London, Oct. 4.
To the Editor of "The Daily Telegraph."
Sir – permit me to suggest, in reference to the tragedies that are at present occupying the mind of everyone –

1. That the idea that the letters attributed to the murderer could have been "a practical joke" or "hoax" is quite untenable. It is inconceivable that any human being, even the most degraded, could joke on such a subject. Rather, the more degraded the class, the more sympathy there would be with these unfortunate women. Besides, the letters breathe the very spirit of such a murderer.
2. It is unlikely that the man's dress or exterior is at all in keeping with his crimes. Probably he is well dressed, and his entire appearance is such as to totally disarm suspicion, otherwise women would not trust themselves in his company in the way they seem to do.
3. His letters favour far more of American slang than of home. They are the exact reprint of the Texas rough's style, and probably the Texas solution of the mystery is the true one. – I am, &c.

OBSERVER.

Another appeared in the *Daily News* of Friday 5 October 1888, which stated that it had been received by the Central Press and bore an EC postmark. The article noted that "The manager of the Central Press, immediately on receipt of the above extraordinary communication, placed it at the disposal of the Scotland-yard authorities." The letter is still in the police files and is one of the earliest inspired by the 'Dear Boss' letter. It was written in red ink, but in a different hand, and dated 2 October:

2 October

Dear Boss

Since last splendid Success . two more & never a squeal. oh I am master of the art. I am going to be heavy on the guilded whores now, we are. some dutchess will cut up nicely & the lace will show nicely. You wonder how! oh we are masters no education like a butchers

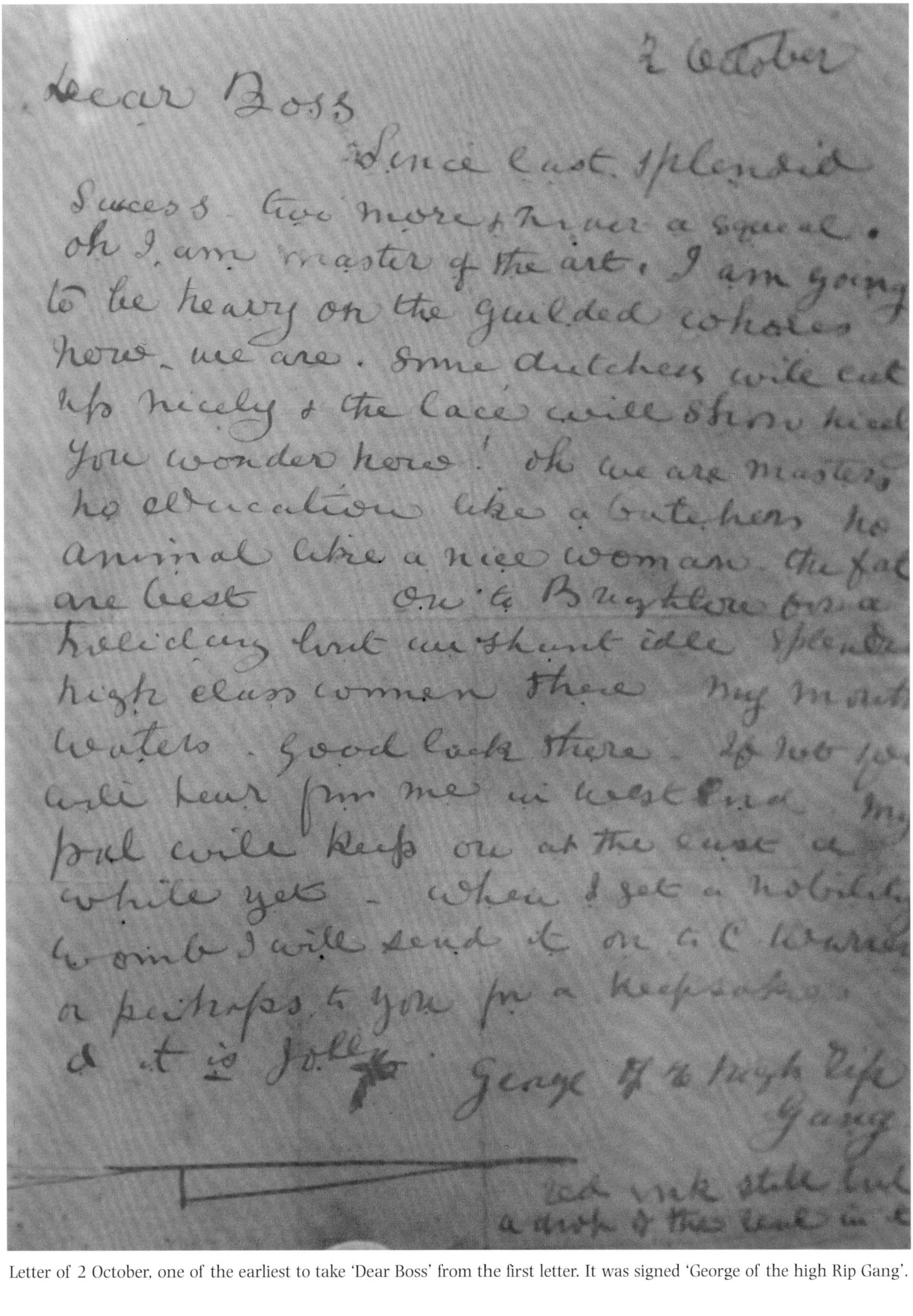

2 October
Dear Boss
Since last splendid
success two more & never a squeal.
oh I am master of the art. I am going
to be heavy on the guilded whores
now we are. Some dutchess will cut
up nicely & the lace will show nicely
You wonder how! oh we are masters
no education like a butchers no
animal like a nice woman the fat
are best On to Brighton for a
holiday but we shant idle splendid
high class women there my mouth
waters. Good luck there. If not you
will hear from me in West End. My
pal will keep on at the east a
while yet. When I get a nobility
womb I will send it on to C Warren
or perhaps to you for a keepsake.
O it is jolly George of the high Rip
Gang
Red ink still but
a drop of this left in a

Letter of 2 October, one of the earliest to take 'Dear Boss' from the first letter. It was signed 'George of the high Rip Gang'.

no animal like a nice woman. the fat are best on to Brighton for a holiday but we shant idle splendid high class women there my mouth waters. good luck there. If not you will hear from me in West End. My pal will keep on at the east a while yet . when I get a nobility womb I will send it on to C. Warren or perhaps to you for a keepsakes o it is jolly.

George of the high Rip
Gang
red ink still but
a drop of the real in it

An interesting letter which shows how closely the Victorian mind linked the arch-villain of earlier years, 'Spring Heeled Jack', with the newly named 'Jack the Ripper' was found on 4 October in the front area of 6 Vincent Square, Westminster. The letter, in which the unknown correspondent claims to be an American, was written in pencil as follows:

October 4th 1888
Spring Heel Jack
The Whitechapel Murderer

I am an american I have been in London the last ten months and have Murdered no less than six women I mean to make a dozen of it now while I am about it I think I may as well have six men in blue to make the number as I see there is a few too many knocking about the East End looking for me but I am close upon their heel every day and will be for some time yet and I was in the crowd at Berners Street watching the blue boy's wash the blood marks away sorry to give you so much trouble but what I have sworne to do I will do at the cost of my own life at nights I have been sleeping in Bow cemetary one thing I have to tell you know is the policemen who has found the women it is those
[second page] I mean settleling as they will not get the chance of giving evidience against me
I shall shortly have to shift or sh[illegible] my quarters from Bow cemetary a[gain?] I have enlightened you a bit a[illegible] I have written this on the Embankment near Waterloo

Jack the Ripper
I will rip a few more
So help my God I
will

Another letter postmarked London W. OC 4 88 and addressed 'Superintendent, Scotland Yard, Whitehall' was received by the Criminal Investigation Department on 5 October. It read:

I beg to inform the police I am the Whitechapel murder I intend to commit two murders in the Haymarket tonight take note of this Withechape is to warm for me now my knife has not
[second page] been found yet for I still have the knife I intend to keep it untill I finish 20
then try & find me

This again shows the influence of the publicity and the threat of further murders to be committed, a theme introduced in the original correspondence.

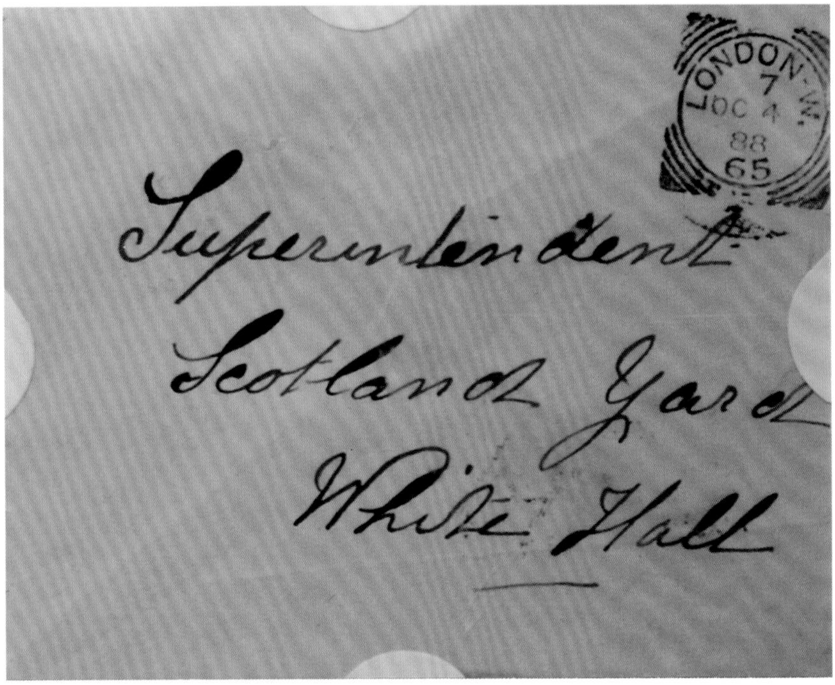
LONDON W
7
OC 4
88
65

Superintendent
Scotland Yard
White Hall

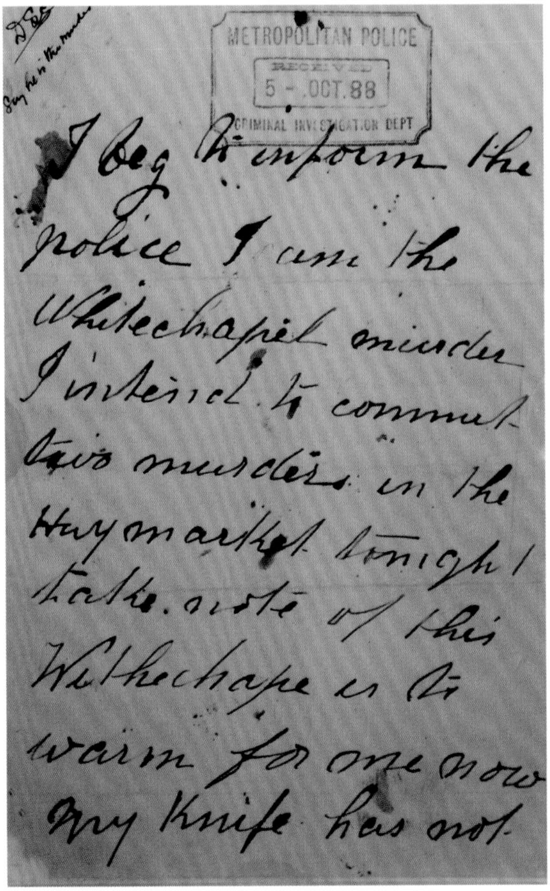
METROPOLITAN POLICE
RECEIVED
5 - OCT.88
CRIMINAL INVESTIGATION DEPT

I beg to inform the
police I am the
Whitechapel murder
I intend to commit
two murders in the
Haymarket tonight
take note of this
Withechape is to
warm for one now
my Knife has not

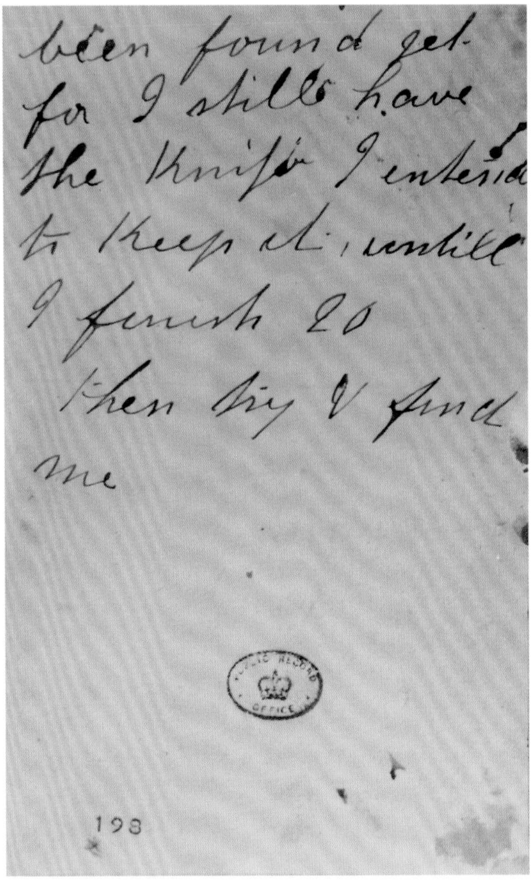
been found yet
for I still have
the Knife I intend
to keep it untill
I finish 20
then try & find
me

198

Letter of 4 October to 'Superintendent, Scotland Yard', stating an intention to commit two murders in the Haymarket.

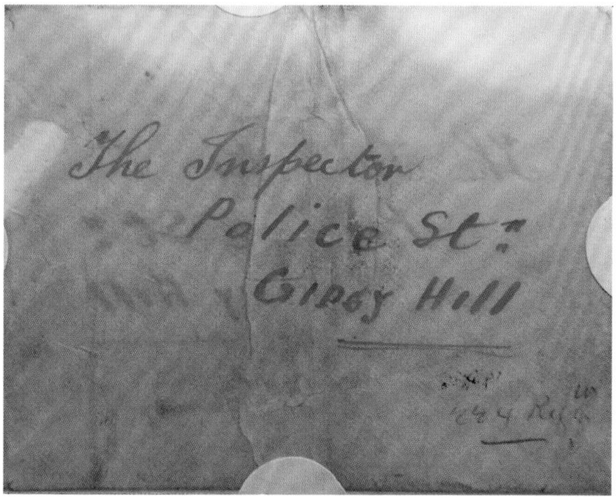

The Inspector
Police St:
Gipsy Hill

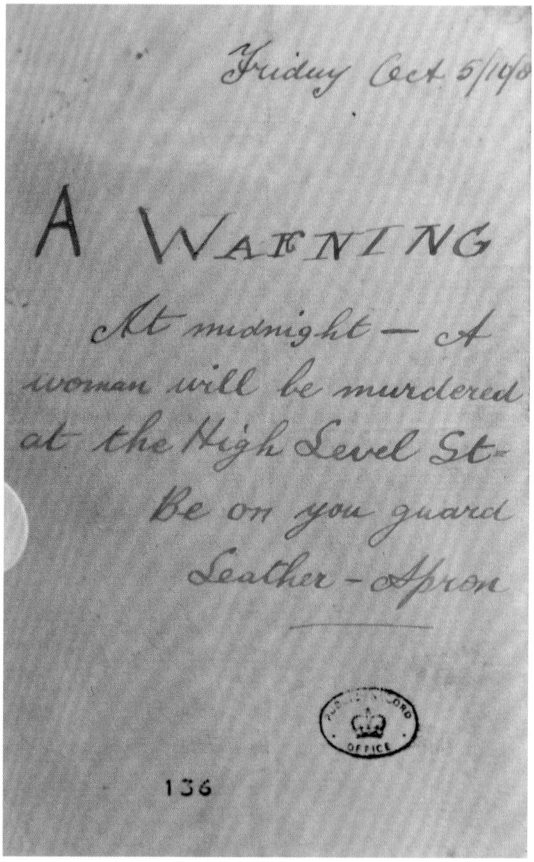

Friday Oct 5/10/8

A WARNING
At midnight – A
woman will be murdered
at the High Level St-
Be on you guard
Leather-Apron

136

Letter dated 5 October sent to the police station at Gipsy Hill. It is signed 'Leather-Apron' and not 'Jack the Ripper'.

A letter and envelope written in red ink were found between Princess Road and Selhurst Railway Station on 6 October, and showed that the earlier nickname of 'Leather Apron' was still remembered despite the new popularity of 'Jack the Ripper'. The envelope was addressed: 'The Inspector, Police St:, Gipsy Hill', and the letter read as follows:

Friday Oct 5/10/8

A WARNING
At midnight – A woman will be murdered at the High Level St.
Be on you guard
Leather – Apron

A noteworthy development in October, which also attracted much press attention, was the idea of the police using trained bloodhounds to track the killer. It resulted in the much-publicised trials of two bloodhounds in London, involving Sir Charles Warren – a gift for the press and letter-writers alike. A postcard written in black ink and addressed to Sir Charles Warren himself was posted on 5 October. It read:

Dr Boss
You have not found me yet I have done another one and thrown it in the river and I mean doing another one before the weeks out. You can put as many bloodhounds as you like but you will never catch me Yours Truly
Jack Ripper

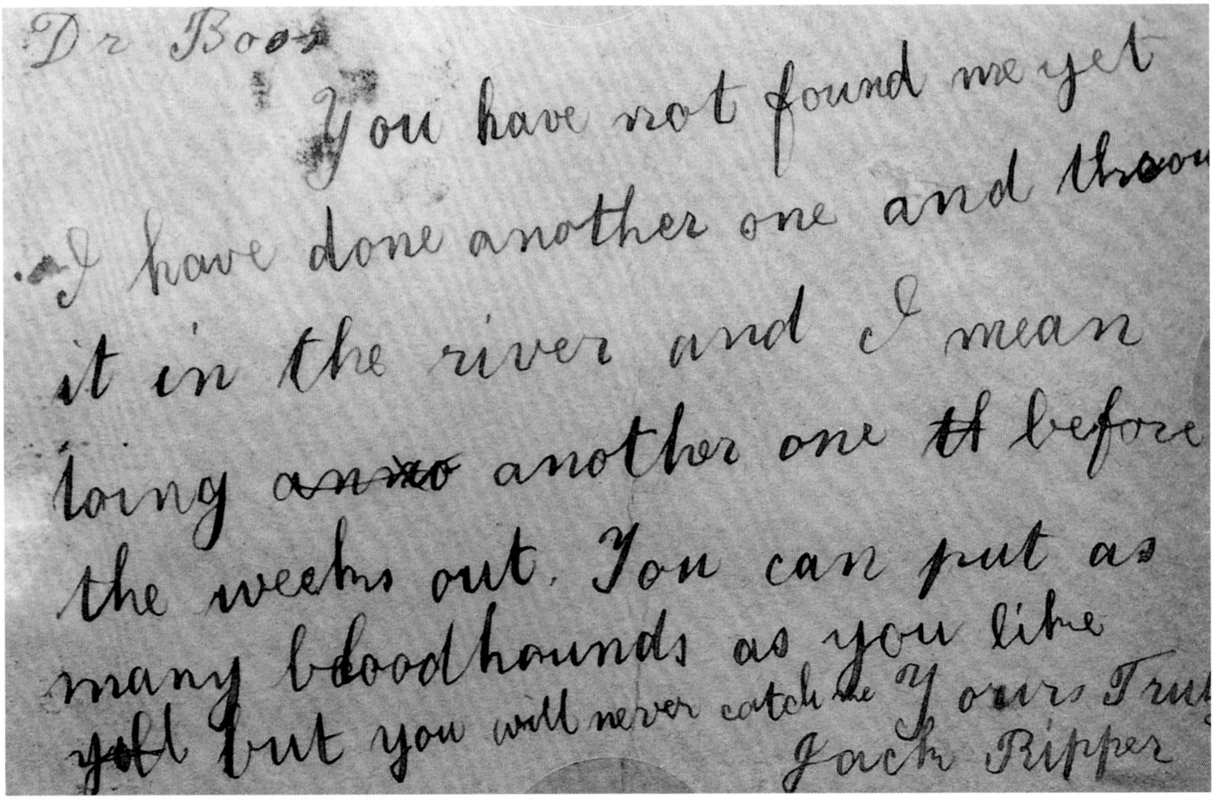

Dr Boss
You have not found me yet
I have done another one and throw
it in the river and I mean
loing ~~anno~~ another one ~~tt~~ before
the weeks out. You can put as
many bloodhounds as you like
~~yell~~ but you will never catch me Yours Tru
Jack Ripper

Postcard dated 5 October and sent to Sir Charles Warren. The writer claims to have thrown a victim in the river and to have killed another. The note mentions bloodhounds.

The Central News Agency apparently also thought that the idea of the bloodhounds had some merit for it is a little known fact that they obtained dogs themselves. No doubt they felt that the ultimate scoop would be theirs if they could actually catch 'Jack the Ripper' themselves. They spent much money, time and enterprise in the attempt to obtain such an 'exclusive'. It was one idea, however, that was not to 'come off'. At the time of the murders two big bloodhounds were installed on the Central News premises in readiness to be put on the track of the murderer on the occasion of his next crime. This must have been in early October, about the same time that the police experimented with their hounds, for a few weeks passed with no renewal of the murders. It was assumed that the murderer had ceased his 'business' and the Central News hounds, like the police ones, were returned to their kennels in the country. Two nights later there was another murder but there were no hounds in London to put on the killer's track.*

Another letter, dated 6 October 1888 but postmarked the 8th and posted in the London NW district, ran as follows:

6 Oct 1888

You though your-self very clever I reckon when you informed the police But you made a mistake if you though I dident see you now I know you know me and I see your little game, and I mean to finish you and send your ears to your wife if you show this to the police or help them if you do I will finish you. It no use your trying to get out of my way Because I

* H. Simonis, *The Street of Ink* (London, Cassell, 1917).

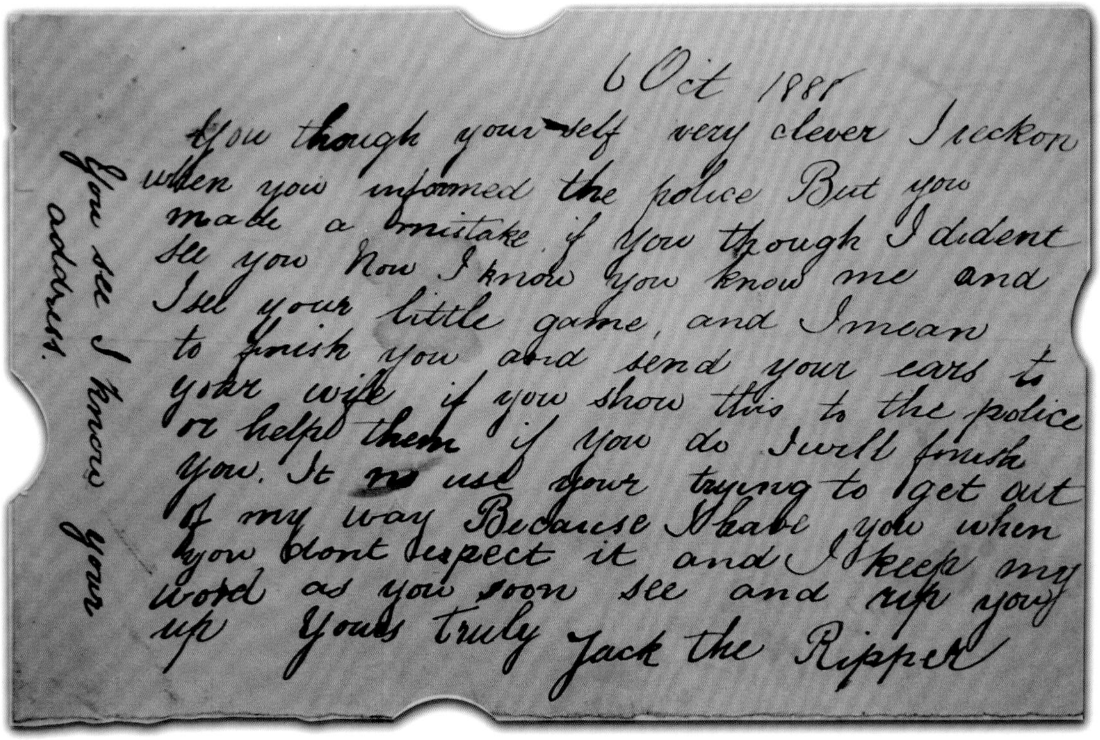

6 Oct 1888

You though your self very clever I reckon
when you informed the police But you
made a mistake if you though I dident
see you Now I know you know me and
I see your little game, and I mean
to finish you and send your ears to
your wife if you show this to the police
or help them if you do I will finish
you. It no use your trying to get out
of my way Because I have you when
you dont expect it and I keep my
word as you soon see and rip you
up Yours truly Jack the Ripper

You see I know your address.

Letter of 6 October making threats to an unknown person. It is postmarked 8 October and was posted in north-west London. Similarities between the writing and signature of this letter and the 'Dear Boss' one have been noted.

> have you when you don't expect it and I keep my word as you soon see and rip you up
> Yours truly Jack the Ripper

Written at right angles down the left margin was – 'You see I know your address.'

The handwriting of this letter is similar, but not identical, to the 'Dear Boss' letter (*see* illustration). It, like so many, also contains echoes from that letter in 'little game', 'send your ears' and, of course, 'Yours truly Jack the Ripper'. It was written in black ink. By this date facsimiles of the 'Dear Boss' letter were widely published, and copying was an easy matter. The writer clearly had some sort of agenda with the recipient who, unfortunately, is not identified. The letter is contained in the MEPO 3/142 files as folio 139 with no other comment.

The increasing volume of correspondence allegedly from the killer is evidenced in a report from the *Star* of Saturday 6 October:

> **Telegram from 'Jack the Ripper.'**
>
> The Press Association says: – The following postal telegram was received by the Metropolitan Police at 11.55 p.m. last night. It was handed in at an office in the Eastern District at 8 p.m.: – Charles Warren, Head of the Police New Central Office. 'Dear Boss, – if [you] are willing enough to catch me I am now in City-road lodging, but number you will have to find out, and I mean to do another murder to night in Whitechapel. 'Yours, Jack the Ripper.'

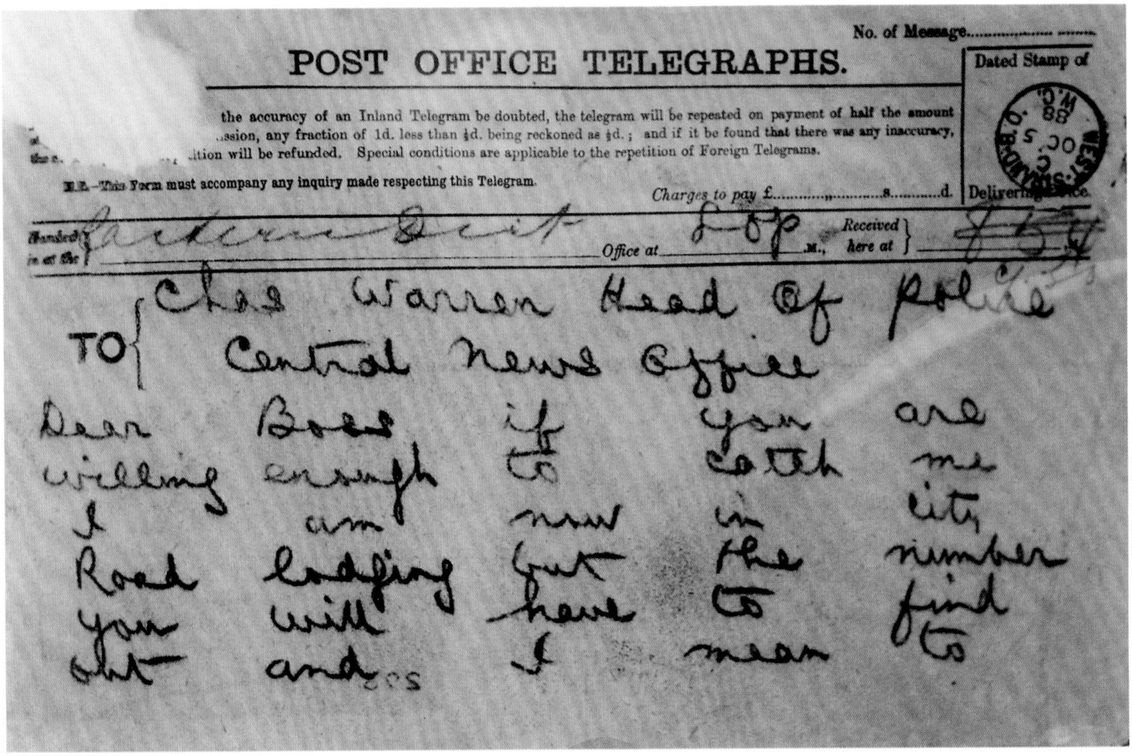
No. of Message.................

POST OFFICE TELEGRAPHS.

Dated Stamp of

...the accuracy of an Inland Telegram be doubted, the telegram will be repeated on payment of half the amount ...ssion, any fraction of 1d. less than ½d. being reckoned as ½d.; and if it be found that there was any inaccuracy, ...ition will be refunded. Special conditions are applicable to the repetition of Foreign Telegrams.

N.B.—This Form must accompany any inquiry made respecting this Telegram.

Charges to pay £..............s...........d. Delivering Office.

Handed in at the Eastern Dist Office at 8 0p M., Received here at 8 5

TO { Chas Warren Head Of police Central news Office

Dear Boss if you are willing enough to catch me I am now in City Road lodging but the number you will have to find out and I mean to

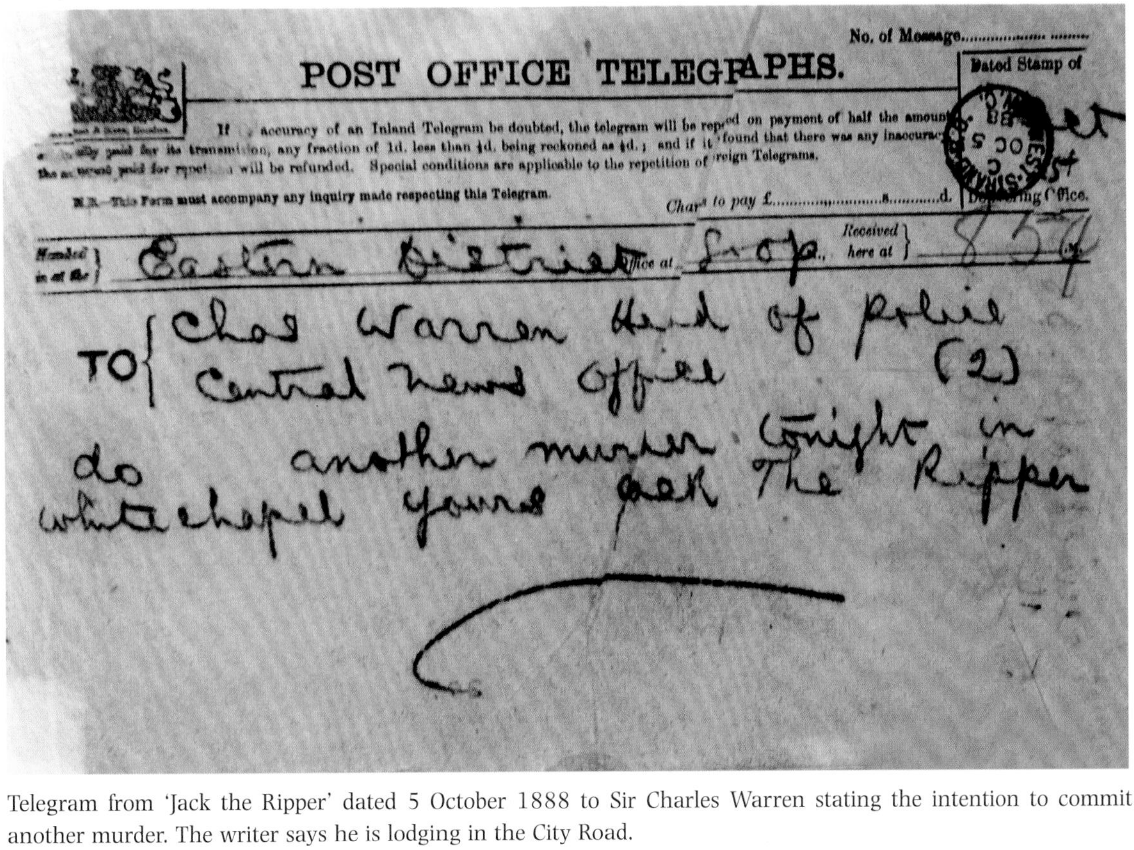
No. of Message.................

POST OFFICE TELEGRAPHS.

Dated Stamp of

If ... accuracy of an Inland Telegram be doubted, the telegram will be repeated on payment of half the amount ...ally paid for its transmission, any fraction of 1d. less than ½d. being reckoned as ½d.; and if it found that there was any inaccuracy, the amount paid for repetition will be refunded. Special conditions are applicable to the repetition of Foreign Telegrams.

N.B.—This Form must accompany any inquiry made respecting this Telegram.

Charges to pay £..............s...........d. Delivering Office.

Handed in at the Eastern District Office at 8 0p M., Received here at 8 5

TO { Chas Warren Head of police Central news Office (2)

do another murder tonight in whitechapel yours Jack The Ripper

Telegram from 'Jack the Ripper' dated 5 October 1888 to Sir Charles Warren stating the intention to commit another murder. The writer says he is lodging in the City Road.

> The telegram has been proved to have been handed in at the chief office of the Eastern District in Commercial-road, but no information is forthcoming as to how it came to be accepted by the telegraphic authorities, or by whom it was handed in.
>
> A letter was also received at the Commercial-street Police-station by the first post this morning. It was written in black lead pencil and signed 'Jack the Ripper.' It is couched in ridiculous language, and the police believe it to be the work of a lunatic.

The above mentioned telegram is preserved in the MEPO files as folios 296–9.

The *Liverpool Daily Post* carried some reports on the 'Jack the Ripper' correspondence on Monday 8 October. One of particular interest ran:

> Information was given to the City police on Saturday morning that Messrs. Bryant and May had received a letter from a person signing himself John the Ripper, couched in the following terms:–
>
> "I hereby notify that I am going to pay your girls a visit. I hear that they are beginning to say what they will do with me. I am going to see what a few of them have in their stomachs, and I will take it out of them so that they will never have no more to do on the quiet. – signed JOHN RIPPER.
> P.S. I am in Poplar today."

The Bryant & May match factory girls had, of course, risen to fame the previous July when 672 women downed tools in support of a colleague who had been unfairly sacked on the 5th of that month. They were joined by 1,200 girls from the wood match-making department at the Bow factory and 300 from the box-making section. The strike was soon over but the 'Match Girls' had gained immortal fame and a place in the history of British trade unionism. The wording given in the above report is not quite true to the original letter and 'stomachs' was substituted for 'bellies', obviously because it was felt to be more acceptable. The letter was dated 'Friday Oct. 5 88/'. At the bottom of the note are the words 'Dear Boss' and 'RIPPER', but the name 'John' is not apparent.

London was not the only place of origin for the letters. The following two-page example, dated 8 October 1888, was addressed from Galashiels. Posted at Innerleithen, it was received by the Criminal Investigation Department at Scotland Yard and was, as a result, initialled 'DSS' in the top left corner by Chief Inspector Donald Sutherland Swanson himself. It ran as follows:

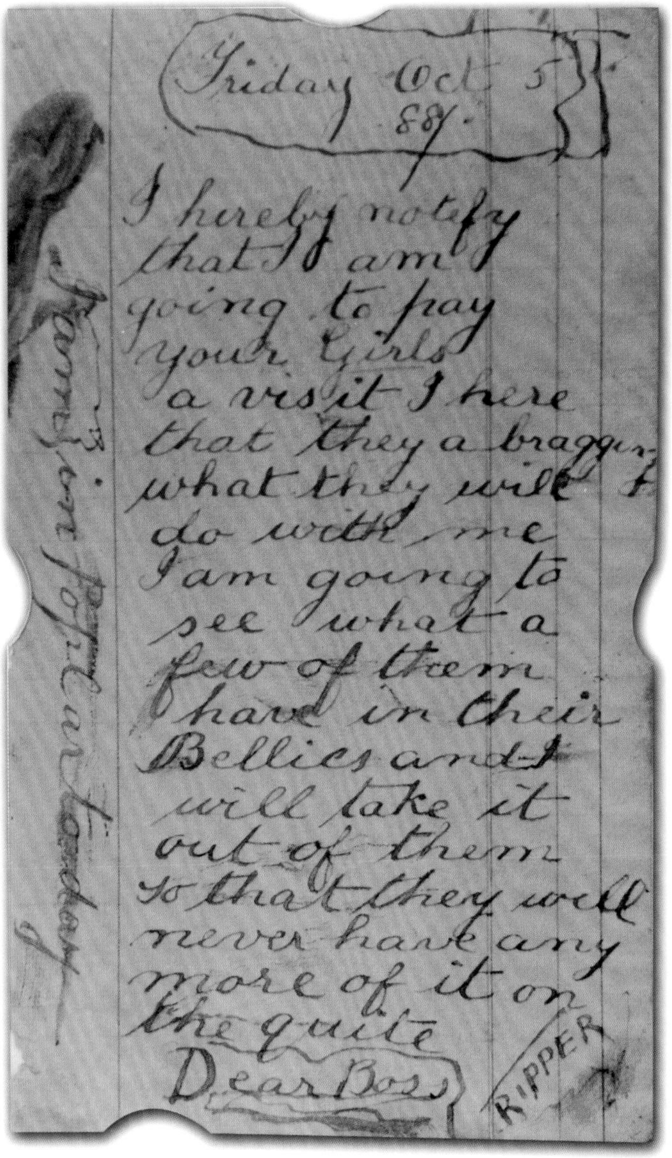
Friday Oct 5
88.

I hereby notefy
that I am
going to pay
your Girls
a visit I here
that they a bragger
what they will
do with me
I am going to
see what a
few of them
have in their
Bellies and I
will take it
out of them
so that they will
never have any
more of it on
the quite
Dear Boss

RIPPER

Letter dated 5 October threatening the girls at the Bryant & May match factory.

8/10/88
Galayshiels

Dear Boss,

I have to thank You and my Brother in trade, Jack the Ripper for your kindness in letting me away out of Whitechapel I am on my road to the tweed Factories. I will let the Innerleithen Constable or Police men know when I am about to start my nice Little game. I have got my Knife replenished so it Will answer both for Ladies and Gents Other 5 Tweed ones and I have one my wager

[reverse] I am Yours
Truly
The Ripper

Other letters, while still bearing the familiar signature, used police officers' and street names made familiar by the press reports. Predicting further murders was a common theme. Another letter written in red ink was found pinned to the passage wall at 22 Scott Street, Brady Street, Bethnal Green:

Berner Street
E.
Oct. 9th. '88.

To Sir C. Warren,
Another dreadful murder will be committed by me to-morrow morning.
Jack the Ripper

Not only did the writers have a field day exercising their literary bent; the artistic among them added elaborate sketches to some of their letters. A particularly striking example (*see* frontispiece) was received by the CID at Scotland Yard on 9 October. It was headed by a skull and crossbones device, complete with halo, crossed daggers, coffin and a skeleton, all in black ink. Posted in Birmingham on 8 October, it was in red ink, and like so many others it purported to come from 'Jack the Ripper' himself. It bears Swanson's initials and is filed as folio 160:

I am as you see by this now amongst the slogging town of Brum and mean to play my part well & vigorously amongst its inhabitants. I have already spotted from its number 3 girls and before one week is passed after receiving this 3 Families will be thrown into a state of delightful mourning. Ha,Ha. My Bloody whim must have its way do not be surprised 15 murders must be completed then I kill myself to cheat the scaffold. For I know you cannot catch me & may I be ever present in your dreams
Jack the Ripper

The widespread effects of 'Jack the letter-writer' were also seen in Ireland. The following report is from the *Star of the East*, Tuesday 9 October:

"JACK THE RIPPER" ABOUT TO
VISIT DUBLIN.

The *Irish Times* says a number of constables have been sent to London on detective duty in connection with the Whitechapel murder. The Dublin police authorities have received a letter, purporting to be from "Jack the Ripper," stating that he intends visiting Dublin this week.

The following letter was postmarked 10 October 1888, South Lambeth, SW, and made mention of the bloodhounds and of female hygiene:

Jack the
Sir Ripper

You had better be carefull, How you send those Bloodhounds about the streets, because of the single females wearing stained napkins . women smell very strong when they are unwell

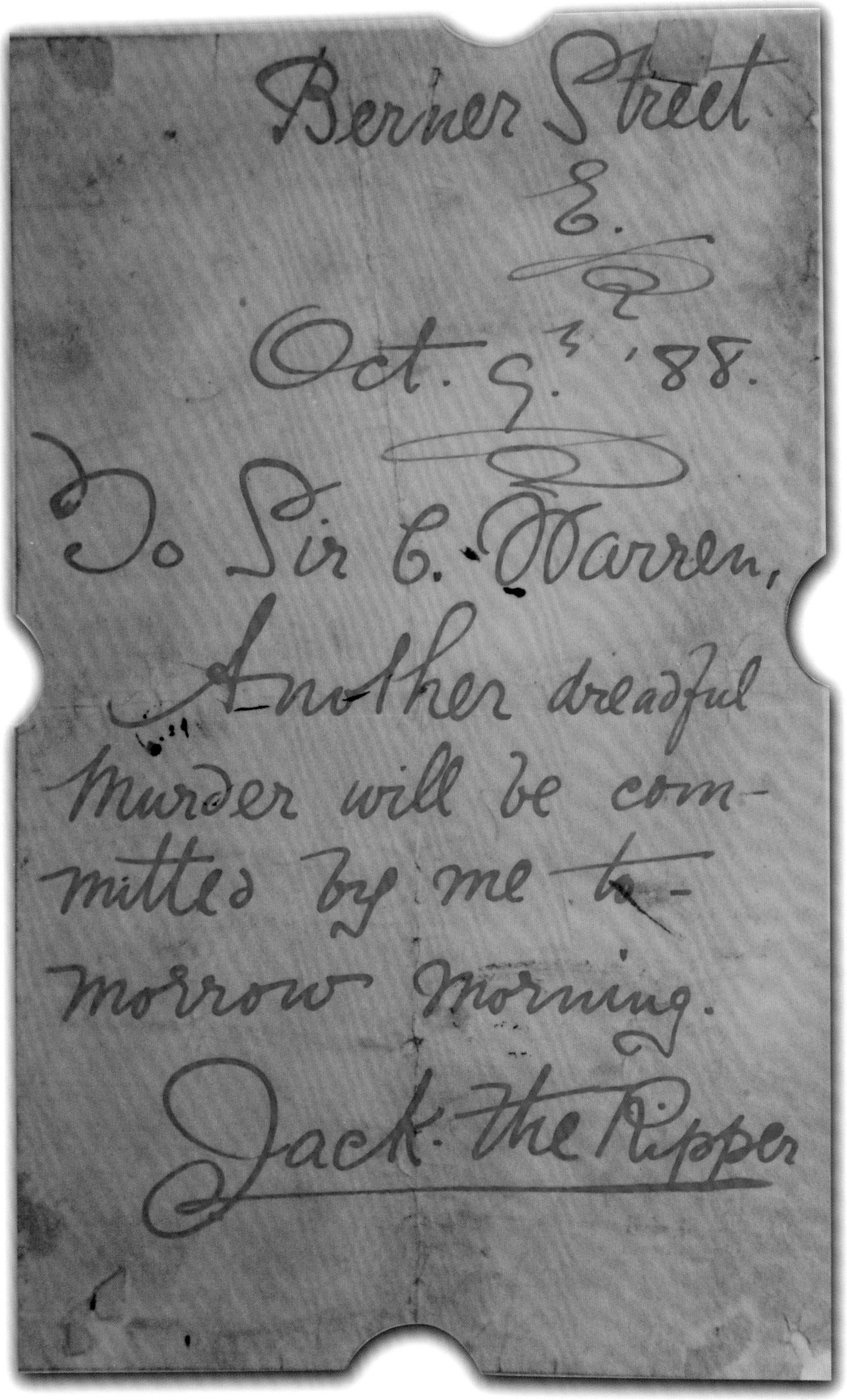
Berner Street
E.
Oct. 9th '88.
To Sir C. Warren,
Another dreadful
murder will be com-
mitted by me to-
morrow morning.
Jack the Ripper

Letter of 9 October from 'Jack the Ripper'. It is addressed from 'Berner Street E.' and threatens another murder the next day. It was found pinned to a passage wall in Bethnal Green.

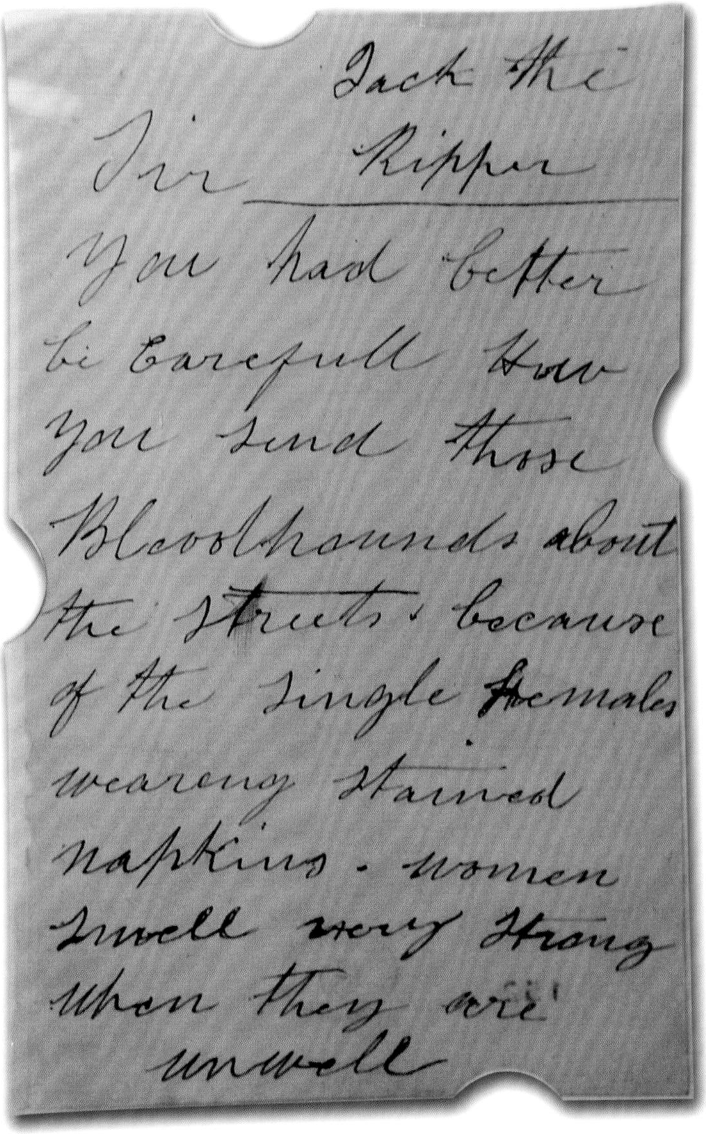
Jack the
Sir Ripper
You had better
be carefull How
you send those
Bloodhounds about
the streets because
of the single females
wearing stained
napkins - women
smell very strong
when they are
unwell

Letter of 10 October from 'Jack the Ripper'. It mentions bloodhounds and female hygiene.

On Saturday 13 October the *East Anglian Daily Times* reported that the letter-writing fad had spread to France:

MURDER CRAZE IN PARIS.

The Whitechapel murders, says a Paris correspondent, have not only been here a newspaper sensation of the first magnitude, but have got on weak brains and set madmen and lovers of practical jokes writing to the Prefect of Police. M. Goroen, the head of the Criminal Investigation Department, has received the following, among other letters: "Sir, – You must have heard of the Whitechapel murders. This is the explanation of their mysterious side. There are partners, I and another, in this business. One is in England and the other in France. I am at Brest, and am going to Paris to operate as does my London colleague in London. We are seeking in the human body that which the doctors have never found. You will try in vain to hunt us down. Our next victim will be a woman between 20 and 30. We will cut her

> carotid artery, disembowel her, amputate four fingers of her left hand, leaving the thumb only. Meanwhile you will hear of me, and in three weeks at most. Look out. Signed-H.L.P.C."

Back in the East End of London the *Borough of Hackney Standard* of 13 October made the following comment:

> The newspaper received a postcard threatening to murder a girl in Hackney Churchyard on Saturday night. The postcard had a knife and cross drawn on it.

The *Standard* handed the postcard over to the police and it is preserved as folio 180 (*see* illustration below). Written in red ink, it was addressed to: 'Hackney Standard, Clapton Road, E.' and was posted in London on 5 October:

> 55, Flower & Dean Street
> Whitechapel
>
> Get your type ready my boys I ll give you a job for your paper I m going to vissit Hackney on Saturday night Ill have a corpse in the Churchyard for parson Sundy morning Glorious fun. 14 more to make the twenty. Good luckk
>
> Jack the Ripper

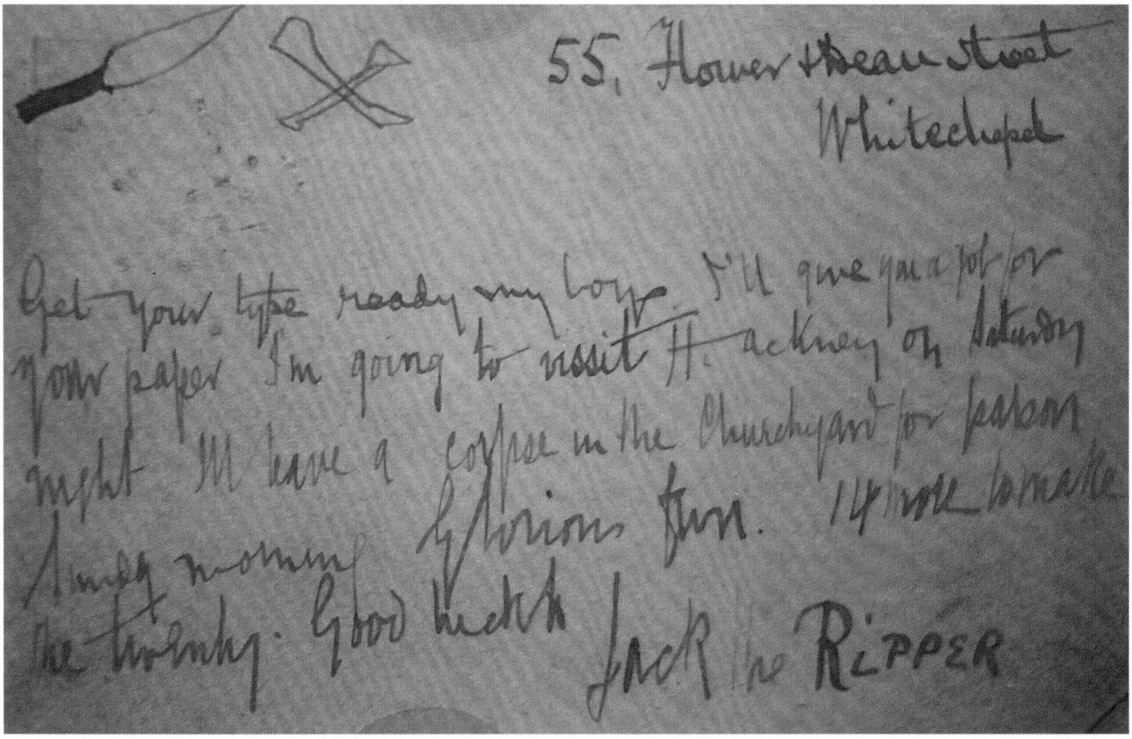
55, Flower & Dean Street
Whitechapel

Get your type ready my boys I'll give you a job for your paper I'm going to vissit Hackney on Saturday night Ill have a corpse in the Churchyard for parson Sundy morning Glorious fun. 14 more to make the twenty. Good luckk

Jack the Ripper

Postcard of 5 October to the *Hackney Standard*. It is addressed from 55 Flower & Dean Street (Eddowes' lodging house) and threatens a murder in Hackney.

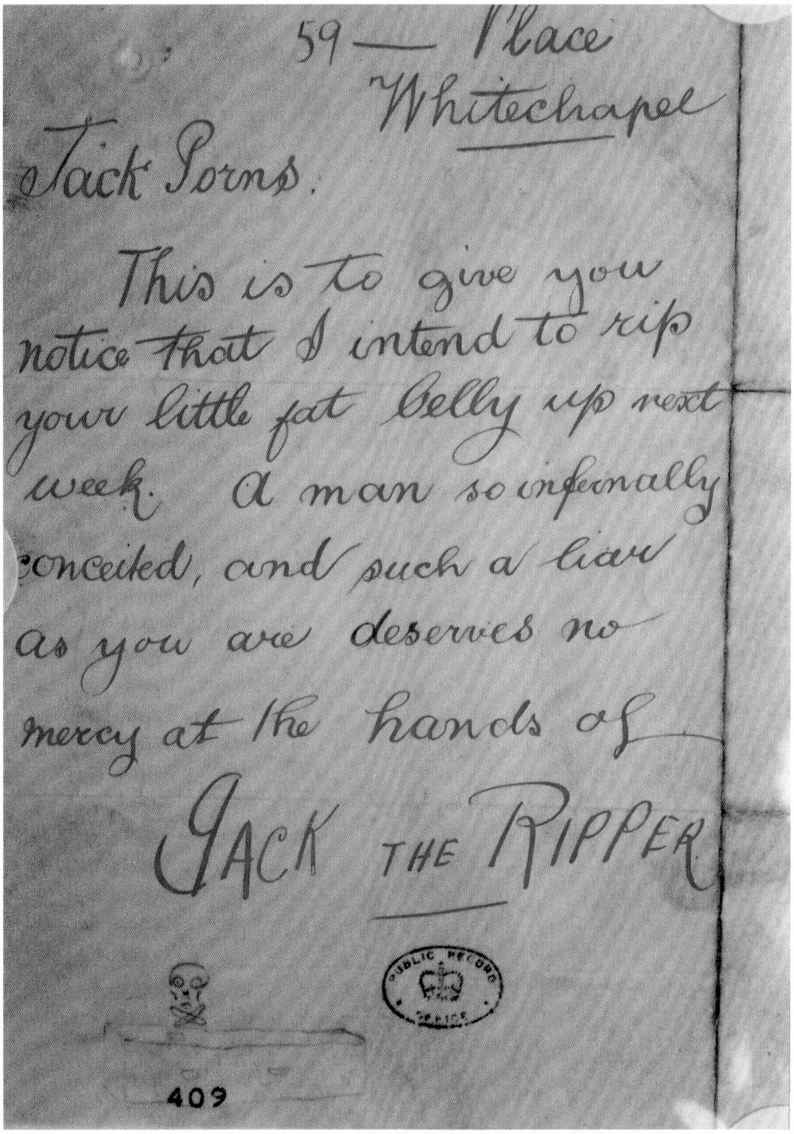

59 — Place
Whitechapel

Jack Porns.

This is to give you notice that I intend to rip your little fat Belly up next week. A man so infernally conceited, and such a liar as you are deserves no mercy at the hands of

JACK THE RIPPER

409

Letter of 13 October threatening an unknown person.

It is interesting to note that 55 Flower & Dean Street was the address of the lodging house where Eddowes lived with her common-law husband John Kelly.

Another red-ink letter-writer posted the following cryptic epistle – to someone who had apparently upset him – at New Cross on 13 October:

> 59 — Place
> Whitechapel
>
> Jack Porns.
>
> This is to give you notice that I intend to rip your little fat belly up next week. A man so infernally conceited, and such a liar as you are deserves no mercy at the hands of
>
> JACK THE RIPPER

The name 'Jack the Ripper' was perceived to guarantee to strike fear into the heart of any man or woman who received a communication signed by him. It was an opportunity too good to miss for the writers of malicious letters.

The circulation of the facsimiles of the 'Dear Boss' letter and 'saucy Jacky' postcard by the Metropolitan Police also resulted in suspects being investigated by the police and led to great public excitement. The *Star* of Tuesday 16 October reported:

> A Poor Joke
>
> Early this morning some 'Jack the Ripper' writing in chalk was found on the gate of a stable at Lewisham-road, near Blackheath Railway Station. "Dear Boss," it says, "if you wish to find the head of the body on the Embankment it is in a sack on the water. I have done another to-night. Jack the Ripper. Revenge." A policeman is guarding the gate, though in all probability the writing is only that of someone playing a stupid joke.
>
> A Unionist Idiot in Southwark
>
> A little girl named Maggie Smith, living at 17, Arnott-street, New Kent-road, picked up a parcel in New Kent-road, and took it to her mother. The covering consisted of a copy of the *Echo* of 5 Oct., and a part of a piece of music entitled 'Grandfather's Clock.' Inside was the upper portion of a pair of blood-stained grey-mixture trousers, attached to which was a piece of paper, on which was written the words, "Jack the Ripper's work."

It is now a well-known fact that, contrary to popular mythology, none of the murders was committed in foggy weather. However, October 1888 was a particularly foggy month in London, and one writer saw the advantage of committing a murder in such weather conditions. A letter dated the 18th of the month was sent to 'The Supt, Vine St, Police Station, W.' and ran as follows:

> Oct 18th 1888.
> Albany Road
>
> Sir,
> Look out to night for me in the neighbourhood of London Road they are some hot ones there if these fogs continue what a chance I shall have I am getting tired of my rest and I want to get to work again I shall not write anymore. Yours truly
> J the R

The episode of the 'From hell' letter to George Lusk provided further material for the letter-writers. As early as 19 October a letter combining phrases from both the 'Dear Boss' communication and the letter to Lusk was found in a letter-box at 37 West Ham Lane. Written in pencil, the letter was folded up and addressed 'To the Occupier'. It had a crude drawing of a stamp on the corner of the addressed section and was couched in the following terms:

> From Hell I am
> <u>somewhere</u> <u>19/10/88</u>
> <u>To the finder</u>
> <u>Dear Sir or Madam</u>
> I hope you are pretty well Dear old <u>Boss</u> I shall visit you shortly in about 3 or 4 weeks time I can write 5 hand writings if anybody recognises the writing I shall kill the first female I see

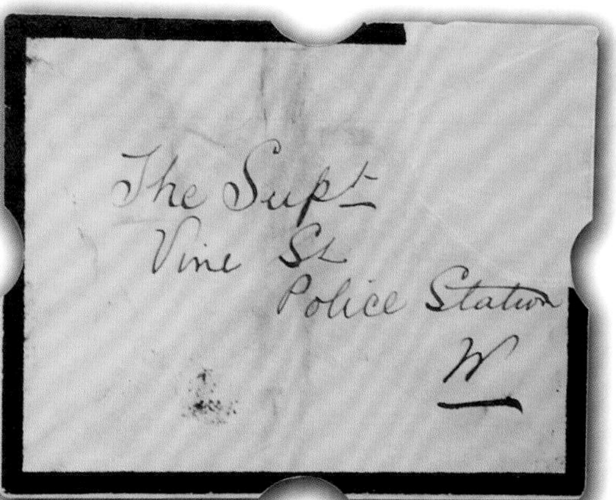

The Supt
Vine St
Police Station
W

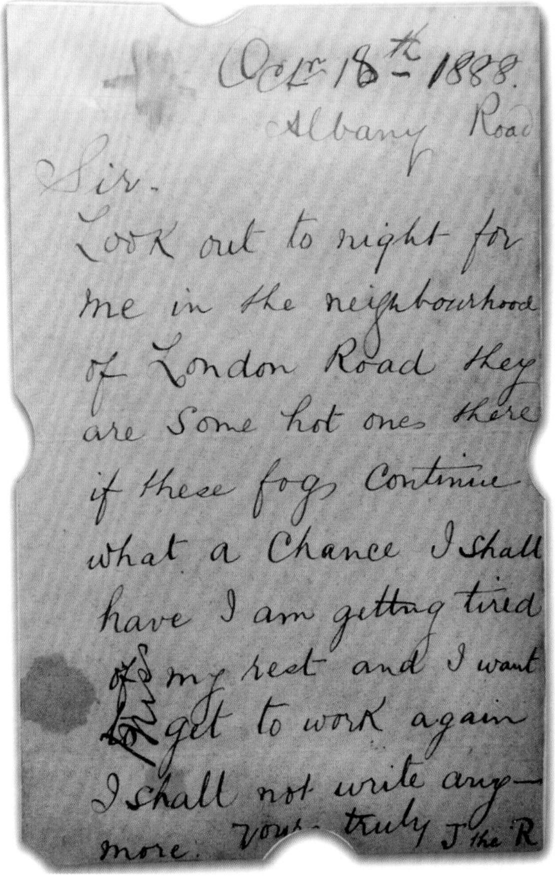

Octr 18th 1888.
Albany Road

Sir.
Look out to night for me in the neighbourhood of London Road they are some hot ones there if these fogs continue what a chance I shall have I am getting tired of my rest and I want to get to work again I shall not write any-more. yours truly J the R

Mourning envelope and letter of 18 October, signed 'J the R'. It states that the writer will be 'in the neighbourhood of London Road tonight' and mentions October fogs.

Below: Letter dated 19 October and found in a letterbox at 37 West Ham Lane threatening the occupants of the house. It echoes the 'From hell' letter to George Lusk.

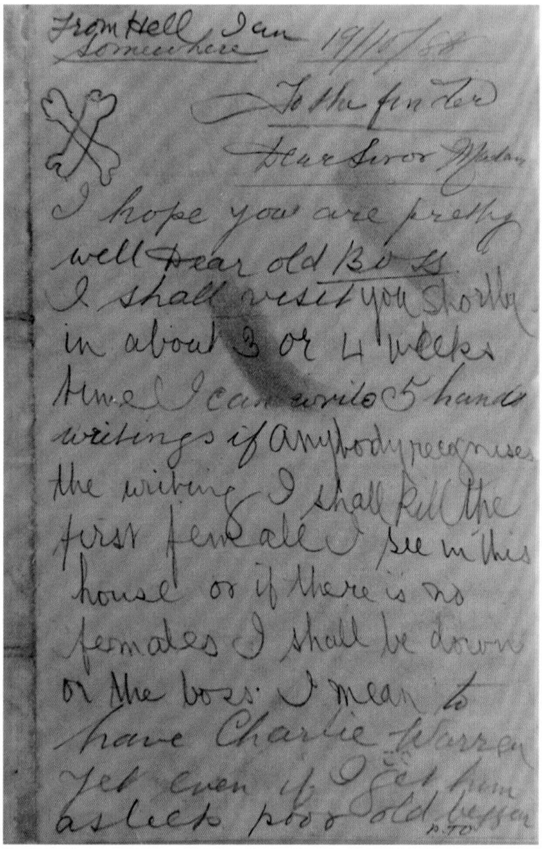

From Hell I am somewhere 19/10/88

To the finder
Dear Sir or Madam
I hope you are pretty well ~~dear~~ old Boss I shall visit you shortly in about 3 or 4 weeks time I can write 5 hand writings if anybody recognises the writing I shall kill the first female I see in this house or if there is no females I shall be down on the boss. I mean to have Charlie Warren yet even if I get him asleep poor old beggar P.T.O.

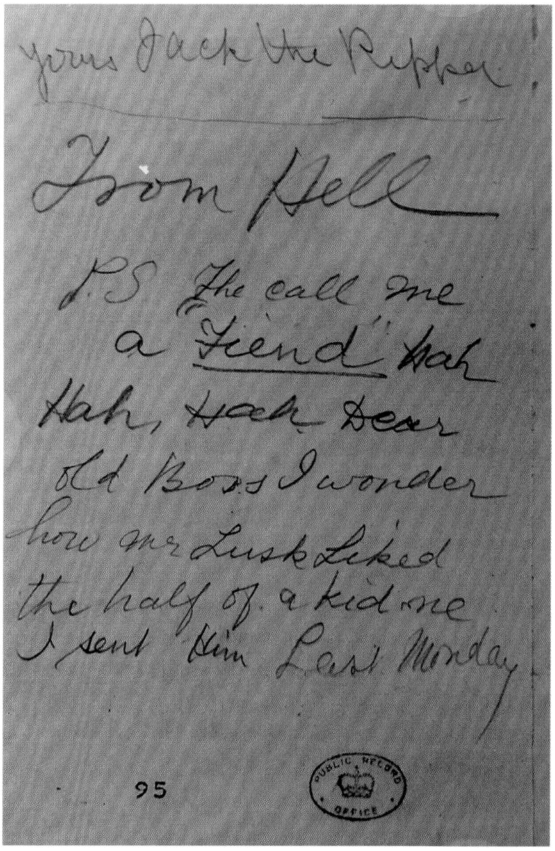

yours Jack the Ripper

From Hell

P.S. The call me a "Fiend" Hah Hah, Hach Dear old Boss I wonder how Mr Lusk Liked the half of a kidne I sent him Last Monday

95

PUBLIC RECORD OFFICE

> in this house or if there is no females I shall be down on the boss I mean to have Charlie Warren yet even if I get him asleep poor old beggar
>
> P.T.O.
>
> [second page] Yours Jack the Ripper
>
> From Hell
>
> P.S. The call me a "Fiend" Hah Hah, Hah, Dear old Boss I wonder how Mr Lusk Liked the half of a kid ne I sent Him Last Monday.

Albert Bachert, aged twenty-eight years, an art engraver of 13 Newnham Street, Whitechapel, was another Whitechapel Vigilance Committee member who received press publicity and did not seem to mind it. In early October he had featured in stories in several newspapers concerning a suspicious man with a black bag. *The Times* of Monday 1 October had reported:

> A man named Albert Bachert has made the following statement:– "I was in the Three Nuns Hotel, Aldgate, on Saturday night when a man got into conversation with me. He asked me questions which now appear to me to have some bearing upon the recent murders. He wanted to know whether I knew what sort of loose women used the public bar at that house, when they usually left the street outside, and where they were in the habit of going. He asked further questions, and from his manner seemed to be up to no good purpose. He appeared to be a shabby genteel sort of man, and was dressed in lack clothes. He wore a black felt hat and carried a black bag. We came out together at closing time (12 o'clock) and I left him outside Aldgate Railway Station."

The location of this incident has also been reported as the Three Tuns Hotel, and both establishments were located within the City boundary. To further confuse the issue there was yet another Three Tuns at 1 Whitechapel High Street.

Bachert's raised profile after his press appearance did not go unnoticed, and a 'Jack the Ripper' communication, although undated, was recorded on the file as sent to him on 20 October. It was posted in the EC district, if the folio reference is correct. It was a postcard addressed to Mr Toby Baskett, 13 Newman Street, Whitechapel. The text ran:

> Dear Old Baskett
>
> You only tried ter get yer name in the papers when yer thought you had me in the Three Tuns Hotel I'd like to punch yer bleeding nose
>
> Jack the Riper

The postcard was written in red ink and was heavily blotted. If the writer knew Bachert, which seems possible, then this may tip the balance in favour of the establishment involved being The Three Tuns. Bachert featured intermittently in the press stories of the Whitechapel murders and later claimed to be chairman of the Whitechapel Vigilance Committee. He was the London-born son of German-born parents who were British

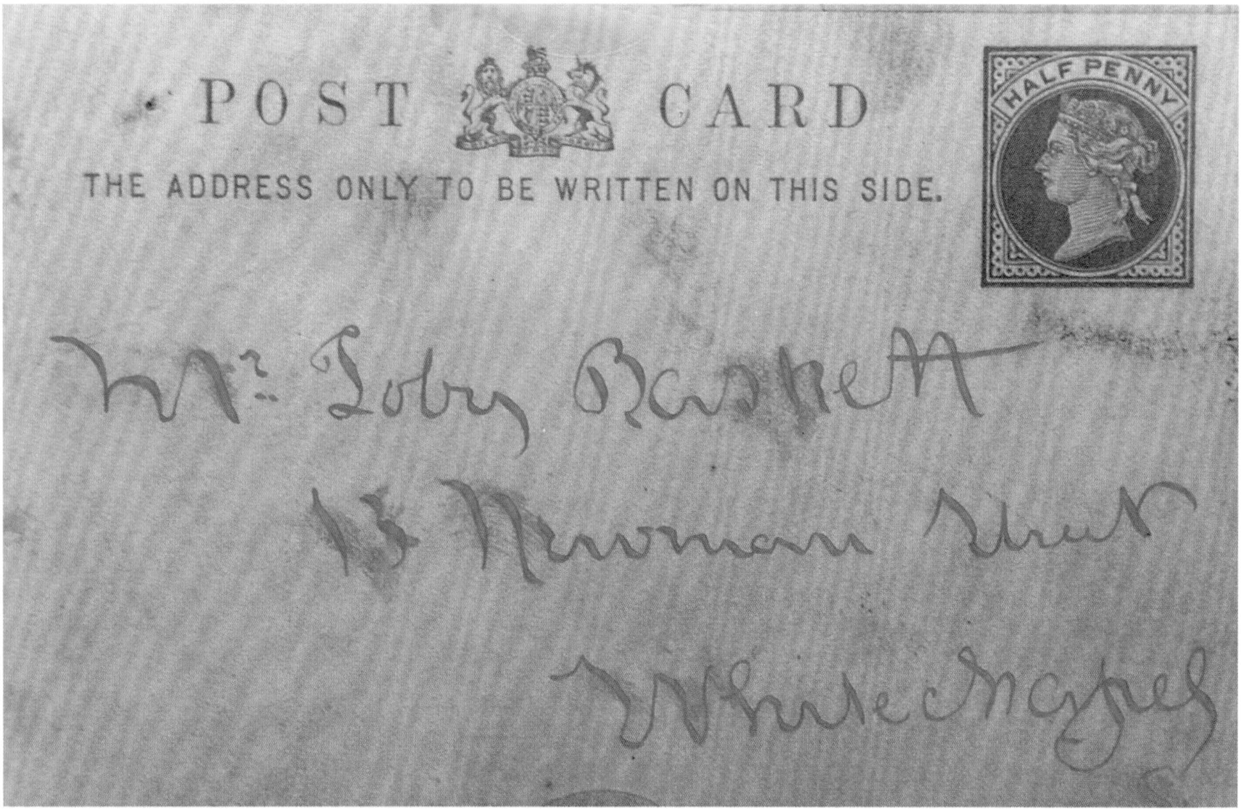

POST CARD

HALF PENNY

THE ADDRESS ONLY TO BE WRITTEN ON THIS SIDE.

Mr. Toby Baskett
13 Newman Street
Whitechapel

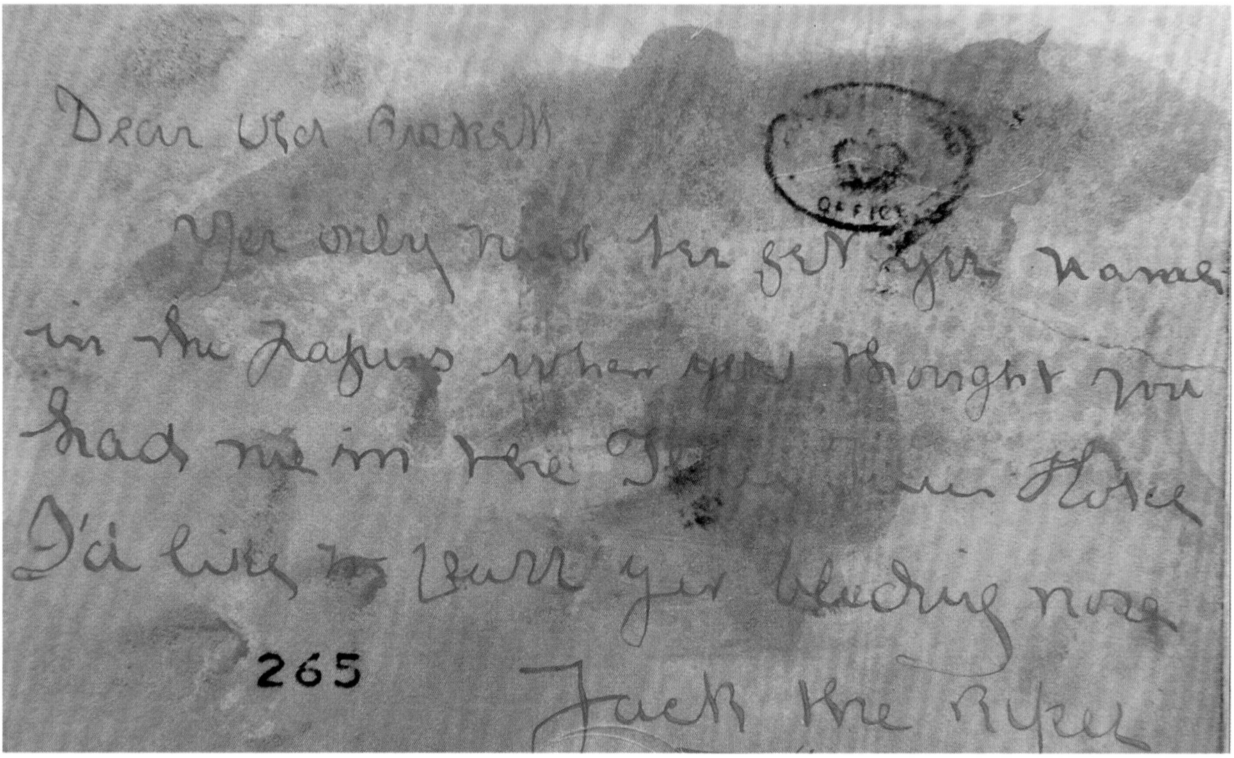

Dear Old Baskett
Yer only had ter get yer name in the papers when yer thought you had me in the Three Tuns Hotel
I'd like to punch yer bleeding nose
Jack the Ripper

OFFICE

265

Postcard of 20 October received by Albert Bachert of the Whitechapel Vigilance Committee, threatening him and mentioning The Three Tuns pub. It is addressed to 'Mr Toby Baskett'.

subjects, presumably immigrants who had been granted British nationality.* Bachert seemed, for a young man, to be very sure of himself and thought nothing of challenging those in authority. The *Eastern Post and City Chronicle* of Saturday 20 August 1887 had reported an appearance he made before the magistrate of the Thames Police Court:

Singular Charge Against The Police

A Mr. Albert Bechart [*sic*], of Gordon House, Newnham Street, Whitechapel, made a complaint to Mr. Lushington respecting the conduct of two police constables. Last Thursday fortnight he saw two constables interfering with a respectable woman, who was talking with her brother-in-law in the Commercial Road. Applicant told the officers he knew the woman and asked them for their numbers. They struck him, and afterwards knocked him down. The officers took him into custody, and having dragged him along the road afterwards let him go, saying they had made a mistake. Although he had since seen a number of constables, and had been in communication with the inspector, he had been unable to identify the two men in question. Applicant had since heard that there was a conspiracy amongst the police to raise a trumpery charge against him and take him into custody. His object in coming to the magistrate was to make him acquainted with the facts of the affair in case a trumpery charge might be brought against him.

Mr. Lushington replied that if any case came before him he would remember applicant had been there.

Applicant thanked his worship and withdrew.

In December 1889 Bachert faced a charge of uttering counterfeit coin with others but was acquitted. In March 1893, his age given as twenty-six years, he was found guilty of obtaining bread and flour by false pretences and received three months' imprisonment.

Another October 1888 letter, unfortunately the exact date is not recorded, resumed the American theme and was posted from Philadelphia:

Honorably Sir

I take great pleasure In giving you my preasent whereabouts for the benefit of the Scotland Yard Boys. I am very sorry that I did not have time to finish my work with the London Whores and regret to state that I must leave them alone for a <u>short while</u> I am now safe in New York and will travel over to Philadelphia and when I have the lay of the locality I might take a notion to do a little ripping there. Good bye ,, dear friend" I will let you here from me before long with a little more Culling and Ripping I said so and I fancy I will make it 40 on account of the slight delay in operations

Yours lovingly
,,Jack" the ripper

A neatly written, red-ink, three-page letter took not only the chance to goad the police but also to air the writer's own answer to the reason for the mysterious murders. Posted in London SW on 23 October, it ran:

* See census returns for 1881, RG11/447/f.109/p.17.

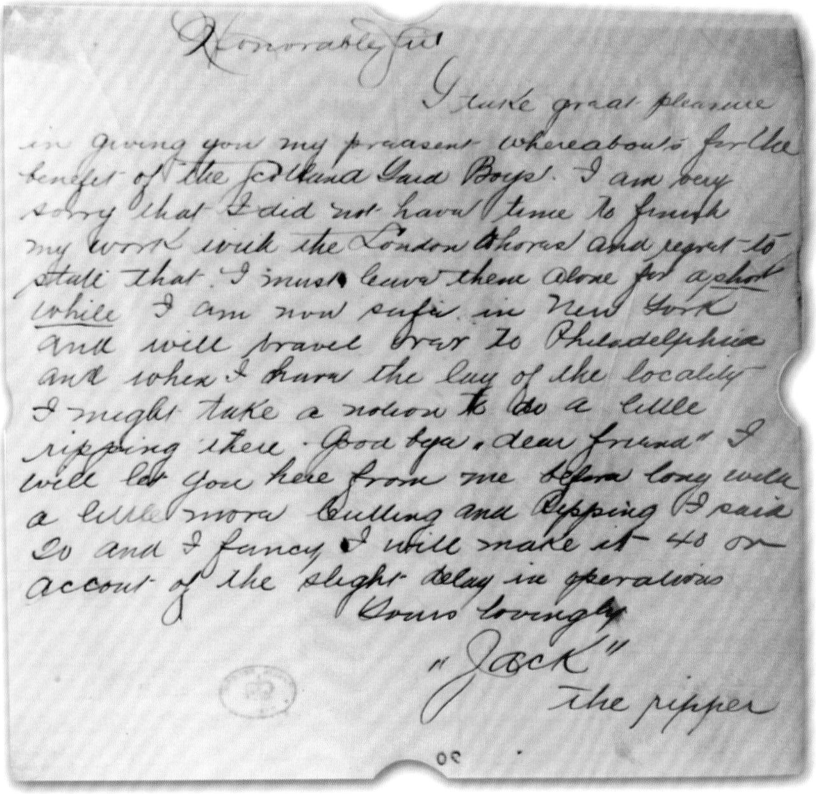

Honorable Sir

I take great pleasure in giving you my present whereabouts for the benefit of the Scotland Yard Boys. I am very sorry that I did not have time to finish my work with the London whores and regret to state that I must leave them alone for a short while I am now safe in New York and will travel over to Philadelphia and when I learn the lay of the locality I might take a notion to do a little ripping there. Good bye, dear friend" I will let you here from me before long with a little more Cutting and Ripping I said 20 and I fancy I will make it 40 on account of the slight delay in operations

Yours lovingly

"Jack"

the ripper

Letter of October 1888 sent from Philadelphia, USA, signed ' "Jack" the ripper'. The writer claims to be in New York and threatens 'ripping' in the USA.

23/10/88

Dear Sirs

I Jack the Ripper thanks you for your trouble in trying to catch me, but it won't do. I suppose you would like to know why I am killing so many women, the answer is simply this. 'When I was at San Francisco in July 1888, I lent three women from London about £ 100 sterling to pay some debts they had got into. promising to pay me back in a months time, and seeing that they had a ladylike look I lent the money. Well when the month passed by I asked for my money but I found that they had sneaked off to London

[second page] so I swore that I would have my revenge, the revenge was this. that I would go to London and kill as many women as possible I've killed 9 as yet you've not found all the corpses yet. Ha. Ha. I've told Sir C. Warren that in a letter of the 22nd inst. In the last women I killed I cut out the kidneys and eat them. You'ill find the body in one of the sewers in the East End. The ['corpse' deleted] leg you found at Whitehall does not belong to the trunk you found there. The police alias po-lice, think themselves devilish clever I suppose they'ill never catch me at this rate you donkeys, you double- faced asses, you had better take the blood-hounds away or I will kill them. I am on the

[third page] scent of these women that swindled me so basely, living like well to do ladies on the money they sneaked from me, never mind that, I'll have em yet, afore I'm done, damn em, To tell you the truth you ought to be obliged to me for killing such a deuced lot of vermin, why they are ten times worse than men.

I remain etc.
Jack the Ripper
alias H.I.O. Battersea

The witness Matthew Packer was kept in the news with an article in the *Evening News* of Wednesday 31 October:

> Last night, Mr. Matthew Packer, who keeps a fruit shop next to the gateway where the Berner-street murder was committed, stated that this last night or two he has felt greatly alarmed owing to his having seen a man exactly like the one who bought the grapes off him for the unfortunate murdered woman, Elizabeth Stride, a short time before the murder was committed. He alleges that he had often seen the man before the murder, as well as the woman who was murdered in Berner-street, but he had not seen any one resembling the man since the murder till he saw him again last Saturday night.
>
> He was then standing with his fruit stall in the Commercial-road when he caught sight of him staring him full in the face. He kept calm and collected for a little time, hoping that a policeman would come by, but not one came. After passing and repassing him several times, the man then came behind him in the horse road looking in a very evil and menacing manner at him. He was so terrified that he left his stall and ran to a shoeblack that was near, and, pointing to the man, asked him to keep his eye on him and watch him.
>
> His great fear was that the fellow was going to stab him to prevent him from identifying him, should anything be brought against him, or his arrest take place. No sooner, however, had he called the shoeblack's attention to him, than he ran away as fast as he could and succeeded in getting on a passing tram. He would have followed the tram had he been able to run, or if he could have left his stall, but he could not as he had several pounds of fruit on it. He has little doubt about him being the man, as he knew him again in a moment.

Packer certainly seemed to enjoy the publicity he attracted and this incident, allowing that it did occur, may indicate that he was also the victim of pranksters out to frighten this newly created celebrity.

The same article also reported on a further letter received by the police from the alleged murderer:

> THREATS OF MORE MURDERS.
>
> By the last post last night a letter, purporting to come from the assassin, was received by the police at the Poplar Police Station, in which the writer said he was going to commit three more murders. The following is said to be the wording : "Oct. 30, 1888. – Dear Boss – I am going to commit three more murders, two women and a child, and I shall take their hearts this time. – Yours truly, (signed) JACK THE RIPPER."
>
> The letter was enclosed in an envelope which, in addition to the Poplar post-mark, also bore the Ealing post-mark, and was directed to the sergeant.
>
> Though the police do not attach serious importance to it, a copy was sent to the Commissioner of Police. The information, with accompanying instructions, were at once telegraphed to the different stations, ordering every possible vigilance to be used in case of an attempted repetition of the crimes. It is stated that an endeavour will be made at Ealing to discover the sender, and already various inquiries are going on to-day.

Even the aristocracy did not escape the attentions of unknown penmen. The *Daily Telegraph* of Saturday 3 November reported:

From *Illustrated Police News*, this cartoon shows the arrival of a letter from 'Jack the Ripper' at Poplar Police Station.

Threatening to Murder an Earl. – The following letter, bearing the Uckfield postmark of Oct. 27, has been received by the Earl of Sheffield: "England, Oct. 27, 1888. – Dear Lord Sheffield – I am sorry, but, feeling it my duty to let you know as I do not think you do or you would not have the Heart to turn an old Tennent like poor old Mrs. Grover out of her Home after such an hard struggle to maintain and bring up her family not only that but not allowing anyone to get an honest living there in the Butchering line as they have done for a great number of years, but it seems to me as though you and your faithful Steward want it all, and if you had my wish you would get more than you wanted. Remember this is a warning to you, but at the same time I should be much obliged to you if you could arrange it for your Steward to sleep under the same roof as yourself on Monday night, Oct. 29, or else I shall have to bring an assistant. My knife is nice and sharp. Oh for a gentleman this time, instead of Lady. I am sorry for troubling you, but don't forget the 29th. – I remain, yours truely, Jack the Ripper." Lord Sheffield has for some time past been so frequently annoyed by anonymous letter-writers that he has resolved to make a special effort upon this occasion to capture his cowardly assailant. The above letter has therefore been reproduced in facsimile, and his Lordship has offered a reward of £250 for information leading to the arrest of the writer.

The writer of the letter to his lordship was identified in a piece in the *Star* dated 27 November 1888 which read:

Lord Sheffield Satisfied Now.

Edward Grover was remanded at Uckfield yesterday on a charge of inciting several persons to attempt to murder Lord Sheffield. The prisoner was formerly a butcher at Fletching, living with his mother. Lord Sheffield recently gave the mother notice to quit. Grover was arrested on Thursday night at East Grinstead, but, obtaining leave to go upstairs for a coat, let himself out of a bedroom window by means of a blanket, and escaped barefooted across country to Fletching, where he was re-arrested on Sunday. The prisoner is suspected of having written the threatening letters by which Lord Sheffield has been of late so annoyed.

The then rising and successful lawyer Edward Marshall Hall was engaged to prosecute the culprit, according to Hall's biographer, Edward Marjoribanks MP, in his book *The Life of Sir Edward Marshall Hall* (1929, pp. 48–9). The outcome of the case is unknown to the authors.

October 1888 was a busy month for the letter-writers. They were an annoyance to the police who, in the main, could do little to trace the originators. Indeed, it would seem that most of the letters were merely read, checked for clues for possible authenticity or source, and then filed. Where offenders were traced, as we have seen, they were dealt with by the police.

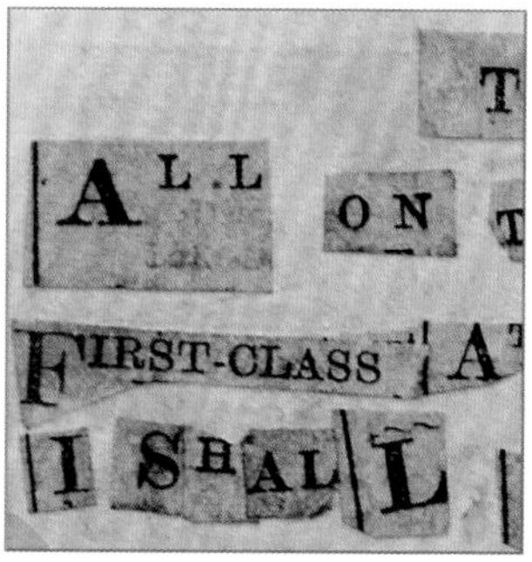

— NINE —

'I am still knocking about Down Whitechapel'

BY the beginning of November 1888 the East End had not witnessed a murder for over a month. However, sporadic press reports, the 'Lusk letter' episode, and the receipt of further letters allegedly from the killer ensured that recent events were not forgotten. The pseudonymous letters continued to flow in November, with their predictions of further murders. The anonymous writers did not realise it but there was a worse horror to come, one that would make the previous murders seem rather less terrible.

In the meantime letters continued to arrive composed in the same vein as those already received. A scribe wrote from Neath, in a letter dated 3 November, as follows:

> Nov. 3rd 1888.
>
> To Mr Charles warren head Police Scotland yard detectives.
>
> I hame pleased to year that I was caught at neath on saturday night at the falcon hotel old market st but you have not had the pleasure of catching me yet by the time you have had this one ore two more will feel my knife I have been helpin the police in the seacret with blood – hounds and rejoiced in heering them say they were on the right track
>
> J.T. Ripper
>
> ah! ah
>
> [second page] next one I copp I.ll send the toes and earoles to you for supper
>
> J.T. Ripper

This was typical of its kind, with the taunts to the police and the threat to send body parts. The bloodhounds were also mentioned because they remained a popular topic for the press.

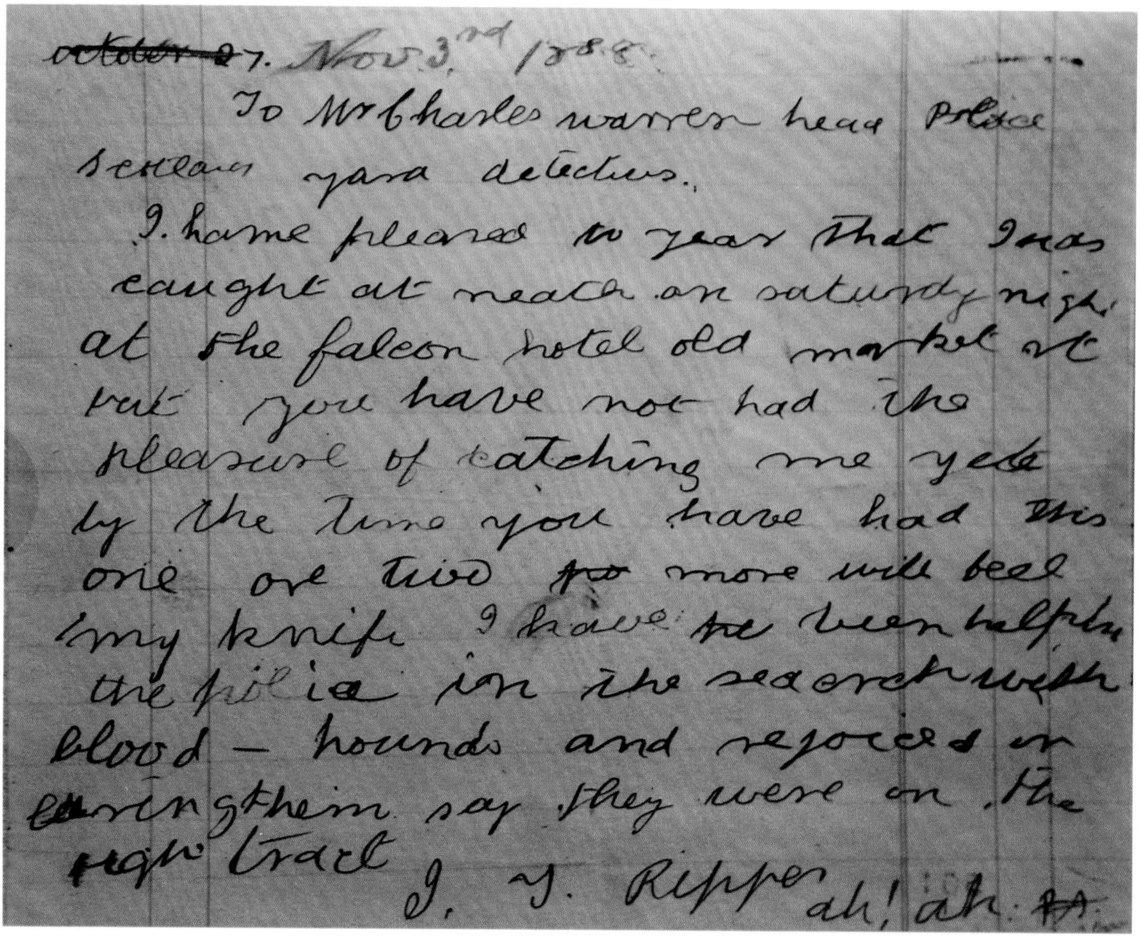

~~October 27.~~ Nov 3rd 1888

To Mr Charles warren head Police Scotland yard detectives..

I. hame pleased to year that I was caught at neath on saturdy night at the falcon hotel old market st but you have not had the pleasure of catching me yet by the time you have had this one ore two more will feel my knife I have been helping the police in the search with blood – hounds and rejoiced in hearing them say they were on the right track

J. T. Ripper ah! ah!

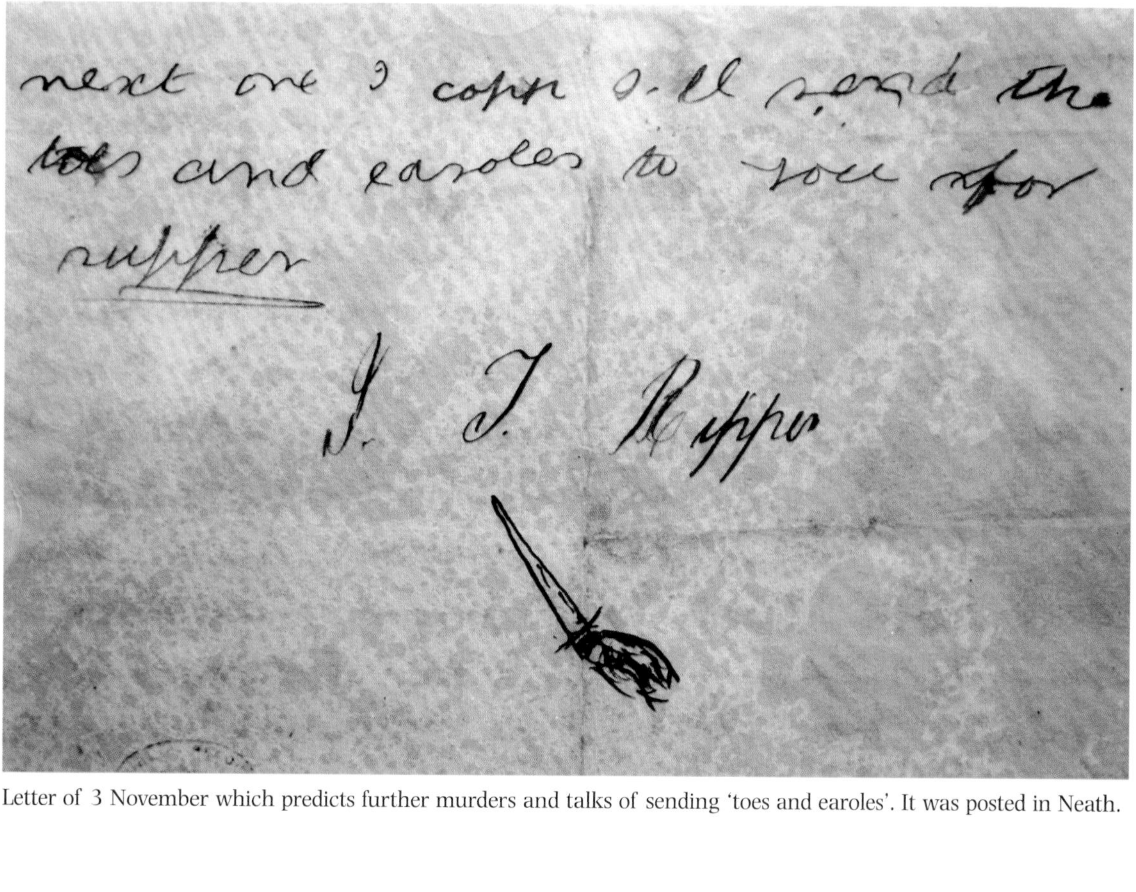

next one I copp I'll send the toes and earoles to you for supper

J. T. Ripper

Letter of 3 November which predicts further murders and talks of sending 'toes and earoles'. It was posted in Neath.

Another letter, postmarked 5 November and posted in the London EC area, was addressed to Leman Street Police Station. It bore no stamp and carried the usual *2d* postal charge. It ran:

> Keep a extra look out in Whitechapel tonight
>
> Jack the Ripper
>
> P.S. THERE IS ONE OLD WHORE WHO I HAVE GOT MY EYE ON SO LOOK OUT
>
> J.T.R.

Was the unknown killer unwell and thus prevented from committing further crimes until he felt better? This thought had obviously occurred to one letter-writer. He set pen to paper and made threats in a letter dated 7 November:

> 7 . 11 . 88
>
> Dear Boss,
>
> I am writing you this while I am in bed with a sore throat but as soon as it is better I will set to work again. on the 13th of this month. and I think that my next Job will be to polish you off and as I am a member of the force I can soon settle accounts with you I will tear your liver out before you are dead and show it to you
>
> [second page] and I will have your kidneys out also and fill them with pepper and salt and send them to lord Sallisbrury as it is just the sort of thing that will suit that old Jew and I will cut of your toes and slice of your behind and make macaroni soup of them and I will hide your body in the houses of parliament so you grey headed old pig say your prayers before I am ready
>
> [third page, at right angles] I cannot say any more at present boss yours truly
>
> Jack the Ripper

The murders were still very much in the public and official eye, although with the October hiatus a general feeling that the horrors might be over began to take hold. Although it cannot be doubted that the majority wanted to see an end to the series of murders, there was a small minority who did not. These included some of the letter-writers and some pressmen who had seen the sale of their newspapers increase with each successive story of horror. The true climax of the series occurred on Friday 9 November with the murder of a 25-year-old prostitute, Mary Jane Kelly, in her room at 26 Dorset Street, Spitalfields. It was a murder that came to epitomise the horrific true nature of 'Jack the Ripper' and set the seal on a future of endless notoriety, speculation and theorising. It was also a further boost for the letter-writers; 'Jack the Ripper' was still alive and well and operating in the East End of London.

One of the anonymous writers provided an ominous and well-timed warning on Thursday 8 November when the following letter was posted in London E. 'To Kingslands Road Police Station':

> Your friend
>
> Jack the ripper
>
> I am very please to send you this little as I am your friend I have been having a nice rest but now my rest is over I am going to make a fresh start again.

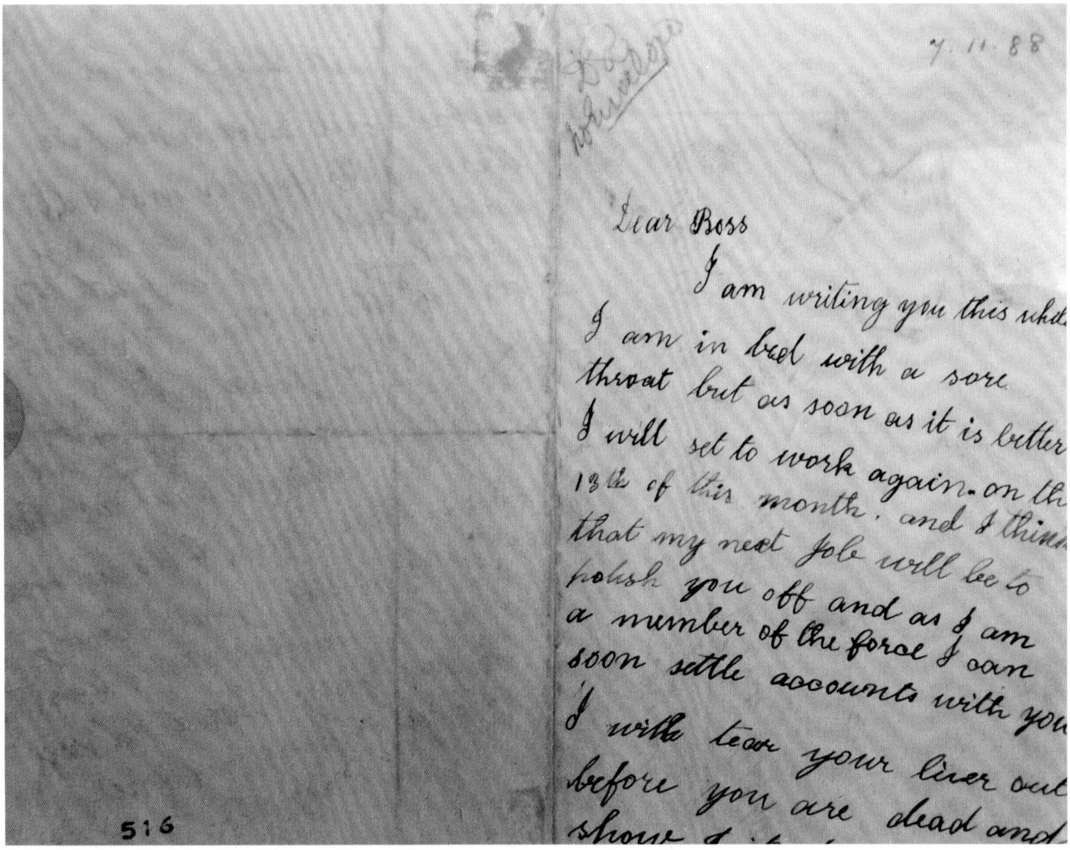

7.11.88

Dear Boss
I am writing you this while
I am in bed with a sore
throat but as soon as it is better
I will set to work again. on the
13th of this month. and I think
that my next Job will be to
polish you off and as I am
a member of the force I can
soon settle accounts with you
I will tear your liver out
before you are dead and
show

516

and I will have your
kidneys out also and frie
them with pepper and salt
and send them to lord
Salisbury as it is just the
sort of thing that will suit
that old Jew and I will
cut of your toes and slice
of your behind and make
macaroni soup of them and
I will hide your body
in, the houses of parliament
so you grey headed old pig
say your prayers before
I am ready

a I cannot say any more at
present boss Yours truly
Jack the Ripper
this is your portrait

515

Letter dated 7 November to 'Dear Boss'. The writer claims to have been in bed with a sore throat. It is signed 'Jack the Ripper' and includes a drawing of a man in a uniform coat.

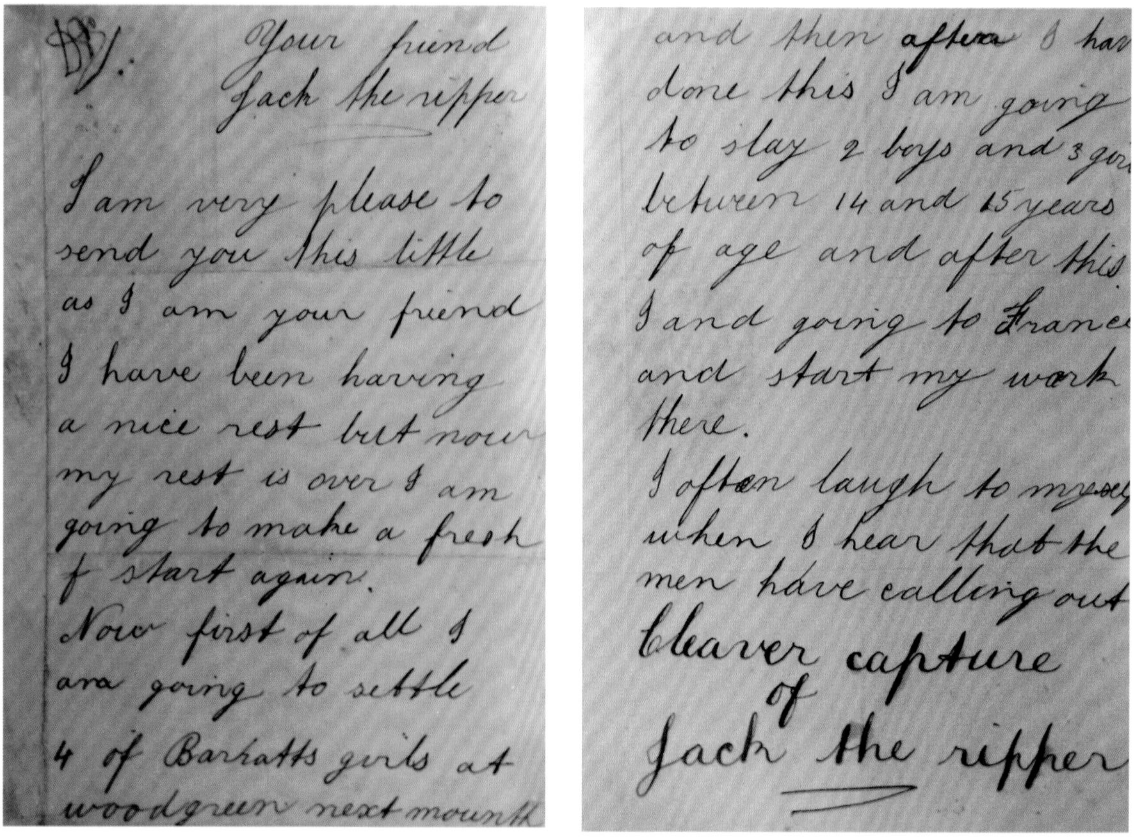
Your friend
Jack the ripper
I am very please to
send you this little
as I am your friend
I have been having
a nice rest but now
my rest is over I am
going to make a fresh
f start again.
Now first of all I
ara going to settle
4 of Barratts girls at
woodgreen next mounth
and then aftera I hav
done this I am going
to slay 2 boys and 3 gir
between 14 and 15 years
of age and after this
I and going to France
and start my work
there.
I often laugh to myself
when I hear that the
men have calling out
Cleaver capture
of
Jack the ripper

Letter of 8 November threatening the murders of two girls and three boys.

Now first of all I am going to settle 4 of Barratts girls at woodgreen next mounth [second page] and then after I have done this I am going to slay 2 boys and 3 girls between 14 and 15 years of age and after this I and going to France and start my work there.

I often laugh to myself when I hear that the men have calling out Cleaver capture of

Jack the ripper

An obscene letter of the same date also warned of an intention to recommence the murders and revealed that the writer closely followed the newspaper reports. It was posted in the London EC district on 8 November and was addressed to 'Sir Charles Warren, Scotland Yard, Whitehall, W.":

Whitechapel
8/11/88

Dear Boss,

I am still knocking about Down Whitechapel I mean to put to Death all the dirty old ores because I have caught the pox and cannot piss, I have not done any murders lately But you will find one done before long I shall send you the kidney and cunt so that you can see where my prick has been up I am in one of the lodging houses in Osborn street, but you will have a job to catch me shoudent advise any copper to catch hold of me because I should do the same to him ass I have done others [second page] Old packer the man I bought the grapes off of saw me the other night and was to frighten to say anything to the police he must have been a fool when there is such a reward offered never mind the reward will not be given. You will hear from me a little later on that I have done another murder. But not just yet.

Dear Boss if I see you about I shall cut you throat, the Old Queen is none other But- one of those old ores I have Been up her arse and shot sponk up her.

I remain Dear
old Boss
Jack the ripper

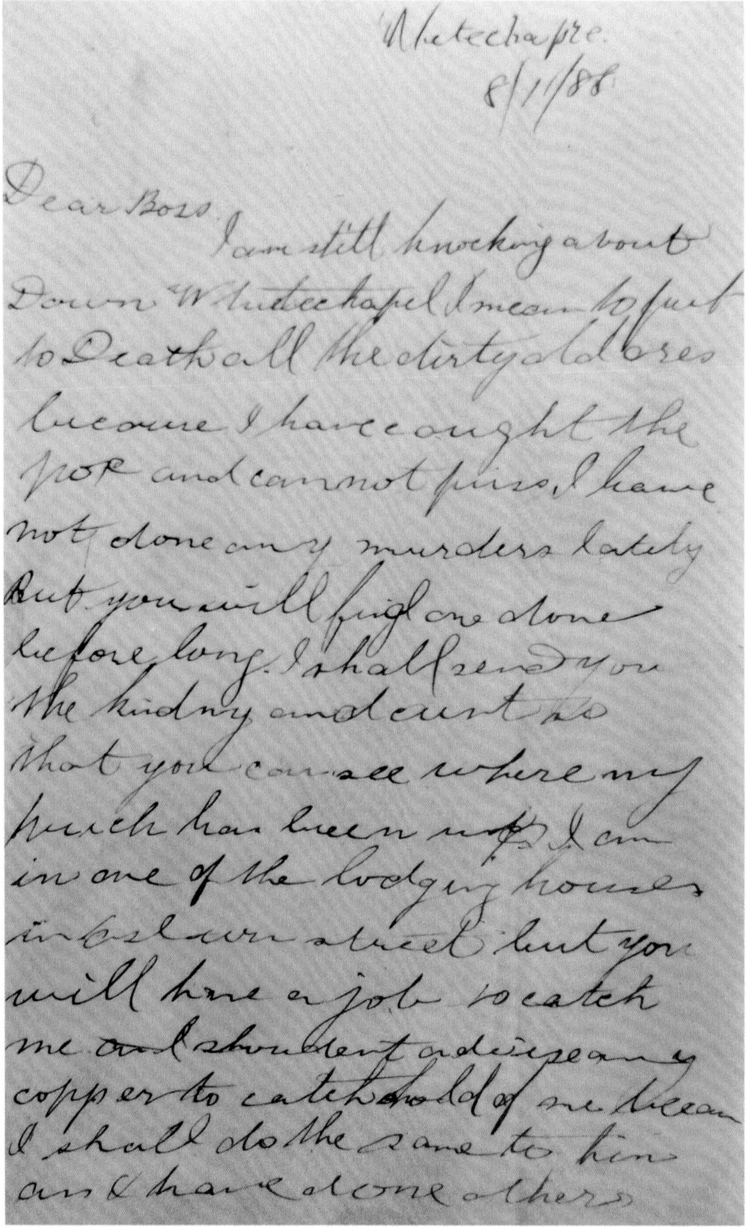

Whitechapre.
8/11/88

Dear Boss,
I am still knocking about Down Whitechapel I mean to put to Death all the dirty old ores because I have caught the pox and cannot piss, I have not done any murders lately But you will find one done before long. I shall send you the kidney and cunt so that you can see where my prick has been up. I am in one of the lodging houses in Osborn street but you will have a job to catch me and shouldent advise any copper to catch hold of me becau I shall do the same to him as I have done others

Letter of 8 November to Sir Charles Warren, warns of killer still 'knocking about Down Whitechapel' stating he has 'caught the pox'.

Friday 9 November 1888 was the day of the Lord Mayor's Show and the new Lord Mayor, the Right Honourable James Whitehead, drove in state to the Royal Courts of Justice to take his oath. It was a festive day in the capital and crowds thronged the streets to witness the pageantry. It was not for this reason, however, that the date was to be remembered in history, and the Lord Mayor's Show was eclipsed by news of an horrific nature.

At 10.45 a.m. Thomas Bowyer was sent by John McCarthy, the landlord of dwellings in Miller's Court, 26 Dorset Street, to collect rent from Mary Jane Kelly who tenanted room 13 on the ground floor to the rear of the property. She was 29*s* in arrears. There was no reply to a knock on the door so Bowyer went round the corner, reached through a broken window and pulled aside the curtain. He was horrified to see a bloody corpse on the bed and lumps of flesh on the bedside table next to the door. Bowyer then informed McCarthy who took a look through the window before they sped to Commercial Street Police Station to alert the police. Inspector Walter Beck and other officers were quickly upon the scene pending the arrival of the Scotland Yard investigators. The door to the room was locked and no entry was gained until the door was forced at 1.30 p.m. Photographs were taken and the body later removed to the mortuary. It had been horrifically mutilated, the face had been partially skinned and hacked about so that the features were unrecognisable. The throat was cut down to the vertebrae, and the thorax had been opened up and eviscerated. The heart was absent. News of this latest terrible East End murder rapidly spread throughout the capital, across the land and beyond British shores.

No immediate suspect of any merit came to light although Kelly's recent live-in lover, Joseph Barnett, was closely questioned by the police. He had split up with her at the end of October and the window had been broken when the couple had a row. However, they were apparently still on good terms. There were previous men friends mentioned, notably a man called 'Morganstone' and a Joseph Flemming. A hurried inquest was held at Shoreditch on Monday 12 November, and a verdict of murder against a person or persons unknown was returned.

That same evening another witness emerged: George Hutchinson was a local man who claimed to know Kelly and to have seen her in the early hours of the morning of her murder. Hutchinson described seeing her in Commercial Street at 2.00 a.m. and she asked him to lend her sixpence. Hutchinson was broke and Kelly moved on, meeting a stranger near the junction with Thrawl Street. They spoke and laughed together and Kelly made her way with the man to her room in Miller's Court. The curious Hutchinson followed and saw the couple enter number 13. Hutchinson waited in Dorset Street, opposite the entrance to Miller's Court, for three-quarters of an hour but the couple did not reappear again and he left. Hutchinson's description of the man, seen under the street lamp of the Queens Head public house, was very detailed: aged about thirty-four or thirty-five, 5 feet 6 inches tall, pale complexion, dark eyes and eyelashes, slight moustache curled up at each end, and dark hair. He was very surly looking, dressed in a dark coat with collar and cuffs trimmed with astrakhan, and a dark jacket under. He also wore a light waistcoat, dark trousers, dark felt hat turned down in the middle, button boots and gaiters with white buttons. He had a very thick gold chain, white linen collar, and a black tie with a

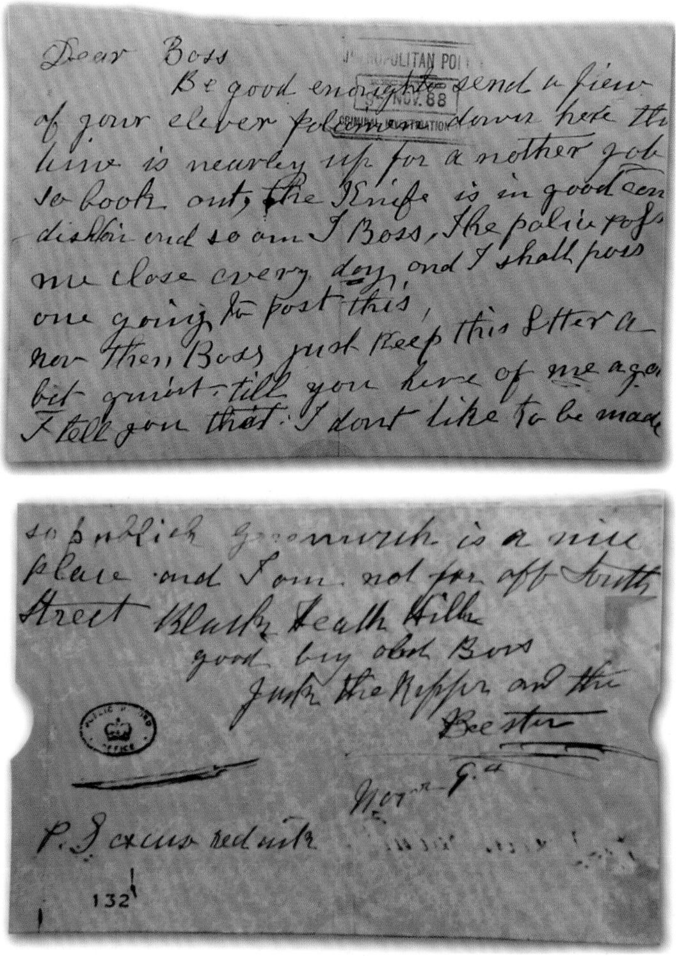
Dear Boss
Be good enough to send a fiew
of your clever policmen down here the
time is nearly up for a nother job
so look out, the Knife is in good con
dishion and so am I Boss, the police pass
me close every day, and I shall pass
one going to post this,
now Then Boss just keep this letter a
bit quiet till you here of me agen
I tell you that I dont like to be made
so public Greenwich is a nice
place and I am not far off Smith
Street Black Heath Hill
good buy old Boss
Jack the Ripper and the
Beester
Nov 9th
P.S excuse red ink
132

Letter of 9 November including the words 'send of fiew of your clever policmen down here . . . time is nearly up for a nother job'. It mentions Blackheath and Greenwich and is signed 'Jack the Ripper'.

horseshoe pin. He seemed respectable and had the appearance of a Jew. He walked very sharply.*

This description was important to the police and it was soon published in the hope that someone would recognise the man. Despite the arrests of several suspects, the Kelly murder, like those committed previously, remained unsolved. Meanwhile, the renewed press coverage and general excitement resulted in a further boost for the writers who wasted no time in putting pen to paper.

Needless to say the scribes were keen to mock the police. One writer posted his letter addressed 'on her majyster's service, To the Comessisur of Police, Scotland Yard, London'. It had a London EC postmark dated 9 November:

> Dear Boss
>
> Be good enough to send a fiew of your clever policmen down here the time is nearly up for a nother job so look out, the Knife is in good condishion and so am I Boss, the police pass me close every day, and I shall pass one going to post this.

* MEPO 3/140 ff. 227–9.

Now then Boss just keep this letter a bit quiert till you here of me again I tell you that I don't like to be made
[second page] so publick Greenwich is a nice place and I am not far off South Street Black Heath Hills.

good buy old Boss
Jack the Ripper and the Beester

Nov 9th

P.S. excuse red ink

The letter is written in black ink, and the postscript is no doubt intended as an apology for not writing in red.

A note printed in black ink, postmarked London EC Nov 10 88 and addressed 'On Her Majesty's Service The Inspector, Leman St Police Station', warned the police as follows:

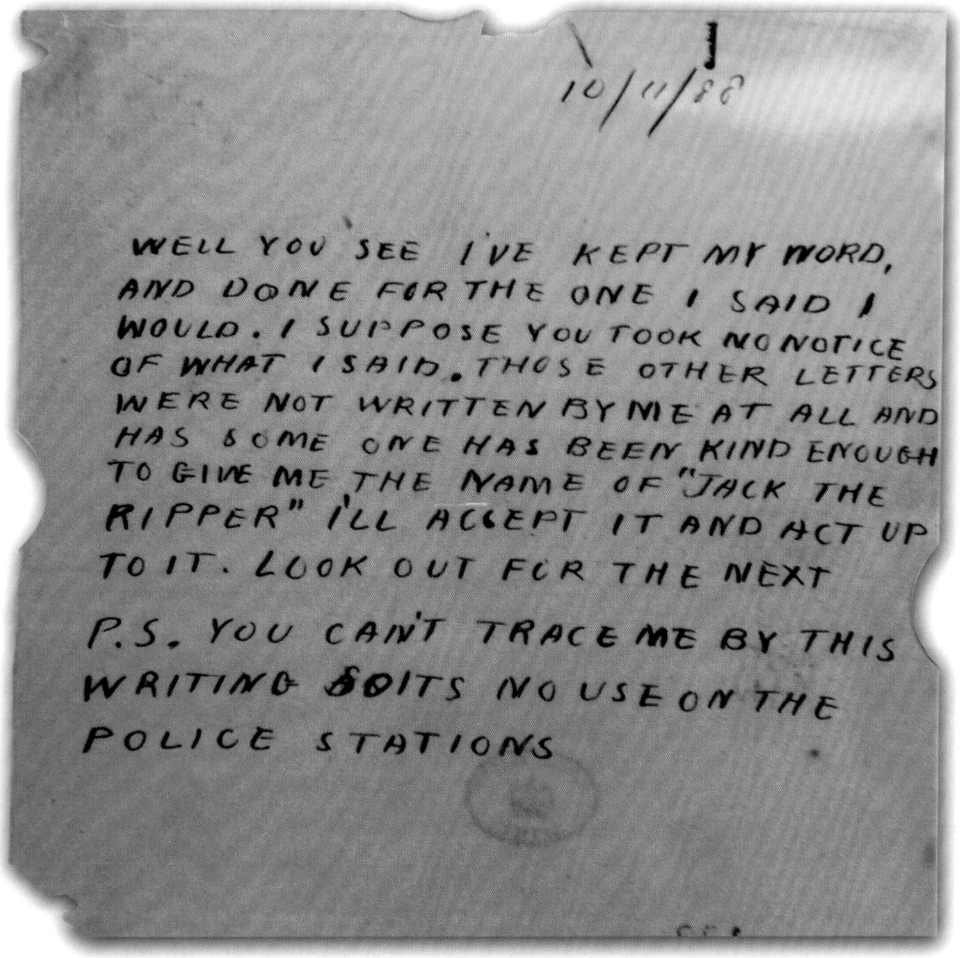
10/11/88

WELL YOU SEE I'VE KEPT MY WORD, AND DONE FOR THE ONE I SAID I WOULD. I SUPPOSE YOU TOOK NO NOTICE OF WHAT I SAID. THOSE OTHER LETTERS WERE NOT WRITTEN BY ME AT ALL AND HAS SOME ONE HAS BEEN KIND ENOUGH TO GIVE ME THE NAME OF "JACK THE RIPPER" I'LL ACCEPT IT AND ACT UP TO IT. LOOK OUT FOR THE NEXT

P.S. YOU CAN'T TRACE ME BY THIS WRITING SO ITS NO USE ON THE POLICE STATIONS

Note dated 10 November. The writer states he has 'done for the one I said I would' and denies writing other letters.

It is interesting to note that this scribe, while claiming to be the killer, denied having written the previous letters. He also accepted his 'christening' and claimed he would live up to the name.

The *Daily Telegraph* of Saturday 10 November ran the story of a young woman named Mrs Pannier (*sic* – Paumier) who sold roast chestnuts at the corner of Widegate Street, a short distance from the scene of the murder in Miller's Court. The report told of a suspicious man and repeated in full detail Albert Bachert's account of the individual he had encountered in the Three Nuns Hotel:

> . . . Mrs. Pannier is reported to have stated that shortly after noon yesterday a man, dressed like a gentleman, said to her, "I suppose you have heard about the murder in Dorset-street?" and that when she replied that she was aware of it he said, "I know more about it than you." He then proceeded down Sandy's-row, a narrow thoroughfare which cuts across Widegate-street, looking back as if to see whether he was watched. Mrs. Pannier described this person as a man about 5ft 6in high, with a black moustache, and wearing a black silk hat, dark coat, and speckled trousers. He carried a black shiny bag about eighteen inches long and a foot deep. It will be remembered that this description agrees fairly with a personage previously described, and that the black bag has more than once figured in the evidence given. It may be worth while to recall that at the inquiry into the Berner-street murder Mrs. Mortimer said, "The only man I had seen pass through Berner-street previously was a young man who carried a black shiny bag." [In fact the man spotted by Mrs Mortimer was seen by the police and turned out to be an innocent passer-by.] Similarly Arthur [*sic*] Bachert deposed: "On Saturday night, at about seven minutes to twelve, I entered the Three Nuns Hotel, Aldgate. While in there an elderly woman, very shabbily dressed, came in and asked me to buy some matches. I refused, and she went out. A man who had been standing by me remarked that these persons were a nuisance, to which I responded "Yes." He then asked me to have a glass with him, but I refused, as I had just called for one myself. He then asked a number of questions about the women of the neighbourhood, and their ages &c. He asked if I could tell him where they usually visited. He went outside and spoke to the woman, and gave her something, I believe. He was a dark man, height about 5ft 6in or 5ft 7in. He wore a black felt hat, dark clothes, morning coat, black tie, and carried a black shiny bag." But the point in Mrs. Pannier's statement which engaged the greatest amount of attention, and which, if corroborated, might unquestionably possess real significance was her further averment that she had seen the same man on the previous evening, and that he had accosted three young unfortunates in Dorset-street, who chaffed him, and asked what he had in the bag, and he replied, "Something that the ladies don't like." . . .

The significance of such detailed and evocative stories of suspicious characters lies in the fact that they were eagerly devoured by readers and subject matter raised was used in the 'Jack the Ripper' letters that followed.

The landlord of 26 Dorset Street, John McCarthy, had received prominent mention in the press reports of the Kelly murder. As a result a postcard was sent to Mrs McCarthy, bearing a Folkestone postmark dated 11 November. It was addressed to 'Mrs McCarthy, No 28 Dorset St, London, East End'. The text ran as follows:

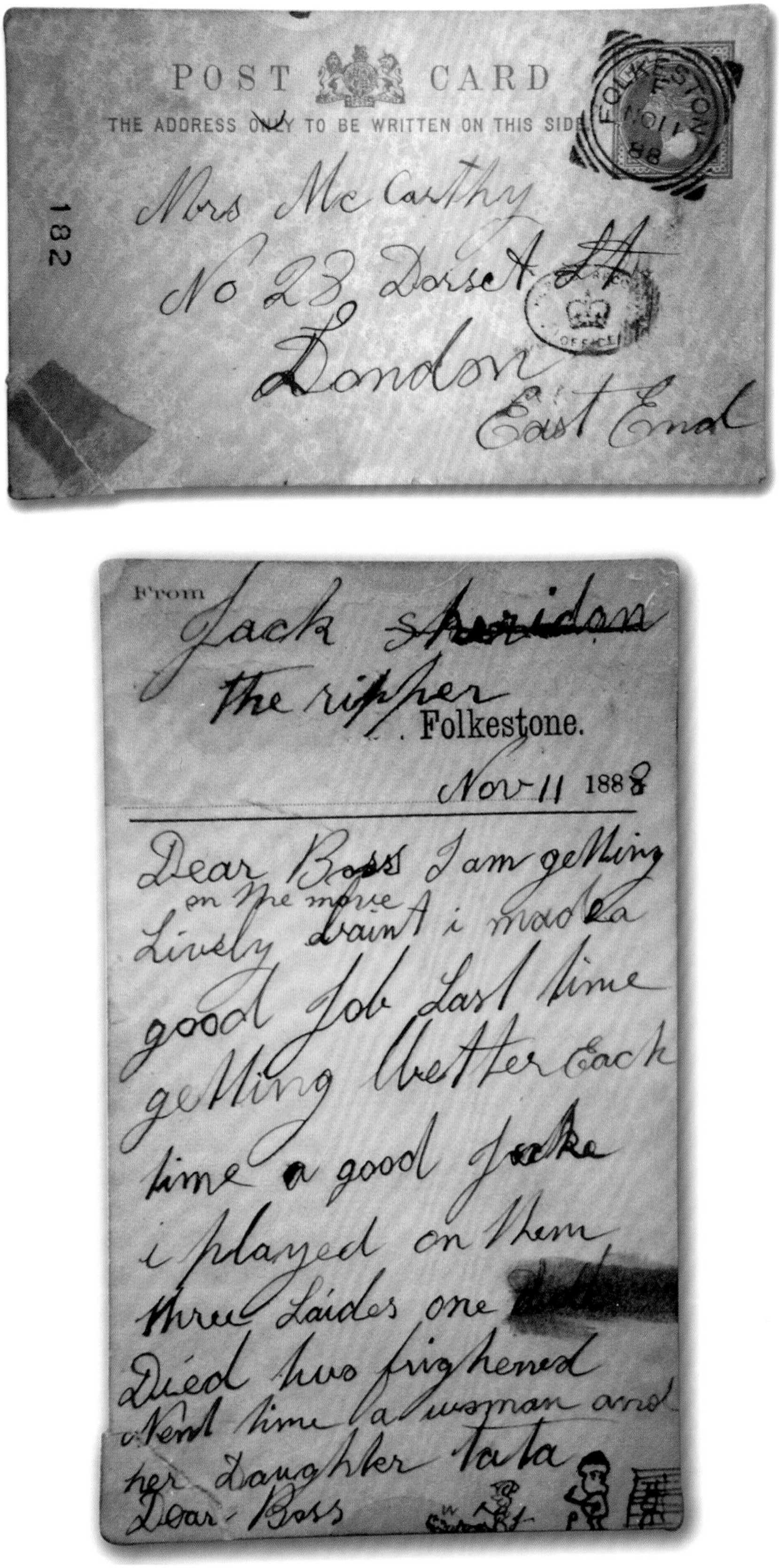
POST CARD
THE ADDRESS ONLY TO BE WRITTEN ON THIS SIDE
FOLKESTONE
NO 11
88
182
Mrs McCarthy
No 23 Dorset St
London
East End
From
Jack Sheridan
the ripper
Folkestone.
Nov 11 1888
Dear Boss I am getting
on the move
Lively aint i made a
good Job Last time
getting better each
time a good Joke
i played on them
three Laides one
Died two frighened
Next time a woman and
her Daughter tata
Dear Boss

Postcard of 11 November sent to Mrs McCarthy, wife of Mary Kelly's landlord, from Folkestone. It threatens 'next time a woman and her daughter'.

> From Jack ['sheridan' deleted]
> the ripper
> Folkestone.
> Nov 11 1888
>
> Dear Boss I am getting on the move Lively baint i made a good Job Last time getting better each time a good Joke i played on them three Laides one Died two frighened Next time a woman and her daughter ta ta
> Dear Boss

In 1935 a French Ripper book, *Jack L'Eventreur*, by Jean Dorsenne was published and it featured a few Ripper letters. Dorsenne claimed that a retired policeman was his source. He mentions one of the letters received by Lusk, the press version of which included the term 'box of toys' (*see Jack L'Eventreur*, page 84). Dorsenne obviously did not understand that 'box of toys' was Cockney rhyming slang for boys. The text of this particular letter to Mr Lusk was printed in several newspapers, and Dorsenne supplied his own version. He stated that the ex-policeman had told him:

> Three days later, George Lusk – who seemed to have become Jack's favourite correspondent – received a new letter. Hold on, I've got it here, with my papers:
>
> *I say, Boss, you seem to be jolly frightened. I really wanted to play a little joke on you all but I haven't got enough time left to let you play cat and mouse with me. Even so, I do hope to see you, if I'm not too busy.* Au revoir, *Boss.*
>
> *Jack the Ripper.*

Dorsenne quotes a further letter, and adds:

> a pill-box was found at the corner of Marylebone Road – one of the pill-boxes which Jack always planted at the scene of his crimes. Folded inside was a letter addressed to the police in these terms:
>
> *Dear Boss, Tomorrow night I shall be at my work in Marylebone.*
> *Jack the Ripper. P.S. Look out, at ten o'clock on the dot.*

The text from which this letter is taken would appear to be that published in the *Evening Post* of Saturday 10 November:

> LETTER FROM "JACK THE RIPPER."
>
> Last night, in the pillar-box at the corner of Northumberland-street and Marylebone-road, was found a letter directed to the police, and its contents were as follows: 'Dear Boss, – I shall be busy tomorrow night in Marylebone. I have two booked for blood and guts. – Yours, JACK THE RIPPER. Look out about 10 o'clock, Marylebone-road."

The authors note that Dorsenne apparently did not know what a 'pillar-box' was and thus deducted that it meant a simple pill-box, containing a letter, which the killer left at the scene of each murder! Dorsenne also wrote:

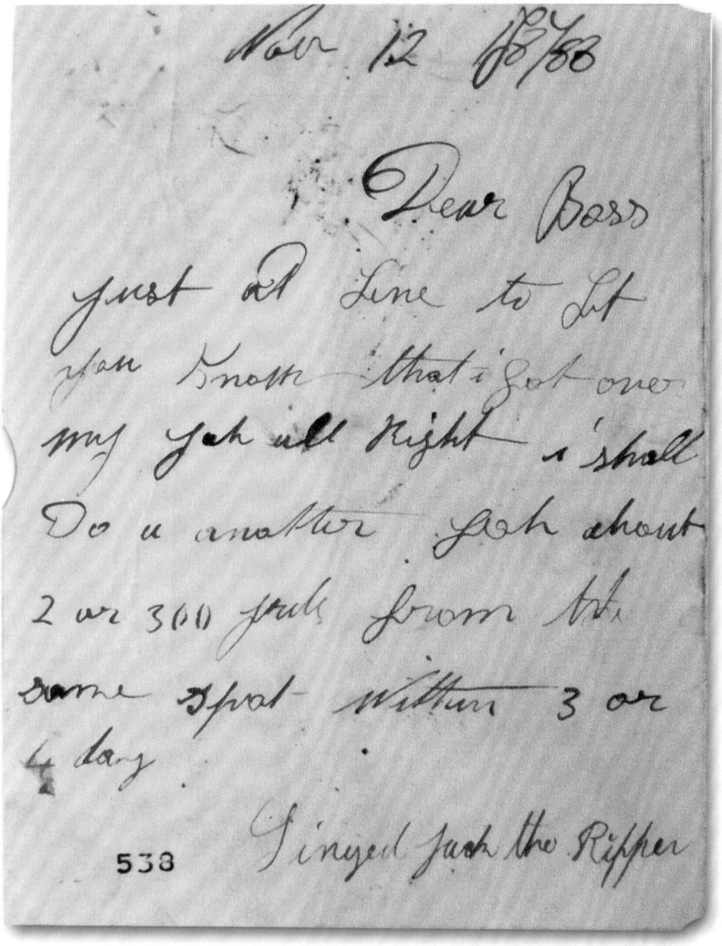
Novr 12 18/88

Dear Boss

just a line to let you know that i got over my job all right i shall Do another job about 2 or 300 yards from the same spot within 3 or 4 day.

538 Singed Jack the Ripper

Letter of 12 November including a threat to do 'another job'. This letter is mentioned in the 1935 French book *Jack L'Eventreur*.

A little later, the police-station at Leman Street received another letter from Jack:

Dear Boss, Just a line to let you know that I love my work. Three or four days from now, I shall do another one, three or four hundred yards from my latest. Jack the Ripper.

This would appear to refer to a letter, now in the police files, posted in the London EC district on 12 November and written in purple ink:

Novr 12 18/88

Dear Boss

just a line to let you know that i got over my job all right i shall Do another job about 2 or 300 yards from the same spot within 3 or 4 day.

Singed Jack the Ripper

The *Globe* published details of this letter (together with another one) on Wednesday 14 November:

"JACK THE RIPPER'S" CORRESPONDENCE.

The police at Leman-street, Whitechapel, received by post the following letter; – Dear Boss – Just a line to let you know that I got over that job allright, I shall do another job about 200 or 300 yards from the same spot within three or four days. JACK THE RIPPER.

A fourth letter quoted by Dorsenne, also claimed to have been sent to Lusk, ran:

> I'm writing this letter to you in black ink, since I haven't got the right stuff. I'm going to show you something tomorrow, Saturday night, while you are all fast asleep at Scotland Yard with your dogs. I shall do another double murder, but not in Whitechapel this time. It's become too hot for me now. Time for me to move on. No more for the moment until you hear about me again.
>
> Jack the Ripper.

The authors identified this letter as being a variant of the one quoted by Professor Francis Camps in his article in *The Criminologist*, February 1968:

> The Boss,
> Central News Office,
> London City.
> *Received 12th Oct.*, 1888.
>
> *To Mr. Lusk*,
> I write you a letter in black ink, as I have no more of the right stuff. I think you are all asleep in Scotland Yard with your bloodhounds, as I will show you tomorrow night. I am going to do a double event but not in Whitechapel. Got rather too warm there. Had to shift. No more till you hear me again.
>
> JACK THE RIPPER

To date the authors have not traced the original source for this letter. Dorsenne's texts may have become altered in translation, but the essential content is there and would seem to confirm the material's origins. However, these particular letters do not prove that he had any unique source for they had appeared in newspaper reports.

The second letter referred to in the *Globe* report mentioned above read as follows:

> The police of the H or Commercial-street Division have received by post a letter bearing yesterday's date, and which reads as follows: – "Dear Boss, – You shall have a nice parcel when I do the next job in N.E. I have 13 booked for blood, and will give myself up. – JACK THE RIPPER."

A letter posted in the London E district on 15 November was addressed to 'The Boss, Leman St. Police Station, Whitechapel E.'. It bore no postage stamp, but had a drawing of a 1*d* stamp on it. The usual excess post of 2*d* was duly stamped on the envelope by the Post Office. The letter read:

> 14/11/1888
> 5-20 P.M.
>
> Dear Boss,
> I gave you warning that I would clip the lady's ears off, grand work it was, Had plenty of time, finished her straight off. Shall not keep you waiting long. Will try & clear 3 woman

Letter of 15 November sent to Leman Street police station. It contains clear echoes of the original 'Dear Boss' letter.

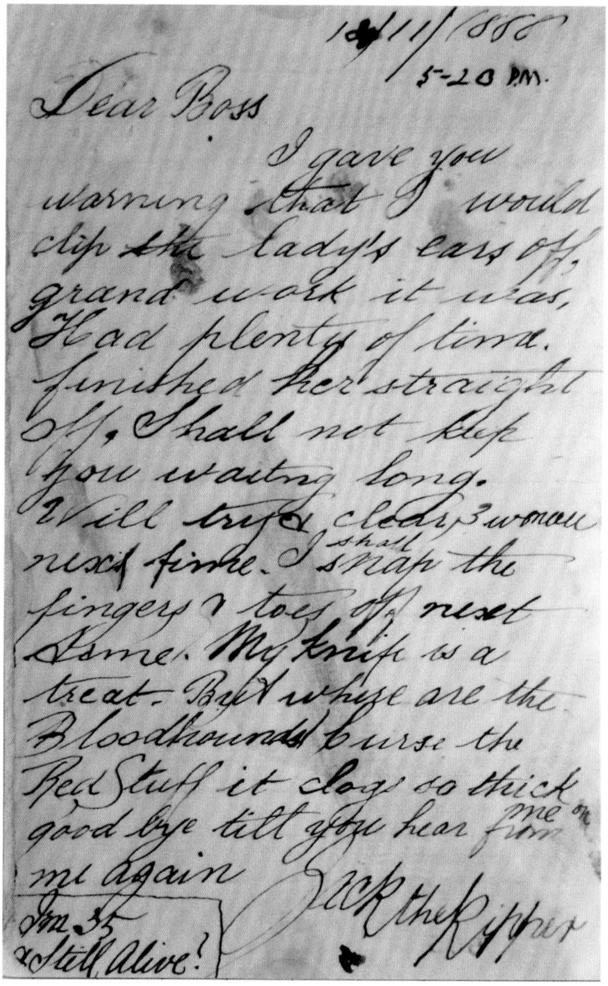
1[illegible]/11/1888
5-20 P.M.
Dear Boss
I gave you warning that I would clip the ladys ears off, grand work it was, Had plenty of time. finished her straight off, Shall not keep you waiting long. Will try & clear 3 woman next time. I shall snap the fingers & toes off next time. My knife is a treat. But where are the Bloodhounds Curse the Red Stuff it clogs so thick on me good bye till you hear from me again
Jack the Ripper
I'm 35 & Still Alive!

> next time. I shall snap the fingers & toes off next time. My knife is a treat. But where are the Bloodhounds Curse the Red Stuff it clogs so thick on me
> good bye till you hear from me again   Jack the Ripper
> I'm 35 & Still Alive?

This drew strongly from the original 'Jack the Ripper' letter, although it was written in a different hand and in black ink.

As if to supply the letter-writers with yet more subject matter the *Daily Telegraph* of Thursday 15 November ran another story on the ever-popular witness Matthew Packer:

> Mr. Matthew Packer, the fruiterer who sold some grapes to a man in company with the murdered woman just before the Berner-street murder, has made the following extraordinary statement:
>
> On Tuesday evening two men came to my house and bought 12s worth of rabbits of me. They then asked me if I could give an exact description of the man to whom I sold the grapes, and who was supposed to have committed the Berner-street and Mitre-square murders, as they were convinced they knew him and where to find him. In reply to some questions, one of the men said: "Well, I am sorry to say that I firmly believe it is my own cousin. He is an Englishman by birth, but some time ago he went to America, stayed there a

few years, and then came back to London about seven or eight months ago. On his return he came to see me, and his first words were, "Well, Boss, how are you?" He asked me to have some walks out with him, and I did round Commercial-street and Whitechapel. I found that he was very much altered on his return, for he was thorough harem scarem. We met a lot of Whitechapel women, and when we passed them he used to say to me, "Do you see those ——? How do you think we used to serve them where I came from? Why, we used to cut their throats and rip them up. I could rip one of them up and get her inside out in no time." He said, "We Jack Rippers killed lots of women over there. You will hear some of it being done over here soon, for I am going to turn a London Jack Ripper." The man added, "I did not take much notice then of what he said as he had had a drop of drink, and I thought it was only his swagger and bounce of what he had been doing in America, at some place which he mentioned, but I forget the name; but," continued the man, "when I heard of the first woman being murdered and stabbed all over I then began to be very uneasy, and to wonder whether he really was carrying out his threats. I did not, however, like to say anything about him, as he is my own cousin. Then, as one murder followed after another, I felt that I could scarcely rest. He is a perfect monster towards women, especially when he has a drop of drink. But in addition to what he said to me about these murders in America, and what was going to be done here, I feel certain it is him, because of the way these Jack the Ripper letters which have appeared in the papers begin. They all begin "Dear Boss," and that is just the way he begins his letters. He calls everybody "Boss" when he speaks to them. I did not want to say anything about him if I could help it, so I wrote to him, but he did not answer my letter. Since this last murder I have felt that I could not remain silent any longer, for at least something ought to be done to put him under restraint." Packer states he feels sure the men are speaking the truth, as they seemed very much concerned, and hardly knew what to do in the matter. He knows where to find the men. One is employed at some ironworks and the other at the West India Docks, and the man they allude to lives somewhere in the neighbourhood of Whitechapel.

The reporter to whom the above statement was made at once sent off a copy of it to the Home Secretary, and also Sir William [*sic*] Fraser, the Chief Commissioner of the City Police. Sir William Fraser immediately acted on the information, and sent Detective-sergeants White and Mitchell to investigate it. They read the letter to Packer, who said it was true, and then took the detectives to the man's house. On being questioned by the police he stated where his cousin was generally to be found. It transpired that he is sometimes engaged on the Thames, and late last night a search was, it is said, being made for him upon the river.

On inquiring early this morning we were officially informed that the above statement had not led to any satisfactory result.

This reappearance of Packer as a press celebrity seems to have been another red-herring. No result is recorded but it bears all the signs of being a prank played by the two men on Packer that, in the end, went rather wrong. Detective Sergeant White was the officer who dealt with Packer's first dubious witness statement, and it would appear that here, again, he had been led on a wild goose chase. The interesting aspect of this story is that it shows the great influence the letters had on people's behaviour, and how the pranksters gleaned their information from the press. As far as the journalists themselves were concerned this was clearly sensational stuff and sold even more

2D
8.B
Inspector
Leman St. Police
Court
Whitechapel.

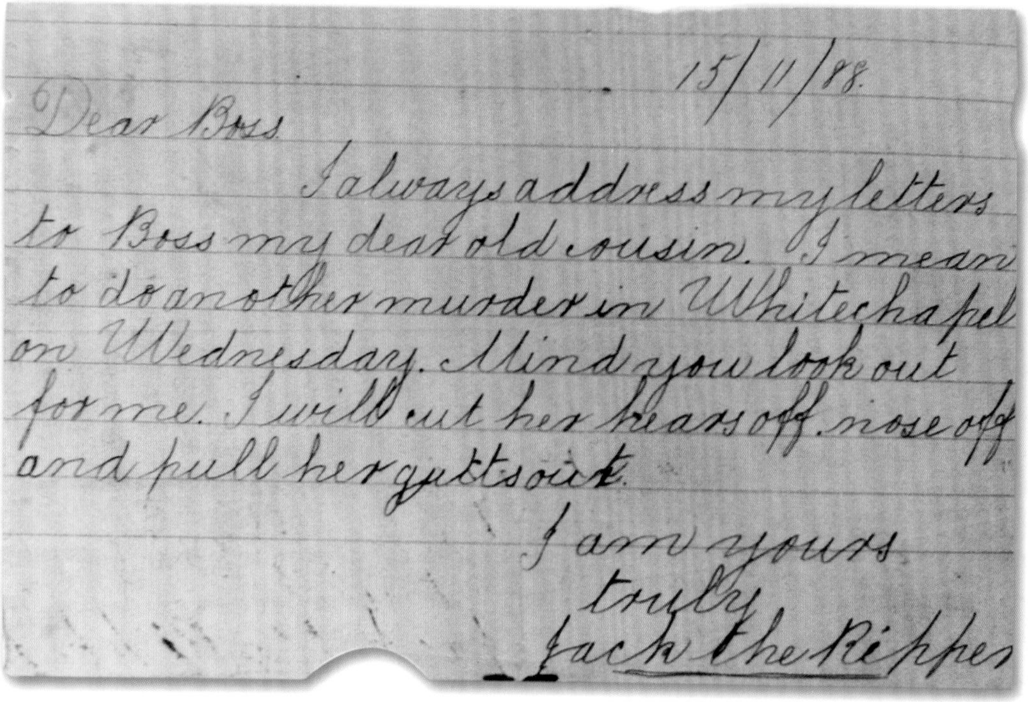

15/11/88.
Dear Boss.
I always address my letters to Boss my dear old cousin. I mean to do another murder in Whitechapel on Wednesday. Mind you look out for me. I will cut her ears off. nose off and pull her gutts out.
I am yours truly
Jack the Ripper

Letter of 15 November which drew on the witness Packer's story, as well as threatening another murder and bloodthirsty mutilation. This letter was mentioned in the *Eastern Post* of 17 November.

newspapers. Indeed, this latest Packer story did not go unnoticed for long by a letter-writer. The *Eastern Post* of Saturday 17 November reported:

> The police received another letter from "Jack the Ripper." It commenced with "Dear Boss," and went on to explain that the writer always addressed his cousin in those terms. He threatened to perpetrate another murder in the locality on Wednesday next, on which occasion he would inflict injuries on his victim, identical to those of his last.

The letter referred to here is preserved in the police files. Bearing a Hackney E postmark dated 15 November (the very day the Packer story appeared in the newspapers), it was addressed to 'Inspector, Leman St. Police Court, Whitechapel'. Written on lined paper, the letter actually reads:

15/11/88.

Dear Boss

I always address my letters to Boss my dear old cousin. I mean to do another murder in Whitechapel on Wednesday. Mind you look out for me. I will cut her hears off nose off and pull her gutts out.

I am yours.
truly
Jack the Ripper

Packer thus found his place in Ripper lore firmly established, despite the dubious nature of his evidence. He remained at 44 Berner Street for many years after the murders and died at the age of seventy-seven on 13 April 1907 at 24 Severne Street. He was survived by his wife Rose Ann Packer. His death certificate gives his occupation as a costermonger.

The *Glasgow Herald* of Friday 16 November reported another horror story relating to 'Jack the Ripper' letters under the heading 'THE WHITECHAPEL MURDERS':

A STRANGE AND THREATENING LETTER.

An extraordinary story was told yesterday of two ladies, well known in society, who have had to seek the special protection of the police. The other day they were walking out of curiosity through the East End, and the conversation turning upon the recent murders, they expressed a hope that the assassin, if caught, would be handed over to the women of the neighbourhood to be lynched. The next day they both received communications signed "Jack the Ripper", informing them that they had been overheard and traced to their respective homes, and assuring them of a speedy visit from their mysterious correspondent. At Scotland Yard the missives were declared to be in the same handwriting as the more important of those received previous to the Mitre Square and Berner Street tragedies.

On Saturday 17 November the *Weekly Budget* reported on its front page:

"Jack the Ripper's" Epistles.

"Jack the Ripper's" epistles are again in circulation. Mrs. McCarthy, the wife of the landlord of the house, has been amongst the last recipients of a communication from the mysterious individual whom the public already connect with the authorship of these crimes. In this letter the writer declares that he means "to have another mother and daughter." The writing of the letter resembles that of the letter previously published by the police.

Another communication from "Jack the Ripper" is of rather a curious character. It was found in Palatine-road, Stoke Newington, and was written in ink on a piece of wood cut in the shape of a cross. It was as follows; "This is a *fac-simile* knife with which I committed the murder. – JACK THE RIPPER." On the other side was written, "I will visit Stoke Newington next Friday. – JACK THE RIPPER." A recent letter – bearing the same signature – which the Commercial-street police received, was written on ordinary note-paper. It ran: "Dear Boss, – I am coming to do another on Sunday night in the City-road. Then I will let you know when I will give myself up. It will be Tuesday, about 12 o'clock, at the Kingsland-road police station. Good-bye till Tuesday. – JACK THE RIPPER."

Some days since the Chief Constable of Great Yarmouth (Superintendent Brogden) received the following letter, bearing the London post-mark, signed "Jack the Ripper." Of course no notice was taken of the matter at the time, as similar letters have been received by the police authorities throughout the country. However, upon the news of last Friday's tragedy coming to hand several people in Great Yarmouth were struck by the coincidence that the Chief Constable's correspondent dated from 14, Dorset-street. The letter, which was unstamped, was directed thus – "To the Head Constable of Yarmouth," and was as follows; "14, Dorset-street, Spitalfields, London, 29/10/88. Look-out for me on Thursday night at either of the piers, where I intend to rip up two Norwich women before closing time, so distinguish yourself better than the London coppers. – "JACK THE RIPPER." The letter appeared to have been written in red ink with a quill pen.

With such a large amount of 'Jack the Ripper' correspondence being received by the police there were sure to be some lucky coincidences struck by some of the writers, and this is but one example. However, such coincidences would result in much more importance, or attention, being accorded to the communication than otherwise might have been the case. As was to be expected, the Kelly murder had resulted in another flurry of letters.

On 19 November 1888, a correspondent in Scotland mailed a postcard in Glasgow. In true anonymous letter fashion the whole is comprised of cuttings from newspapers. It was addressed 'Metropolitan Police Office London' and read as follows (*see* below and the top of the opposite page):

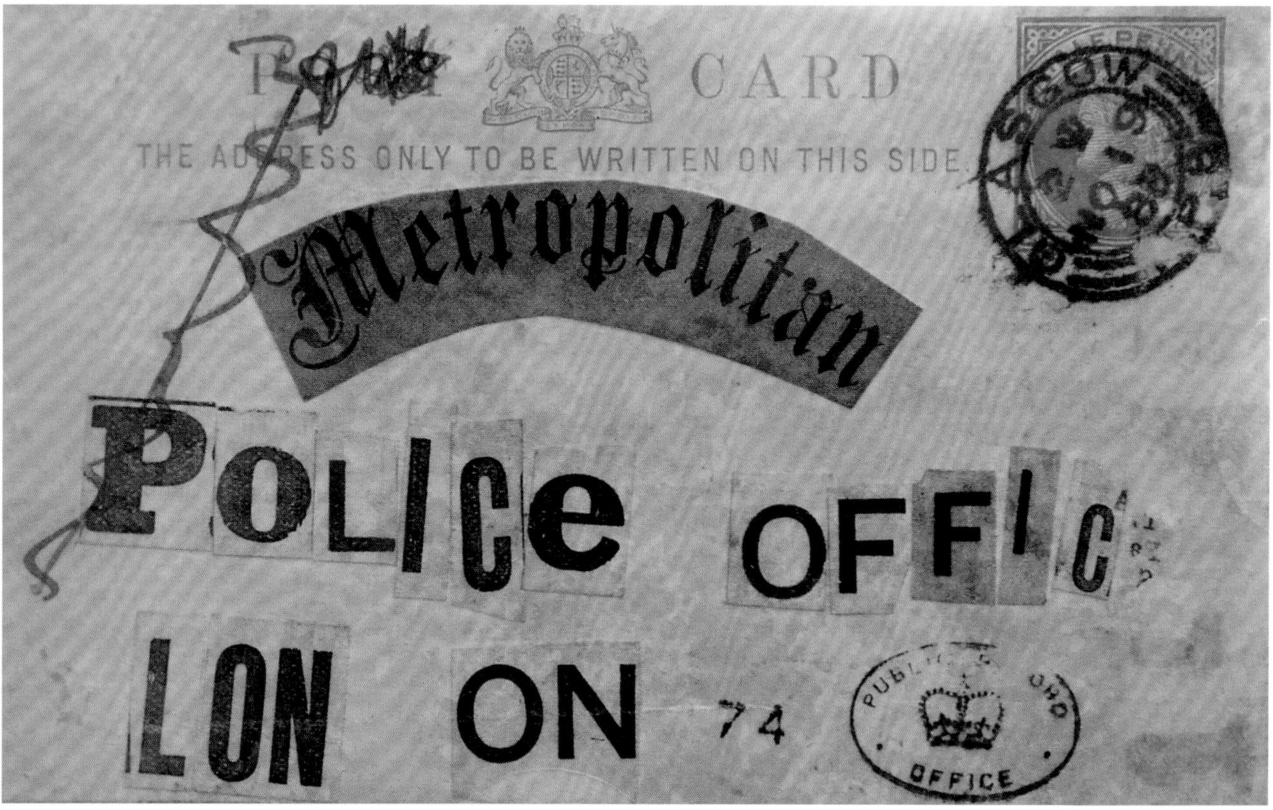

THE WHITECHAPEL ATROCITIES.
A L.L ON THE WRONG SALVAGE! I AM IN
FIRST-CLASS AT GOVAN WANTED young lady the 24th instant.
I SHALL CLEAR GLASGOW AND GOVAN AND
POLLOKSHIELDS, OF 16 ENGLISH
LADIES AND GENTLEMEN THE LORD WIL
DO HIS Guaranteed WOrk BY SCUTCHER. 300 Pieces
REQUIRED,
NO CLUE

A card posted in Glasgow on 19 November and composed of press cuttings, a rarity among the 'Ripper' letters. It was sent to the Metropolitan Police in London.

The description given by the witness George Hutchinson of the man he had seen with Kelly shortly before her murder was published in the newspapers and appeared as a sketch in the *Illustrated Police News*. A prominent feature of this description was the fact that the suspect was wearing 'a long dark coat collar and cuffs trimmed astracan [*sic*]'. A letter posted at Stratford on 19 November was addressed: 'please send this to Scotland Yard The Headquarters of the police'. The letter had a drawing of the back of a man wearing such a coat and the words:

> I am Jack the ripper catch me if you can
> [reverse] shall have one in Woolwhich This week Look out for me at Woolwhich

Another posted in Weston-Super-Mare on 19 November even purported to give the address where the sender was staying. It read:

> Royal Hotel
> Weston-S-M.
> 11/17/88
>
> Dear Old boss.
> I am now going to make my way to Paris and try my little games them as you aint sharp

Illustrated Police News picture of the suspect described by the witness George Hutchinson. He is wearing an astrakhan-trimmed coat and such a coat also appeared in a drawing on a letter of 19 November.

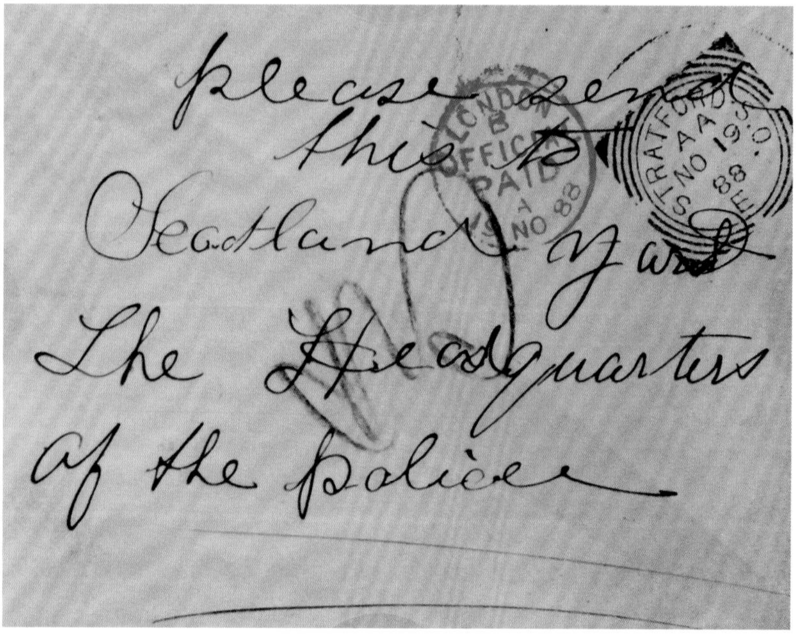

please send this to Scotland Yard The Headquarters of the Police

Envelope (*opposite*) and letter posted in Stratford on 19 November and illustrated with a drawing of a man wearing an astrakhan coat, as described by the witness George Hutchinson.

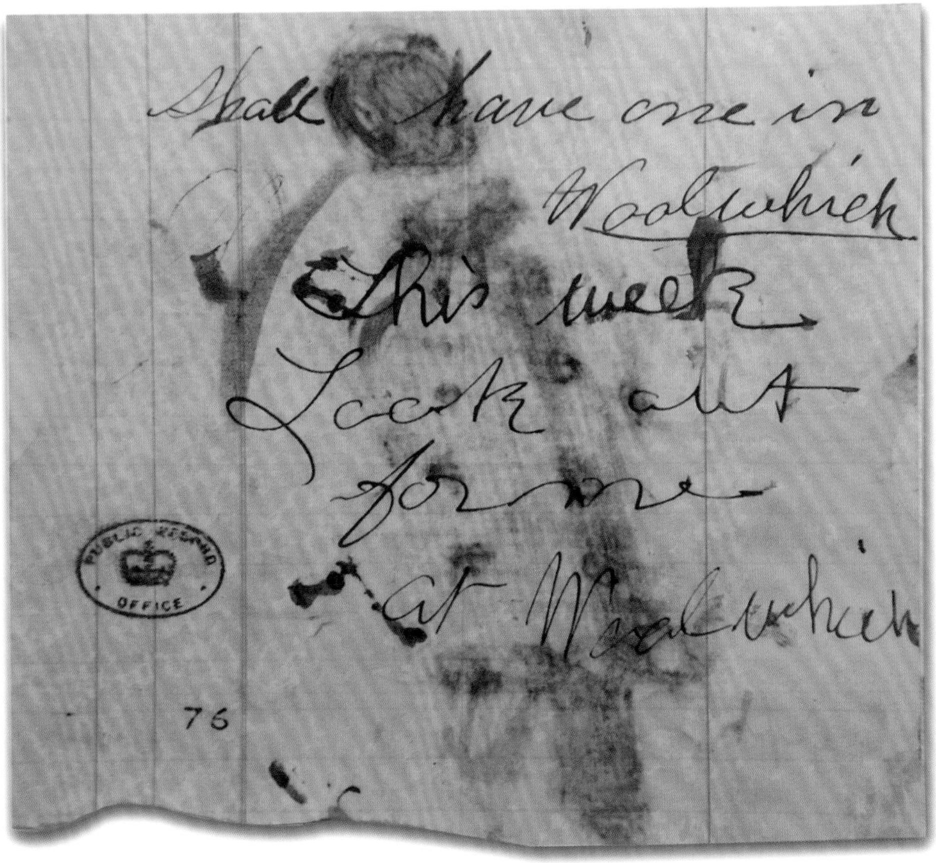
Shall have one in
Woolwich
This week
Look out
for me
at Woolwich

PUBLIC RECORD OFFICE

76

enough for me here I have done eleven murders so you aint found them out after al. Two gone down suers.

God bless you
Good by I'm of to Paris.
Believe me ever
Yours affectionatly

Albert Bachert again appeared in the press at this time. The *Manchester Evening News* of Monday 19 November carried the following report:

MORE WRITING ON THE WALL.

The blank wall of a house in Newnham-street, Whitechapel, in which Albert Bachert, who gave a description of the supposed Whitechapel murderer, lives, was found this morning to have had the following chalked upon it: 'Dear boss, – I am still about. Look out. – Yours, "JACK THE RIPPER." The words were afterwards partly obliterated to avoid attracting a crowd.

The *Portsmouth Evening News* of 26 November carried the following startling report:

ANOTHER THREATENING LETTER.

Yesterday the police authorities were informed that a Mrs. M'Kean, the wife of a City merchant, living at 18, Hilldrop-crescent, Camden-road, had received the following communication by post at nine p.m. the previous evening:–

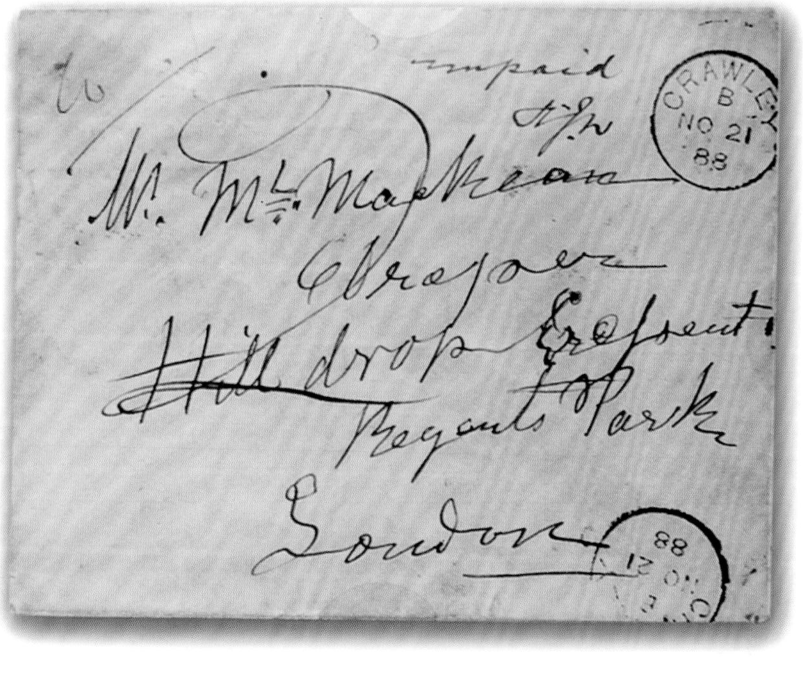

Envelope and letter (*opposite*) of 21 November sent to Mr MacKean of Hilldrop Crescent and threatening a visit to his City shop. Signed 'Jack Riper', it featured in the *Portsmouth Evening News*.

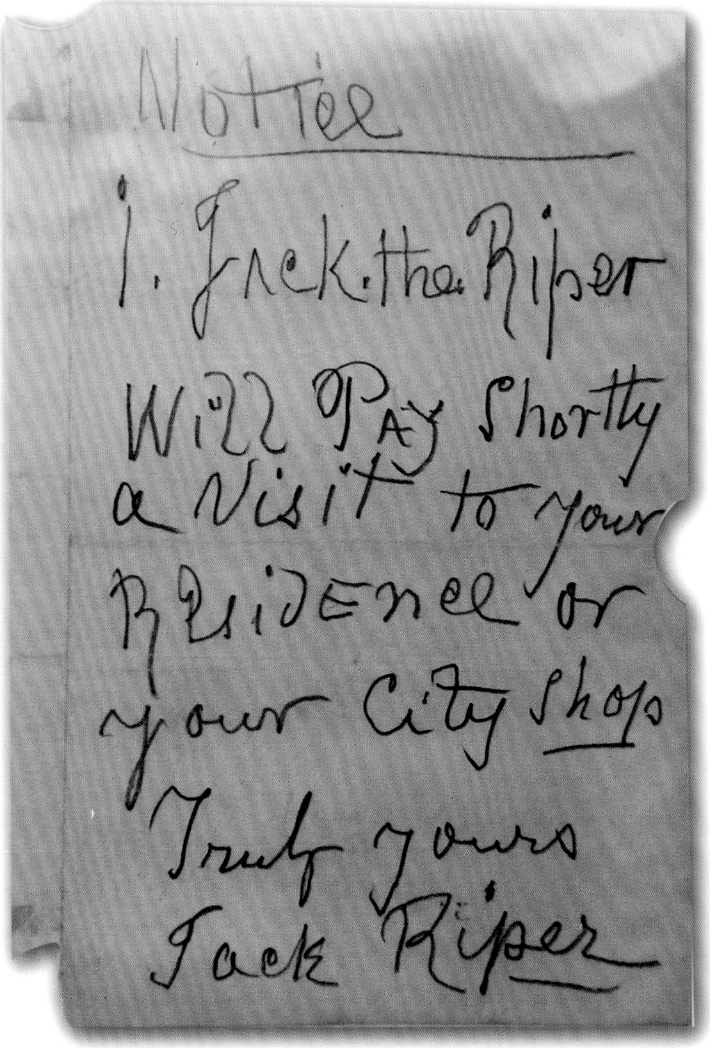
Notice

I. Jack. the. Riper
Will Pay Shortly
a Visit to your
Residence or
your City Shop
Truly yours
Jack Riper

> "I, Jack the Ripper, intend shortly giving you a visit at your residence or at your City shop
> Yours truly,
> JACK THE RIPPER."
>
> As may be supposed, the letter has caused some amount of alarm in the household, but by some of the members of the family it is put down as a silly hoax, or for annoyance by some discharged employee of Mr. M'Kean's.

This letter and envelope are preserved as folios 31–4 in the MEPO file and the postmark is 21 November, Crawley. The address on the envelope reads 'Mr. MacKean, 6 [illegible], Hilldrop Crescent, Regent's Park, London'. The back of the envelope is annotated 'not known at 6 Hilldrop Cres Holloway'. The letter is written in pencil in a spidery print and the only differences to the published version are the word '*Notice*' at the top and the phrase 'I . Jack . the . Riper Will Pay shortly a visit to your Residence or your City shop Truly yours Jack Riper'. The letter obviously eventually reached its intended destination. It is interesting to note that twenty-two years later, in 1910, number 39 Hilldrop Crescent was to become one of the infamous criminal addresses – the home of wife murderer and mutilator Dr Crippen.

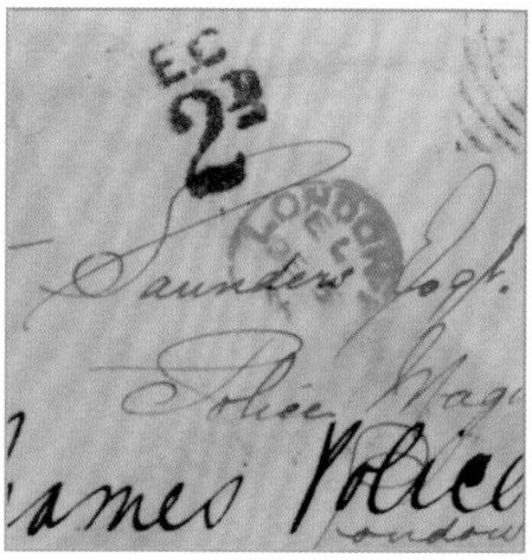

— TEN —

'Good Bye old fellow til i return'

AFTER the Kelly murder and the spate of correspondence it generated there were a few more incidents to ensure that the Whitechapel murders story could be kept alive, thus allowing the press to sustain public interest. However, the incidents became more sporadic and the last two noteworthy events of 1888 could not be directly linked with the 'Jack the Ripper' story.

The first was an alleged attack on a 'dissolute woman', Annie Farmer aged about forty years, in a common lodging house at 19 George Street, Spitalfields, on the morning of Wednesday 21 November. Briefly sensationalised in the press as another 'murderous outrage', the assault occurred at about 9.30 a.m. in a room apparently taken by Farmer and a man for immoral purposes. The woman suffered slight injuries only to the throat, which may have been self-inflicted. Her 'client' made off and she screamed blue murder. The incident was probably the result of a dispute over payment for services. However, it did not go unnoticed by one 'Jack the Ripper' correspondent. Written in red ink, the letter was sent from Rea Street Lodging House, Birmingham on 23 November. It read:

> Dear Sir
>
> I beg to inform you that I have read about that bungling affair yesterday morning in Whitechapel, this is to say that I have had no hand in it, but I think it must be one of my apprentices who has been practising, while I have been away, I am pleased to say that I arrived safe in B'ham last friday, where I have been since, I come to record my vote last saturday in [second page] support of the Bible candidate, for the school board election I am taking a holiday for a week I will again give you a standby visit, but I am going to try my luck here, before I come over, as I can see good chances for my practise, regretting you have been compelled to retire, wishing you better luck from the
>
> Old Original Jack the Ripper
>
> PS Kindly let the public know how disgusted I am with that offer, but I will make out next time

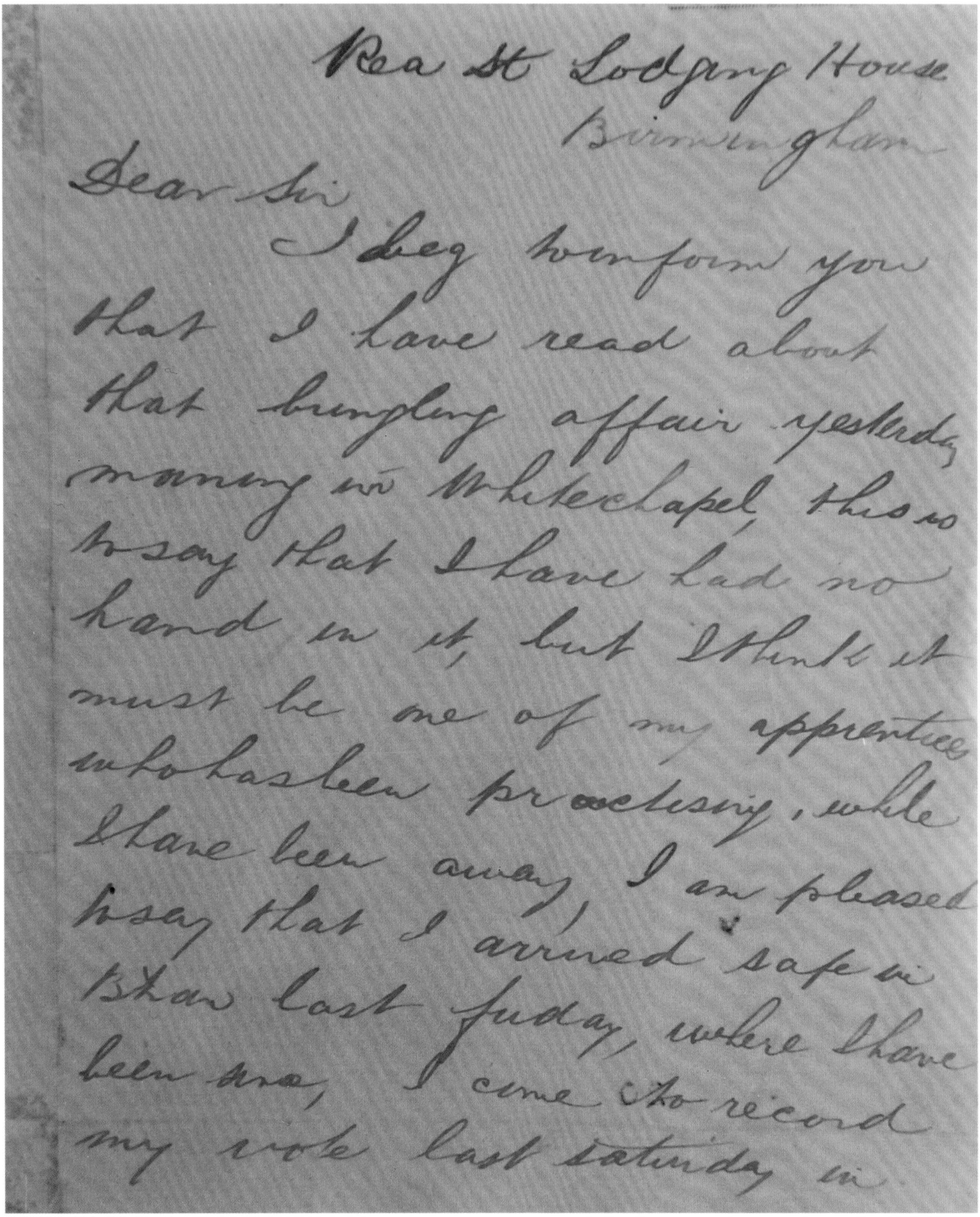

Rea St Lodging House
Birmingham

Dear Sir
I beg to inform you
that I have read about
that bungling affair yesterday
morning in Whitechapel, this is
to say that I have had no
hand in it, but I think it
must be one of my apprentices
who has been practising, while
I have been away, I am pleased
to say that I arrived safe in
Bham last friday, where I have
been since, I came to record
my vote last saturday in

Letter sent from 'Rea St Lodging House, Birmingham' on 23 November. It mentions the attack on Annie Farmer.

A taunting telegram, written with red ink, was sent on 21 November from London EC:

TO Inspector Abberline
Scotland Yard
Jack the Ripper wishes to give himself up will Abberline communicate with him at number 39 Cutler Street Houndsditch with this end in view.
FROM Jack the Ripper

Inspector Frederick Abberline, the high-profile Scotland Yard detective who headed the investigation at Whitechapel in 1888.

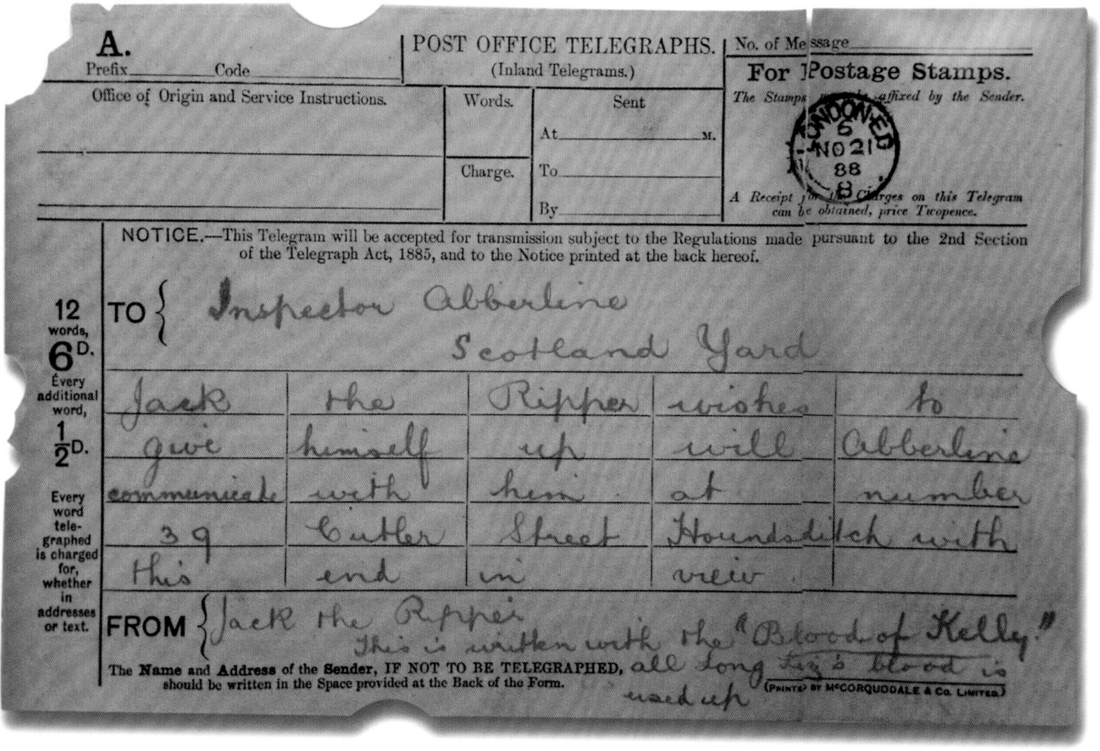

A.
Prefix______ Code______

POST OFFICE TELEGRAPHS.
(Inland Telegrams.)

No. of Message______

For Postage Stamps.
The Stamps ... affixed by the Sender.

LONDON E.D. 5 NO 21 88 8

A Receipt for the Charges on this Telegram can be obtained, price Twopence.

Office of Origin and Service Instructions.

Words.

Charge.

Sent
At______M.
To______
By______

NOTICE.—This Telegram will be accepted for transmission subject to the Regulations made pursuant to the 2nd Section of the Telegraph Act, 1885, and to the Notice printed at the back hereof.

12 words, 6D. Every additional word, ½D.

Every word telegraphed is charged for, whether in addresses or text.

TO { Inspector Abberline
Scotland Yard

Jack	the	Ripper	wishes	to
give	himself	up	will	Abberline
communicate	with	him	at	number
39	Cutler	Street	Houndsditch	with
this	end	in	view	

FROM { Jack the Ripper
This is written with the "Blood of Kelly" all Long Liz's blood is used up

The Name and Address of the Sender, IF NOT TO BE TELEGRAPHED, should be written in the Space provided at the Back of the Form.

(PRINTED BY McCORQUODALE & Co. LIMITED.)

Telegram of 21 November sent to Inspector Abberline stating that 'Jack the Ripper' wishes to give himself up and that he is at 39 Cutler Street, Houndsditch.

This is written with the "Blood of Kelly"
all Long Liz's blood is used up

Another letter was sent from Manchester, written in black ink in a small hand, on 22 November and stated:

> Dear Boss
>
> I am staying in Manchester at present but dressed as a poor man a navvie. saw the paper and you have had a letter from someone signed J.Ripper from Portsmouth soon after I did the last job (Kelly) i have been in Manchester since. Had nothing to do since kelly but seen Jervis's girls [?] every day will visit London about Sunday ready to be in time again on Monday. when i will do another i will tell you all when i get copped. Good Bye old fellow till i return.
>
> Yours Truly
>
> Jack the Ripper

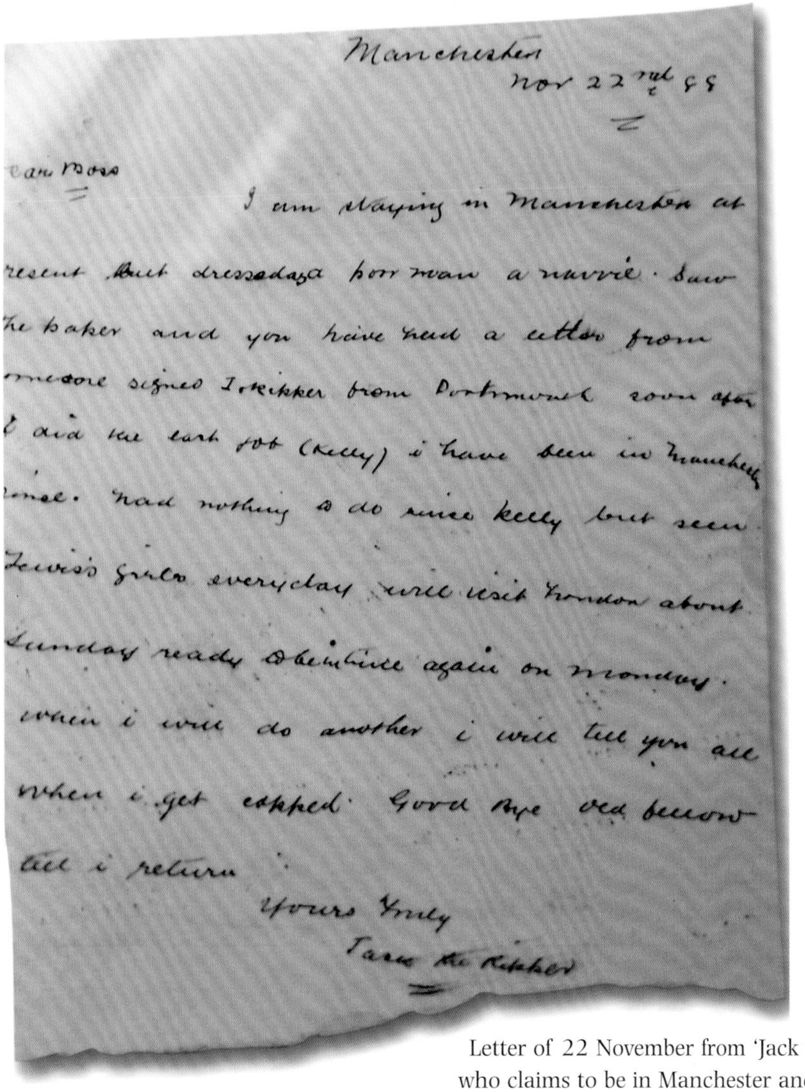

Manchester
Nov 22nd 88

Dear Boss

I am staying in Manchester at present but dressed as a poor man a navvie. saw the paper and you have had a letter from someone signed J.Ripper from Portsmouth soon after I did the last job (Kelly) i have been in Manchester since. Had nothing to do since kelly but seen Jervis's girls everyday will visit London about Sunday ready to be in time again on Monday. when i will do another i will tell you all when i get copped. Good Bye old fellow till i return

Yours Truly
Jack the Ripper

Letter of 22 November from 'Jack the Ripper' who claims to be in Manchester and threatens to return to London.

On Thursday 22 November the *Manchester Evening News* reported:

ANOTHER LETTER FROM "JACK THE RIPPER."

Yesterday, Mr. Saunders, the sitting magistrate at the Thames Police Court, London, received a letter purporting to come from "Jack the Ripper." The envelope bore the Portsmouth postmark, and was directed as follows: "To the head magistrate, Police Court, Whitechapel, London." It read as follows:–

"No. 1, England, 1888.

"Dear Boss, – It is no good for you to look for me in London, because I am not there. Don't trouble yourself about me till I return, which will not be very long. I like the work too well to leave it long. Oh, it was such a jolly job the last one. I had plenty of time to do it properly. Ha! ha! The next lot I mean to do with a vengeance – cut off their head and arms. You think it is a man with a black moustache. Ha! ha! ha! When I have done another you can catch me, so good bye, dear boss, till I return. – Yours, "JACK THE RIPPER."

The letter has been handed over by Mr. Sayer, the chief clerk, to the police.

The publication of this letter no doubt resulted in Mr Saunders receiving another one a short time later. Preserved in the police files, the letter and envelope are written in purple ink and were posted on 4 December in the London EC district. The envelope was addressed: 'Saunders Esqr. Police Magistrates London', written over, in black ink, at the bottom: 'Thames Police Court E'. The letter was written on a newspaper cutting, as follows:

England

Dear Boss

Look out for 7th inst. Am trying my hand at disjointing and if can manage it will send you a finger

Saunders Esqr Yours

Police Magistrate Jack the Ripper

The minor popularity of Mr Saunders resulted in a third communication. The *Monmouthshire Merlin and South Wales Advertiser* of Friday 7 December reported:

ANOTHER LETTER FROM "JACK THE RIPPER."

. . . In the meantime Mr. Saunders, the presiding magistrate at the Thames police court, Monday received a letter addressed to "Mr Saunders, chief magistrate, Whitechapel." The letter read as follows. – "Dr Pal, – I am still at liberty, the last job in Whitechapel was not bad; but I mean to surprise them on the next. Shall joint it. Ha, ha, ha! After that shall try on the lazy lounghers who live on unfortunates. We have just enrolled several for the job. I am in the country for my health. I met the super (Wellingboro') the other day, and like him immense. Shall try a job here next. So look out for news from –

JACK THE RIPPER."

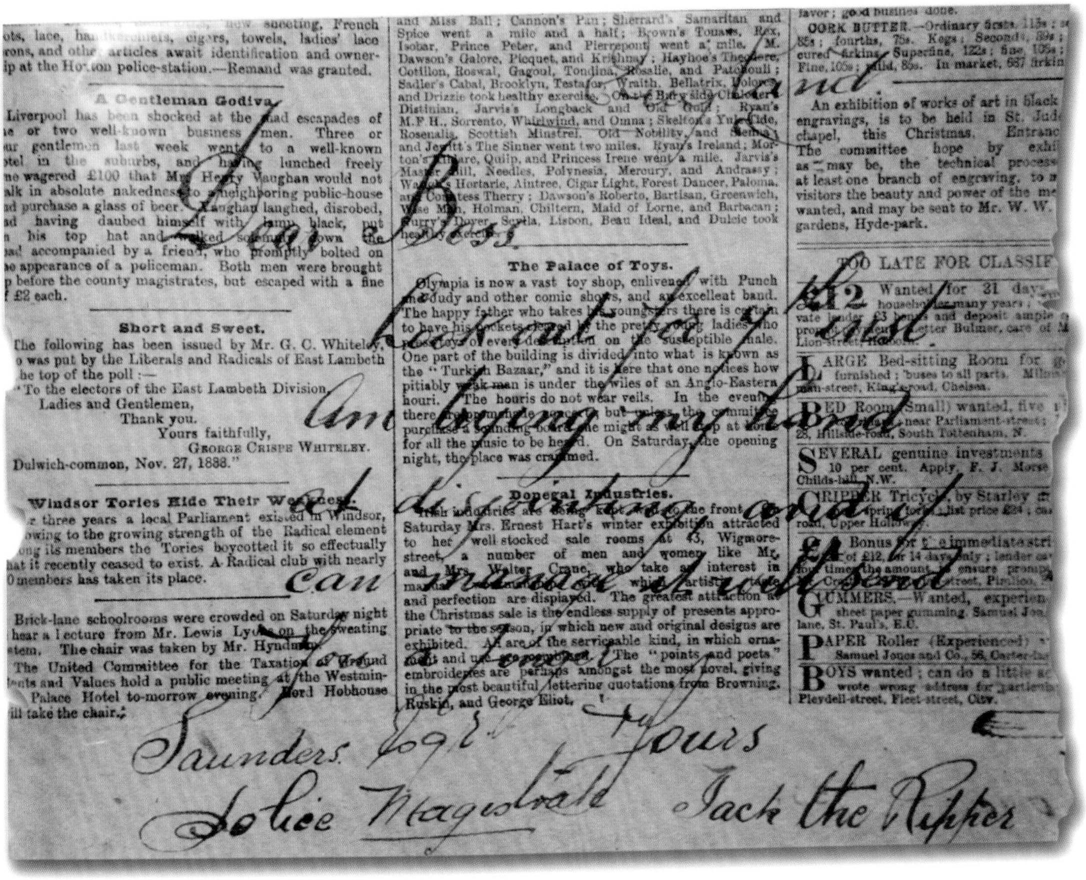

Letter of 4 December written on a press cutting to Mr Saunders, the Thames Police Court magistrate.

We have evidence of a 'Jack the Ripper' letter even being sent in the USA at this time. In New York, the *Sun* of Friday 14 December reported that Mayor Hewitt had received the following letter:

> New York, Dec 12 1888.
>
> Hon. Abram. S. Hewitt, Mayor,
>
> Sir. It is folly for the police and the newspapers to speculate on my being in Montreal or any other part of Canada. I am right here in their midst, and will begin operations immediately after Christmas.
>
> JACK THE RIPPER

There was a further alleged murder on Thursday 20 December when the body of another prostitute, Rose Mylett, alias Lizzie Davis, was found at about 4.00 a.m. by a patrolling police officer in Clarke's Yard, High Street, Poplar. She had apparently been strangled but there were no cuts to the body whatsoever, and it was even claimed by Assistant Commissioner Robert Anderson to be a death from natural causes.

On 29 December the murdered body of a small boy, seven-year-old John Gill, was found at Manningham, Bradford. His legs had been hacked off, his abdomen slashed open from the neck to the pubis, exposing the intestines, his heart cut out and placed with the intestines and his left ear was missing. This led, for a short while, to press speculation that it may have been another Ripper crime. The boy had last been seen alive aboard the milk cart of one William Barrett, whom the boy was assisting with his deliveries. Barrett was soon arrested on suspicion of murder but denied all knowledge of the crime. Initially there was insufficient evidence and the prisoner was released after court hearings. However, new information quickly came to light at the inquest and Barrett was re-arrested. His trial was scheduled for Leeds winter assizes in March 1889 but Barrett was again released when the evidence against him was again found to be insufficient. The identity of the murderer was never established.

James Monro, Commissioner of the Metropolitan Police from November 1888 to 1890.

This killing was also referred to in a 'Jack the Ripper' letter sent to C Division of the Metropolitan Police on 15 January 1889 in which the writer claimed 'I riped up little boy in Bradford . . .'. Another letter sent the following day stated 'I am still in London After my trip to Bradford.'

The first six months of 1889 seemed to pass normally enough but at about 12.50 a.m. on Wednesday 17 July beat officer PC 272H Walter Andrews discovered the body of another murdered prostitute in Castle Alley, Whitechapel. The victim was Alice McKenzie, who rejoiced in the nickname 'Clay Pipe Alice'. This time there were similarities with the previous Whitechapel murders: her throat had been cut and there were deep lacerations to her abdomen. Initially the Police Commissioner, James Monro, believed it to be another 'Ripper' murder and the press sensationalised the case. Another flurry of letters to the police resulted. One of these letters was apparently sent to Albert Bachert, and the *Hemel Hempstead Gazette* of Saturday 20 July reported:

> "JACK THE RIPPER" LETTERS.
>
> It is stated that the police have during the past few weeks received letters, signed "Jack the Ripper," intimating that he would recommence his horrible work in July: and Mr. Albert Backert [*sic*], who took a leading part in the Vigilance proceedings of last year, received a similar letter about three weeks ago.

There are no letters preserved in the police files that substantiate this story but it does indicate the continuing press interest in Bachert.

The early days of 1889, from January to March had resulted in a mere seven dated letters which may be found in the police file. However, the McKenzie murder, and its obvious similarities to the 1888 killings, resulted in a resurgence of 'Ripper' mail. There are fourteen dated letters on file that were sent between 19 July and 4 September. One of these letters, addressed to 'The head one of the policemen, Scotland Yard, London', was posted in London SW on 19 July:

> I will cut Whitechapel
> out There Three women done me
> Abdomen wrong in Whitechapel
> I dare say you So I will kill every
> Know what women there. 20 because of
> That means Them
> I am Jack the Ripper.
> I am going to have another women in two more days time
> in Whitechapel near castle alley. I am a mark on the women
> [This paragraph is written in pencil.] The police ant artfull enough for me.
> I do it when I get a chance not when I see police coming I will do it one of
> those times when a copper looking and the I'll do the same to him
> I live in
> Whitechapel Yours Truly
> I have been Jack the Ripper [signature in pencil]
> over in
> america
> all the
> summer
> I am in [illegible and torn]
> They searched all them barrows and carts Near the castle
> alley But they didnt search the one I was in I was looking
> at the police all the Time.

The only example that the authors have come across of a 'Jack the Ripper' letter in private hands is from this time. It is dated 22 August 1889 and is written in red crayon to an unknown newspaper. It is, unfortunately, in quite poor condition, some of the crayon having come off over the years. The letter reads as follows:

> My Dear Sir would you just put in your paper a word for me just to put the police on my trail i mean to have a nice young woman [illegible] in Dalston lane i have been on my [deletion] Holiday at A Ramsgate i mean to pay my visit in Dalston lane August 22 i think that i have been very good up to now i mean to have a nise time of it i have no no more to say this time i think i shall have a [deletion] truble
> [second page] this time so Good By
>
> So I am yours
> Truly Jack The
> Riper Ar Ar

This letter is owned by Roy Deeley, Director of the Universal Autograph Collectors Club, who tells an interesting tale of how it came into his possession: 'About fifteen years ago a man working for a firm I give sub contract work to knew I collected autographs and brought this to work for me. Unfortunately he had it in his wallet for several days. He told me that he had bought an old desk at a sale, and found that it had a secret door, which when he opened it he found this letter inside. So I was able to buy it from him because he had no interest in autographs.' The letter was contained in a torn envelope with 'On His Majesty's S[ervice]' printed at the top, and written thereon was 'G. FitzGibbon Esq., [L]etter from "Jack the Ripper"'. The envelope obviously post-dates the letter by may years, if the date on the letter is correct. No other provenance is known and this letter remains another minor mystery.

A message in a bottle dated 2 September was found washed ashore on the Channel coast between Sandwich and Deal, Kent. The piece of paper measured 6¼ inches wide by 2 inches and on it was written the following cryptic message: 'S.S. Northumbria Castle Left ship – am on trail yours Jack the Ripper'.

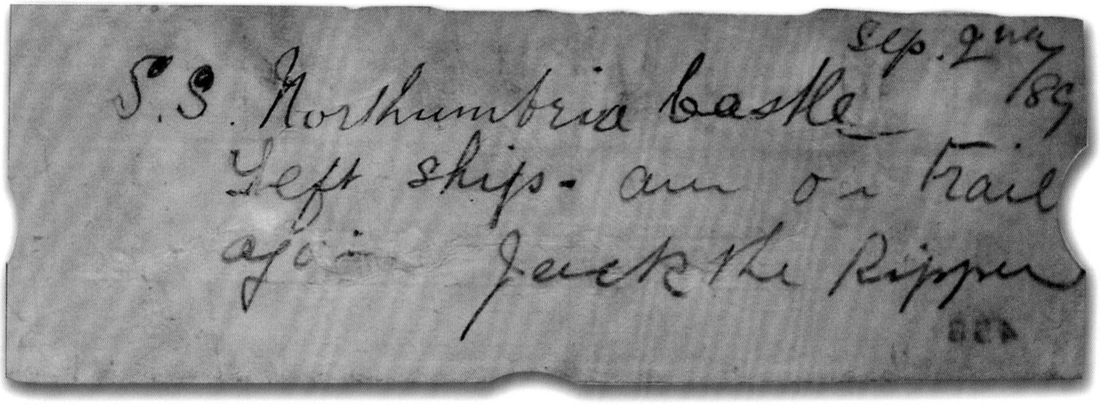

Message dated 2 September 1889 and found in a bottle washed ashore between Sandwich and Deal in Kent.

On the morning of Tuesday 10 September a female torso, minus the head and legs, was found under a railway arch in Pinchin Street, St George's-in-the-East, in the Whitechapel Division of the Metropolitan Police. Initially billed by the press as another 'Ripper' scare, it quickly became obvious that it was nothing at all to do with the previous murders. The case remained unsolved and the remains unidentified. However, it did result in the sending of further letters and there are some twenty-six dated between 10 September and 29 November. One writer claimed to be 'Jack the Ripper' but not the author of the Pinchin Street crime. Posted in London E on the very day of the discovery of the remains the postcard, written in pencil and addressed to the *Evening News and Post*, ran:

> Whitechapel Sept. 10
>
> Dear Boss
> The Ripper scare this morning is an infernal scandal on me you know. I never do my ripping in that fashion but give them a chance to catch me ha ha I'd show you again soon wont be long but this will delay my opperations untill it bloodhounds [?]
>
> Jack the Ripper

On Thursday 12 September a letter was posted in the London N area addressed to 'Mr. Monro, Chief Commissioner of Police, Scotland Yard'. The writer appears to have been of a particularly sadistic turn of mind. Possibly impressed by the details of the Pinchin Street torso case, on the reverse of the envelope he wrote 'shall write the next letter in Blood implements of torture' and followed this with drawings of a gun, razor and knives. The text was written in black ink:

> Jack the rippers
> hole Whitechapel
>
> Dear Boss
> I shall certainly have you wife or Daughter of theirs leg Before another month she will be mutilated in a cruel manner But I can't help that
>
> Signed [illegible]

The Sunday Times of 29 September 1889 reported:

> Last evening the Press Association received a letter bearing the East London post-mark, purporting to be from the notorious "Jack the Ripper." The envelope was apparently written by a different person from the text of the note, which was written on a torn single sheet of note paper, and which ran as follows:–
>
> "E., 29 Sept.
> Dear Editor,
> I hope to resume operations about Tuesday or Wednesday night. Don't let the coppers know.
> JACK THE RIPPER."
>
> The envelope is smeared with red ink, and the words "Jack the Ripper" are underlined with red ink.

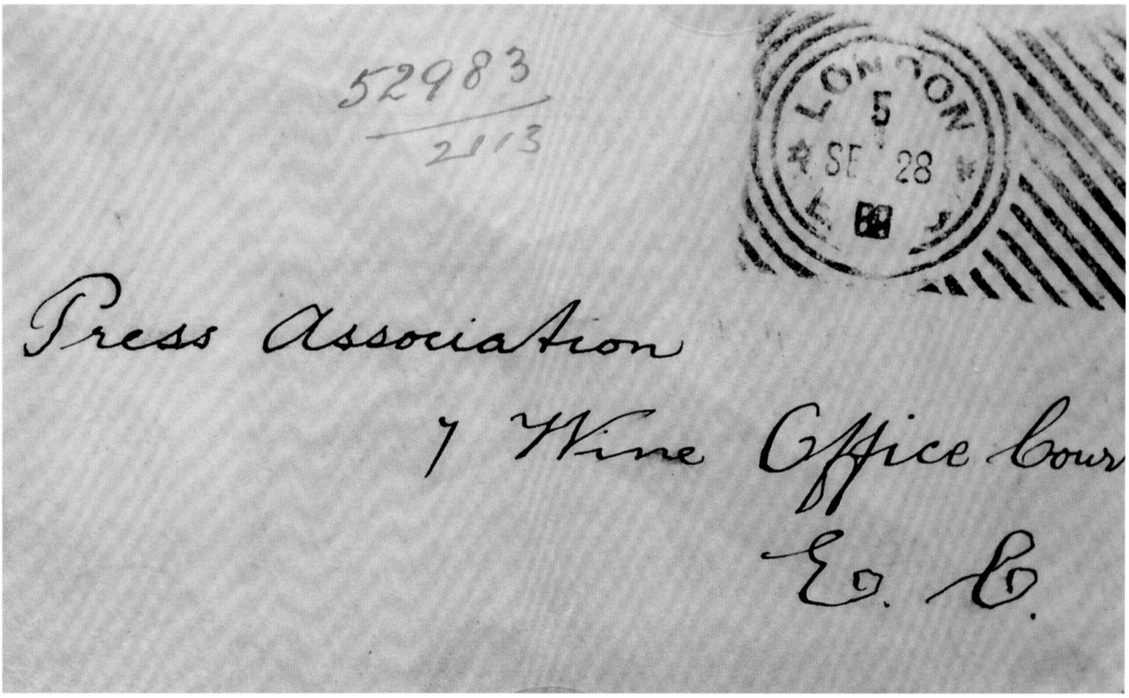
52983
2113

Press Association
7 Wine Office Cour
E. C.

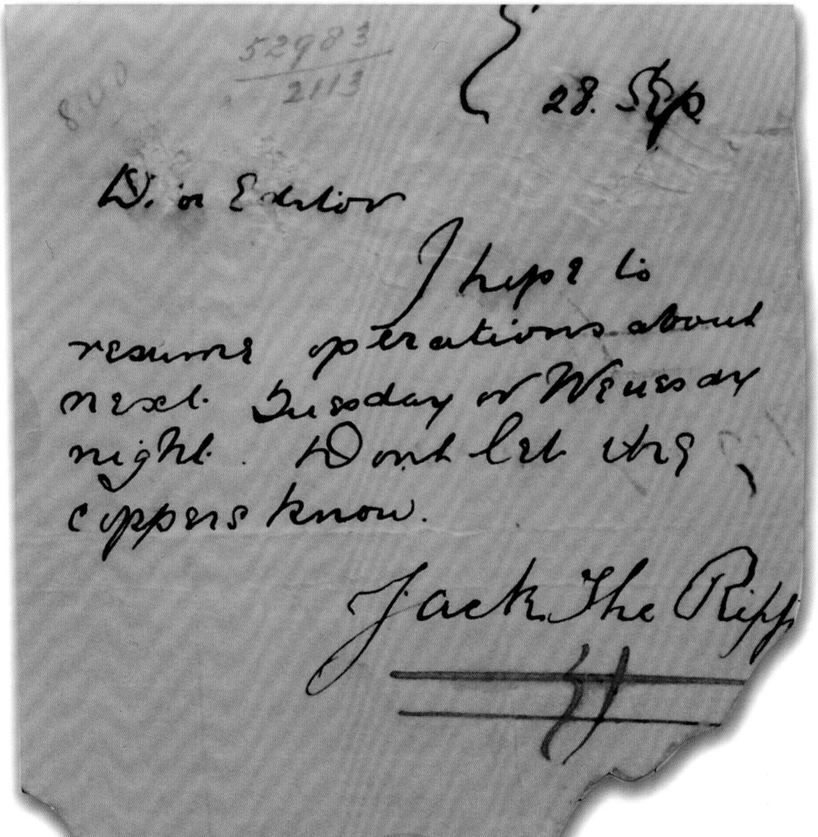
52983
2113

28. Sep

Dear Editor

I hope to resume operations about next Tuesday or Wednesday night. Dont let the coppers know.

Jack The Ripp

Letter of 28 September 1889 sent to the Press Association from 'Jack the Ripper'. The writer threatens that he will 'resume operations' and urges the recipient: 'Don't let the coppers know'. It was mentioned in *The Sunday Times* of 29 September.

A letter from a writer in America was posted in Boston, Massachusetts, on 30 October and sent to the editor of *The Times*. Written in black ink, it disparaged the English police while favourably commenting on American officers and stated that such a 'series' of murders would not be possible in the United States:

> Editor of the London Times. As I was obliged
> to go to America that murder which was promised within
> a week failed to be performed. There's plenty of time
> yet in which to complete the fifteen. Some of your police
> regulations are so absurd that I have to laugh at them. Here
> [deletion] the officers are armed and allowed to use their
> discretion. There the whole system is stupid. I did not see it
> so much till I came here where such a series would not be possible.
> However I hope you won't wake up until I am through. I will
> follow this one week later. Then look out——
> Jack the Ripper

Although much of the 'Ripper' literature features rhymes allegedly written by the killer, the actual files do not bear out the impression which has been created that this was a strong feature of the writings. There was the 'I'm not a butcher, I'm not a Yid' verse and it is perhaps the most famous of the rhymes that can actually be accorded any authenticity. However, the original is not known to exist and we have only Melville Macnaghten's rendering of it in *Days of My Years*. It is probably this published verse that has led to subsequent writers utilising such material to enhance their books. The official files include only one real poem, albeit a lengthy one, signed 'J. Ripper'. It was posted to Scotland Yard on 8 November 1889, from London SW. Written in black ink with a postscript in red ink, the text can be seen on pages 288–90 and it is too lengthy to reproduce here. This rhyming letter referred to the theories of Dr Forbes Winslow, see Chapter Thirteen.

There are only six letters on file for 1890 and the year was a quiet one in Whitechapel with no murder or scare attributable to the Ripper. The last Whitechapel murder on the police files is dated Friday 13 February 1891, and this was the final crime to be briefly attributed to 'Jack the Ripper'. The body of Frances Coles, a prostitute aged twenty-six years, was found by PC 240H Thompson at about 2.15 a.m. under a railway arch at Swallow Gardens, Whitechapel, an alley that ran between Chamber Street and Royal Mint Street. Her throat had been cut twice. A male friend of hers, James Thomas Sadler, a ship's fireman, was arrested on suspicion of her murder. He was briefly believed by the police to be 'Jack the Ripper' and an attempted identification was carried out using the Mitre Square murder witness, Lawende. No evidence could be adduced against him for the Coles murder, however, and he had been at sea at the time of the previous killings. He was eventually released. This was the last time that a real 'Ripper' scare appeared in the press. There are only two dated letters – one from March and one from April – in the police file relating to the Coles murder, indicating something of a decline in public interest, presumably because this, the last of the Whitechapel murders, was not widely regarded as a return of 'Jack the Ripper' and the dark days of 1888–9.

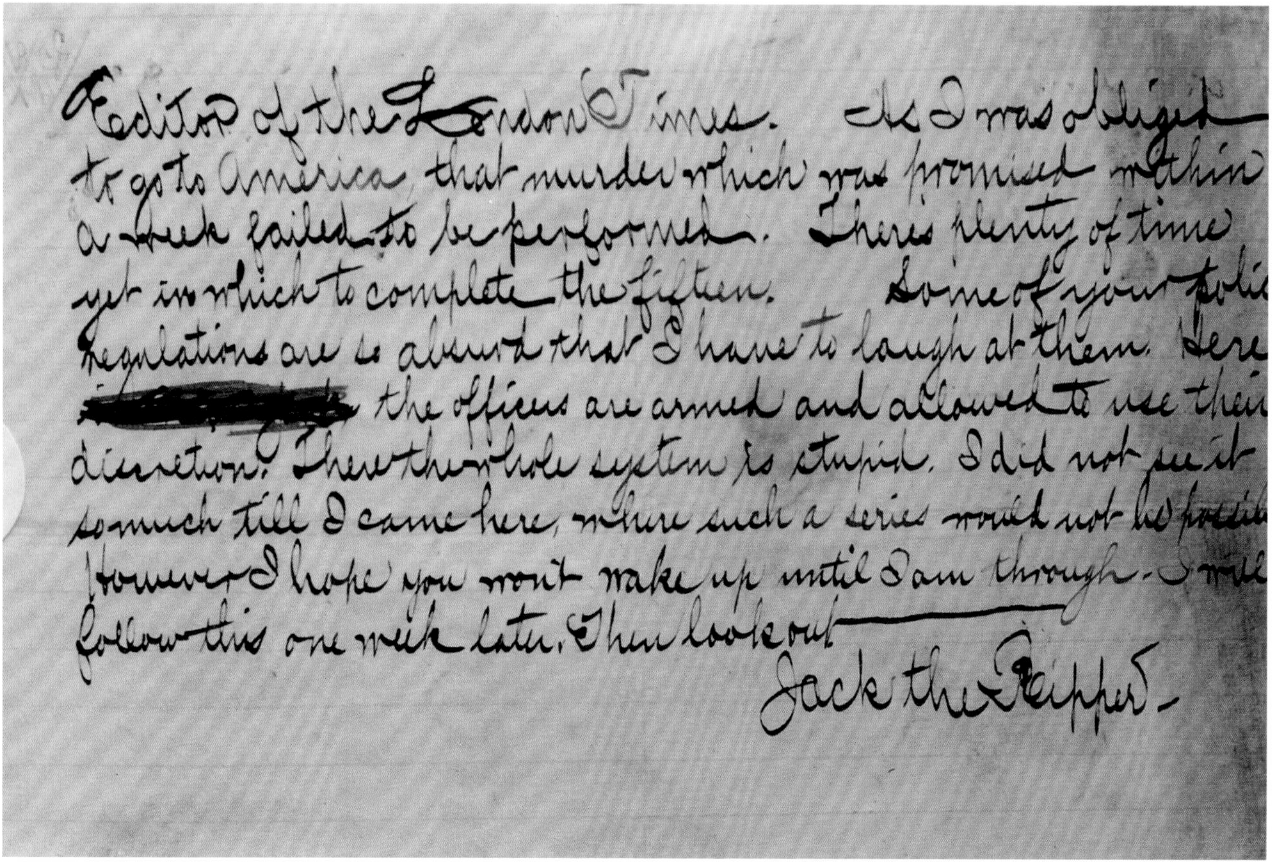
Editor of the London Times. As I was obliged
to go to America, that murder which was promised within
a week failed to be performed. There's plenty of time
yet in which to complete the fifteen. Some of your police
regulations are so absurd that I have to laugh at them. Here
[redacted] the officers are armed and allowed to use their
discretion. There the whole system is stupid. I did not see it
so much till I came here, where such a series would not be possible.
However I hope you wont wake up until I am through. I will
follow this one week later. Then look out

Jack the Ripper -

Letter of 30 October 1889 sent to the editor of *The Times* from Boston, Massachusetts. 'Jack the Ripper' claims to be in the USA.

Another brief 'Jack the Ripper' mention came on 6 May 1893 when a short article appeared in the *East London Observer*. Entitled 'Jack the Ripper Once More', the piece stated that the Detective Department at Scotland Yard was engaged in making enquiries about another letter received on the previous Monday by Mr Mead, a magistrate of the Thames Police Court, which was signed 'Jack the Ripper'. The letter stated that the 'Ripper' had again arrived in London and would directly resume operations. It bore the outline of a coffin drawn with blood or red ink, and in a piece of tissue paper was a fragment of dried liver.

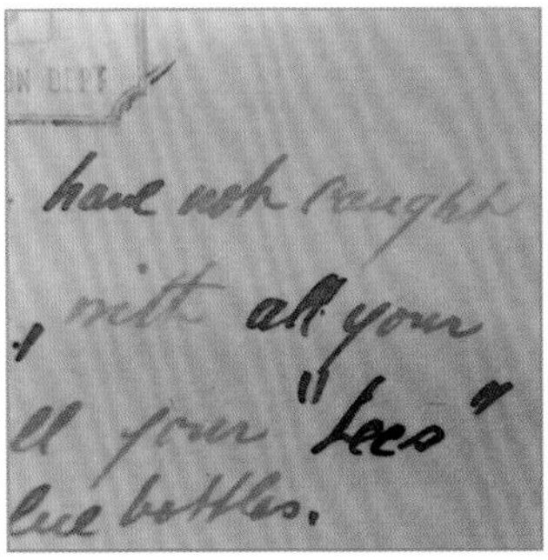

— **ELEVEN** —

'They summoned the spirit'

ONE of the persistent legends in the Ripper story concerns the medium and clairvoyant Robert James Lees (1849–1931). In 1888 he was resident in Peckham and had already established a reputation as a prominent Christian Spiritualist. That he took an interest in the murders cannot be in doubt for his diary, lodged at Stansted Hall, records that he made an approach to the police on Tuesday 2 October 1888: 'Offered services to police to follow up East End murders – called a fool and a lunatic. Got trace of a man from the spot in Berner Street. Wednesday 3rd October. Went to City police again – called a madman and fool. Thursday 4th October. Went to Scotland Yard – same result but promised to write to me.' There is no other known contemporary evidence to associate him with the murders.

That this mysterious series of killings attracted the attention of the spiritualists is not in doubt. Indeed, a story in the *Star of the East* on Monday 8 October stated:

> A MESSAGE FROM THE SPIRIT WORLD.
>
> An extraordinary statement bearing upon the Whitechapel tragedies was made to the Cardiff police on Sunday by a respectable-looking elderly woman. She stated that she was a spiritualist, and that she and five other persons held a *séance* on Saturday night. They summoned the spirit of Elizabeth Stride. After some delay the spirit came, and in answer to questions, stated that her murderer was a middle-aged man whose name she mentioned, who resided at a given number in Commercial Road or Street, Whitechapel, and belonged to a band of 12.

A further report in the same newspaper added:

> THE SPIRITUALIST AND THE MURDERER.
>
> At another Spiritualistic *séance* held at Bolton yesterday, a medium claims to have obtained a description of the Whitechapel murderer, which she has given, and adds that he will be caught in the act of committing another murder.

The *Evening Post* of Saturday 10 November carried a spiritualist story on its front page:

> A SPIRITUALISTIC UTTERANCE.
>
> At last a spiritualistic medium, one Mrs. Charles Spring, has made a deliverance in reference to the Whitechapel murders. Here it is:– "He is not English. Go to Florence, in Italy. We do not know his name, but there are more than one in hiding now. He goes in and comes out of his home like a gentleman, and sometimes has a disguise like an old woman, going about. Look well after the military medicals, also the foreign secret societies. They consider our bodies do not matter, and that such as us will not be missed from the world, and our bodies suit the purpose better than other women's, as they want our bodies for a particular reason, which will be seen by-and-bye. Yes, there will be more murders yet, but not in the same place; they are planning now, and the police will have all their work to find it out. They go away out of London, soon after the deed is done, back to their home to carry on their business as usual through the week, and manage the murders on Saturday, to get clear away on Sunday. They use chemicals to wipe off spots of blood from their clothes. They are too respectable-looking to be suspected by those who know them. Foreigners quick with knife, and sure not to make a blunder. How they plot and plan; But look to military medicals, bad, fallen ones now they cannot get bodies from the hospital so soon after death. They have a particular purpose; they want to find something."

To return to Lees, a later story was expounded to the effect that he had received a psychic impression of the murderer. The account ran that the clairvoyant had been riding with his wife on a London omnibus from Shepherd's Bush and the man boarded at Notting Hill. The man alighted at Oxford Street and Lees followed him, pointing the individual out as 'Jack the Ripper' to a police constable in Park Lane. The policeman rejected Lees' story and the man disappeared in a cab. Lees then, allegedly, gave his account to a more receptive police sergeant and then to an inspector at Scotland Yard. After Lees related the details of a 'vision', a postcard was produced by the officer, written in red ink and with two bloody fingerprints on it. It read:

> Tomorrow night I shall again take my revenge, claiming from a class of women who have made themselves most obnoxious to me my ninth victim.
>
> JACK THE RIPPER
>
> P.S. To prove that I am really 'Jack the Ripper' I will cut off the ears of this ninth victim.

This confirmed a second vision Lees had experienced and he 'fainted dead away'. By now the police inspector was convinced of Lees' account. The story went on to say the murder did take place, and the inspector was amazed to hear that one of the victim's ears was nearly severed and the other left hanging from her head by a shred of flesh. Lees went abroad while the murderer went on to claim his sixteenth victim!

Lees then had a vision that another murder had been committed and again went to see the police. The same inspector was impressed by the account and he and his men followed Lees through the streets of London at night as the clairvoyant 'followed the

The clairvoyant R.J. Lees featured in 'Ripper' lore. He was certainly interested in the murders but his role in the case has been greatly enhanced by legend and the tale about his allegedly tracking the murderer was used to bolster the latter-day suspect Dr William Withey Gull.

trail of his quarry like a bloodhound'. Finally Lees pointed out a 'west end mansion' where, he told the police, they could find 'Jack the Ripper'. It was the residence of a celebrated physician. In the morning the police called at the house and saw the doctor's wife who told them she entertained fears about her husband's sanity. The doctor was then examined by two leading experts on mental illness and was accused of the 'Ripper' crimes. He admitted that he was 'unbalanced' and had been suffering bouts of loss of memory. The conclusion was arrived at that the physician was obviously the notorious East End killer and he was removed to a private insane asylum. There he became known simply as 'Thomas Mason, alias No. 124'.

The story of how Lees tracked down 'Jack the Ripper' received wide publicity after his death, and appeared in the *Daily Express* of 7, 9 and 10 March 1931 under the headline 'CLAIRVOYANT WHO TRACKED JACK THE RIPPER'. In 1976 the best-selling book *Jack the Ripper: The Final Solution* by Stephen Knight was published and Knight's theory of a royal/masonic conspiracy was eagerly taken up by both press and public. The Lees story admirably suited Knight because his putative Ripper was the Royal Physician in Ordinary, Sir William Withey Gull. Despite its controversial premise, Knight's work did contain many interesting new facts accessed from the recently released official files. Among others, he examined the MEPO 3/142 'Jack the Ripper' letters file. In so doing he noticed a letter that apparently supported the fact that Lees had indeed been on the track of 'Jack the Ripper'. Here, he felt, was some sort of confirmation that Lees had been involved in the hunt for the killer. Knight wrote:

> Even 1895 [the Lees story made its first appearance in the Chicago *Sunday Times-Herald* in April that year], seven years after the murders, was not the beginning of the Lees story; it was merely the first time it had been committed to print. The story had wide circulation, in London at least, as early as July 1889 – only nine months after the murders. This is confirmed by a note in the *Letters* file at Scotland Yard. Admittedly this is from a crank who signed himself 'Jack the Ripper', but the writer's state of mind is immaterial. Only his knowledge counts. The contents of the letter show that the story of Lees having helped the police run Jack the Ripper to earth was known forty-three years earlier than critics of the story have stated. The letter, received at the Yard on 25th July 1889, says:

> Dear Boss
>
> You have not caught me yet you see, with all your cunning, with all your "Lees" with all your blue bottles.
>
> Jack the Ripper
>
> For the story to have gained this sort of acceptance as early as July 1889 means it must initially have been told (or leaked out) a few weeks after the murder of Kelly, which fits in with Lees taking part in the hunt for the Ripper in November 1888, as the story claims.

This transcription from the 'Lees' letter shows only the first few lines; the whole is three pages long.

A diligent search through the newspapers of late 1888 and the first half of 1889 has failed to reveal any mention of Lees whatsoever, so where did an anonymous 'Jack the Ripper' letter-writer borrow his 'Lees' reference from? Stephen Knight assiduously transcribed dozens of pages of notes from the official files. Unfortunately, and understandably, he made some errors of transcription. Crucially, here, he wrongly transcribed the word 'Lees', which in fact is not 'Lees' at all. An examination of the original letter revealed the word to be 'tecs', the contemporary slang for detectives (*see* illustration opposite). In fact, as can be seen, with this correct reading of the word the sentence makes sense, which it did not before. This may be a minor point, but it is important for it shows just how the letters can play a part in the Ripper story and may be used by an author as a significant building block. In this case an error of transcription led to a repetition of the mistake in later books. The true content of the letter also underlines how important it is for writers and historians to access primary resources, only that way can they avoid perpetuating the errors of others.

Sir William Withey Gull, Bart, MD, FRS, physician to Guy's Hospital, was born in 1816 and so was seventy-two years of age in 1888, the year of the Whitechapel murders. He took his MB degree in 1841 and became a medical tutor at Guy's. He was appointed Assistant Physician to Guy's Hospital in 1851. In 1858 he became full Physician, retired from work at the Hospital in 1868 and in 1871 was made Consulting Physician. He was appointed Lecturer on Medicine at Guy's in 1856, together with Dr Owen Rees, and held this post until 1867. In 1858 he was elected a Fellow of the Royal Society and was a member of its council for many years. In 1871 he treated the Prince of Wales, who was suffering from a severe bout of typhoid fever, and attended him until the Prince was fully recovered. From 1871 to 1883 he represented the Crown and from 1886 to 1887 the University of London on the General Medical Council. In 1871 and 1872 he was President of the Clinical Society. His honours included the honorary degree of DCL, Oxford, 1868; LLD, Cambridge, 1880; and LLD, Edinburgh, 1884.

In 1872 Gull was created a baronet in recognition of his services during the Prince of Wales' severe illness. At the same time he was appointed Physician to the Prince. Subsequently he became Physician Extraordinary, and latterly Physician in Ordinary to Queen Victoria. During a holiday in Scotland in October 1887 he was struck down by paralysis, a stroke, from which he never wholly recovered. A few weeks later he was moved to London, but in January 1890 he was struck by an acute illness and died.

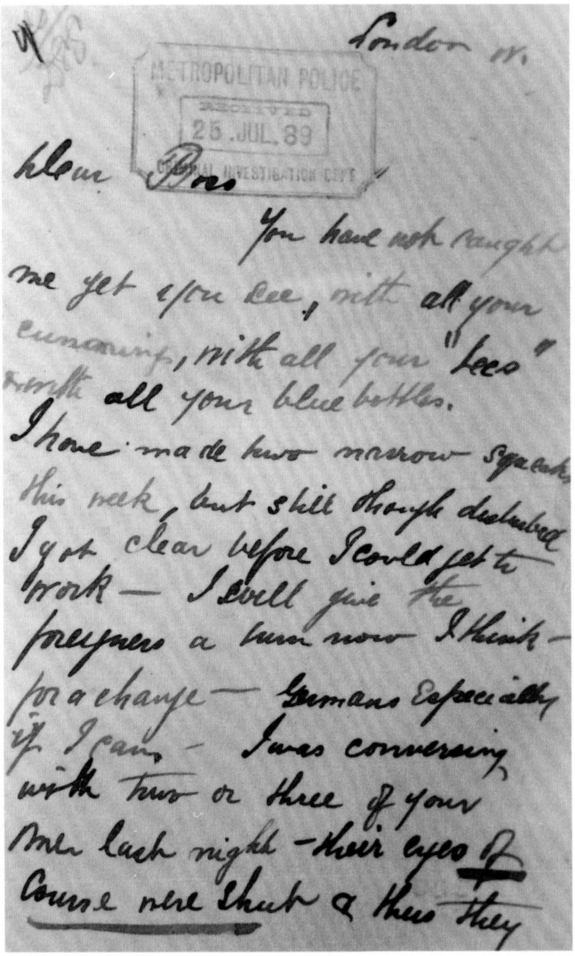

London W.

Dear Boss

You have not caught me yet you see, with all your cunning, with all your "tecs" & with all your blue bottles.
I have made two narrow squeaks this week, but still though disturbed I got clear before I could get to work — I will give the foreigners a turn now I think — for a change — Germans especially if I can — I was conversing with two or three of your men last night — their eyes of course were shut & thus they

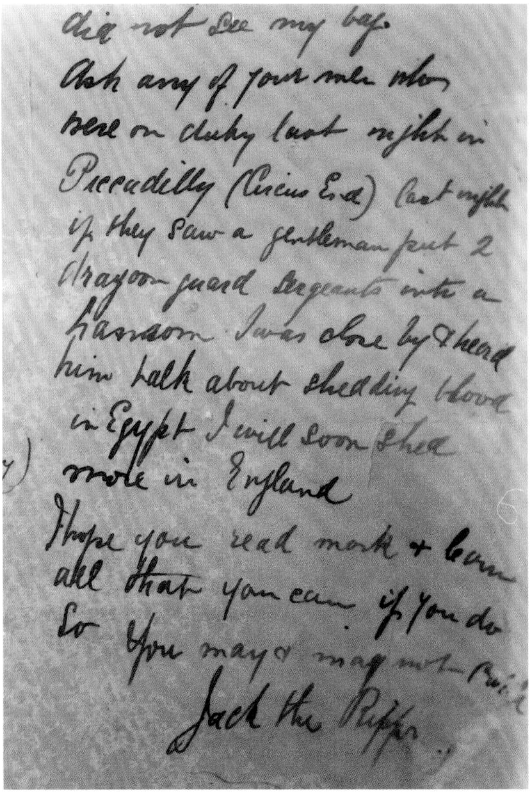
did not see my bag.
Ask any of your men who were on duty last night in Piccadilly (Circus End) last night if they saw a gentleman put 2 Dragoon guard sergeants into a Hansom. I was close by & heard him talk about shedding blood in Egypt I will soon shed more in England
I hope you read mark & learn all that you can if you do so you may & may not catch
Jack the Ripper

The so-called 'Lees Letter' of 25 July 1889 which has been used to support the idea that the clairvoyant R.J. Lees was involved in the Ripper inquiry.

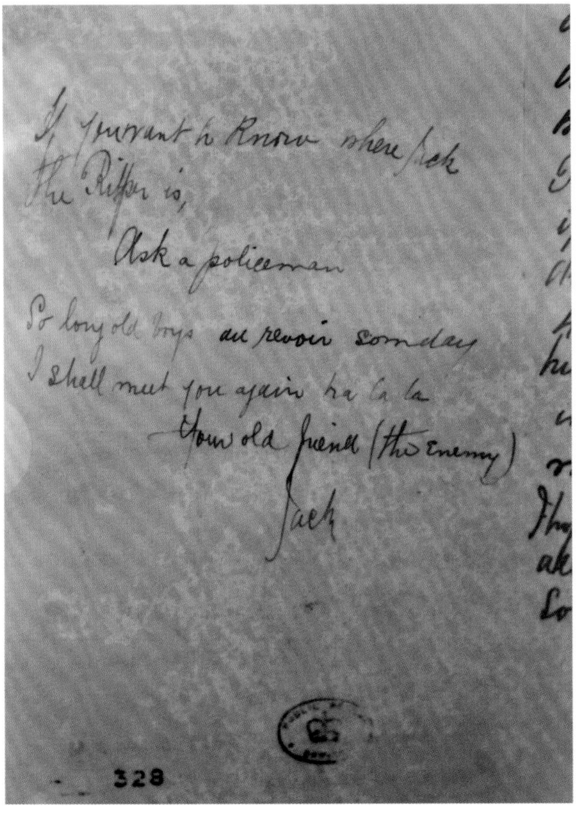
If you want to know where Jack the Ripper is,
Ask a policeman
So long old boys au revoir someday I shall meet you again ta ta ta
Your old friend (the Enemy)
Jack

328

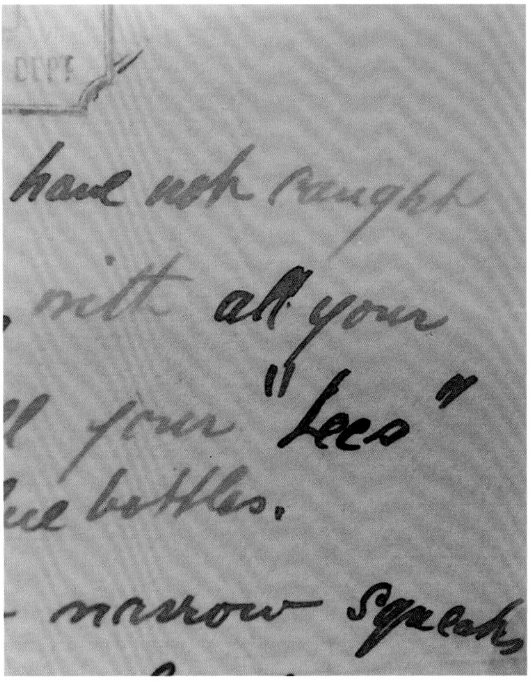
have not caught
with all your
"Lees"
blue bottles.
narrow squeaks

A close-up of the word which Ripper author Stephen Knight interpreted as 'Lees' in his 1976 book *Jack the Ripper: The Final Solution*. Examination of the original letter revealed the word was actually 'tecs'.

Latter-day 'Jack the Ripper' suspect Sir William Withey Gull.

A more distinguished medical career would be hard to imagine. Yet this has not prevented the illustrious man from becoming part of the legend of 'Jack the Ripper' and a suspect in the hunt for this most notorious killer. His name entered the story in November 1970 with the publication in *The Criminologist* magazine of an article by Thomas E.A. Stowell, CBE, MD, FRCS, a noted medical man himself. Stowell's piece gave worldwide exposure to the royal/Ripper connection: he positively linked Gull and Lees' visit with a police inspector to 'the home of a fashionable and highly reputable physician' in the West End. Stowell speculated that the house in question was Sir William's at 74 Brook Street, Grosvenor Square. Although Stowell's Ripper suspect was called only 'S', he was later identified as Prince Albert Victor, Duke of Clarence (1864–92), who was being nursed and protected by Gull. Stowell went on to claim, without supporting evidence, that:

> It was said that on more than one occasion Sir William Gull was seen in the neighbourhood of Whitechapel on the night of a murder. It would not surprise me to know that he was there for the purpose of certifying the murderer to be insane so that he might be put under restraint as were other lunatics apprehended in connection with the murders.

A few years later Sir William was pushed across the line and himself took on the mantle of 'Jack the Ripper.'

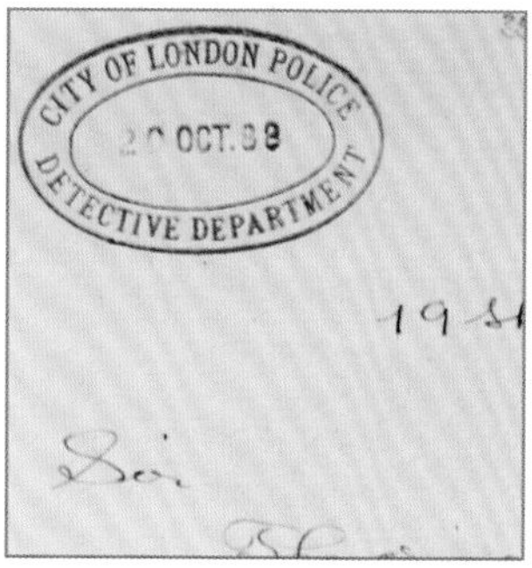

— **TWELVE** —

The City Letters

THE second large collection of letters associated with the Whitechapel murders came from the City of London Police and is held at the Corporation of London Records Office at the Guildhall. This collection was discovered in the late 1960s by Ripper historian and ex-City of London Police Sergeant Donald Rumbelow. It was lodged with the City Records Office in the 1980s. When he discovered the letters Don was collecting material for his history of the City Police, *I Spy Blue*, and he found them in the basement of the former City of London Police headquarters at 26 Old Jewry. They were in an old envelope apparently thrown into a cupboard which had been put in the basement. Don secured them for future generations of historians and researchers.

This fascinating collection comprises about 363 communications sent by some 301 correspondents. The vast majority of the writers are concerned individuals offering their suggestions and suspicions to the police. The letters, in the main, are signed by identifiable correspondents. These include a couple of men whose names crop up as suspects – Nikaner Benelius and Major R.D.O. Stephenson.

A most interesting letter dated 5 October 1888 and signed M.P. refers to the writer having seen the actor Richard Mansfield appearing in the stage play *Dr Jekyll and Mr Hyde*. He '. . . felt at once that he was the Man Wanted' for the murders. The writer was so impressed that he had '. . . not been able to get this feeling out of my head'. M.P. also noted that he thought it strange '. . . this play should have commenced before the murders for it is realy something after the same stile'. He had also '. . . read in the Globe the outher night that the same fritfull murders took place in America & was never discovered. Mr M is I think A American but weather he comes from there I dont know.' He signed off 'Yours one who prays for the murderer to be caught. M.P.'

Other notable correspondents were E.K. Larkins (customs officer and amateur Ripper hunter), Percy Lindley (prominent in encouraging the police to use bloodhounds),

John Moore (manager of the Central News Agency), Edward Terry (of Terry's Theatre), and Dr Forbes Winslow and his wife Florence.

However, the section of the City letters most relevant to our study is the 'Anonymous' group, which comprises sixty-three senders and a total of seventy letters (they have been included in the overall tally quoted above). Many in this section also relate to suggestions for the police, including some fascinating accusations against various parties. Only eight purport to come from the killer and one from 'An Accessory'. Many are undated but all are in a similar vein to their counterparts in the MEPO files.

One of the 'Ripper' letters was posted on 1 October 1888 to the *Daily News* office and the staff there forwarded it to the City Police the following day:

> London E.
> Monday
>
> I am so pleased to see another chance of ripping up a dear creature.
>
> I shall be in Bucks Row or very close to ['at' deleted] between 12 & 2 in morning on Wednesday
>
> I have got
>
> [second page] the girl set & as I have been offered dooble money for her woomb and lower part of body mean to have them at any price
>
> I do like to find them nice parts.
>
> I do pity Leather Apron.
>
> I've got some
>
> [third page] ['some' deleted] Some one to write this for me.
>
> Yours truly
> Boss
> Ripper

The *Daily News* letter accompanying this missive commented to Sir James Fraser, the City of London Police Commissioner: 'The enclosed was no doubt the work of some stupid person, but I think it as well to forward them to you.'

The next item to be found in the City files is a postcard stamped 'LONDON E.C. 3 OC 88' and addressed to Sir James Fraser. Written in black ink, it reads:

> I will write to you again soon
>
> Just a card to let you know that I shall (if possible) do some more of my business in the West part of London & I hope to be able to send you my victims ears. I was not able to last time. My bloody ink is now running out so I must get some more. It amuses me that you think I am mad you will see when I am caught but it is death to the first man who touches me. It will be most probaly the end of October or it may be before all depends Jack the Ripper

These communications show that the City Police also received the attention of the hoaxers soon after the Eddowes murder. The anonymous letter signed by 'An Accessory' was sent in an envelope addressed to 'Inspector, Detective Dept, 26 Old Jewry, City, E.C.'. Written in black ink and bearing a penny lilac stamp postmarked 'LONDON [?] 19 OC 88', it contains the following cryptic message:

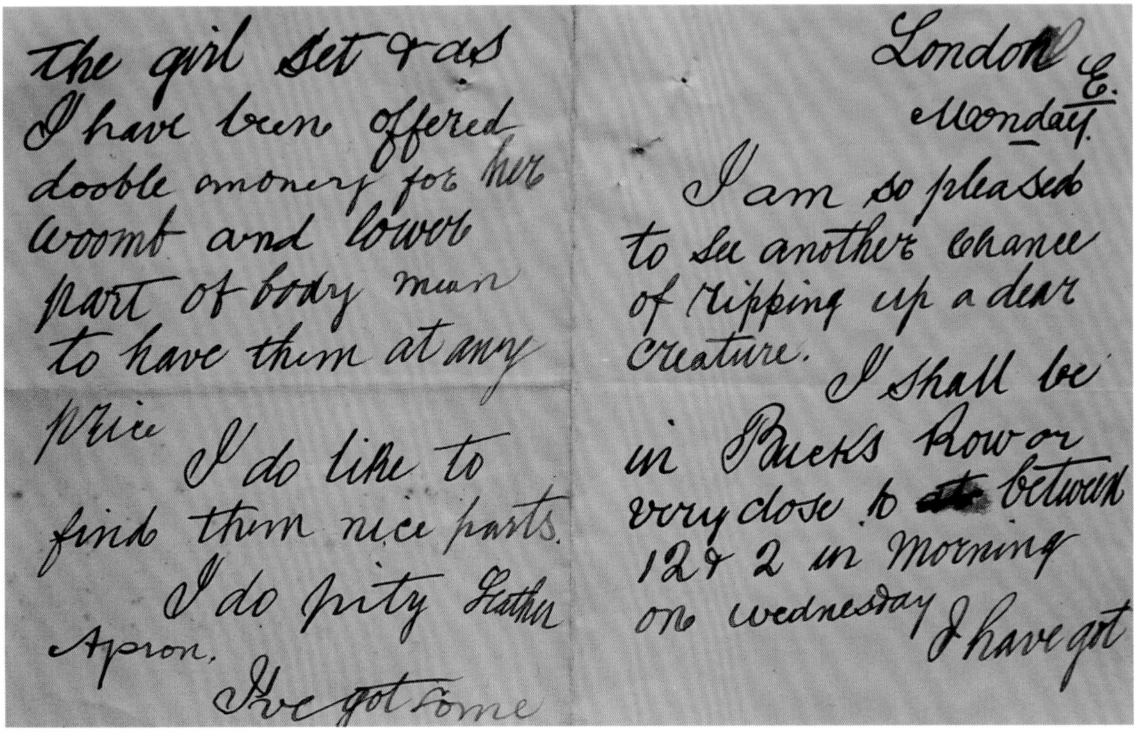
London E.
Monday.
I am so pleased
to see another chance
of ripping up a dear
creature. I shall be
in Bucks Row or
very close to between
12 & 2 in morning
on wednesday I have got

the girl set & as
I have been offered
dooble money for her
woomb and lower
part of body mean
to have them at any
price
I do like to
find them nice parts.
I do pity Leather
Apron.
I've got some

Letter sent to the City of London Police by the *Daily News*. It was received on 1 October; it mentions a future murder and selling body parts.

19th Oct 1888

Sir,

The crime committed In Mitre Square City and those in the district of Whitechapel were perpetrated by an Ex Police Constable of the Metropolitan Police who [second page] was dismissed the force through certain connection with a prostitute The motive for the crimes is hatred and spite against the authorities at Scotland Yard one of whom is marked as a victim after which the crimes will cease

Yours truly
An Accessory

The third page bears the annotation 'Copy sent to Scot. Yard 20.10.88'. This was, no doubt, the anonymous writer's method of communicating to the police a theory he had developed. It is interesting to see that the allegation was sent to the City Police and not the Metropolitan force, against whose ex-officer the accusation was levelled. It would be intriguing to know which ex-officer the writer had in mind, if anyone in particular.

On the same date, 19 October, an address pre-printed postcard was mailed in Dublin to 'Messrs. Bensdorp & Co., Manufacturers of the Royal Dutch Soluble Cocoa, ['30, & 31, Newgate Street' deleted] London, E.C.'. It was written in pencil and read:

> Please send 1 Bottell Whiskey I intend to murder one in Dublin to night Grand job I made of the last Goodby Dont forget to meet me in Patrick st J the R Yours truly Jack the Ripper

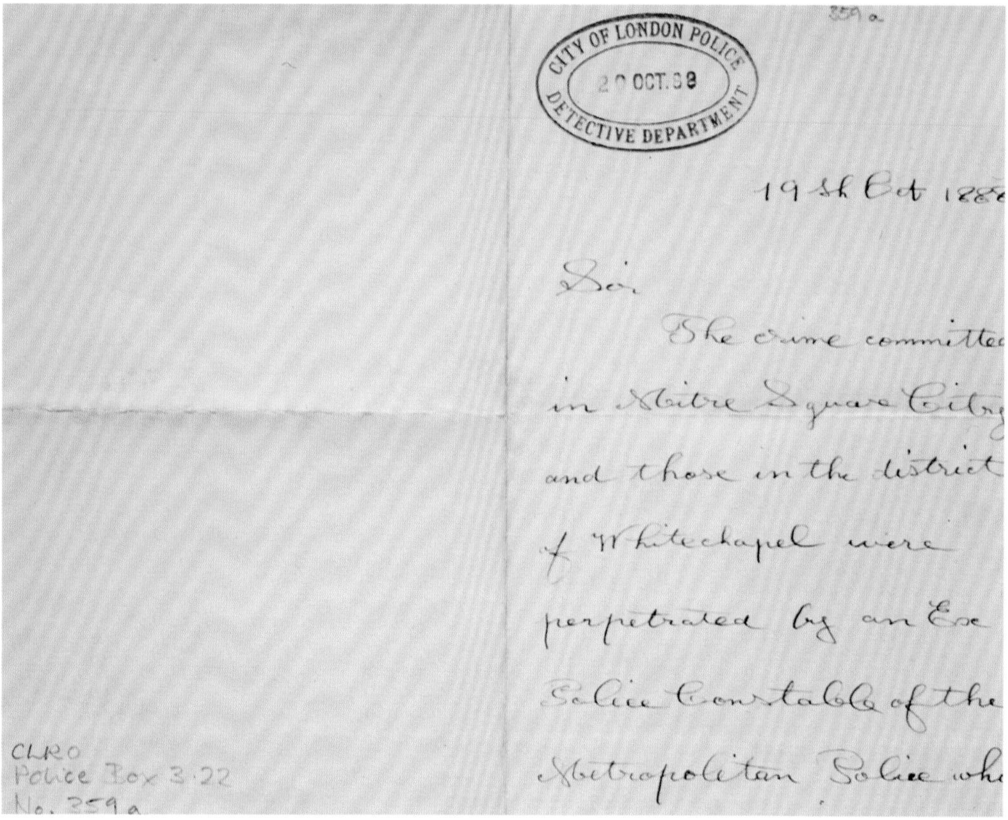
359a

CITY OF LONDON POLICE
20 OCT. 88
DETECTIVE DEPARTMENT

19th Oct 188

Sir

The crime committed in Mitre Square City and those in the district of Whitechapel were perpetrated by an Ex Police Constable of the Metropolitan Police who

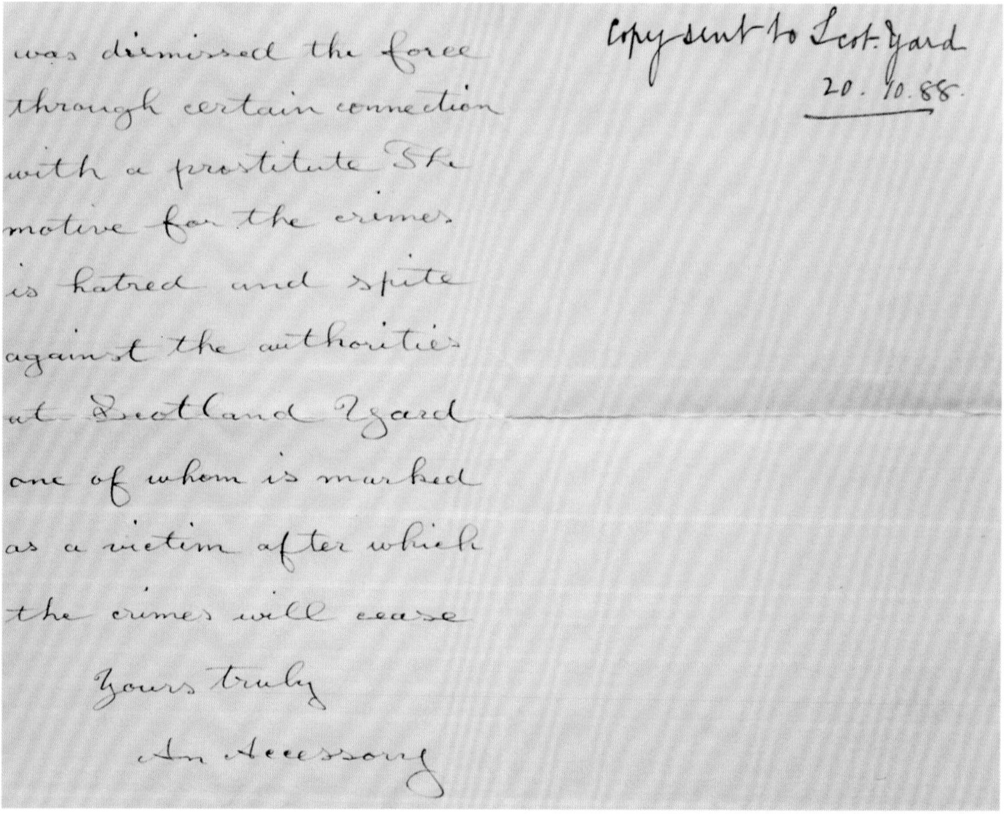
was dismissed the force through certain connection with a prostitute The motive for the crimes is hatred and spite against the authorities at Scotland Yard one of whom is marked as a victim after which the crimes will cease

Yours truly

An Accessory

Copy sent to Scot. Yard
20. 10. 88.

Letter of 19 October to the City Police from 'An Accessory'. It states that the Mitre Square murder was committed by 'an Ex Police Constable of the Metropolitan Police' and states that the officer in question was dismissed for 'certain connection with a prostitute'.

The card was forwarded 'To the Superintendent of The City Police, Old Jewry, E.C.' by Messrs Bensdorp on 23 October with a covering letter stating:

> Dear Sir,
>
> Enclosed we beg to hand you p.c. received last Saturday morning. purporting to come from "Jack the Ripper"
>
> Evidently some one has got possession of one of our post-cards & made above use of it. therefore we think it better to hand it over to you.
>
> Yours truly
>
> Bensdorp

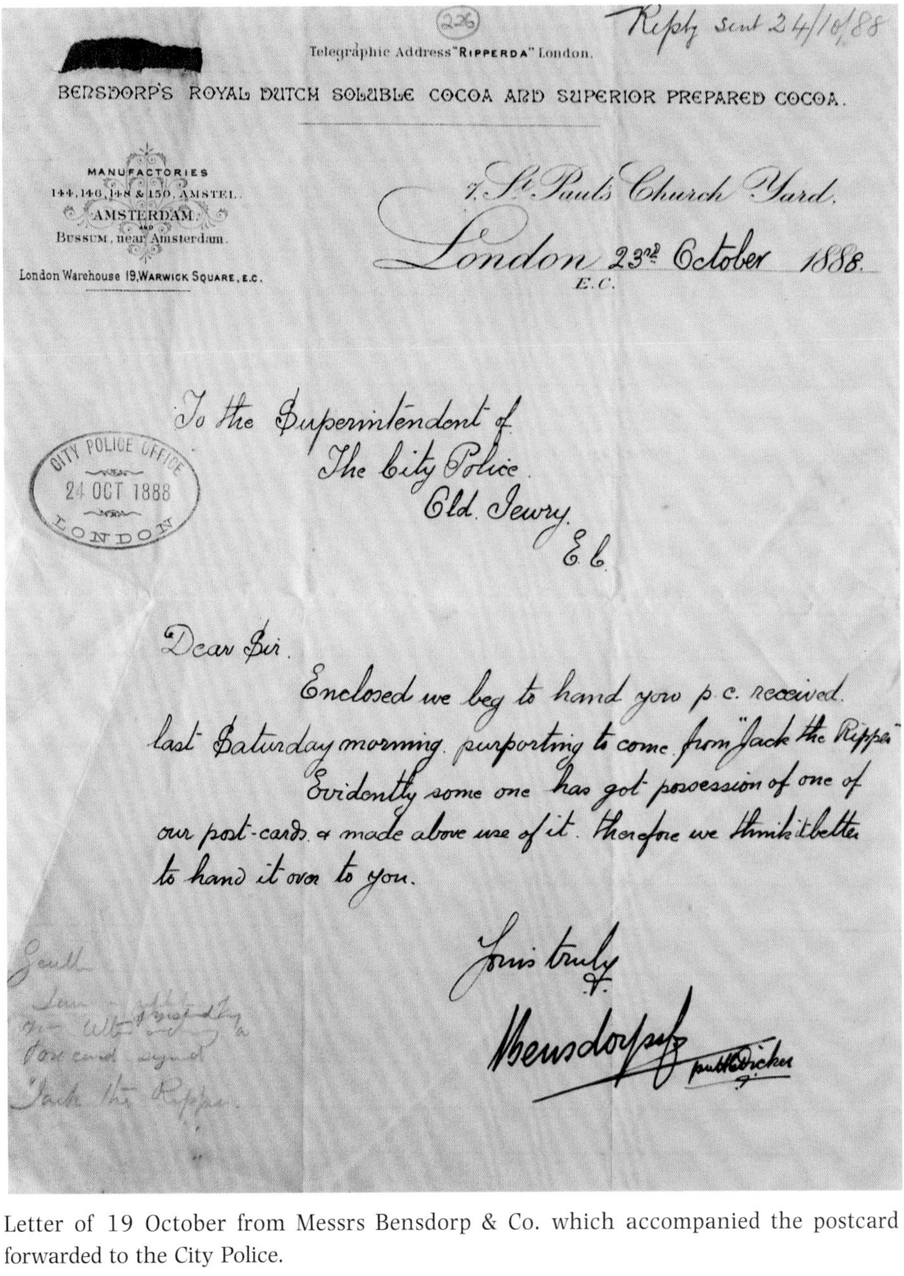

(226) Reply sent 24/10/88

[redacted]

Telegraphic Address "RIPPERDA" London.

BENSDORP'S ROYAL DUTCH SOLUBLE COCOA AND SUPERIOR PREPARED COCOA.

MANUFACTORIES 144, 146, 148 & 150, AMSTEL. AMSTERDAM. AND BUSSUM, near Amsterdam.

London Warehouse 19, WARWICK SQUARE, E.C.

7, St. Paul's Church Yard, London E.C. 23rd October 1888.

To the Superintendent of The City Police. Old Jewry. E.C.

CITY POLICE OFFICE 24 OCT 1888 LONDON

Dear Sir.

Enclosed we beg to hand you p.c. received last Saturday morning. purporting to come from "Jack the Ripper"

Evidently some one has got possession of one of our post-cards & made above use of it. therefore we think it better to hand it over to you.

Yours truly

Bensdorp

Letter of 19 October from Messrs Bensdorp & Co. which accompanied the postcard forwarded to the City Police.

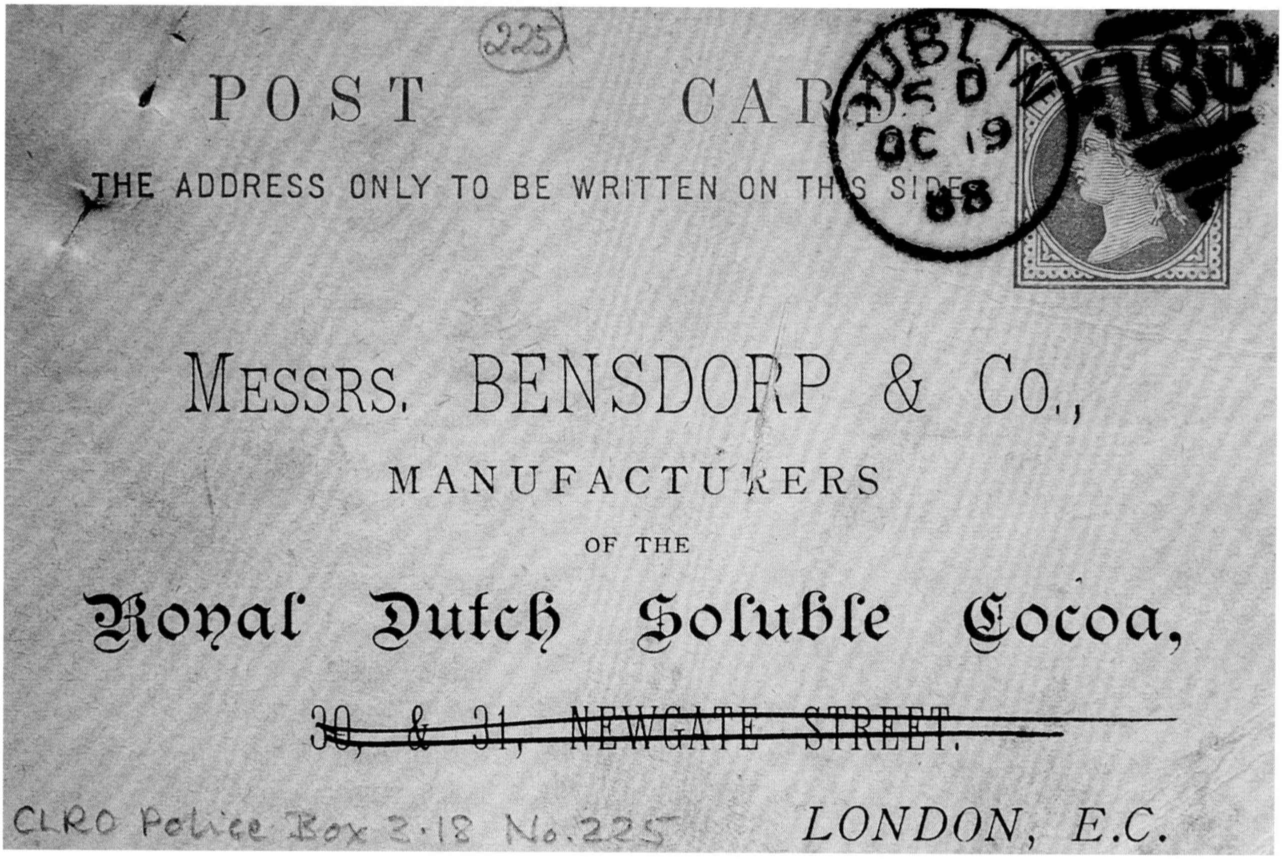
POST CARD
THE ADDRESS ONLY TO BE WRITTEN ON THIS SIDE
DUBLIN OC 19 88
MESSRS. BENSDORP & Co.,
MANUFACTURERS
OF THE
Royal Dutch Soluble Cocoa,
30, & 31, NEWGATE STREET.
CLRO Police Box 3.18 No.225
LONDON, E.C.

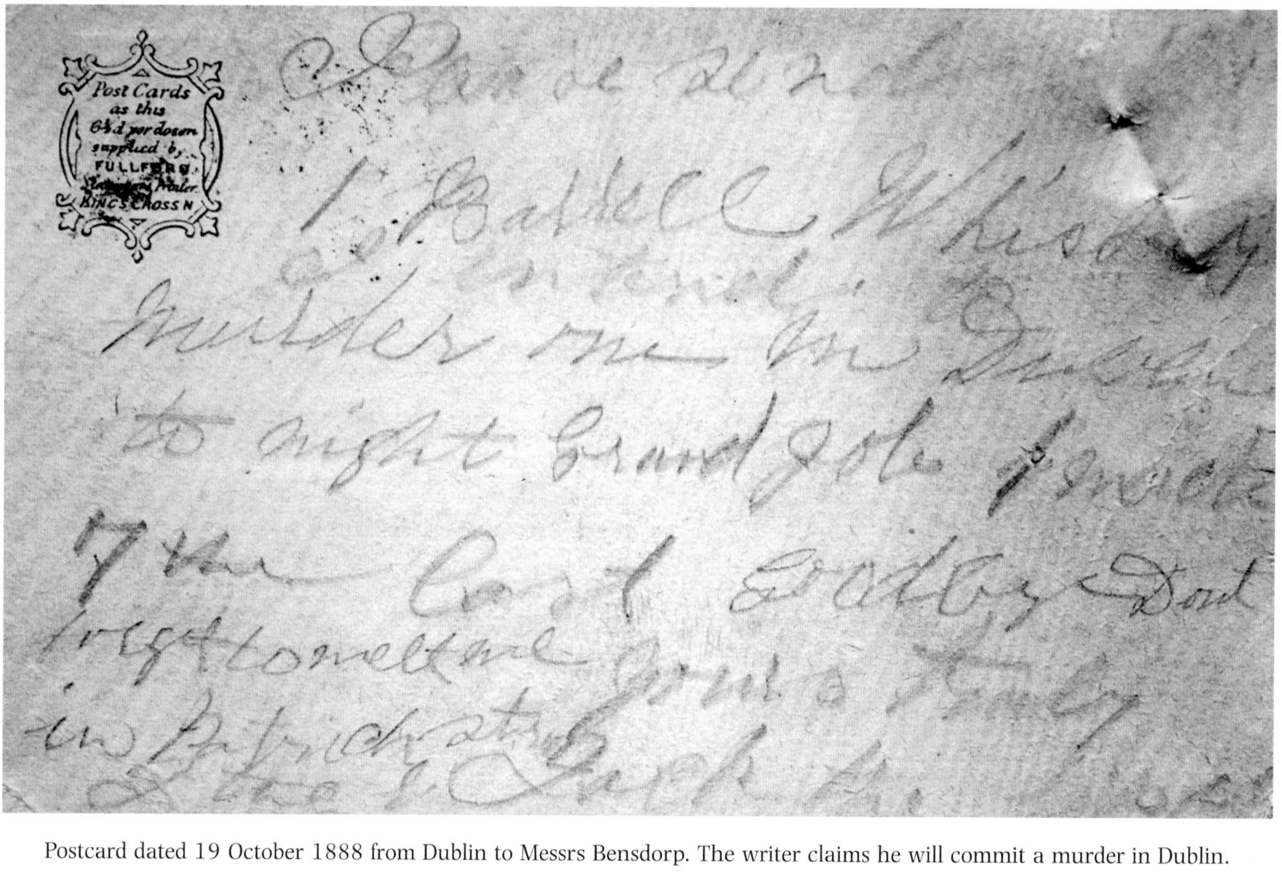

Postcard dated 19 October 1888 from Dublin to Messrs Bensdorp. The writer claims he will commit a murder in Dublin.

There is an unstamped and undated envelope and letter, written in black ink, in the same section as the Bensdorp card and addressed 'Mr. Boss, Desford Industrial School, Near Liecester'. The letter reads:

> Dear Boss
> I write these few lines to you That the ripper is coming over on the 9th Novr. don't? . . forget
> Mr Boss
> Desford Industrial School
> Near Liecester

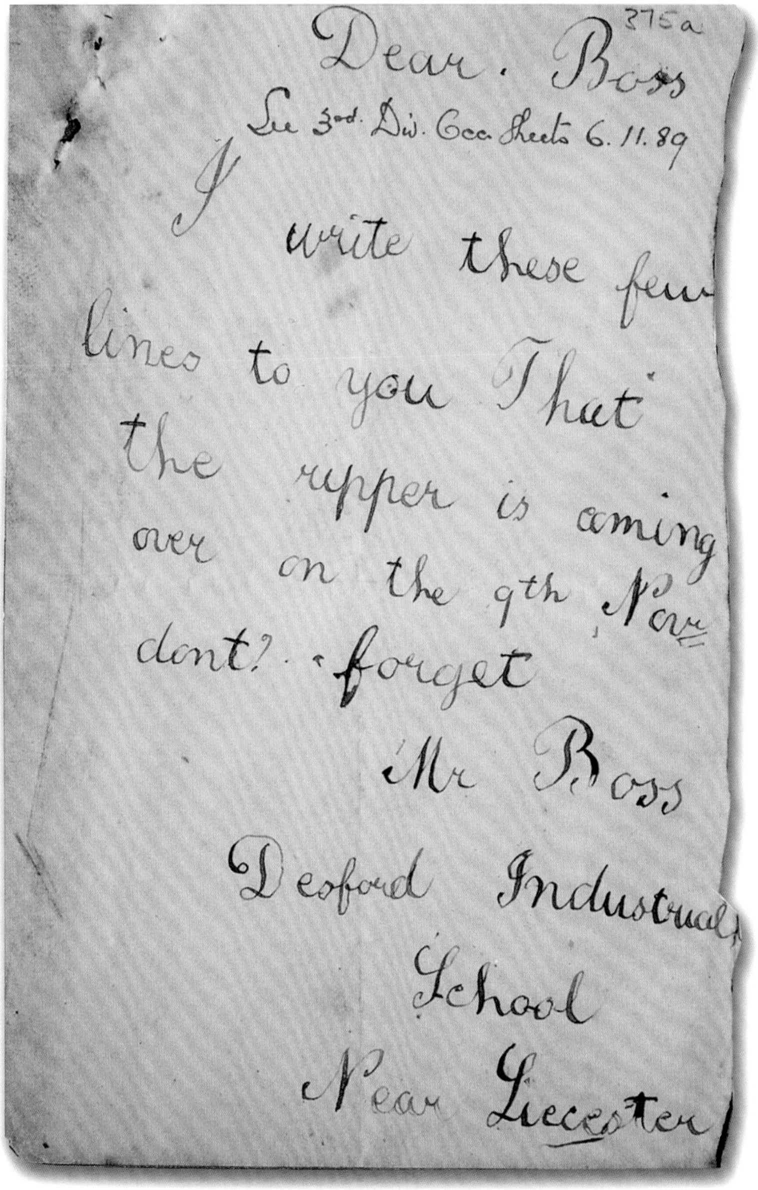
375a
Dear. Boss
See 3rd. Div. Occ. Sheets 6.11.89
I write these few lines to you That the ripper is coming over on the 9th Novr dont? . forget
Mr Boss
Desford Industrial School
Near Liecester

Undated letter sent to 'Dear Boss' at Desford Industrial School, near Leicester, stating that 'the Ripper is coming over on the 9th Novr. [1889]'.

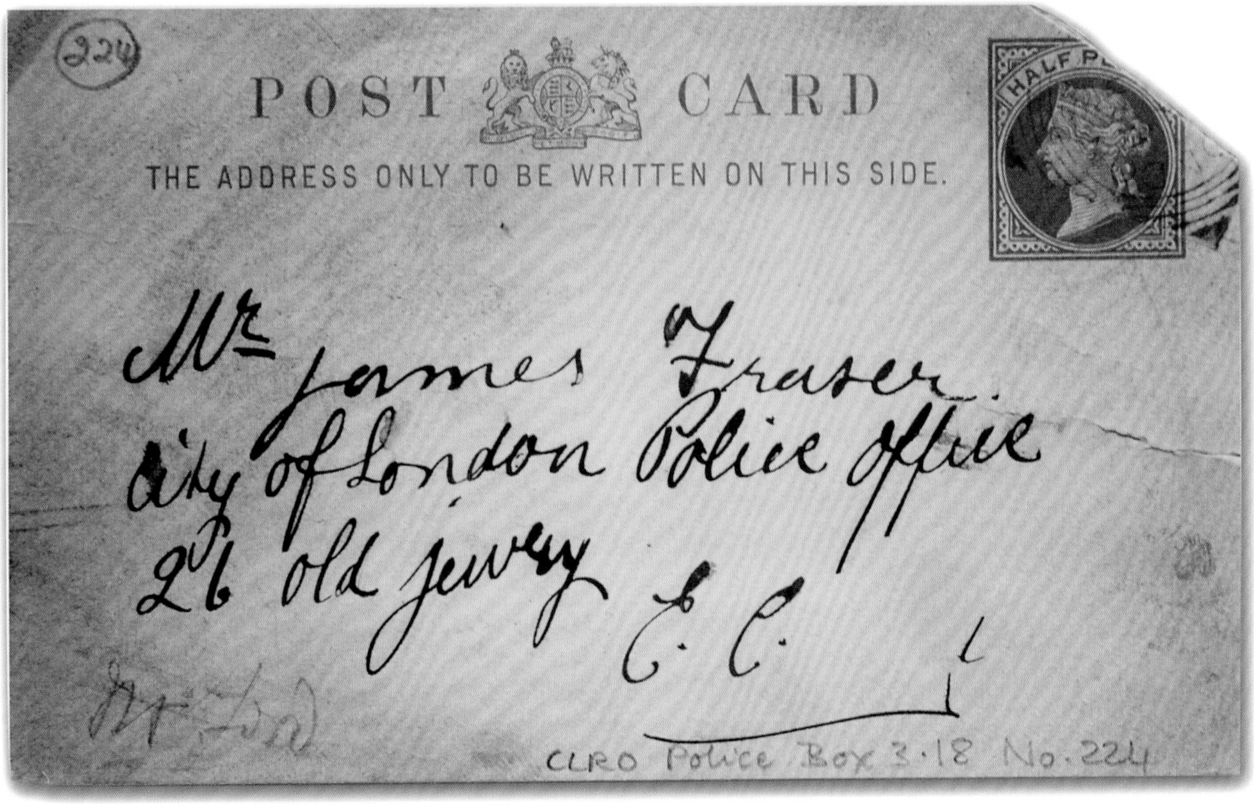

(224)

POST CARD

THE ADDRESS ONLY TO BE WRITTEN ON THIS SIDE.

HALF P

Mr James Fraser
City of London Police Office
26 Old Jewry
E.C.

CLRO Police Box 3.18 No. 224

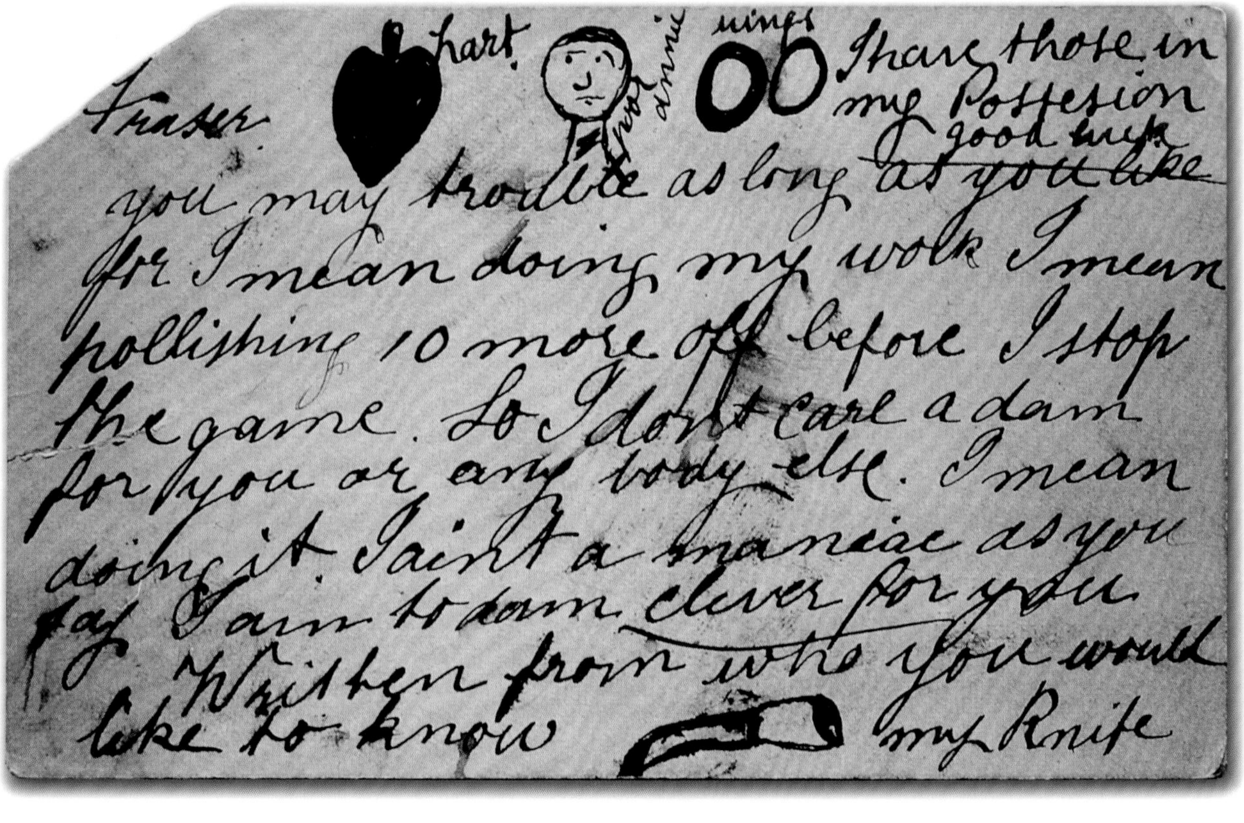

heart. poor annie rings

Fraser

I have those in my Possesion

you may trouble as long ~~as you like~~ good luck
for I mean doing my work I mean
pollishing 10 more off before I stop
the game. So I dont care a dam
for you or any body else. I mean
doing it. I aint a maniac as you
say I am to dam clever for you
Written from who you would
like to know my Knife

An intriguing but undated postcard sent to the City Police. It includes drawings of a heart, 'poor annie' and two rings. There is no signature.

A communication like this appears to have been sent only to cause consternation at the address where it was received. It was obviously forwarded to the City Police. Another postcard, in black ink, addressed to 'Mr James Fraser, City of London Police Office, 26 Old Jewry, E.C.' read:

> Fraser [drawing of heart] hart [drawing of face] poor annie [drawing of rings] rings
> I have those in my Possesion
> good luck
>
> You may trouble as long as you like for I mean doing my work I mean pollishing 10 more off before I stop the game. So I dont care a dam for you or any body else. I mean doing it. I aint a maniac as you say I am to dam clever for you
> Written from who you would like to know [drawing of knife] my knife

The card bears a London postmark, but the corner is missing and the date is not visible. Another letter in black ink, no date, reads:

> Dear Boss
> The police will not Get me, they think they Will, I hope they do I am sure that they will not I will ripp some more up soon, I am taken them away
> Jack the RIPPER
> [second page] It is nice to go home with a woman it is only 2/4 sometimes they charge more
> But Farwell
> yours
> Jack the RIPPER and Gang
> PS We are paying a visit all over th <u>count. ry</u>

Another undated letter was written in bright red ink and has a large red blot at the top of the page:

> Whitechapel
>
> I come from Boston You spanking ass. Glad you prented my last letter. Having no more of the right sort I wright with red ink You'll hear of another murder before the month is out. Yes, you'll hear of Saucy Jacky very soon Will send next ears I clip to Charly Warren Nice work isnt it. Ye damned fool are the ['perlise' deleted] police.
> <u>Jack the Ripper</u>

A postcard in pencil and clearly postmarked 'LONDON S.E. FE 4 89' was addressed to 'Mr Monro, City Superintendent Of, Police Authoritys' and received by the City Police on 4 February 1889:

> Dear Boss
> Be on the look out . as I am coming to visit Mile-end and do for the rest to number 15 then I give myself up to the Police Yours – Jack the Ripper returned from America

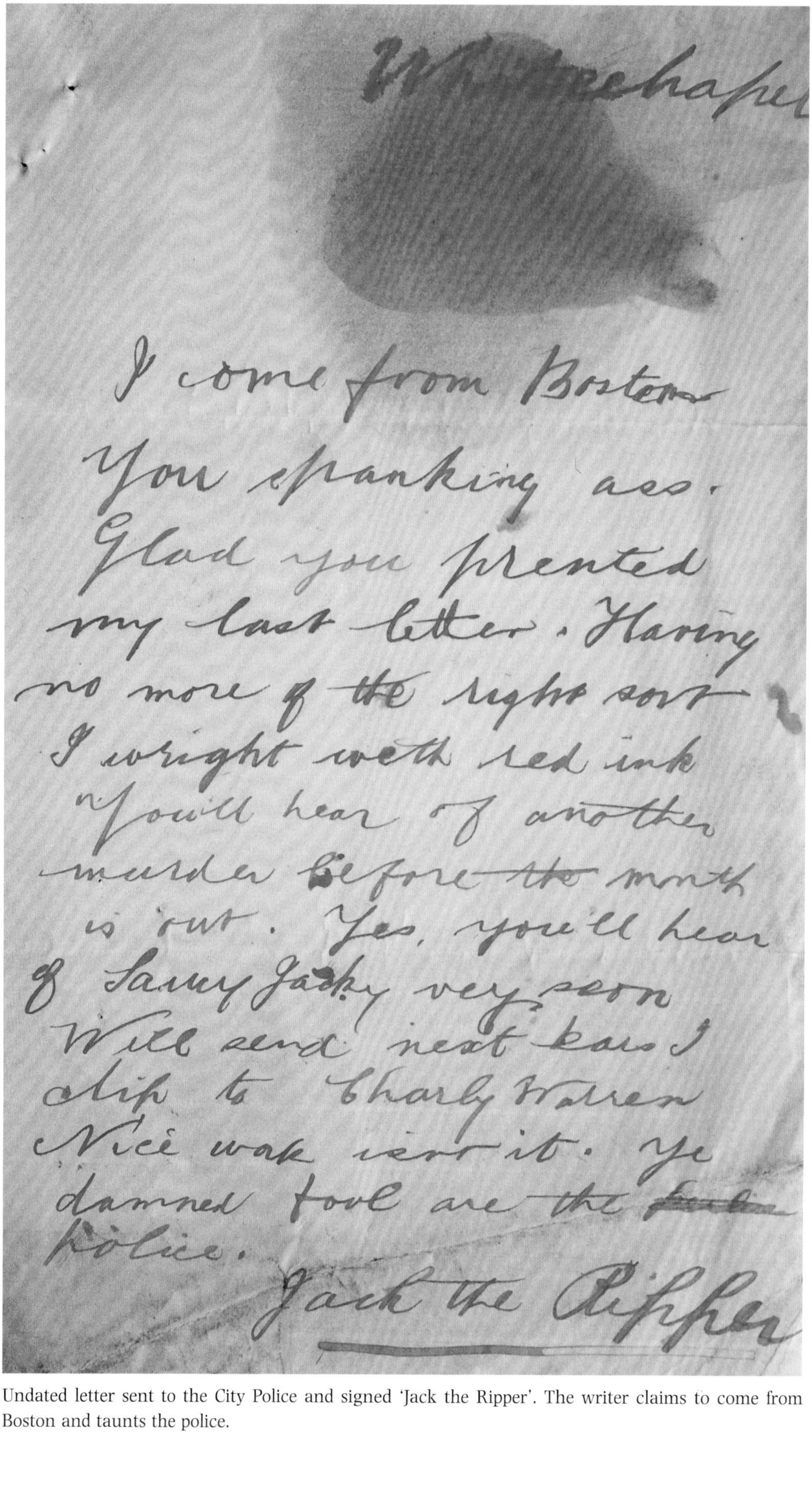

Whitechapel

I come from Boston
You spanking ass.
Glad you prented
my last letter. Having
no more of the right sort
I wright with red ink
you'll hear of another
murder before ~~the~~ month
is out. Yes, you'll hear
of Saucy Jacky very soon
Will send next ears I
clip to Charly Warren
Nice wak isn't it. Ye
damned fool are the ~~[illegible]~~
Police.

Jack the Ripper

Undated letter sent to the City Police and signed 'Jack the Ripper'. The writer claims to come from Boston and taunts the police.

The recurring themes found in the newspapers can be seen and easily recognised in these communications. The religious message was also popular and the City Police received an envelope dated and postmarked 'LONDON JY 30 89' which contained the following red printed words:

All the other communications in the City Police files make suggestions to the police as to suspects or methods of capturing the killer; they come from some identifiable and some anonymous writers. If these were all the communications purporting to come from the offender that the City Police received, then they escaped more lightly than their Metropolitan counterparts.

However, Henry Smith, Acting Commissioner of the City Police in 1889, does mention a suspicious man who wrote to him (*From Constable to Commissioner*, pages 155–6) suggesting he had knowledge of the murderer:

> The Ripper certainly had all the luck. Three or four days after the murder in Mitre Square, a letter addressed to me by name – and for which I, or rather the Corporation, had to pay twopence sterling – was delivered at my office. The writer was complimentary to myself personally. He said he was anxious to see me, as he had a lot to tell me about the murders; that he was not afraid to meet me, but that he was on ticket of leave, and hadn't reported himself, and that if he came to Old Jewry the "tecs" – of whom he evidently had a very low opinion – would apprehend him, and send him back to work out the remainder of his sentence; that he was living on the earnings of his wife, who by the kindness of the missioner, had got a laundry and was doing well; that if I wanted to write to him, a letter addressed to a certain place in Hoxton – a large, and, generally speaking, disreputable district – to be left till called for, would find him.
>
> Besides being a convict, the writer was evidently an ex-soldier. "You're not on the right scent at all," he said; "the man you want is not in London, he's in Manchester. What you think is his writing isn't. He writes just like an orderly-room clerk." (A facsimile of the writing of the purloiner of the kidney – whence obtained I know not – had appeared in an evening paper.)

Smith then went on to recount how he had replied to the letter and arranged to meet the writer in a West End Square. Smith waited and spoke with a man who arrived at the agreed location. The stranger denied being there to meet him and walked away! Smith claimed he received another communication from the man stating that he now knew he could trust Smith and told him that he would come to Old Jewry (the City Police headquarters) to see him. The man never came.

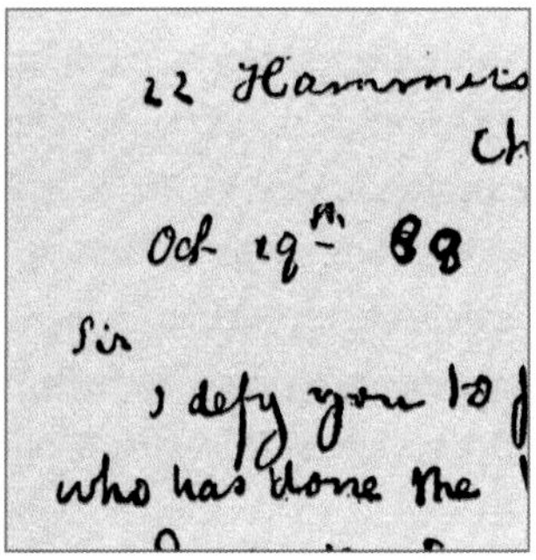
22 Hammers
Ch
Oct 19th 88
Sir
I defy you to
who has done the

— **THIRTEEN** —

The Alienist

DR Lyttleton Stewart Forbes Winslow LLB, LLM, MB, MRCP (Lond.), DCL (Oxon), LLD (Cantab.), forty-four years of age in 1888, was a celebrated alienist of his day. He had a long history of working with the mentally ill and felt himself qualified to comment on the psychological make-up of the unknown Whitechapel killer. He was one of the very early Ripper theorists and did not hesitate to make his opinion known. His frequent appearances in the press guaranteed him a high public profile and ensured that he was on the mailing list of the 'Jack the Ripper' letter-writers.

Winslow was a frequent correspondent in the newspapers but his first real clash with officialdom came after an article was published in the *New York Herald* in September 1889. A reporter from the London office of that newspaper had interviewed Forbes Winslow who had produced a large pair of boots from under his table, saying 'Here are Jack the Ripper's boots. The tops of these boots are composed of ordinary cloth material, while the soles are made of indiarubber. The tops have great bloodstains on them.' These 'noiseless coverings' were supplemented, according to the doctor, with 'ordinary walking boots, which are very dirty, and the man's coat which is also bloodstained'. A woman had been in communication with Winslow and had given him details of a suspect who had accosted her, and who had subsequently been followed to 'a certain house', the location of which Winslow would not divulge. Allegedly the woman had previously seen the suspect acting strangely and had seen him washing his hands in the yard of the house on the morning after the murder of McKenzie. The suspect, according to Winslow, lived with a friend of his and Winslow was sanguine of an early arrest. Winslow stated that the suspect was suffering from 'a violent form of religious mania which attacks him and passes off at intervals'. He concluded with the confident words, 'I am as certain that I have the murderer as I am of being here.'

Winslow was interviewed by Chief Inspector Swanson, who submitted his report on the matter on 23 September 1889. Swanson saw Winslow at his home address at

The Victorian alienist Dr Lyttleton Stewart Forbes Winslow, who took great interest in the murders and claimed to have received letters from 'Jack the Ripper'.

70 Wimpole Street on that date and Winslow claimed that he had been misrepresented by the *New York Herald* reporter. Swanson reported that Winslow '. . . produced a pair of felt galoshed boots such as are in common use in Canada, and an old coat. The felt boots were motheaten, and the slough of the moth worm remained on one of them.' Winslow named the source of his information as Mr E. Callaghan of 20 Gainsborough Square, Victoria Park, who had told him the story on 8 August 1889. Mr Callaghan's story was as follows:

> In April 1888, my wife and myself were residing at 27 Sun Street, Finsbury Square, the upper part of our house was let off to various gentlemen. In answer to our advt: we put in Daily Telegraph a Mr. G. Wentworth Bell Smith, whose business was to raise money for the Toronto Trust Society; applied and took a large bed sitting room. He said that he was over here on business and that he might stay a few months or perhaps twelve. He told us that before he had come to us he had an office at Godliman Street at the back of St Pauls. Whilst at home he occupied himself in writing on religious subjects; sometimes as many as 60 sheets of foolscap were filled up with such material. Whenever he went out of doors he would wear a different suit of clothes to what he did the day before. He had many suits of clothes and quite eight or nine hats. He kept very late hours and whenever he came in it was quite noiseless. He had also a pair of India rubber boots to put over his ordinary ones to deaden any possible sound. On Augt 9th (altered to 7th) the date of one of the murders, Mrs. Callaghan was in the country, and her sister kept house in her absence. She was

however expected home that evening and we sat up for her till 4 a.m. at which hour Mr. Bell Smith returned stating that he had had his watch stolen in Bishopsgate Street, which on investigation proved to be false. Shirts were found hanging on his towel horse he having washed them himself, and marks of blood on the bed. This I saw myself. Two or three days after this murder of Augt. 9th, with the stated reason of returning to Toronto [*sic*]. I however found that he had not done so, but he did not return to my house. He was seen getting into a tramcar in Septr. Of 1888. We all regarded him as a lunatic and with delusions regarding "Women of the streets," who he frequently said ought to be all drowned. He told me that he was greatly impressed with the amount of immorality in London; and said that a number of whores walked up and down St. Pauls Cathedral during the service. He also said that women in the East End especially ought to be drowned. He also had delusions respecting his wealth stating that he had large wealth at his command. At night he would talk and moan to himself frequently. One day he said, "Physically I am a very weak man, but the amount of my willpower is so great that I am able to outwork several men." Implying that he had great brain power. Frequently on his return he would throw himself down on a sofa and groan. He kept concealed in a chest of drawers in his room three loaded revolvers. He would if taken by surprise by anyone knocking at his door rush and place his back against this chest. The following post card came on[e] day for him signed 'Dodger,' we can't get through it. Can you give us any help.' I gave this information to the police in August after the man left my house, and curiously enough the detectives came over to my house to make enquiries also about this same man, at the instigation of a lady from the Surrey side of the water. The writing of Bell Smith is in every way similar to that sent to the police & signed Jack the Ripper. I am positive he is the man. He is about 5ft 10in in height walks very peculiarly with his feet wide apart, knees weak and rather bending in, hair dark, complexion the same, moustache and beard closely cut giving the idea of being unshaven, nice looking teeth probably false, he appeared well conducted, was well dressed and resembled a foreigner speaking several languages, entertains strong religious delusions about women, and stated that he had done some wonderful operations. His manner and habits were peculiar. Without doubt this man is the perpetrator of these crimes.
Sept. 9. 1889

Swanson included in his report: 'The foregoing is the information he possesses.' This indicates Forbes Winslow's lack of specific information. Tellingly, the story related to events that were already a year old. The mention of 'Dodger', however, is very interesting for preserved in the MEPO files is the following letter [ff. 393–5], posted 23 September 1889 in London SW. The timing is surely beyond coincidence:

To The Inspector of Police
Scotland Yard

Dear Boss

I write these few lines to you hoping you are quite well as it [illegible] me at present the bloke that thinks that he is on my track is right off scent and now I have got my eye on four or five young girls from ponton road nine [illegible] Lane Vauxhall 2 of which I must have this week commencing [illegible] 2 to the 29 or [illegible]

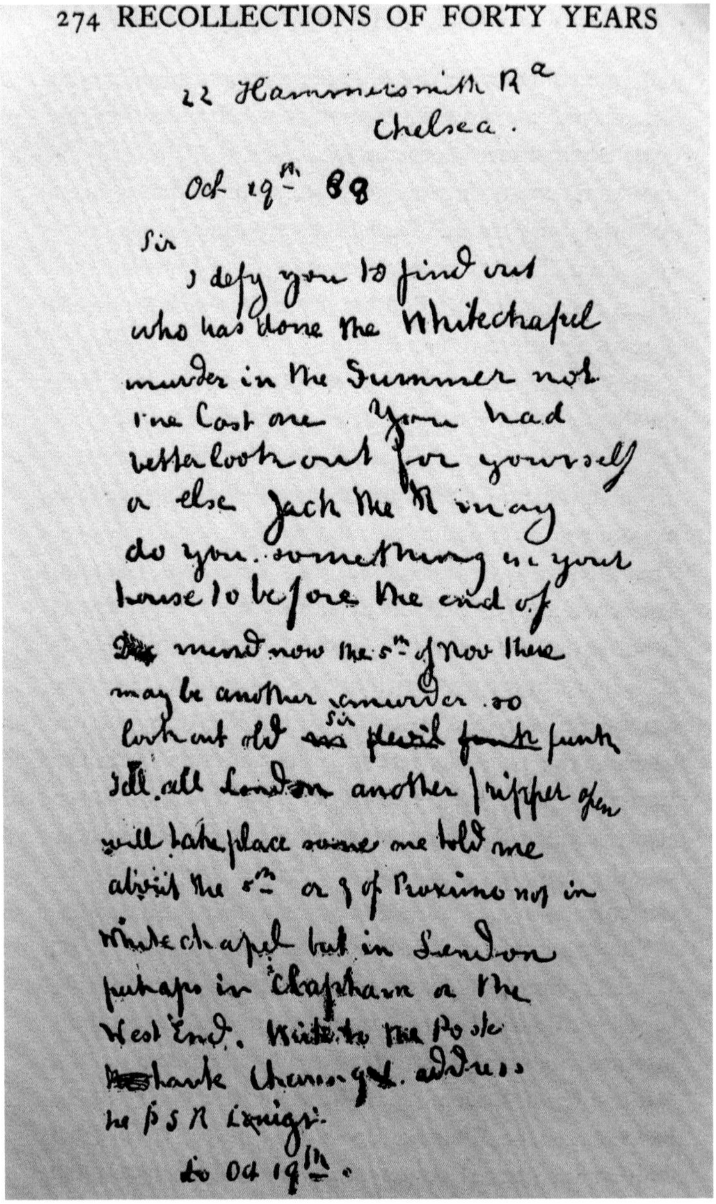

274 RECOLLECTIONS OF FORTY YEARS

22 Hammersmith Rd
Chelsea.

Oct 19th 88

Sir
I defy you to find out
who has done the Whitechapel
murder in the Summer not
the last one You had
better look out for yourself
or else Jack the R may
do you. something in your
house to before the end of
[illegible] mind now the 5th of Nov there
may be another murder so
look out old sir [illegible] funk
till all London another ripper open
will take place some one told me
about the 5th or 9 of Proximo not in
Whitechapel but in London
perhaps in Clapham or the
West End. Write to the Post
[illegible] Charing X. address
the P S R [illegible]
to Oct 19th.

Letter dated 19 October 1889, sent to Dr Forbes Winslow and reproduced in his book. The date has been altered from 1889 to 1888. It is addressed from 22 Hammersmith Road.

> [second page] [illegible] others later as [illegible] & good bye for the present From the Ripper and the [‘dogg’ deleted] dodger
>
> In the time that you receive this note I shall have my knife well sharpened and on my way there . you will hear [rest illegible]

Forbes Winslow’s 1910 book, *Recollections of Forty Years*, devoted a whole chapter to ‘Jack the Ripper’ and it was the first publication to consider the Ripper correspondence at length and reproduce facsimiles. Winslow lists the Ripper murders, counting the killing of Alice McKenzie on 17 July 1889 as the final crime in the series. He considered the murderer to be ‘a homicidal monomaniac of religious views who considered he had a destiny in the world to fulfil; and that he had chosen a certain class of society to vent his vengeance on'. His lunacy theory was built around his claim that the murders were committed when the new moon rose, or when the moon had entered upon its last quarter, barring the Kelly murder, which did not fit this timing. In relation to the killing of Kelly, Winslow stated:

> In only one murder was this proved to be incorrect – that is, the murder of 9th November, 1888, the one in which I received a letter warning me of what would happen. The murder was just one day beyond its time, and, to accord with the theory I am now stating, the murder should have been committed on the 7th November; but I will draw attention to the fact that it was evident that the murder was contemplated about that time, as in the letter I received in October 1888 the writer told me that the murder would be committed either on the 7th or the 9th. This will establish to a certain extent the theory that lunatics are subject to lunar influences.

On the correspondence Winslow wrote:

> During the month of August 1888 a man was seen whose description, as then given to me, corresponded with the man who was found writing on a wall under an archway. The inscription read: "Jack the Ripper will never commit another murder."
>
> On 4th October I received a letter purporting to come from Jack the Ripper, and expressing an insane glee over the hideous work he was carrying out. This letter was in the same handwriting as the writing found under the archway. Another letter was received by me on 19th October, also in the same handwriting, which informed me that the next murder would be committed on 9th November.

Another reference to the mysterious 'writing found under the archway' is made by Winslow in an article published in the *Pall Mall Gazette* of 19 April 1910:

> I have in my possession the actual letter sent me by Jack the Ripper in the same writing as that which Sir Robert Anderson alludes to as being found under the arches, and which the police rubbed off. When in New York at a subsequent period I was highly complimented by the judicial bench on the lucidity of my clue and the way I had worked out the same.

Winslow's New York visit had taken place in August/September 1895 when he attended the Medico-Legal Congress to preside over the Department of Insanity and Mental Medicine. A reporter for the *New York Times* interviewed him in the Westminster Hotel on the evening of 31 August. Winslow gave the reporter his theory on 'Jack the Ripper':

> Jack the Ripper was a medical student, of good family. He was a young man, of slight build, with light hair and blue eyes. He studied very hard, and his mind, being naturally weak, gave way. He became a religious enthusiast and attended early service every morning at St. Paul's.
>
> His religious fervor resulted in homicidal mania toward the women of the street, and impelled him to murder them. He lodged with a man whom I knew, and suspicion was first directed toward him by reason of the fact that he returned to his lodgings at unseasonable hours; that he had innumerable coats and his hats stained with blood.

> I have in my possession now a pair of Canadian moccasins stained with blood that the 'Ripper' wore while on his murderous expeditions. I notified the Scotland Yard authorities, but at that time they refused to co-operate with me. Subsequently the young man was placed in confinement and removed to a lunatic asylum, where he is to-day. Since his incarceration there has been no repetition of the horrible murders that he perpetrated.
>
> These facts are all known to the English authorities, and it is conceded that the man now in the asylum is 'Jack the Ripper.' It was deemed desirable, however, to hush the matter up. The details were too horrible to be made the subject of a public trial, and there was no doubt of the man's hopeless insanity.
>
> [*New York Times*, 1 September 1895, page 16]

The congress under the management of the New York Medico-Legal Society opened on Wednesday 4 September and lasted for three days. Winslow read a paper entitled 'Suicide considered as a Mental Epidemic'.

Winslow enlarges on the subject of the correspondence he received, purportedly from the murderer, on page 70 of his book:

> The peculiarity of my correspondence with Jack the Ripper was that his letters were never stamped. One was written on half a sheet of cheap notepaper; it was in a round, upright hand, and evidently written by someone who was not accustomed to using the pen. The writing is distinct, with an absence of flourish, but written with deliberation and care. The scrawl is not a hurried one; the address on the envelope is even more hurriedly written, with less care, than the letter. It bears the postmark of the Western district, whereas the previous letter I received was from the Eastern. There was a smudge upon it which I was always under the impression was blood, and which, by the use of a magnifying glass, proved to be the case.

The envelope and letter are interesting. The former is addressed simply, 'Dr Forbes Winslow, London, W' and is postmarked London WC A7 OC7 89. There is no postage stamp and the Post Office 2*d* surcharge stamp has been put on it. The letter reads, 'This week you will hear of me — Jack the Ripper.' That Winslow attached relevance to this letter, and probably no little measure of self-importance that the alleged killer should write to him, is evidenced in an article written by a *Cassell's Saturday Journal* correspondent which appeared on 14 March 1894:

> In addition to a number of interesting, though scarcely pleasing, mementoes, the eminent specialist possesses the autographs of a number of proven murderers, and, hanging in a frame in his study, is the famous letter supposed to have been written by "Jack the Ripper," of Whitechapel notoriety. This letter (which was posted without a stamp) was addressed "Dr Forbes Winslow, London," and bears the post-mark October 7th, 1889.
>
> The letter runs:
>
> 'Dear Sir, – You will hear of me.
>
> "JACK THE RIPPER."
>
> It is a significant fact (and one which bears out the theory that the murders were committed by someone suffering from homicidal mania), that although a murder was

264 RECOLLECTIONS OF FORTY YEARS

and started exploring the common lodging-houses in the East End, clad in heavy boots, a fustian jacket,

with a red handkerchief around his head and a pick-axe in his hand.

During the month of August 1888 a man was seen

The 'Jack the Ripper' letter and evelope sent to Dr Forbes Winslow and which he kept hanging in a frame in his study. It was dated 7 October 1889.

> committed soon after the receipt of the above letter, the crimes ceased as soon as it became known that Dr. Forbes Winslow had taken up the matter.

Winslow appears to have unquestioningly accepted these epistles as genuine communications from the killer. Possibly it suited him to do so as they gave credence to his account of his investigation of the murders.

The letter about the November murder is reproduced on page 274 of Winslow's book. It is ostensibly dated 19 October –88 but closer examination reveals that the figures '88' appear to have been overwritten and were actually '89' (*see* illustration on page 163). It seems very unlikely that anyone other than Winslow himself could be responsible for altering the date from 1888 to 1889. Winslow says of it:

> The other letter I received was signed P. S. R. Lunigi, giving his address as "Poste restante, Charing Cross"; this is the one in which my correspondent informed me that a murder would take place on the 8th or 9th of November. He requested the reply to be sent to the Charing Cross post-office, giving his address as 22 Hammersmith Road, Chelsea. On making inquiries, however, I found that no such road existed.

Winslow remained convinced that the lodger in his story was the killer, stating:

> In my opinion, there was no doubt the murderer was the one who, on quitting his lodgings in Finsbury, left behind him a pair of silent rubber shoes, stained with blood, which I had in my possession for a considerable period. The landlord subsequently called upon me and asked me to return them, which I believe he then handed over to the police.

The authors note with interest that the address 22 Hammersmith Road, and other references to Winslow's theory, appear in a four-page rhyming letter dated 8 November 1889 and transcribed in the second part of this book.

Winslow claimed that no more murders were committed after the publication of his researches, although he later abandoned the idea that his suspect had been incarcerated in an asylum. He stated that a young man had been arrested for attempted suicide, and was found to be insane by the police surgeon. The man was placed in an asylum where the authorities noticed that 'his description tallied with that of Jack the Ripper' given in Winslow's published statements. The man suffered from 'a despondent madness, breaking out at times into violent homicidal mania'. Investigations resulted in a theory that the mysterious lodger, Jack the Ripper and the asylum inmate were one and the same man, but this was disproved.

> This man was found to come of a well-to-do and respectable family, and evinced considerable ability in his college career. His speciality was anatomy, and he studied so hard that his mind, never very strong, gave way under the strain. Always of a religious turn of mind, he became afflicted with religious mania. But it was found that he was not Jack the Ripper.

Winslow claimed in his 1910 book that the latest development in his connection with Jack the Ripper was a letter received on 19 July of that year from Melbourne, Australia. This had been sent to him, he said, as a result of articles he had published in the press following the well-known claims of Sir Robert Anderson earlier that year that the identity of the Ripper was known to the police and that he was a 'poor Polish Jew' who had been 'caged in an asylum'. The letter-writer, a lady, claimed that the Ripper had been 'frightened away' by Winslow and had sailed for Australia '. . . in a ship called the *Munambidgee*, working his passage to Melbourne, arriving here in the latter part of 1889'. She claimed the man was a native of Melbourne, Victoria, who had been in South Africa for several years. She stated that he was a friend of the late Dr Blair from whom he had gained his surgical knowledge attending post-mortems. The woman claimed that the man read of sensational crimes in London in the newspapers and that she had the following conversation with him:

> I said to him, "Why do you buy those horrid papers? They are only full of police reports of terrible crimes." He said, "I want to see how things are in London." . . . I then said, "What about Jack the Ripper?" He said, "Strange those crimes ceased once I left England." I was astounded at his remark, and said, "My God! Jack, I believe you did those crimes," he having told me about living in that part of London previously. I tried to banish the thought from my mind, as I loved him; but I referred to it many times after, and finally he told me he did do them. I said, "Why did you do those crimes?" He first said, "Revenge," then said, "Research." I said, "But you never made use of the portions you removed from those women; what did you do with them?" He said, "Oh, there are plenty of hungry dogs in London."

The woman claimed to have written to Scotland Yard telling them her story, and that she received an answer from Sir Robert Anderson:

> . . . but as I had told him all I had to say, I did not write again until last year [1909], but have heard nothing from them. It is my opinion they all bungled this matter up and do not like owning up to it. I even gave him up in Melbourne in 1894. The police examined him; he told them he was in Melbourne in 1890, so they found this was true, and without asking him where he was in 1889, they let him go. He laughed, and said, "See what fools they are. I am the real man they are searching the earth for, but they take me in one door and let me out of the other." I even gave one detective a letter of his, but he only laughed at me. I asked him to have the writing compared with that at home signed 'Jack the Ripper' but he did nothing. Now I have burnt his letters long since, but the monster's name is —, called Jack by relatives and friends. His brother told me he is in Durban, South Africa, employed by the South African Railway Co. He left here for South Africa about six years ago.

The lady correspondent continued in a similar vein denouncing the idea that the Ripper could possibly be the recently named suspect William Grant or Anderson's Jew and totally agreeing with Winslow. Indeed, Winslow became something of a champion of Grant in showing he could not be the Ripper. Winslow confidently concluded in his book:

> That Jack the Ripper is the man in South Africa, who left London after I drove him away by publishing my clue in 1889, I believe; and, to complete this weird account of him, I have every reason to hope I shall be the means of bringing his capture about.

What the story of Dr Forbes Winslow and his interest in the Whitechapel murders shows us, and therein lies its importance, is how the letters could be used to the advantage of the writer and theorist. Forbes Winslow died in 1913, his ambition to be the man to lay the Ripper by his heels unfulfilled.

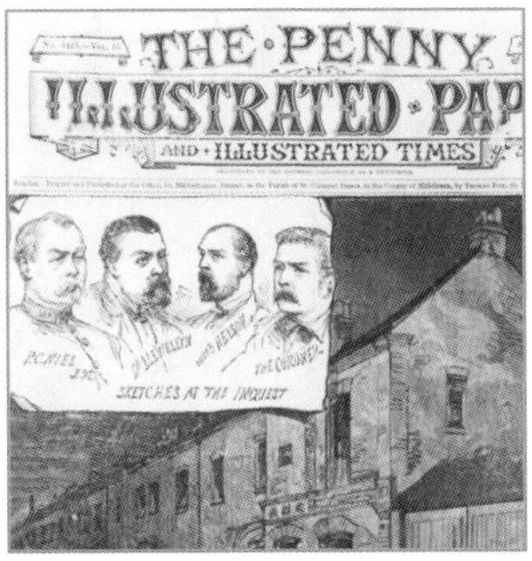

— **FOURTEEN** —

A View from Fleet Street

THE phenomenon, unique at the time, of so many letters allegedly being sent by a series murderer served the press well. The letters were received by the police, journalists themselves and private individuals, and they were being left in public places. What more could the sensational element of the press ask for? As we have seen, George R. Sims, writing for the *Referee*, had much to say about the letters and even at an early stage believed them to be a press invention. They were a staple ingredient for newspaper sensationalism surrounding the case and endowed the unknown killer with an ironic and mocking persona.

Joseph Hall Richardson (1857–1945) was a Londoner, an East-Ender 'born within the sound of Bow Bells', and a journalist for most of his adult life. He was first involved in the press as a freelance writer and served on various provincial papers, but he joined the staff of the *Daily Telegraph* in 1881. His early interest in crime and the police is evidenced by an entry in the visitors' book at the Police Museum ('Black Museum') dated 5 August 1886. He not only took an especial interest in criminal cases, but also reported on many trials. Richardson co-authored two books, *Police!* and *The Rogues' Gallery*, both with ex-police officer, Charles Tempest Clarkson, and published by Field & Tuer, The Leadenhall Press, in 1890. The former was an interesting history of the police with a useful, concise summary of the CID at the time of the murders (*Police!*, pages 260–1):

> The Detective, or Criminal Investigation, Department is under the control of Dr. Anderson, who, having had four years' experience of the prisons branch of the Home Office, and much knowledge in the ways in which secret service money is expended, took Mr. Monro's place, when the latter resigned. Mr. Monro having since been appointed commissioner, Dr. Anderson is now responsible to him, he having the assistance of Mr. Williamson, who joined the force in 1850, and who of late years has exchanged his post as superintendent of the Detective Department for that of Chief Constable. Mr. Shore, who has been thirty years

J. Hall Richardson, a journalist who covered the Whitechapel murders for the *Daily Telegraph* and who later wrote the book *From the City to Fleet Street*.

in the Metropolitan Police, succeeded to the vacancy, and he now directs a staff of chief inspectors and of inspectors. In June 1889, Mr. Melville Leslie Macnaghten was appointed chief constable of the Criminal Investigation Department. There are five chief inspectors, but one of these, Mr. Neame, is in charge of the Convict Supervision Office, and another, Mr. Littlechild, has command of a little body of what may be termed political police.

Besides these officers, there are local inspectors, one of whom is attached to each division, and he has several detective sergeants to assist him. In this way, at the beginning of 1889, a total force of about three hundred men was composed, of whom thirty were first-class inspectors, and seven were second-class inspectors. We may state upon authority that there are proposals for the strengthening of the Detective Department, in the direction of augmenting the number of men attached to the local divisions.

This early book also made some very relevant observations on the Whitechapel murders and indicated Richardson's long and detailed knowledge of the subject. On page 273 of *Police!* he wrote:

. . . It was not until five or six of the Whitechapel series of murders and mutilations had gone by without any real clue having been obtained, that the police thought it advisable to photograph the corpse, before removal, and thus preserve a permanent record of its position. But even in this matter they erred in the other direction, for whilst they were engaged in the necessary formalities, and waiting for bloodhounds, which were not available – and if the dogs had been at hand they would have been useless, as the trail had been frequently crossed – they were allowing the residents in the locality, whose evidence was valuable, to be interviewed by reporters. Thus frequently it happened that statements appeared in print before they were committed to writing in the detectives' room.

The book was written while the series of Whitechapel murders was still current, and gives a unique pressman's view of the police and the investigation as perceived in Fleet Street. The above passage obviously refers to the murder of Mary Jane Kelly and further comment is made about this killing on page 277:

. . . One of the most energetic coroners in London is Mr. Wynne Baxter. He has sifted the testimony relating to all, except one, of the Whitechapel murders. Mr. Baxter steadfastly set his face against suppression of facts, and in one of the earlier inquests it was only under pressure that the divisional surgeon of police disclosed what his post-mortem had revealed. In the case which did not come before Mr. Baxter, the coroner took the course of abruptly closing the inquiry, without asking for the detailed medical evidence, the result being that the injuries inflicted upon the seventh victim, Mary Janet Kelly [*sic*], in Miller's Court, Dorset Street, have not been placed on public record. One result was to put into circulation a number of statements which may or may not have been in accordance with the truth, but which were misleading because not authorised. "Crowner's 'quest law" unmistakably sets out the necessity of recording the nature of *all* the wounds, the description of the weapon by which they were produced, and the circumstances under which they were inflicted, so that the action of Dr. Macdonald in the Dorset Street case cannot be taken as a safe precedent.

The 'Jack the Ripper' letters reflected what the press wrote, and the fertile imaginations of the writers capitalised on all the press speculation. Richardson and Clarkson went even further, suggesting that newspaper coverage led to copycat murders (*Police!*, pages 277–8):

. . . But . . . the cup of horrors was already overflowing, and there was reason to believe that the publication of details would lead to imitation, something of the sort having already happened at Gateshead [the murder of Jane Beetmore by a spurned suitor]. That there was reason in this view was subsequently shown by the fact that similar atrocities were committed at Havant, Bradford, and Yeabridge – the victims being children – not long after the mutilations in London, whilst attempts to kill women were elsewhere reported. Indeed, it was remarkable to what an extent the infectious influence of these diabolical outrages was felt, not only in England, but on the Continent.

The fame of "Jack the Ripper" spread far and wide. It is probable that nothing would have been heard of this cognomen had it not been for the indiscretion of Scotland Yard in publishing a facsimile of sensational letters sent to a news agency, which thereby gave to these interesting documents the stamp of official authority.

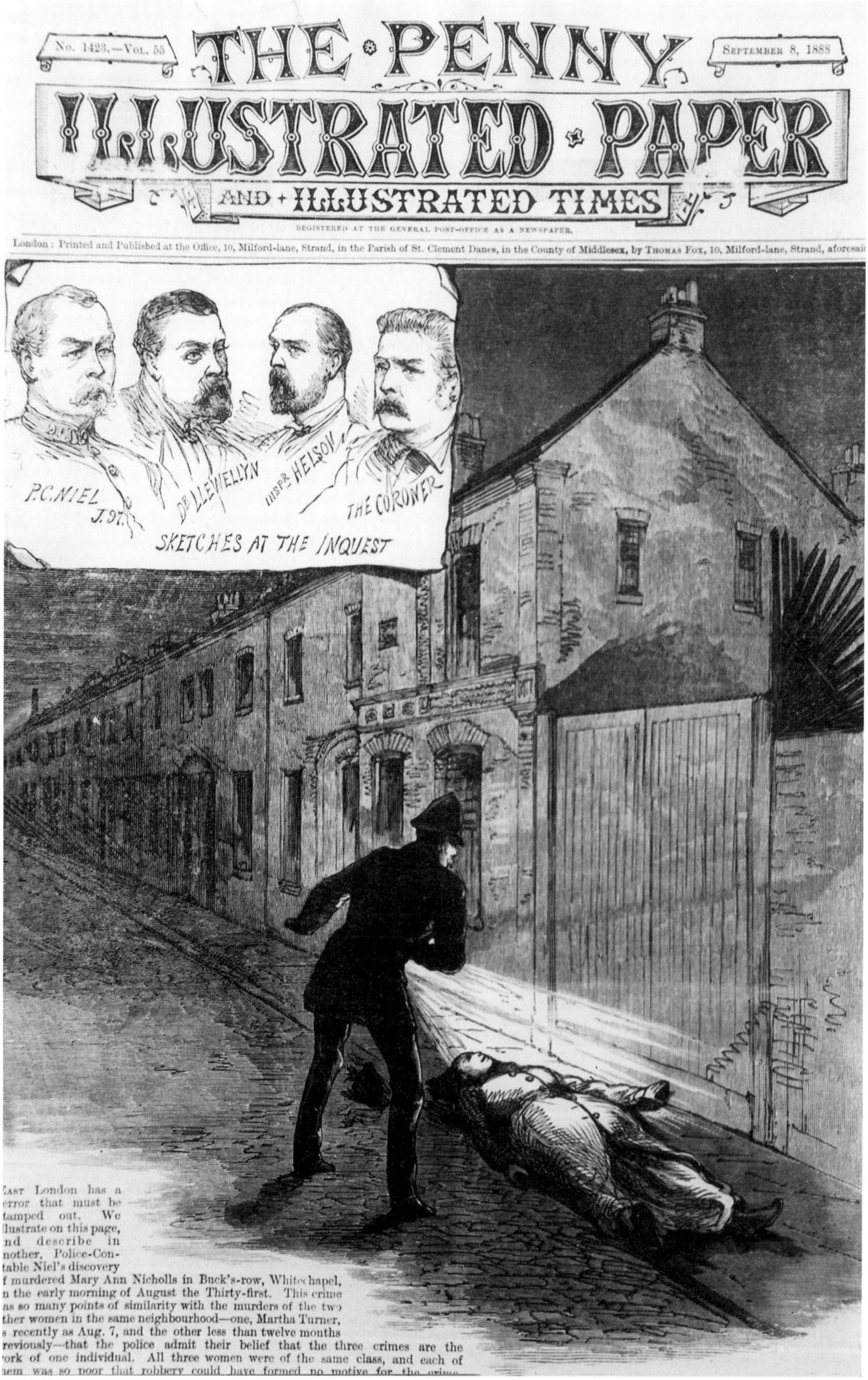

No. 1423.—Vol. 55

THE PENNY ILLUSTRATED PAPER AND ILLUSTRATED TIMES

September 8, 1888

REGISTERED AT THE GENERAL POST-OFFICE AS A NEWSPAPER.

London: Printed and Published at the Office, 10, Milford-lane, Strand, in the Parish of St. Clement Danes, in the County of Middlesex, by Thomas Fox, 10, Milford-lane, Strand, aforesai

East London has a error that must be tamped out. We llustrate on this page, nd describe in nother, Police-Constable Niel's discovery f murdered Mary Ann Nicholls in Buck's-row, Whitechapel, n the early morning of August the Thirty-first. This crime as so many points of similarity with the murders of the two ther women in the same neighbourhood—one, Martha Turner, s recently as Aug. 7, and the other less than twelve months reviously—that the police admit their belief that the three crimes are the ork of one individual. All three women were of the same class, and each of hem was so poor that robbery could have formed no motive for the crime

The prominence afforded the murders is shown here on the front page of *The Penny Illustrated Paper* of 8 September 1888 which featured the Nichols murder in Buck's Row.

> Neither the police nor coroner, however, foresaw all this. They distrusted the newspapers. The police had especial reason to resent the publicity given by the press, which unhesitatingly exposed their short-comings, whilst at the same time they hampered the detectives. It will be remembered that suspicion attached to a man nicknamed "Leather Apron," chiefly on account of the wild stories told by the women of Spitalfields. The man was detained for inquiries for two days, the police making no charge. "Leather Apron" was perfectly innocent, but the police by their reticence were really responsible for the deductions that were drawn from their conduct. Henceforward, under pain of dismissal, the detectives refused information even to the accredited representatives of London papers. But there was suspicion that there was favouritism exercised.

After many years' experience on the journalistic side of the *Daily Telegraph*, Richardson was appointed its general manager. He retired in this position at the end of 1927. Like many journalists he wrote his reminiscences, and any involvement in the Jack the Ripper story was too good to omit. In 1927 Richardson published *From the City to Fleet Street* (Stanley Paul & Co.). In Chapter XV, 'Mysteries Still', he wrote of his memories of the 'Whitechapel murders'. The *Daily Telegraph* had carried many detailed reports on the crimes, but Richardson obviously had his own views on aspects of the case and regarding the Goulston Street wall writing he said:

> I do not propose to follow these horrors in detail, but there were one or two incidents which cannot very well be forgotten. For example, it would scarcely be believed that the Metropolitan Police held the clue to the identification of the murderer in their own hands and deliberately threw it away under the personal direction of the then Commissioner of Police, Sir Charles Warren, who acted in the belief that an anti-Semitic riot might take place if a certain damning piece of writing were permitted to remain on the walls.
>
> Following the murder in Mitre Square, which is within the precincts of the City and, therefore, came under the direct cognisance of the City Police, the murderer threw away a portion of the apron of the murdered woman, upon which he had wiped his bloodstained hands, in the doorway of some model dwellings in Goulstone [*sic*] Street, not far from Petticoat Lane, and then some freak of fancy had led him to write upon the wall this sentence: "The Jewes are not the men to be blamed for nothing."
>
> I have never learned that any photographic record was made of this inscription, and when the City Police came to hear of it they were horrified that their colleagues in the Metropolitan Force had wiped away what might have been an important piece of circumstantial evidence as to the class to which the murderer belonged.

Richardson then gave Assistant Commissioner Robert Anderson's view on the erasure of the message:

> In April, 1916 [*sic* – 1910], Sir Robert Anderson, who was then writing his reminiscences, objecting to criticism, wrote to one of the daily papers:
>
> "In your notice of my article in this month's *Blackwood*, you refer back to what I wrote last month about the Whitechapel murders, and you add: 'In that connection he might have

> recalled – but did not – the crass stupidity of Scotland Yard men, who wiped out from the wall of the labourers' buildings in Goulstone [*sic*] Street, the only tangible piece of evidence ever obtained pointing to the identity of Jack the Ripper.'
>
> "I beg to assure you that here you do an injustice, not only to me, but to the Criminal Investigation Department. The night on which the murder in question was committed I was on my way home from Paris, and great was my indignation when, next day, I heard of what you rightly call an act of 'crass stupidity.' But the Scotland Yard men were in no way responsible for it – it was done by the officers of the uniform force in the division, upon an order issued by one of my colleagues. The exact words of 'the mural inscription' which the murderer chalked upon the wall were, 'The Jewes are not the men to be blamed for nothing.'
>
> "May I add that all this was in the MS. of my article, but a wish to avoid what seemed to reflect upon others, led me to strike out the paragraph."

Richardson also made comment on the letters allegedly from the Ripper, and is responsible for preserving the text of one that otherwise appears not to have survived. He wrote (*From the City to Fleet Street*, page 219):

> The Police and Press received many letters from the "Ripper," mostly written in red ink, and I give one:
>
> "Liverpool,
>
> "29th inst.
>
> "BEWARE I shall be at work on the 1st and 2nd inst. in 'Minories' at 12 midnight and I give the authorities a good chance but there is never a Policeman near when I am at work.
>
> "Yours,
>
> "JACK THE RIPPER."
>
> "Prince William St., L'pool.
>
> "What fools the police are I even give them the name of the street where I am living.
>
> "Yours,
>
> "JACK THE RIPPER."

It is important to note that this correspondence quoted by Richardson is shown as one letter only, the taunt about the address appearing as a sort of postscript to the main text warning of intended 'work' in the Minories. (The Minories is immediately south of Aldgate High Street (and Mitre Square), and principally situated in the City area.) The letter is signed 'Jack the Ripper' and must, in fact, post-date the Stride and Eddowes murders of 30 September as the infamous nickname had not then gained public currency.

The reason for taking careful note of Richardson's quoting of this letter is the fact that it was subsequently reproduced in a popular Ripper book. The single letter became two, and the date became 29 September 1888. This misrepresentation and contamination of Richardson's letter was effected by Donald McCormick in his 1959 book *The Identity of Jack the Ripper*. It was subsequently copied in other works. We may be certain that Richardson was McCormick's source for this letter as he quotes Richardson just two pages previously.

Richardson continued his memoirs with a discussion of some of the suspects of the time (1927). He mentioned William Le Queux's Russian surgeon candidate 'Alexander

Pedachenko' (later favoured by Ripper author Donald McCormick), and Sir Basil Thomson's (ex-Assistant Commissioner) 'insane Russian medical student whose body was found floating in the Thames immediately after the last of the outrages'. Richardson also made mention of the suspect suggested by coroner Wynne Baxter at the Annie Chapman inquest: the 'American medical specialist . . . issuing a book on anatomy, for each copy of which he required parts of the human body'. His conclusion was:

> I, therefore, remain of the conviction that the police never knew and are never likely to know who actually was the Whitechapel murderer. The Commissioner at that time, Mr. Monro, was a great personal friend of mine, and I am sure that if he could possibly have given me the faintest clue he would have done so.

It was Richardson's newspaper, the *Daily Telegraph*, that had reported the attempted identification of James Sadler, arrested on suspicion of the Coles' murder, as the culprit for the earlier murders. And on pages 277–9 of *From the City to Fleet Street* Richardson added a postcript on Sadler that indicated how closely he worked with the police. As far as we know this is the first time that this information has been included in a book about 'Jack the Ripper':

> Two or three years subsequent to the series of "Jack the Ripper" atrocities in the East End (not one of them occurred in Whitechapel) [*sic*] there was a peculiarly brutal tragedy of a similar class in the same district. It revived the belief that the "Ripper" had been in safe custody for a while, had regained his liberty and resumed his old career of outrage and murder. Consequently when a ship's fireman [Sadler] was arrested his guilt was too readily assumed.
>
> The detective police were not quite so sure about it. They had small scruple in using two reporters – one of them was myself – to secure their own ends.
>
> One day a detective-sergeant beckoned to the pair of pressmen and then communicated in strict secrecy the address of the ship's fireman in a naval port, not at any great distance from London [Chatham].
>
> Initiative was not denied to me. My friend and I were as speedily as can be en route for this port, and without much difficulty found the ship's fireman's wife – a virago who, in no unmeasured language, gave the man away.
>
> It seemed a sure thing – sure enough to pursue inquiries in the shipping centre of London and at the Board of Trade offices. Registers were examined, dates compared, and, finally, an ingenious string of facsimile signatures produced – the object being to show that each time the accused man "signed on" it was within a day or two of the latest "Whitechapel" murder.
>
> I recollect accompanying Wilson [Harry Wilson the Bow Street solicitor] and Marshall Hall after the police court proceedings.
>
> In the sequel the ship's fireman was discharged.
>
> I don't suppose that it would have occurred to him that he had a ground of action against anybody.
>
> The ship's fireman's case was at once taken up by a newspaper which made the most of it – the *Star*. Its editor, none other than "T.P." who founded it, was keen to take a rise out of another journal. In 1894 "T.P." admitted that crime had sent up the circulation of his paper at that period. It always does.

They say in Fleet Street that "dog doesn't eat dog." It was not so in this case.

"T.P." lost no time in taking the ship's fireman to Harry Wilson, who as a police court lawyer had a rising reputation, and he did not think twice about briefing counsel, Marshall Hall, also of rising reputation, and, in the end, the case came for trial and was settled on payment of damages so moderate that the expenditure from the paper's point of view was nominal.

In the editorial offices of the benevolent paper which had instituted the campaign against its contemporary the ship's fireman, the solicitor, the editor and his colleague, drank champagne to celebrate the event.

The fireman was new to the liquor. The first glass or two made him genial.

"What have you done with all that money?" asked the newspaper men.

"Got it in my cap," was the reply.

"But you'll lose it. Better give it to Mr. — to be put in his safe until you want it."

The man complied, but after a glass or two more of champagne he grew quarrelsome and demanded it back, as he "wasn't going to be robbed."

What became of him? Did he go back to his spouse? Not at all.

A day later the man was outside the lawyer's office, waiting to settle up. The solicitor was engaged with a gentleman who projected a gun-running expedition to South America, where two Republics were at war.

"A ship's fireman did you say! Just the man I want! Let me see him!"

"But," said the lawyer, "it's a dangerous game."

"Not a bit. I'll make him chief stoker."

Next day he sailed for the Spanish Main and never has been heard of since.

Joseph Hall Richardson thus gives us a clue as to the fate of the suspect Sadler.

— FIFTEEN —

The Mysteries of McCormick

STEWART EVANS*

AS we have shown, the material provided by the 'Jack the Ripper' correspondence is just too good for authors to miss. Until the release of the official files, writers of Jack the Ripper books were confined to using only letters that had been reproduced in the press, or those they themselves had invented. If invented by an enterprising author, such correspondence provided excellent Ripper fodder. We witness a strange phenomenon with Donald McCormick, perhaps the 'father' of modern Ripper writing. Undoubtedly the inventor of much Ripper fiction, it would appear that McCormick did not hesitate to create Ripper correspondence of his own. Some subsequent authors accepted McCormick at his word and reproduced material for which no provenance can be found prior to McCormick's 1959 book, *The Identity of Jack the Ripper* (Jarrolds, London). Prime sources were not sought; many of McCormick's inventions became part of Ripper lore and accepted as fact. McCormick used letters allegedly penned by the killer to endow the unknown criminal with a persona and a dark sense of humour and irony. It was an appealing formula which other authors have imitated and which has added immeasurably to the myth of 'Jack the Ripper'. McCormick is thus the originator of many literary mysteries.

George Donald King McCormick was born on 11 December 1911 at Rhyl; his father was a journalist. He was educated at Oswestry School and after leaving school took up a career as an investigative journalist at the age of nineteen. He was married three times

* Authors' note – In a rare departure from their normal working relationship, during the writing of this book the authors were unable to reach consensus about the work of Donald McCormick. It is the extent of Mr McCormick's invention they cannot agree upon. To this end it was felt better that the following two chapters be printed under the name of only one author.

and had a son by his second wife. During the Second World War McCormick served in the Royal Naval Volunteer Reserve and was a skipper of landing craft. In 1942, serving in Combined Operations, he met naval intelligence officer and former journalist Ian Fleming. The two became friends – Fleming, of course, later went on to great fame as the creator of James Bond. After the war Fleming became foreign manager of *The Sunday Times* and other Kemsley newspapers. McCormick was then managing editor of the *Gibraltar Chronicle* and Fleming appointed him as North African correspondent for the Kemsley group. In 1949 Fleming had McCormick appointed Commonwealth correspondent for *The Sunday Times*, then in 1963 McCormick was appointed to the position of foreign manager (previously occupied by Fleming) and held the post for the next ten years.

During his postwar journalistic career McCormick pursued an interest in the secret service, inspired by Fleming, and in crime mysteries. His own works were essentially factual, although he wrote in an age where primary sources were not quoted and facts were not too strictly adhered to when they might have affected the appeal of the book. Factual books were more 'novelised' in McCormick's early days than would be acceptable now and even included invented conversations. McCormick wrote histories of the world's secret services and used the pen name Richard Deacon in addition to his own. Among his publications were *The Hell-Fire Club* (1958); *The Mystery of Lord Kitchener's Death* (1959); a study of Lloyd George; *The Mask of Merlin* (1963); *The Red Barn Mystery* (1967); a study of the Lower Quinton and Hagley Wood murders called *Murder By Witchcraft* (1968); a study of Maundy Gregory entitled *Murder By Perfection* (1970); an autobiography, *With My Little Eye: Memoirs of a Spy Hunter* (1982); and a history of Cambridge University's 'intellectual secret society' *The Cambridge Apostles* (1985).

There can be no doubt that McCormick was a gifted writer and his books are certainly entertaining. The one that concerns us here is his 1959 *The Identity of Jack the Ripper* and its 1970 revised reprint. Chapter 7 is entitled 'The Correspondence of Jack the Ripper' and McCormick uses a study of Ripper letters to provide a psychological profile of the killer and add much colour to his study; it is a lengthy account. As McCormick rightly observes, 'But for the correspondence of Jack the Ripper, his name would never have been handed down to posterity and in all probability the crimes he committed would have long ago been forgotten.' Then, tellingly, McCormick states, 'For it was he who created this "grotesque mask" under which he contrived most effectively to "hide his seriousness and reveal his levity".' Next McCormick poses three intriguing questions that are perhaps themselves the answer to why the letters hold so much interest for students of the case. He asks:

> (1) was Jack the letter-writer the East End killer?; (2) or was he a practical joker?; (3) does his correspondence provide any clue as to his identity?

McCormick correctly notes that the name 'Jack the Ripper' received no mention from the police or the press until after the murders of Stride and Eddowes on 30 September 1888 and the subsequent appearance of the 'Dear Boss' letter. However, he incorrectly states the postmark on this letter was 28 September and accepts it, and the 'saucy Jacky'

The broad highway of Whitechapel Road – at the end of the nineteenth century, as now, the main route into London from the eastern counties. The London Hospital, which features prominently in the 'Ripper' story, can be seen on the right.

postcard that followed, as being sent by the actual murderer. He cites the threat to 'clip the lady's ears off' as being the telling phrase in the letter, for the killer was interrupted when he murdered Stride but attempted to carry out the threat on Eddowes. McCormick writes, 'the lobe of the right ear was obliquely cut through', and 'Dr. Bagster Phillips stated that the lobe of Stride's left ear was torn'. What McCormick failed to note was the fact that the injury to Stride's ear was old and healed, and the cut to Eddowes' ear was incidental to a slash across her face. McCormick calls the postcard 'this letter' and states it 'was written and posted on 30 September'. All we know of the date of the postcard is the postmark, which is 1 October. It may or may not have been written and posted on Sunday 30 September because, as we have seen, the first collection for a Sunday post was at 3.00 a.m. on Monday morning.

McCormick also relates the story of the Lusk letter and kidney episode, oddly referring to Lusk as 'Mr. Lark', an error that he corrected in later editions of the book. He argued for the authenticity of the Lusk communication, saying that the piece of kidney with the letter must have come from Eddowes as it was, 'a portion of a human kidney (a "ginny" kidney, that is to say, the kidney of someone who drank heavily). I should say it belonged to a woman aged about forty-five and had been removed from the body within the last two weeks.' We have already seen the truth of this matter: Dr Openshaw was misquoted in the press.

McCormick did not accept the police claims that the author of the correspondence was a journalist: 'I find the hoax theory unsatisfactory. It is far too glib a method on the part of officials to explain away something for which they had no solution.' He asks why, if Anderson knew his identity, was the journalist 'not prosecuted for causing a public mischief?' The truth was, of course, that the senior police officers *believed* they knew who was responsible for the initial 'Jack the Ripper' letters and postcard, but they lacked the necessary proof to put the matter before a court. McCormick also asks why the police poster of the letter and postcard was displayed in the 'Black Museum' at New Scotland Yard, and why the police did not denounce the letters and postcard as the work of a practical joker. As we have seen from Sir Charles Warren's letter to the Home Office, he *did* think that they were the work of a hoaxer, but he was obliged to keep all options open and to prosecute enquiries as to the author. McCormick states that:

> . . . there were many letters sent to the police, to the newspapers, and to various individuals concerning the murders – probably at least 2,000 over a period of years. This does not take into account a dwindling, but still steady stream of letters, including many bogus 'confessions', until as recently as November 1958. Of this correspondence the bulk was of anonymous authorship; there were more than one hundred letters or cards signed 'Jack the Ripper', 'Jack' or 'The Ripper'. A fair percentage of these were obviously imitations of the original Jack and in a totally different handwriting.

McCormick's unsourced estimate of 'at least 2,000' letters has often been misquoted as the number of letters received purporting to have come from the murderer. In fact this figure includes those 'concerning the murders' and suggestions as to the identity of the murderer or how to catch him. In truth there are 210 letters and postcards which purport to have come from the murderer in the Metropolitan Police files, and substantially fewer in the preserved City of London Police letters file. McCormick states: 'According to the police, the letters signed "Ripper" were definitely not in the same handwriting as that of the originals. And at least one epistle signed "Jack the Ripper" was a fake.' He then goes on to relate the story of Maria Coroner to support this. This statement does seem to indicate that McCormick made some sort of inquiry with New Scotland Yard about the letters, and that some official looked at the file for him and noted a difference in the writing of 'Jack the Ripper' and just 'Ripper' in the files. A proper check would have revealed, of course, that there were many examples of 'Jack the Ripper' written in almost as many different hands.

To sum up his conclusions McCormick observed:

> But the correspondence of the original Jack the Ripper is not so easily dismissed. There is no evidence that any single journalist benefited to the extent of a scoop as a result of these letters: had such a journalist wished to benefit himself he would hardly have sent his communications to the editor of a news agency, knowing that the information would eventually be passed on to all newspapers. And it hardly seems feasible that a London journalist should have taken the trouble to travel up to Liverpool to post a letter signed 'Jack the Ripper'.

On 29 September this assiduous scribe wrote from Liverpool:

> 'Beware, I shall be at work on the 1st and 2nd inst. in Minories at twelve midnight and I give the authorities a good chance, but there is never a policeman near when I am at work.
>
> Yours,
>
> JACK THE RIPPER.'

Some time later this was followed by another brief missive:

> 'Prince William Street,
>
> Liverpool.
>
> What fools the police are. I even give them the name of the street where I am living.
>
> Yours,
>
> JACK THE RIPPER.'

McCormick obviously had not considered the possibility that the correspondence may have originated from the Central News Agency itself. One of his sources was J. Hall Richardson's book, *From the City to Fleet Street*, from which he quotes. What is not made clear is his source for the 'Liverpool letters'. The original letter(s) cannot be traced and the only mention of this Liverpool correspondence prior to McCormick was by J. Hall Richardson. The inevitable conclusion is that McCormick *must* have used Richardson as the source for the Liverpool letter(s). And it is here that we see an example of McCormick modifying his source material for effect. The first change is to alter the date from the bare '29th inst.' of Richardson's original to '29 September' with the implied year 1888. Then Richardson's 'one' letter is split into two. And so, via McCormick, another myth entered Ripper lore.

McCormick continues his chapter using various letters and other communications as the work of 'Jack'. He includes the 'I'm not a butcher . . .' rhyme from Macnaghten's book, then two unsourced verses:

> Up and down the goddam town
> Policemen try to find me.
> But I ain't a chap yet to drown
> In drink, or Thames or sea.

And:

> I've no time now to tell you how
> I came to be a killer
> But you should know, as time will show,
> That I'm society's pillar.

These rhymes sound like the inventions of McCormick's fertile mind and they too cannot be found to pre-date his 1959 book. They reflect popular Ripper tales of the killer having 'drowned in the Thames' and the killer being 'a toff'. McCormick deduced that the Ripper was 'an incorrigible joker' with a sense of humour. Thus, via the correspondence, he was able to endow the main character of his book (a total unknown) with a sense of identity, and with some sort of appeal for his readers.

McCormick recounted the story of Dr Forbes Winslow – as we have seen, an independent, qualified medical man who interested himself in tackling the great mystery and whose views on the case were given in his own book. It is here that McCormick introduces his own amateur Ripper sleuth, Dr Thomas Dutton of Westbourne Villas, Bayswater. McCormick tells us that Dutton:

> . . . compiled over a period of sixty years three volumes of handwritten *Chronicles of Crime*, based on his experience as a doctor. Prior to the East End murders he had been a leading figure in the Chichester and West Sussex Microscopic Society and had specialised in micro-photography.

Dutton is then developed as a leading character in McCormick's book. This has special significance to the study of the 'Jack the Ripper' correspondence, for McCormick continues with the words of Dutton:

> 'I made micro-photographs of 128 specimens of the alleged correspondence of "Jack the Ripper" to the police and other institutions and individuals. Of these at least 34 were definitely in the same handwriting. This is not to assert that all the remaining letters and verses were fakes, or written by other persons. Some undoubtedly were, but the authentic letter-writer was, to judge from the micro-photographs, deliberately disguising his true method of caligraphy, and, in doing so, he not unnaturally fell into the error of frequently forming his C's, H's, R's and T's in a variety of ways.
>
> 'Some letters appeared to be in a different handwriting when looked at with the naked eye. It was only by comparing a large number of letters and noting the frequency with which certain letters were formed differently and by examining the micro-photographs that one could detect positively minute similarities in writing which, superficially at least, seemed as though it could not have been the work of the same man.
>
> 'I often thought that the police paid too little attention to these letters, and it is certain that, had the crimes been committed today, our highly specialised detective force would have made more of them. They assumed that several hoaxers were at work and therefore regarded every new letter or warning received as of no significance.
>
> 'The fact that there was more than one letter-writer does not detract from the importance of the 34 which were in the same handwriting. And 34 were the minimum number of letters which Jack wrote. Micro-photography in the 'eighties was still in its infancy, and I was only an amateur at it. But I dare say that modern methods would have shown many more to be the same man's work.
>
> 'The writing was disguised to appear to be that of an uneducated man on some occasions; on others it was that of a painstaking clerk. The same with the phraseology. But even that was marked by "lapses" into literacy, especially in Jack's effective essays into verse. To quote one example:
>
> Eight little whores, with no hope of heaven,
> Gladstone may save one, then there'll be seven.

> Seven little whores begging for a shilling,
> One stays in Henage Court, then there's a killing.
>
> Six little whores, glad to be alive.
> One sidles up to Jack, then there are five.
> Four and whore rhyme aright,
> So do three and me,
> I'll set the town alight
> Ere there are two.
>
> Two little whores, shivering with fright,
> Seek a cosy doorway in the middle of the night.
> Jack's knife flashes, then there's but one,
> And the last one's the ripest for Jack's idea of fun.'
>
> 'It may not be verse in the accepted sense, but this is certainly not the composition of an illiterate. Jack would sometimes misspell words deliberately, then forget later on and write a word correctly. It was the same with his punctuation. He wrote "Jewes" with an extra *e* when he scrawled his message in chalk on the wall, and which the police so stupidly washed off. But he also spelt the word correctly in some letters.
>
> 'I was asked by the police to photograph the message on the wall before it was washed off, but Sir Charles Warren was so insistent that the message must not be preserved in any form that he ordered the police to destroy the prints I sent them. But the micro-photograph which I took definitely established that the writing was the same as that in some of the letters.'

It should be noted that a micro-photograph, used in the photography of minute objects, could not possibly have been taken of such wall writing.

McCormick spends some time examining and then dismissing Forbes Winslow's theories on the murderer and his motives. Obviously impressed with Forbes Winslow as a character, McCormick was determined to go one better with his own sleuthing doctor. According to McCormick, Dutton was a friend of Inspector Abberline, an officer who frequently consulted with the good doctor for his advice. In his summation McCormick reached the erroneous conclusions that:

> . . . only in the original Jack's letters was there information which only the killer could have obtained. It might be argued that it was a mere coincidence that the writer forecast the murders of 9 November, 1888, and 17 July, 1889 [as falsely claimed by Forbes Winslow]. It could equally be claimed that when he said he would 'be at work on the 1st and 2nd inst. in Minories at twelve midnight' he prophesied wrongly as the murders were committed at least a day earlier. Yet his second murder on this night was carried out very close to the Minories and he would be unlikely to give the police the exact time and place of his intended crimes, nor in fact would it be possible for him to do so. But his indication that he would clip off the ears of one victim and his undoubted attempt to do so, coupled with an apology for failure, are surely more than coincidence. When one sets these facts alongside his revelation that Elizabeth Stride cried out and the incident of the kidney, one can scarcely fall back on the excuse of coincidence any longer.

Postmen sitting and relaxing in the Postmen's Park near to St Martin's-le-Grand. (*Living London*)

Having apparently convinced himself and many of his readers of the authenticity of the 'Jack the Ripper' correspondence, McCormick was ready to present his mocking killer. It was a view of the letters that other authors would adopt:

> From this correspondence emerges a picture, if not of the man, at least of the 'mask'. How much of the man is allowed to peep out of the 'mask' one cannot be sure. The 'mask' is that of a crude and moronic joker. The man himself was able to write in a variety of styles, though the outlook was always the same – a hatred of whores and a Puck-like delight in making the flesh creep. There can be no doubt at all that he read his newspapers avidly, that he followed every story published about the investigation of the crimes and was aware (for example, his jibe at Gladstone) of the most scurrilous scandal of the day. But the most remarkable feature of the correspondence and verse, with very few exceptions, is its irrepressible sense of fun. Jack revels in every aspect of the murders, not gloatingly, not pansexually, but in sheer glee and impishness. It is this very impudence which is the most effective disguise of all.

For McCormick, the 'Jack the Ripper' correspondence transformed the killer into a villain with a delightful sense of humour and an avid reader of his press. It revealed that the murderer must be a foreigner or a well-educated Englishman who had travelled abroad: 'He must have had an iron nerve and astonishing confidence in his ability to avoid capture.' And, McCormick states that, according to Dr Dutton, the killer was not a skilled forger because if he had been, there would have been fewer variations in his handwriting: 'Possibly he wanted the police to think that not all his letters were written by the same person. If so, he certainly succeeded in foxing some of them.' McCormick felt that the killer had an intimate knowledge of the East End, as revealed by his references to the Minories and 'such an obscure alley as Henage [*sic*] Court'. He continued:

> That he travelled seems certain, for Dr. Dutton not only confirms that the Liverpool letters were in his hand, but mentions a communication from Glasgow which stated:
>
> '"Think I'll quit using my nice sharp knife. Too good for whores. Have come here to buy a Scotch dirk. Ha! Ha! That will tickle up their ovaries."'
>
> And the doctor adds: 'The only mention in the Press of a specific organ being removed from the Ripper's victim concerned the kidneys. Though the ovaries were on one occasion cut out of a body, the Press merely referred to the removal of "a certain organ".'

McCormick ends by quoting Leonard Matters' opinion on the first 'Jack the Ripper' letter and postcard. In his 1928 book *The Mystery of Jack the Ripper*, Matters had included a chapter on 'Who Wrote the Letters?'. He concluded that the 'Dear Boss' letter was written by an American and the postcard that followed possibly by someone else with a knowledge of the content of the letter. The writer (or writers) was an American sailor just arrived in London. Matters also decided that the author was not the killer and that the correspondence was therefore a hoax. McCormick quotes Matters' opinion:

> 'The caligraphy (of the letter) was excellent. It was the sort of letter that might have been written by a young man after careful tuition at a night school. But it is not the writing of a man of middle age . . . The postcard may or may not have been written by the same person, though the probability is that it was. This is by no means apparent, however. There is striking degeneration in the quality of the penmanship.
>
> 'I should say at the first glance that two different hands had written the two documents. If this is correct, then obviously the second writer must have known precisely what was said in the first communication: otherwise he could not have followed up the argument.'

But it is odd that McCormick does not mention Matters' conclusions that the writer was probably an American and that he was a hoaxer.

In the second edition of *The Identity of Jack the Ripper* (1970), McCormick added two new sections to his correspondence chapter. The first was a reference to 'the Openshaw letter', which Major Smith, in his own book of 1910, claimed had been sent to him. The second mentioned a Ripper handwriting analysis that had been made in an article in *The Criminologist* of August 1968 by C.M. MacLeod, a graphologist. McCormick mentioned that MacLeod had decided that the handwriting revealed 'a propensity to cruelly perverted sexuality to a degree that even the most casual amateur graphologist could hardly mistake'. McCormick did not include the fact that the specimens MacLeod referred to were 'the Lusk letter' and 'the Openshaw letter', and not the original 'Jack the Ripper' correspondence. A mere glance by any layman will reveal that there is no similarity between the handwriting in the original correspondence and the Lusk/Openshaw letters. McCormick said:

> Divining that there were two distinct letter-writers, Mr. MacLeod said that if there was only one real Jack the Ripper he would cast his vote for the writer of the letters [*sic*] to Mr. Lusk: 'he shows tremendous drive in the vicious forward thrust of his overall writing and great cunning in his covering-up of strokes; that is, the re-tracing of one stroke of a letter over another, rendering it illegible while appearing to clarify . . . I would say that this writer was capable of conceiving any atrocity and of carrying it out in an organised way.'

One is left wondering about McCormick's motives in choosing material to quote. Although the Lusk letter is referred to, he does not clarify which correspondence it is being compared with. Forensic document examination and graphology are two different disciplines. The former is legally recognised as a scientific aid, whereas the latter is more of an art. To the detriment of Mr MacLeod's arguments it must be stated that he was using only photocopies of the correspondence, and he was already 'primed' by having seen them in Professor Francis Camps' article about 'the letters of Jack the Ripper'.

McCormick suffered from a coronary attack early in 1973 and was contacted at that time by Paul Bonner who was the producer for the BBC on its Barlow and Watt television treatment of the Jack the Ripper story. McCormick claimed to have thrown out much of his material, even at that time, although he stated that he was 'partially committed on any new J.T.R. material' in that he had just written a foreword to a new book on the subject. This book was due for publication the following September, but failed to materialise. McCormick aptly commented: 'The Ripper, like the Don, flows quietly on.'

— **SIXTEEN** —

'A secret diary of Dr. Thomas Dutton'

STEWART EVANS

DR Thomas Dutton certainly existed and, as a professional man, he would have kept a diary. It cannot be proven, however, that he wrote his *Chronicles of Crime*, or an account of his adventures involving the Ripper case, as described by Donald McCormick. Dr Dutton is an important source for McCormick. Of course the great interest for us is the fact that McCormick uses Dr Dutton as the source for much information on the correspondence of 'Jack the Ripper'.

Dutton died in 1935, and the *Daily Express* reported his death on Wednesday 13 November 1935:

Doctor-Friend Of Princes

Tells Life-Story In 50-Year

Diaries; Dies Near to Poverty

"Daily Express" Special Representative

One of Britain's cleverest bacteriologists yesterday entered the West London surgery of Dr. Thomas Dutton, the aged specialist who was found dead on the floor beside his bed on Monday, and looked at his old colleague's quarters with grief in his eyes.

Every room was littered with books, papers, and unpaid bills. Many had not been used for months. Dust lay thick on floors and furniture.

In extreme old age, Dr. Thomas Dutton, friend of princes, brilliant physician, once wealthy, had lived on the borderline of poverty. He had cooked his own food, looked after his rooms and himself, scorning help. Few of his friends knew.

Two pounds was all the money he possessed. No banking account can be traced.

In death he faced a "parish burial." The friend who stood in his rooms yesterday has saved him from that. He has undertaken to pay all funeral expenses.

Prince Albert Victor Christian Edward (1864–92), from 1891 Duke of Clarence and Avondale, grandson of Queen Victoria, and Heir Presumptive to the throne. Since the early 1960s Prince 'Eddy' has been put forward as a Ripper suspect. It is interesting to note that he was allegedly, according to an article of 1935 in the *Daily Express*, a 'friend' of Dr Thomas Dutton. Other articles at this time suggested that Dutton knew the identity of 'Jack the Ripper'. Could this have been the origin of the idea for a 'Royal Ripper'?

Unmethodical though he was in all that pertained to the mechanical side of living, there was one habit Dr. Dutton never lost. A diary has been found that he kept faithfully for more than fifty years.

Duke Of Clarence

It tells not only of his own medical activities, but records events of importance in the lives of the Royal family.

It goes back to the days when the Duke of Clarence (the King's elder brother) was his friend; to the days when he himself was the possessor of a substantial fortune, keeping his own hunters, playing an active part in the colourful social life of the Edwardian and the late Victorians.

In his diaries Dr. Dutton revealed himself as an enthusiastic racegoer and backer, a keen student of crime and one intensely interested in the affairs of the greater world.

Such names as those of Sir Robert Perks, the engineer, and Lady Cathcart figure in its pages.

The case of Mrs. Rattenbury and her young chauffeur-lover, George Stoner, who killed her husband in their Bournemouth villa early this year, is commented on at length.

Woman Sought

Dr. Dutton took his degrees as long ago as 1878. He made a name for himself as a dietician, and was the author of valuable medical works on obesity and dietetics.

No inquest is considered necessary, but the police are trying to trace a woman whose name appears in his prescription book as one of his few patients.

It is thought she may be able to help the police in certain formal inquiries. She is not known at the address she gave to the doctor.

There is no mention of 'Jack the Ripper' in this piece, and for the first mention of Dutton in that connection we have to turn to the *Sunday Chronicle* of 17 November 1935:

Secret Diary Revelations
Of Dead Doctor
HE KNEW "JACK THE
RIPPER"

"Sunday Chronicle" Special Correspondent

"I KNEW 'JACK THE RIPPER.' I KNOW WHY HE COMMITTED THE WHITECHAPEL MURDERS."

This dramatic revelation in a secret diary of Dr. Thomas Dutton, the eighty-year-old specialist who was found dead at his house in Shepherd's Bush last week, was disclosed to me yesterday by a woman who for years had been one of his few patients.

Miss Hermione Dudley, friend and patient of the doctor, told me the story of his "passionate interest in crime" when I called on her at a Bayswater boarding house.

A CRIMINOLOGIST

"I knew the doctor when I was quite a young girl," she said, "He was then at the height of his fame – an excellent doctor, a brilliant specialist, and an authority on all manner of diseases.

"But it was as a criminologist that he revealed most of his outstanding genius.

"By far the most interesting document he compiled was his *Chronicle of Crime*, three volumes of handwritten comments on all the chief crimes of the past sixty years.

"My father was one of the few men to whom he showed this document, and owing to my own interest in it, Dr. Dutton gave it to me some time ago."

Miss Dudley described to me some of the remarkable entries in these crime diaries. In the first volume there are several pages devoted to the notorious Whitechapel murders – the series of maniacal murders of women during the autumn of 1888.

"I am certain that the doctor assisted with the post mortems on the 'Jack the Ripper' victims. His diary makes this quite clear.

"Often he told me, and he repeats it in his diary – that he knew the identity of 'Jack the Ripper.'

"He described him as a middle-aged doctor, a man whose mind had been embittered by the death of his son.

"The latter had suffered cruelly at the hands of a woman of the streets and the father believed this to be the cause of his brilliant son's death.

"For months after his son's death the father roamed the streets of the East End, where he had been told this particular woman was to be found.

"Dr. Dutton did his best to persuade his colleague that the nature of his son's death was best forgotten, but for a while this embittered man disappeared completely.

"I understood from Dr. Dutton that in the course of a post mortem examination on a 'Ripper' victim he formed his own conclusion as to who committed the murder."

A further article citing Dutton's association with 'Jack the Ripper' featured in the *Empire News* of the same day, 17 November 1935:

TRAGIC LAST DAYS OF A
BRILLIANT
DOCTOR

A FEW days after the last murder committed by that fiend in human guise, "Jack the Ripper," and at a time when the scared but infuriated people in the Whitechapel district were crying out for the life of the assassin, there passed down the Whitechapel-road a man, carrying a small, black bag.

At once he was surrounded by a mob of people and violently hustled, and it required the united efforts of several police officers to save him from the crowd and take him along to Leman-street Police Station amidst cries of "Jack the Ripper – Jack the Ripper." Once inside the police station, however, a few minutes sufficed to prove that far from being the man who had murdered and mutilated no fewer than six women of the unfortunate class, the victim of this outcry was none other than a doctor working in the district who had endeavoured to assist the police by a little amateur detective work in connection with the crimes.

The man was Dr. Thomas Dutton, and this week his dead body was found, lying on the floor beside his bed. He had died in abject poverty after being one of the best-known specialists of his day and numbering among his patients many of the most famous men and women of the past forty years.

The author of a number of standard works on dietetics he was for years the hon. physician to a maternity and child welfare clinic near the surgery in Uxbridge-road where he died, and his last book was called "Every Mother's Book."

In Poverty

Of late he had but few patients and lived alone, a recluse almost in the dusty rooms which he occupied, doing his own cooking and waiting upon himself entirely.

That he had a surgery in New Cavendish-street, Harley-street, was no criterion of the state of his finances, for apparently £2 was all the money he had in the world.

But for the kindness of a friend, this man who had been the friend of princes, had owned his own hunters, and had been a prominent figure in society, might have been buried in a pauper's grave.

Such was the man who, as a young doctor, started out on his career in the East End of London at a time when "Jack the Ripper" was causing a thrill of horror to pass throughout the world.

Like every other person in the district he had taken a keen interest in the efforts of the police and public in endeavouring to round up the murderer and had been quietly making inquiries among his women patients, many of whom were of the class who had been selected by the "Ripper" for his victims, in the hope that he might stumble upon some little clue which might lead to an important discovery.

He was convinced that the man who carried out the crimes was possessed of some anatomical skill if not actual surgical knowledge, and he concentrated on trying to find out whether there was any medical student or doctor in the neighbourhood who appeared to be of an abnormal turn of mind.

The Black Bag

It was undoubtedly his being seen in possession of the little black bag that which caused the mob to suspect him, for over a period of weeks – ever since two murders had been committed on the same night within an hour of each other – there had been a hue and cry for a man with a black bag, and the mere presence of anyone in the district with such a commonplace article as it was then was sufficient for that person to be surrounded and hustled, and arrests were made on a wholesale scale.

It will be recalled that there had been five murders of women, all taking place within the space of a square mile, each victim being a woman of the unfortunate class, and each murder being carried out in precisely the same manner.

First the victim's throat was cut, the head being almost severed from the body. Then the murderer carried out a number of diabolical mutilations on the lower part of the body, disembowelling his victim.

In some cases a certain part of the abdomen had been removed and taken away for what purpose can only be surmised, and it was undoubtedly the medical facts which intrigued Dr. Dutton so much, for he had specialised in the study of women's diseases, and he was interested to discover the reason for the murderer's wanton surgical experiments.

Like many others of that day, including the late Dr. Forbes Winslow, Dr. Dutton endeavoured to find an answer to the question "Who could have done these terrible things?"

Many theories have been presented and demolished one by one. There is no theory which has yet been put forward which fits in with all the facts.

That it was a person – most likely a man with surgical knowledge – is certain. But who?

In the first edition of his book *The Identity of Jack the Ripper*, McCormick did not explain how he obtained his information on Dr Dutton. He did not state whether or not he had met the doctor, nor did he explain how he could quote the writings of Dutton so extensively. However, a new era of Ripper research and interest was approaching and in 1965 two new books appeared on the subject: *Autumn of Terror* by Tom Cullen (Bodley Head), and *Jack the Ripper In Fact and Fiction* by Robin Odell (Harrap). Both examined the correspondence of 'Jack the Ripper' at some length and quoted McCormick on Dr Dutton. The doctor and his 'diaries' or *Chronicles of Crime* had become established in Ripper lore.

At this time the crime author Colin Wilson was also taking an interest in the 'Ripper' and published both articles and books on the crimes. Wilson was the first to raise doubts on the authenticity of Dr Dutton in his 1969 book, *A Casebook of Murder* (Leslie Frewin). Wilson states that McCormick:

> . . . buttresses his theory with many quotations from unpublished diaries and manuscripts of one Dr Thomas Dutton, but he offers no more evidence for the actual existence of Dr Dutton than Matters did for Dr Stanley. In fact Dr Dutton actually existed – Tom Cullen told me he had seen his obituary notice – but until his Chronicles of Crime are published it will be impossible to assess the reliability of any of his facts . . .

Wilson was, of course, correct and indicated the serious doubts over McCormick's transcriptions from the alleged writings of Dr Dutton. Now McCormick's source had been challenged, he was obliged to supply provenance for Dutton's words. In the 1970 edition of *The Identity of Jack the Ripper* (John Long), describing Wilson as 'an imaginative writer with almost telepathic gifts as an amateur detective', McCormick embarked on a defence of his writings:

> . . . But my case rests not so much on Le Queux as on Dr. Dutton, Prince Belloselski and other sources . . . Colin Wilson claims that I offer 'no more evidence for the actual existence of Dr. Dutton than Matters did for Dr. Stanley', though he admits that Dr. Dutton actually existed.
>
> Well this time I will offer some evidence for Dr. Dutton's existence. His biographical details will be found in various editions of the *Medical Directory* and the *Medical Register*. These will show he lived in Bayswater in 1888–9 and that his last days were spent at Shepherd's Bush. I, too, fervently wish that Dr. Dutton's chronicles of his crime researches had been preserved for posterity. He allowed me to take notes from them as long ago as 1932 and they covered a number of other interesting cases. By a lucky chance my notes were safely tucked away, forgotten and then rediscovered after World War II.

To bolster his claims McCormick then went on to cite the *Sunday Chronicle* story of 1935 quoted above. This was artful of McCormick: he provided evidence for the undisputed existence of Dutton, but signally failed to offer any proof for the existence of the Dutton chronicles other than his own providentially preserved notes allegedly made from the said documents. He then went on to quote a further passage from the errant chronicles concerning alleged police interest in a murderous Russian surgeon named Konovalov – this in order to support his own claimed suspect a Russian named Dr Alexander Pedachenko. This is a most unsatisfactory and unfortunate situation. It means that there is a total lack of evidence for the existence of the Dutton chronicles, other than McCormick and the 1935 reports of the death of Dr Dutton.

And what of those 1935 newspaper reports? At that time McCormick was a young reporter, and claims to have met Dutton just three years before his death. Could McCormick actually have been responsible for the 1935 Ripper–Dutton connection? In 1995 author Paul Feldman undertook research into Dr Dutton and the elusive *Chronicles of Crime*. He made contact with McCormick who stated he was unable to help with any information other than that contained in the two editions of his book. McCormick added:

> . . . I either disposed of, or destroyed my various notes and cuttings on the subject a long time ago and memory does help with such items as Dr. Dutton, *whose story I reported in the*

press nearly 60 years ago [author's italics]. I was put on to the Dutton story by a mortuary keeper and that is literally all I can recall. [Letter of 5 May 1995]

1. Between 1935 and 1938 I ran a new agency entitled London & Provincial News from an office in Broadway Chambers, Ludgate Hill. Through this agency my story was put out. I cannot be sure, but I am certain that one of the papers which published it was the Sunday Chronicle, as I also free-lanced for them and did Saturday duties in their office at Kemsley House during that period. I should say the actual date was between September, 1935 and December, 1936.
2. I knew mortuary keepers at Westminster, Paddington and Hammersmith in this period. I should say the keeper in question was at either Paddington or Hammersmith.

It would seem that in some way Hermione Dudley has confirmed my story, but I cannot recollect any more details and, as I have told you, all my records have now gone . . . [Letter of 15 May 1995]

It would appear that probably even the 'corroborative' stories on Dutton's death in the 1935 newspapers were written by McCormick himself. At that time popular, newsy tales involving the 'Jack the Ripper' story were often found in the press.

Both authors advise strict caution when dealing with the writings of Donald McCormick. What is certain, though, is the fact that Dr Dutton and his alleged writings on the correspondence of 'Jack the Ripper' have become an established part of the legend. The full truth will never be known for, sadly, Donald McCormick died in hospital after a stomach operation on Saturday 3 January 1998, taking his secrets with him.

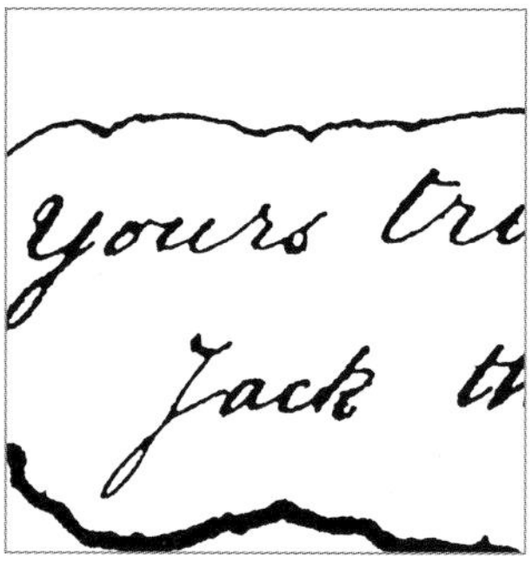

— SEVENTEEN —

'I'm Jack'

IN 1896 all thought of 'Jack the Ripper' and the fraught years of the Whitechapel murders must have been far from the minds of those at New Scotland Yard, the impressive Norman Shaw-designed building on the Embankment. It was four years since anything had been added to the files, and, although still open as an unsolved case, the only recent mention of the murders had been press speculation. However, two veterans of the Ripper hunt were still very much at work with the CID at Central Office. One was Donald Sutherland Swanson, by now a superintendent, who had been the chief inspector in charge of the investigation. The other was the experienced Henry Moore, now a chief inspector, who as a detective inspector had joined Inspector Abberline in the investigation at Whitechapel in September 1888. When Abberline left the Ripper case in the first half of 1889, Moore had assumed control of the East End investigations.

It must, then, have come as something of a surprise when another 'Jack the Ripper' letter was received in the post by the police of H, Whitechapel Division on 14 October 1896. It read:

> Dear Boss,
>
> You will be surprised to find that this comes from yours as of old Jack-the-Ripper. Ha. Ha. If my old friend Mr Warren is dead you can read it. you might remember me if you try and think a little Ha Ha. The last job was a bad one and no mistake nearly buckled, and meant it to be best of the lot curse it, Ha Ha Im alive yet and you'll soon find it out. I mean to go on again when I get the chance wont it be nice dear old Boss to have the good old times once again. you never caught me and you never will. Ha Ha
> [second page] you police are a smart lot, the lot of you could nt catch one man Where have I

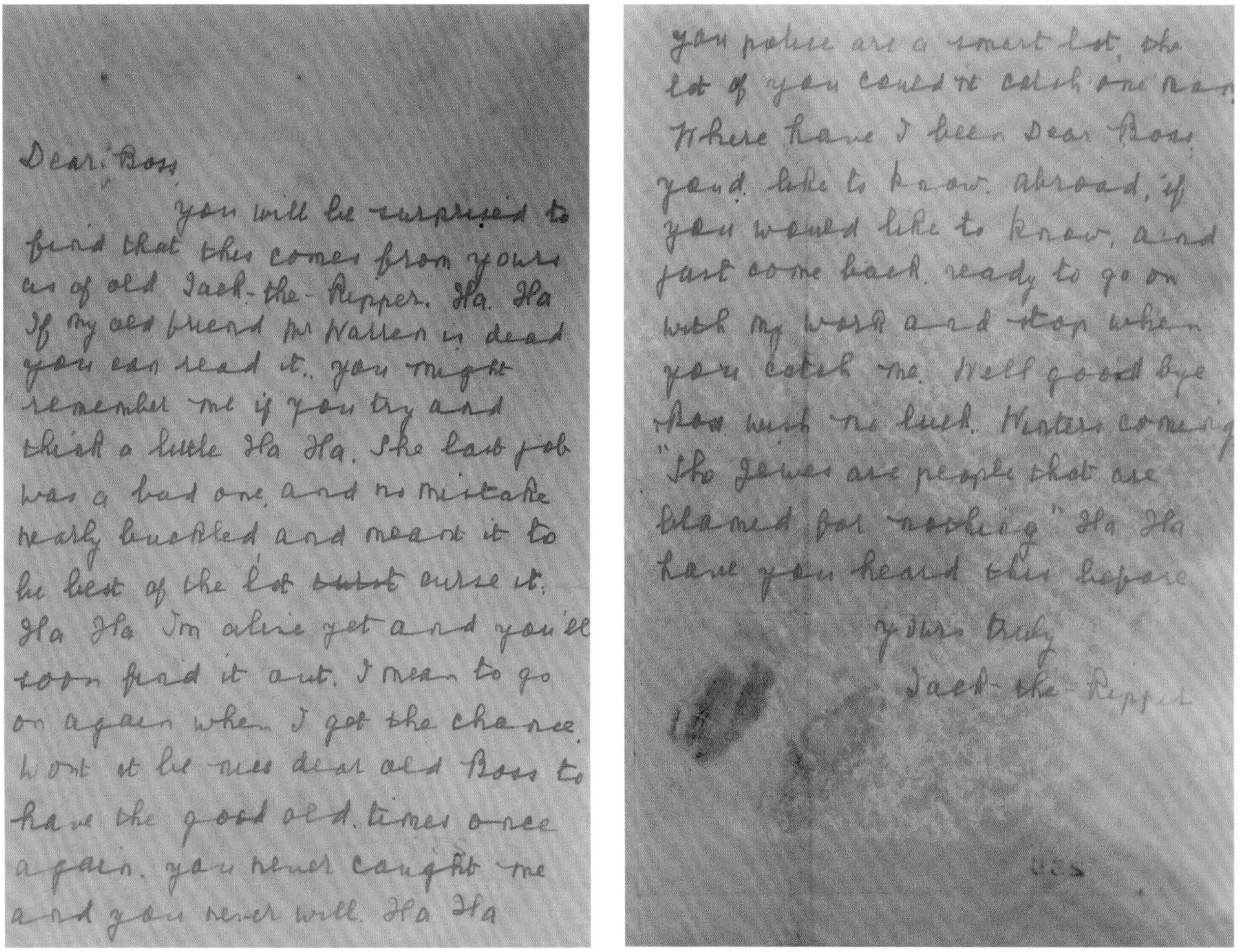
Dear Boss
you will be surprised to find that this comes from yours as of old Jack-the-Ripper. Ha Ha If my old friend Mr Warren is dead you can read it. you might remember me if you try and think a little Ha Ha. The last job was a bad one, and no mistake nearly buckled and meant it to be best of the lot curse it. Ha Ha Im alive yet and you'll soon find it out. I mean to go on again when I get the chance. wont it be nice dear old Boss to have the good old times once again. you never caught me and you never will. Ha Ha

you police are a smart lot, the lot of you could nt catch one man Where have I been Dear Boss you d like to know. abroad, if you would like to know, and just come back. ready to go on with my work and stop when you catch me. Well good bye Boss wish me luck. Winters coming "The Jewes are people that are blamed for nothing" Ha Ha have you heard this before
yours truly
Jack-the-Ripper

The last 'Jack the Ripper' letter in the official files. It was received on 14 October 1896 and begins 'Dear Boss'.

> been Dear Boss you d like to know, abroad, if you would like to know, and just come back. ready to go on with my work and stop when you catch me. Well good bye Boss wish me luck. Winters coming
>
> "The Jewes are the people that are blamed for nothing" Ha Ha have you heard this before
>
> Yours truly
>
> Jack the Ripper

Detective Inspector Payne of H Division was the first to deal with this letter and he immediately gave instructions to his men 'to keep a sharp lookout'. Acting Superintendent Cross, presumably fearing the letter might be genuine, 'caused a telegram to be sent to surrounding Divisions . . . asking that directions be given to police to keep a sharp look out, but at the same time to keep the information quiet'. His strong belief seems to have been that it was probably a hoax; he added: 'Writer in sending the letter no doubt considers it a great joke at the expense of police.'

The report was forwarded to New Scotland Yard with the suggestion that the letter was in different handwriting to the original 'Dear Boss' communication but that a comparison should be made. There Superintendent Swanson examined the new letter and had Chief Inspector Moore submit a report on 18 October. It was immediately felt that the decision to circulate the information to surrounding stations had not been the correct one. Moore's observations make interesting reading:

> . . . having carefully perused all the old "Jack the Ripper" letters, and fail to find any similarity of handwriting in any of them, with the exception of the two well remembered communications which were sent to the "Central News" office; one a letter, dated 25th Septr./88 and the other a post-card bearing the post-mark 1st Oct./88., vide copies herewith.
>
> On comparing the handwriting of the present letter with handwriting of that document, I find many similarities in the formation of letters. For instance the y's, t's, and w's are very much the same. Then there are several words which appear in both documents; Viz: – Dear Boss; ha ha (although in the present letter the capital H. is used instead of the small one); and in speaking of the murders he describes them as his "work" or the last "job"; and if I get a (or the) chance; then there are the words "Yours truly" and the Ripper (the latter on post-card) are very much alike. Besides there are the finger smears.
>
> Considering the lapse of time, it would be interesting to know how the present writer was able to use the words – "The Jewes are people that are blamed for nothing" [Here there is a marginal note by Swanson 'Were not the exact words "The Jewes are not the men to be blamed for nothing"?']; as it will be remembered that they are practically the same words that were written in chalk, undoubtedly by the murderer, on the wall at Goulston St., Whitechapel, on the night of 30th. Sept., 1888, after the murders of Mrs. Stride and Mrs. Eddows; and the word Jews was spelt on that occasion precisely as it is now.
>
> Although these similarities strangely exist between the documents, I am of opinion that the present writer is not the original correspondent who prepared the letters to the Central News; as if it had been I should have thought he would have again addressed it to the same Press Agency; and not to Commercial Street Police Station.
>
> In conclusion I beg to observe that I do not attach any importance to this communication.
>
> Henry Moore, Chf Inspr.

The report was read by Swanson who marked Moore's last sentence with an 'A' and wrote, 'In my opinion the handwritings are not the same. I agree as at A. I beg that the letter may be put with other similar letters. Its circulation is to be regretted.' And there this letter remains to this day.

This is a most interesting incident because of the police comments it attracted. It would appear that Moore had decided that the words on the wall in Goulston Street were actually written by the murderer. However, this was by no means the consensus of police opinion and should not be accepted as such. As in most instances, opinion was divided. The verification of the piece of bloody apron as being from Eddowes and the fact that it was found beneath the graffiti was enough to persuade some, but the status of the wall writing was never decided with certainty.

This letter and the report on it are the last documents to be included in any official file on the mystery of the Whitechapel murders.

It must be obvious to all reading the fascinating correspondence published here for the first time that the murderer very quickly became established in the minds of many as a lone crusader fighting against vice and the forces of law and order. In this sense he acquired the guise of an avenger with mysterious powers of invisibility and incredible luck. He was also a means to taunt the police and the government of the day – both were hated in some quarters – and to use his name as a threat to others who would regard the receipt of a letter from 'Jack the Ripper' with the greatest trepidation. The persona projected through some of the letters into the press of the day ironically gave him a mythical, folk anti-hero status that has endured through the years. Reading only of the crimes in the newspapers, those far removed from the mean streets of the East End were able to absorb details about the hideous crimes with a clinical detachment. They saw them almost as a Grimm's fairy tale, to be enjoyed before going to bed; something to read about with a delightful shudder of fear, an enjoyable *frisson*. Today's tourists may regard the crimes in much the same way when conducted around the East End of London to see the places where the crimes were actually committed, while they enjoy the bloodcurdling commentary of their guides.

Reynolds News of 9 January 1949 carried a report which reveals the perennial interest in 'Jack the Ripper' and his writings. In an article headed 'THIS MAN SAYS: "I AM JACK THE RIPPER"' the newspaper's crime reporter wrote that Scotland Yard had been given two letters received from a man who claimed to be 'Jack the Ripper'. These letters had been written to the manager of the Torch Theatre in London, where a play by Claude Purkiss based on the life of the Ripper was being presented. They were posted in Notting Hill but did not include a sender's address. The writer disagreed with Purkiss's theory that 'Jack the Ripper' was a doctor. 'What a hope,' wrote the anonymous scribe. 'Horse doctor more like it.' The handwriting was shaky and the writer claimed to be eighty-four

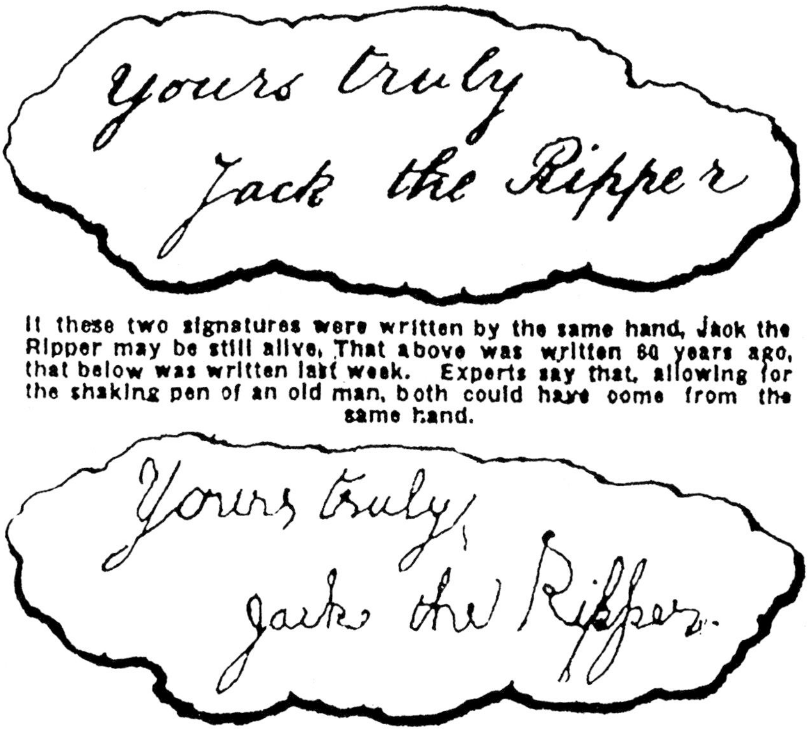

Signatures of 'Jack the Ripper' which appeared in *Reynolds News* of 9 January 1949 when an anonymous person wrote in claiming to be 'Jack the Ripper'.

years old – in 1888 he would have been twenty-two. In the first letter he said that his eyes were as good as they had been and, '. . . whenever I read about myself I have a good laugh, ha ha'. He added that he would like to visit the theatre to see himself, but 'perhaps it wouldn't be wise'. The letter concluded: 'What chances of catching me now?'

In the second letter he boasted about the murders and continued: 'I done another two after, one in 1912 and one in 1916.' This time he concluded: 'Well, all the best, Sir. Here's hoping for 1949. Yours truly, Jack the Ripper.' The *Reynolds News* reporter took one of the documents to Madame Tussaud's where facsimiles of the original 'Dear Boss' letter and postcard in the form of the Metropolitan Police poster were on display in the Chamber of Horrors. The reporter concluded that though the original hand was 'firm and youthful' there were still 'strong similarities' to be seen in the current specimen. His article carried an illustration of the original 'Yours truly, Jack the Ripper' phrase and the same words from the new letter. After comparing the general style and certain characters he decided it was: '. . . possible that the letters were written by the same hand, allowing for the changes that 60 years can bring about . . . "Yours truly" has hardly changed at all, apart from shakiness in the 1949 version, though the signature is a little different.'

Other similarities noted by the *Reynolds News* man were 'a fancy capital "H"' and the phrase 'ha ha', which appeared twice in the old letter and once in the new. The enterprising journalist consulted a handwriting expert who said: 'Allowing for the sixty years there are striking similarities which could make these letters the work of the same man. But I would have to spend days with the original letters before a positive answer could be given.' It is worth noting that many people over the years have simply assumed that the original Central News Agency correspondence was actually written by the murderer. The main reason for this, as we have seen, must be the fact that the Metropolitan Police took the letter and postcard so seriously, which led them to issue the famous poster.

Such is the influence of the Ripper phenomenon that clear echoes of it were seen during the killings by Peter Sutcliffe, the Yorkshire Ripper, between 1975 and 1980. In March 1978 a letter, allegedly from the murderer, was received by the police and another was sent to the editor of the Manchester *Daily Mirror*. The echoes of 1888 were loud and clear. A year later a third letter was sent which was believed to be genuine. It was not. In June 1979 a cassette tape was received by Assistant Chief Constable George Oldfield, who was heading the inquiry into the murders. The taped message purported to come from the killer and began: 'I'm Jack. I see you are still having no luck catching me. I have the greatest respect for you George, but Lord, you are no nearer catching me now than when I started four years ago. I reckon your boys are letting you down George . . .'. There were other phrases similar to those used in the 1888 'Jack the Ripper' communications: 'I warned you in March that I would strike again . . . I'm not sure when I will strike again, but it will definitely be some time this year, maybe September or October, even sooner if I get the chance . . . Yours Jack the Ripper.' The tape had not come from Sutcliffe, but unfortunately Oldfield thought it was genuine. Police inquiries and suspicion shifted. Theories about the identity of the unknown killer moved in the wrong direction – to Wearside instead of Yorkshire. Other murders were committed and it was not until January 1981 that Sutcliffe was arrested in Sheffield. The hoax communications had led the police astray. The hoaxer(s), it would seem, were well versed in the original 'Jack the Ripper' communications and had been influenced by them.

It should now be apparent that the true identity of 'Jack the Ripper', or more correctly the Whitechapel murderer(s), will probably never be known. But some readers may feel that the inventor of 'Jack the Ripper' has now been identified with a degree of certainty.

It is difficult to give an exact figure of how many communications purporting to come from the killer were received. The *Illustrated Police News* of 20 October 1888 commented that upwards of 700 letters had been inquired into by the police, but this figure, of course, would have included suggestions as to the identity of the killer and ideas for capturing him. We have presented here all the letters that were 'signed' by the Ripper and are now preserved in the official files, along with one that is in private hands. Possibly there were dozens more sent to individuals, newspapers and other organisations that were not forwarded to the police, certainly in the provinces. The total probably did not exceed 300 (including the ones on file), although this is very much an informed guess. There may yet be some in circulation and still to come to light.

Did the bloody hand of the actual murderer ever pause, holding his pen, while his troubled mind sought the words to put his thoughts onto paper? Was he literate, intelligent and capable of writing some, any, of the letters we have seen? Did he ever read the words of a 'Jack the Ripper' letter in a newspaper? The questions still hover. The search for new material continues.

The Whitechapel murders of 1888–91 are historical fact. 'Jack the Ripper' is an altogether more intangible entity. It may even be perfectly reasonable and accurate to describe him as literally a press creation. He can be whoever you want him to be. Historians, writers and theorists have inherited the rich legacy of this material in their search to evaluate the killer's motives, to form a profile of his psychology, in short, to build their own 'Jack the Ripper'.

— EIGHTEEN —

Suspects

IN this chapter the term handwriting analysis denotes the forensic comparison of specimens of handwriting to determine whether they were written by the same person. (We do not mean graphology.) Such scientific examination cannot determine the age, sex, or character of the writer and because of the legal implications of such examination, it should only be made by experts accredited in the field. Even then, the result is an expert opinion, and experts are renowned for disagreeing with each other. The subject letter, i.e. the one allegedly written by the murderer in this case, is referred to as 'the questioned document'. The sample of handwriting of known authorship, for comparison, is always referred to as 'specimen handwriting' of the suspect. Such letters and samples, legally, are subject to very strict controls, and only original specimens are acceptable. The dating of such samples is also very important because although the handwriting of a healthy adult may not change much over the years, that of adolescents, or elderly people who are fatally ill, alters materially over short intervals of time. The analysis should contain the comparison of like with like, meaning that cursive, script or block lettering should be compared only with that in the same style. Legally the samples should even be matched in the type and size of paper, and ruling (if any). If possible, the writing instrument should also be similar. For a proper comparison the specimen handwriting should contain all the letters, letter combinations, and figures that appear in the questioned document. Photocopies should never be used for these comparisons.

Finally it should be noted that any writer of 'Jack the Ripper' letters could, and probably did, disguise his normal style of writing. A person's customary, flowing and rapid style can easily be changed by writing carefully and slowly in a script, or school-taught, style such as the 'Dear Boss' letter exhibits, or in a rough scrawling style like the 'From hell' correspondence. This method of disguise can easily be maintained for a whole missive, often with deliberate changes to the structure of the combination of letters or letter groups.

From the paragraphs above it should be obvious that any analysis of letters allegedly written by the Whitechapel murderer of 1888, or 'Jack the Ripper', is going to fall woefully short of the high legal standards required to give such analysis any validity. It is also highly doubtful that any of the letters were actually written by the killer. Ripper authors have often made a case for certain correspondence having been written by the killer himself, usually the original 'Dear Boss' missive or the Lusk 'From hell' letter, and then to use this to bolster their own theory or named suspect. Such 'analysis' is valueless, and the best that may be claimed is that certain similarities exist from which any individual may draw their own conclusions or ideas. To select one or more of the letters as genuine and then to work on from that premise is fraught with danger. Other authors feel that if none of the letters is genuine, what are we left with as a means to identify the character or motives of the killer?

To make any comparison of a letter with the hand of a named suspect we need samples of that suspect's handwriting, and, in certain cases, such handwriting has survived. The following suspects have been selected because their names were linked contemporaneously or near-contemporaneously with the crimes. It should be noted that no hard evidence exists to connect any suspect with the murders.

Montague John Druitt

Druitt was thirty-one years of age in 1888. He was the barrister and teacher named by Chief Constable Melville Macnaghten in his memoranda of 23 February 1894 as one of three suspects the police had identified (the other two being Kosminski, a Polish Jew, and Michael Ostrog, 'a Russian doctor, and a convict'). Druitt committed suicide by drowning in the Thames. His body was discovered floating off Thorneycroft's Wharf, Chiswick on 31 December 1888 having been in the water upwards of a month. Macnaghten stated that Druitt was 'sexually insane and from private inf. I have little doubt but that his own family believed him to have been the murderer'. Unfortunately, Macnaghten made some rather basic errors in his report and his sources were not disclosed. There is a letter written by Druitt to his uncle preserved in the Sussex Record Office. No examples of Kosminski's or Ostrog's handwriting have been located.

Montague John Druitt, a barrister who was found drowned in the Thames at the end of December 1888. He was named by Melville Macnaghten in his report of February 1894.

Dr Druitt.
8 Strathmore Gardens
Kensington Mall
London

WIMBORNE C 16 SP 76

Letter written by suspect Montague Druitt, preserved in the West Sussex Record Office. This letter is dated September 1876 and was posted in Wimborne from the Druitt family home. (Druitt MS.12.f. 27)

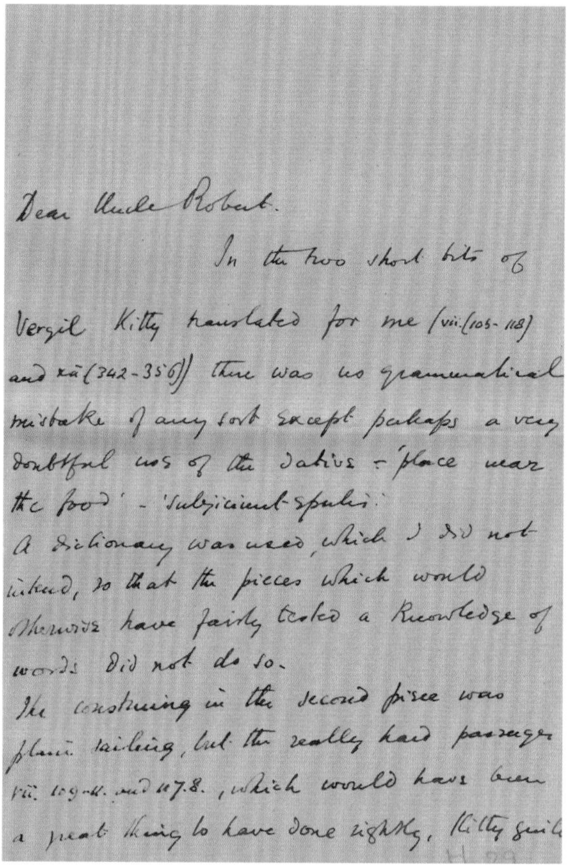
Dear Uncle Robert.

In the two short bits of Vergil Kitty translated for me (vii.(105-118) and xii(342-356)) there was no grammatical mistake of any sort except perhaps a very doubtful use of the dative – 'place near the food' – 'subjiciunt epulis'.

A dictionary was used, which I did not intend, so that the pieces which would otherwise have fairly tested a knowledge of words did not do so.

The construing in the second piece was plain sailing, but the really hard passages vii. 109-11. and 117.8., which would have been a great thing to have done rightly, Kitty quite

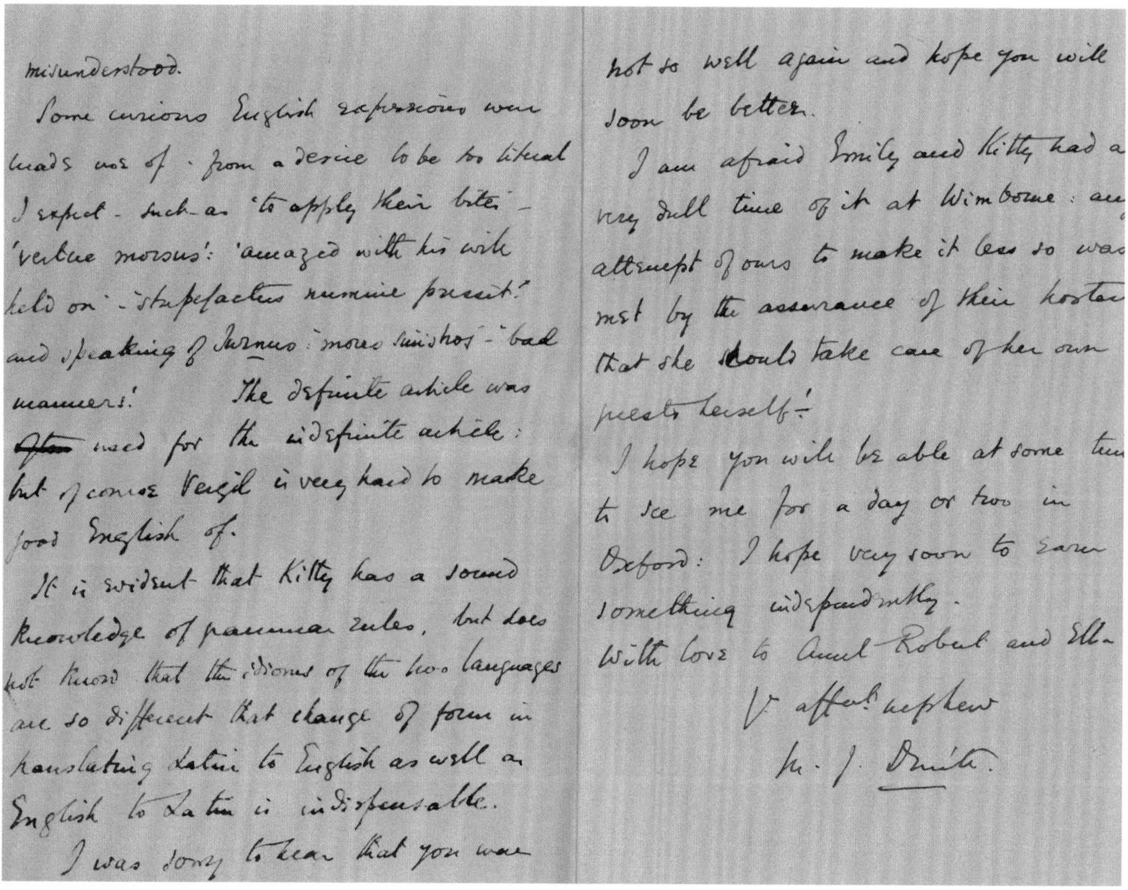
misunderstood.

Some curious English expressions were made use of – from a desire to be too literal I expect – such as 'to apply their bites' – 'vertere morsus': 'amazed with his will held on' – 'stupefactus numine pressit.' and speaking of Turnus 'mores sinistros' – 'bad manners'. The definite article was ~~often~~ used for the indefinite article: but of course Vergil is very hard to make good English of.

It is evident that Kitty has a sound knowledge of grammar rules, but does not know that the idioms of the two languages are so different that change of form in translating Latin to English as well as English to Latin is indispensable.

I was sorry to hear that you were not so well again and hope you will soon be better.

I am afraid Emily and Kitty had a very dull time of it at Wimborne: any attempt of ours to make it less so was met by the assurance of their hostess that she should take care of her own guests herself!

I hope you will be able at some time to see me for a day or two in Oxford: I hope very soon to earn something independently.

With love to Aunt Robert and Ella

Yr affect. nephew

M. J. Druitt.

FRANCIS J. TUMBLETY

Tumblety, fifty-five years of age in 1888, was the wealthy quack Irish-American doctor named by ex-Chief Inspector John George Littlechild of the Special Branch in a letter of 23 September 1913 to George R. Sims as being 'amongst the suspects, and to my mind a very likely one'. History tells us that Tumblety, a practising homosexual, although probably bi-sexual, was arrested for gross indecency on 7 November 1888. The offences, there were finally four of them, were misdemeanours and Tumblety was probably granted police bail. He appeared before the Marlborough Street Magistrate on 16 November 1888 and managed to gain bail under a large surety. While on bail he fled back to the USA where he was pursued to New York by Inspector Walter Andrews of Scotland Yard. Andrews failed to locate Tumblety and returned to England empty-handed in early 1889. Tumblety died in 1903 of heart disease. His letter was written in 1875 to the Manx novelist Hall Caine with whom he was having a relationship at the time. Other letters written by Tumblety survive, deposited in the Manx Museum.

American suspect Dr Francis Tumblety who was named in 1913 by Chief Inspector Littlechild of the Special Branch as 'a very likely one'.

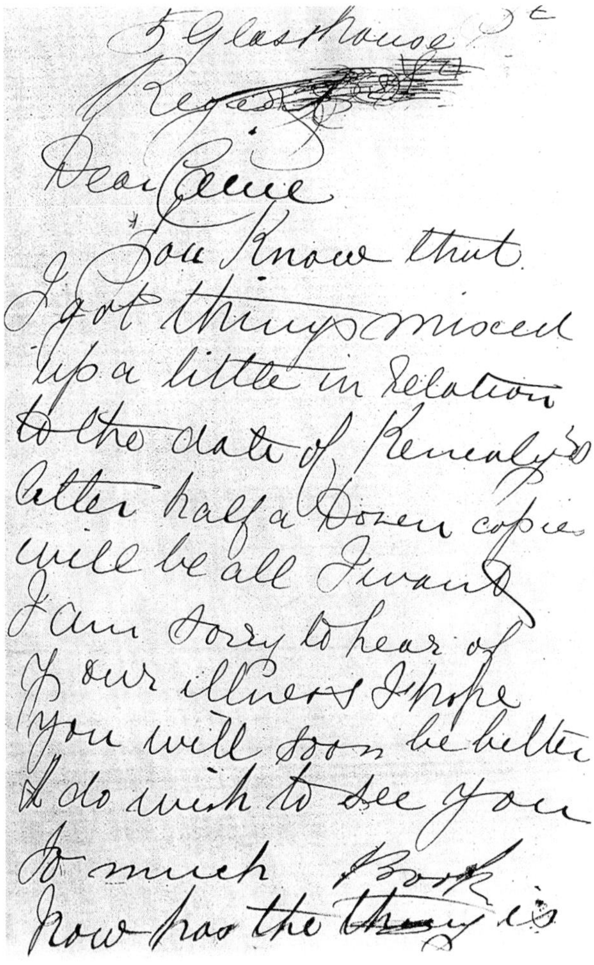

5 Glasshouse St
Regent St

Dear Caine
You know that
I got things mixed
up a little in relation
to the date of Kenealy's
letter half a Dozen copies
will be all I want
I am sorry to hear of
your illness I hope
you will soon be better
I do wish to see you
so much Book
how has the thing is

A sample of Dr Francis Tumblety's handwriting.

Ripper suspect Robert Donston Stephenson was a patient at the London Hospital in autumn 1888. (Phototograph courtesy of Melvin Harris)

ROBERT DONSTON STEPHENSON

Stephenson, also known as Roslyn D'O. Stephenson, forty-nine years old in 1888 and hailing from Hull, was a suspect who injected himself into the police inquiry. At the time of the murders in 1888 Stephenson was a patient in the London Hospital, Whitechapel Road, and he took a keen interest in the murders. He developed a theory on the Goulston Street wall writing which he communicated to the City of London Police. He also wrote an article on his theory about the murders and the wall writing for W.T. Stead's *Pall Mall Gazette* and it appeared on Saturday 1 December 1888 on pages 1 and 2. Further developing his idea that the murderer might be Dr Morgan Davies of the London Hospital he established contact with 'a pseudo-detective named George Marsh, of 24, Pratt St., Camden Town, N.W.' while in the Prince Albert pub, Upper St Martin's Lane. It appears to have been an ill-starred relationship. For Marsh then contacted the police on Christmas Eve and told Inspector Roots that he believed the Ripper was none other than his partner in detection, Stephenson, who was then resident in a common lodging house at 29 Castle Street, St Martin's Lane. Roots had known Stephenson for twenty years and was aware that he was 'a travelled man of education and ability, a doctor of medicine upon diplomas of Paris & New York: a major from the Italian Army – he fought under Garibaldi: and a newspaper writer'. Roots also noted that: 'He has led a Bohemian life, drinks very heavily, and always carries drugs to sober him and stave off delirium tremens.' Stephenson himself went to see Inspector Roots on Boxing Day and wrote a statement regarding his suspicions about Dr Davies. It appears that the police never entertained any serious suspicions against either Dr Davies or Stephenson. It is not known when Stephenson died. A letter written by D'O. Stephenson (Robert Donston Stephenson) survives in the City of London Records Office collection at the Guildhall (CLRO Police Box 3.23, No. 390).

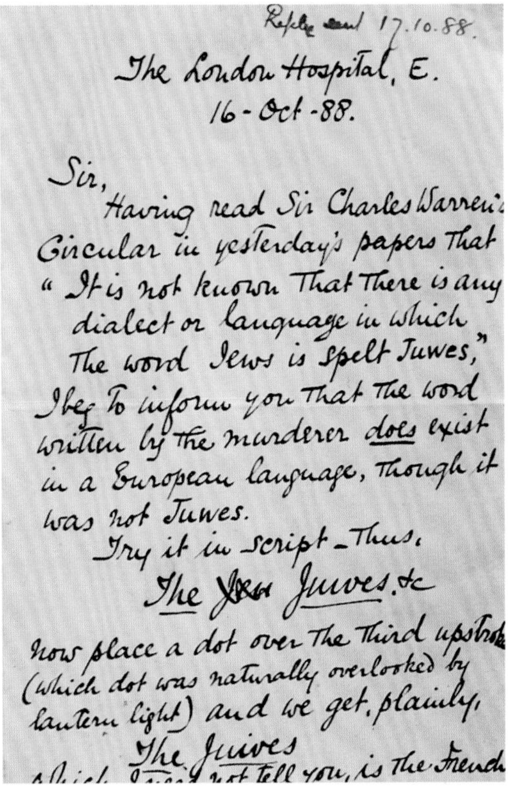

Reply sent 17.10.88.

The London Hospital, E.
16 - Oct - 88.

Sir,
Having read Sir Charles Warren's Circular in yesterday's papers that "It is not known that there is any dialect or language in which the word Jews is spelt Juwes," I beg to inform you that the word written by the murderer does exist in a European language, though it was not Juwes.

Try it in script – thus.

The ~~Jews~~ Juwes &c

now place a dot over the third upstroke (which dot was naturally overlooked by lantern light) and we get, plainly,

The Juives

which I need not tell you, is the French

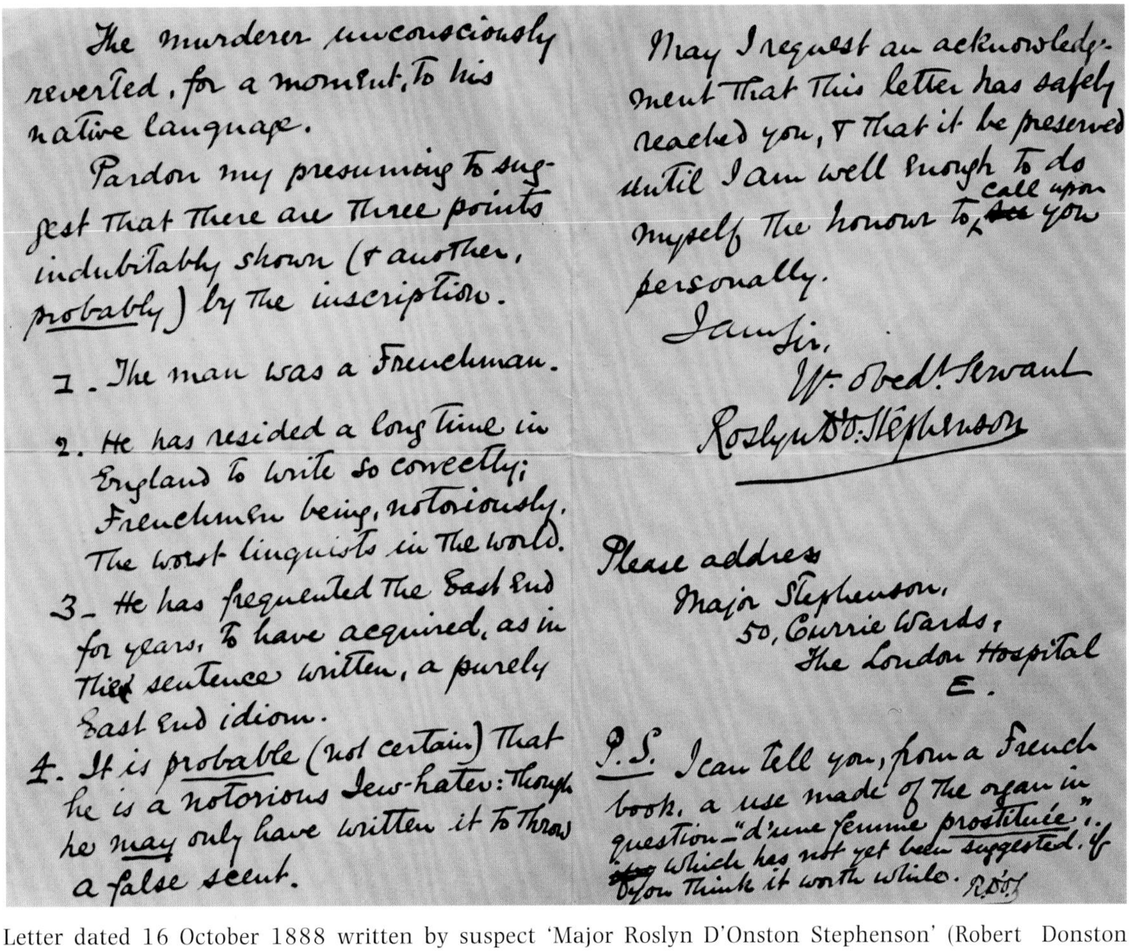

The murderer unconsciously reverted, for a moment, to his native language.

Pardon my presuming to suggest that there are three points indubitably shown (& another, probably) by the inscription.

1. The man was a Frenchman.
2. He has resided a long time in England to write so correctly; Frenchmen being, notoriously, the worst linguists in the world.
3. He has frequented the East End for years, to have acquired, as in the ~~this~~ sentence written, a purely East End idiom.
4. It is probable (not certain) that he is a notorious Jew-hater: though he may only have written it to throw a false scent.

May I request an acknowledgement that this letter has safely reached you, & that it be preserved until I am well enough to do myself the honour to call upon ~~see~~ you personally.

I am Sir,
Yr. obedt. servant
Roslyn D'O. Stephenson

Please address
Major Stephenson,
50, Currie Wards,
The London Hospital
E.

P.S. I can tell you, from a French book, a use made of the organ in question – "d'une femme prostituée", which has not yet been suggested, if you think it worth while. R.D'O.

Letter dated 16 October 1888 written by suspect 'Major Roslyn D'Onston Stephenson' (Robert Donston Stephenson) from the London Hospital where he was a patient.

NIKANER BENELIUS

Benelius was twenty-seven in 1888, a Swedish traveller, who apparently had come to England from America. It would appear he was briefly suspected in connection with the murder of Elizabeth Stride who was of the same nationality. Benelius wrote two letters to the Lord Mayor of London, on 4 and 18 October 1888. The first is a strange document, addressed from 20 Aldgate Street, EC, requesting the Mayor to: 'please inform the young Miss Wilkinson to be in the city to morrow evening. I am pleasantly inform that this is in your power. Be as kind and do it as soon as possible, otherwise let me meet with another lady at the same cathedral.' It would appear that the letter received a reply for Benelius sent the second thanking the Mayor effusively for his reply and stating that:

> I should be very glad to make your personal acquaintance or get introduced in your family circle or any other respectable circ. Then first I would come in my right sphere. During the mean-time I could pursue something. If you know that I have lost something or am about to lose by all means help me. I do and can not fall down because I have tried to get as high moral standing as possible.
>
> Hoping that I very soon will have a kind answer from you.
>
> I am,
> Yours truly,
> N.A. Benelius,
> 19 Goswell Road.

By now the alarm bells were ringing in the Mayor's office, and the letters were sent to Major Smith at the City of London Police Office. On the morning of Saturday 17 November 1888 Benelius was arrested for entering a dwelling house in Buxton Street, Mile End, the home of Harriet Rowe, a married woman, where he confronted the poor woman and grinned at her. She was frightened and ran to the window to get help, at which he fled. Mrs Rowe followed and found Benelius talking with PC 211H Imhoff outside. He gave his address as lodgings at 90 Great Eastern Street and was brought before the Worship Street Magistrates' Court the same day. Detective Sergeant Dew appeared in court and told the magistrate that Benelius' detention had been made under circumstances that required the fullest investigation and that he had previously been questioned in connection with the Berner Street murder. It was stated that his behaviour had been strange and he had been preaching in the streets at times. He was described in *The Times* on Monday 19 November as 'of decidedly foreign appearance, with a moustache, but otherwise cannot be said to resemble any of the published descriptions of men suspected in connection with the Whitechapel murders'. He was detained for further inquiries. The *Star* of the same date reported that full inquiries had been made into the movements of Benelius and Inspector Reid stated that the man's innocence of any hand in the murders had been fully established. It was said that: 'He was arrested on suspicion in connection with the Berners-street [*sic*] murder, and is likely to be arrested every time the public attention is strained to the point of suspecting every man of odd behaviour.' Benelius was duly released free of any suspicion of complicity in the murders, but he certainly was a very strange character. The City branch of the Charity Organisation

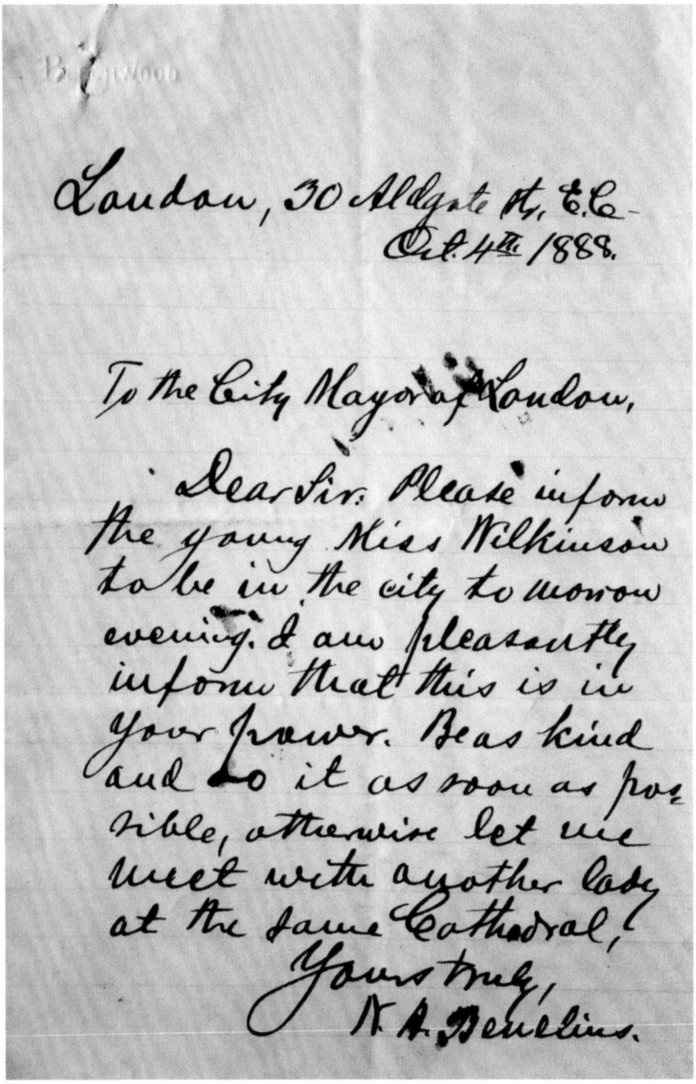

London, 30 Aldgate St, E.C.
Oct. 4th 1888.

To the City Mayor of London,

Dear Sir: Please inform the young Miss Wilkinson to be in the city to morow evening. I am pleasantly inform that this is in your power. Be as kind and do it as soon as possible, otherwise let me meet with another lady at the same Cathedral!

Yours truly,
N. A. Benelius.

Letter dated 4 October 1888 written by Nikaner Benelius to the Mayor of London and forwarded to the City Police.

Society said that it would send him back to America (*Daily Telegraph*, 24 November 1888). Both letters are lodged in the City of London Police files preserved at the CLRO (Police Box 3.19, Nos 241 a–b (including envelope) and 242), among the 'Ripper'-related letters.

William Henry Bury

Twenty-nine-year-old Bury was a resident of Bow in 1888. He had married Ellen Elliott, a known prostitute, in April 1888, and the couple lived in the East End until they moved to Dundee in January 1889. Bury went to the Dundee police on 10 February 1889 stating that his wife had committed suicide. However, investigations revealed that he had murdered her by strangling her with a rope and had then stabbed the body with a knife and stuffed it in a trunk. Chalked on the door of the tenement where the Burys' flat was located were the words 'Jack the Ripper is at the back of this door'. On the stairway wall leading down to the basement were chalked the words 'Jack the Ripper is in this seller'. Deep abdominal cuts were found on the body and the other facts about Bury led to a suspicion that he may have been involved in the Whitechapel murders. He was found guilty of the murder of his wife and Scotland Yard detectives travelled to Dundee to investigate the possible Whitechapel connection. Despite questioning, including a plea for

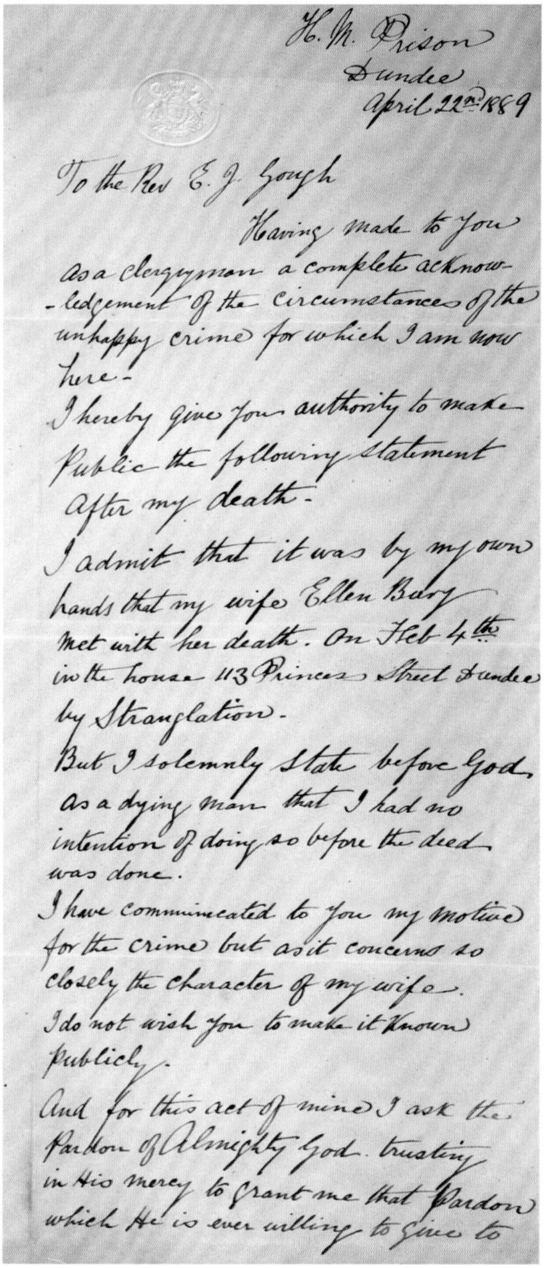

H. M. Prison
Dundee
April 22nd 1889

To the Rev E. J. Gough

Having made to you as a clergyman a complete acknowledgement of the circumstances of the unhappy crime for which I am now here –

I hereby give you authority to make Public the following statement after my death –

I admit that it was by my own hands that my wife Ellen Bury met with her death. On Feb 4th in the house 113 Princes Street Dundee by Strangulation.

But I solemnly state before God, as a dying man that I had no intention of doing so before the deed was done.

I have communicated to you my motive for the crime but as it concerns so closely the character of my wife I do not wish you to make it known publicly.

And for this act of mine I ask the Pardon of Almighty God. trusting in His mercy to grant me that Pardon which He is ever willing to give to

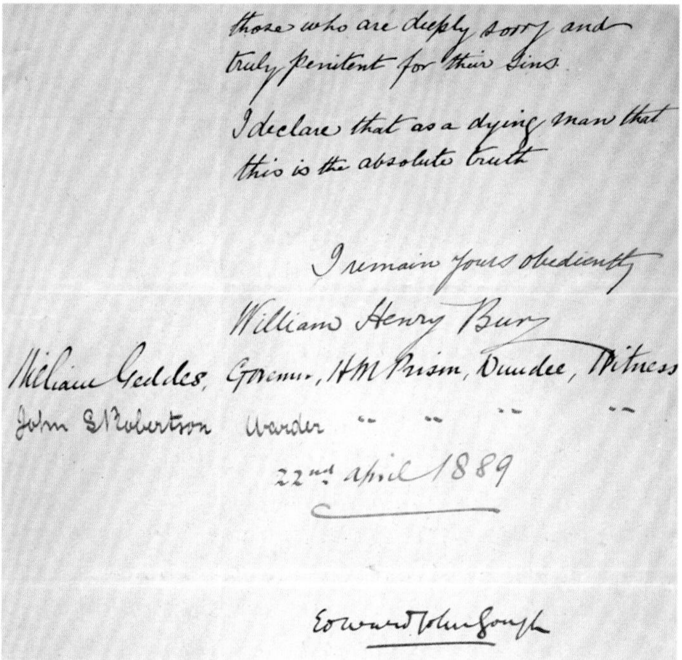

those who are deeply sorry and truly penitent for their Sins.

I declare that as a dying man that this is the absolute truth

I remain yours obediently
William Henry Bury

William Geddes, Governor, HM Prison, Dundee, Witness
John S Robertson Warder " " " "
22nd April 1889

Edward John Gough

Letter of 22 April 1889 written by suspect William Henry Bury from Dundee Prison. Hangman James Berry questioned him about the Whitechapel murders. (National Archives of Scotland)

Suspect William Henry Bury was executed at Dundee for the murder of his wife. He lived in the East End of London at the time of the Whitechapel murders.

a confession to the Whitechapel murders from the hangman James Berry, Bury failed to admit any connection with the London crimes. He was hanged on 24 April 1889.

Bury wrote a letter at Dundee Prison to the Reverend E.J. Gough in which he confessed the murder of his wife (*see* illustration above). The popular idea that Bury and 'Jack the Ripper' were one and the same person continued to be propounded by Berry. The Secretary for Scotland received a letter, dated 28 March 1908, from a student of the Ripper murders. Ernest A. Parr, a journalist from Newmarket, requested more information on this allegation and said: 'In the course of my inquiries I have several times come across details wch appear to point to this man as having committed the crimes, and during a conversation with Berry the ex-Public Executioner, that individual told me explicitly that Bury was known to have been Jack the Ripper.' A letter written by William Henry Bury survives in the Scottish Record Office.

THOMAS NEILL CREAM

Cream was thirty-eight in 1888. He was also serving a lengthy prison sentence for murder in the Illinois State Penitentiary, Joliet, at this time. This has not prevented him from being named as a 'Ripper' suspect. Indeed, there is much to commend him. He was a doctor, a serial killer of prostitutes, a peddler of pornography, and parallels with the 'Ripper' were noted after his arrest in London for the murder of four prostitutes in 1892. He was born in Glasgow on 27 May 1850 but emigrated with his family to Canada in 1854 or 1855. His father was a manager in the shipbuilding industry and was wealthy. In 1872 the young Cream entered McGill College, Montreal, to study medicine. He gained his MD diploma in March 1876. The same year he travelled to London where he studied until 1878 at St Thomas' Hospital. In 1879 he obtained the double qualification of the Royal College of Physicians and of Surgeons at Edinburgh. He returned to Canada, starting a practice in London, Ontario. It was at this time that he embarked on a career of murder, medical malpractice and other crimes, including illegal abortions. After a short while he moved to Chicago in the USA where he continued his shady career.

Cream was awarded a life sentence in 1881 for murdering a 61-year-old man named Daniel Stott with strychnine. Stott's wife, Julia, was attractive and only thirty-three years old; she had become Cream's mistress. Cream was not released from prison until July 1891, so he could not possibly have committed any of the Whitechapel murders, or could he? Various theorists have invented wonderful stories about the wealthy Cream – his father had died in 1887 leaving a large legacy – bribing his way out of prison. Having gained his release he would have been free to commit the London murders before returning to Joliet for his 'official release' in 1891. There was also a theory, held by Sir Edward Marshall Hall, that he had a double with whom he was often confused. There is absolutely no reason to believe the theory and no evidence to suggest such a thing happened. What is certain is that in October 1891, within months of his release, he returned to England, arriving at Anderton's Hotel in Fleet Street on 5 October 1891. He signed in as 'Dr. Neill'. Two days later he found lodgings at 103 Lambeth Palace Road, the area where he had lived during his student days in London. Here he became the notorious 'Lambeth Poisoner'.

On 13 October 1891 Ellen Donworth – an 'unfortunate', only nineteen years old – was murdered by fluid poison and on 20 October Matilda Clover, a prostitute, died by means of poisoned capsules. Both had fallen to the ministrations of Cream. A peculiar habit exhibited by Cream at the time of these murders was the writing of letters under false names in an attempt to cast suspicion elsewhere or to blackmail. In approximately early December 1891, Cream became engaged to a young woman, Miss Laura Sabbatini, who lived in Chapel Street, Berkhamstead. In January 1892 he returned to Canada for a short visit and came back to England on 1 April. He then poisoned two more 'unfortunate' girls – Alice Marsh, twenty-one years old and Emma Shrivell, aged eighteen, who both lived in the lodging house at 118 Stamford Street, off Blackfriars Road. Yet another young woman, Louisa Harris (known by the name Lou Harvey), had been the victim of a failed attempt. She did not take the pills Cream had given her (for spots on her forehead), and she proved an important witness for the prosecution. She met Cream in October 1891

Suspect Dr Thomas Neill Cream. Despite the fact that he was in prison in the USA in 1888 he has still been suggested as 'Jack the Ripper' and handwriting comparisons have been made to back the claims.

and he had given her the pills, telling her to take them. She had pretended to do so but had passed them into her other hand, later throwing them away.

On the final day of the inquest into the death of Matilda Clover the coroner, Mr A. Braxton Hicks, produced a 'Jack the Ripper' letter which shows that the two cases were linked very early. *The Times* of Thursday 14 July 1892 reproduced the text of the letter, which had been addressed to the coroner himself: 'Mr. Hicks, Vestry-hall, Tooting':

> Dear Sir, – The man that you have in your power, Dr. Neill, is as innocent as you are. Knowing him by sight I disguised myself like him and made the acquaintance of the girls that have been poisoned. I gave them the pills to cure them of all their earthly miseries and they died. Miss L. Harris has got more sense than I thought she had, but I shall have her yet. Mr. P. Harvey might also follow Loo Harris out of this world of care and woe. Lady Russell is quite right about the letter, and so am I. Lord Russell had a hand in the poisoning of Clover. Nellie Donworth must have stayed out all night, or she would not have been complaining of pains and cold when Annie Clements saw her. If I were you, I'd release Dr. T. Neill, or you might get into trouble. His innocence will be declared sooner or later, and when he is free he might sue you for damages. Yours respectfully, JUAN DE POLLEN, *alias* JACK THE RIPPER. Beware all. I warn but once..

The reading of this letter caused laughter in the court, and Cream heartily joined in. With his penchant for writing, this is just the sort of communication Cream himself would have invented in an attempt to divert attention and help extricate him from the charge that held him. The evidence indicates that he was a true sadist who enjoyed the agonising deaths suffered by his victims, whereas his earlier counterpart, 'the Ripper', had inflicted a swift death with the minimum of suffering.

Cream was tried at the Old Bailey in October 1892, and found guilty. He was hanged at Newgate on 15 November. The executioner was James Billington and it is in relation to this execution that another 'Ripper' story emerged. According to the account in *The Times* of Wednesday 11 November, all went smoothly enough at the execution. Those

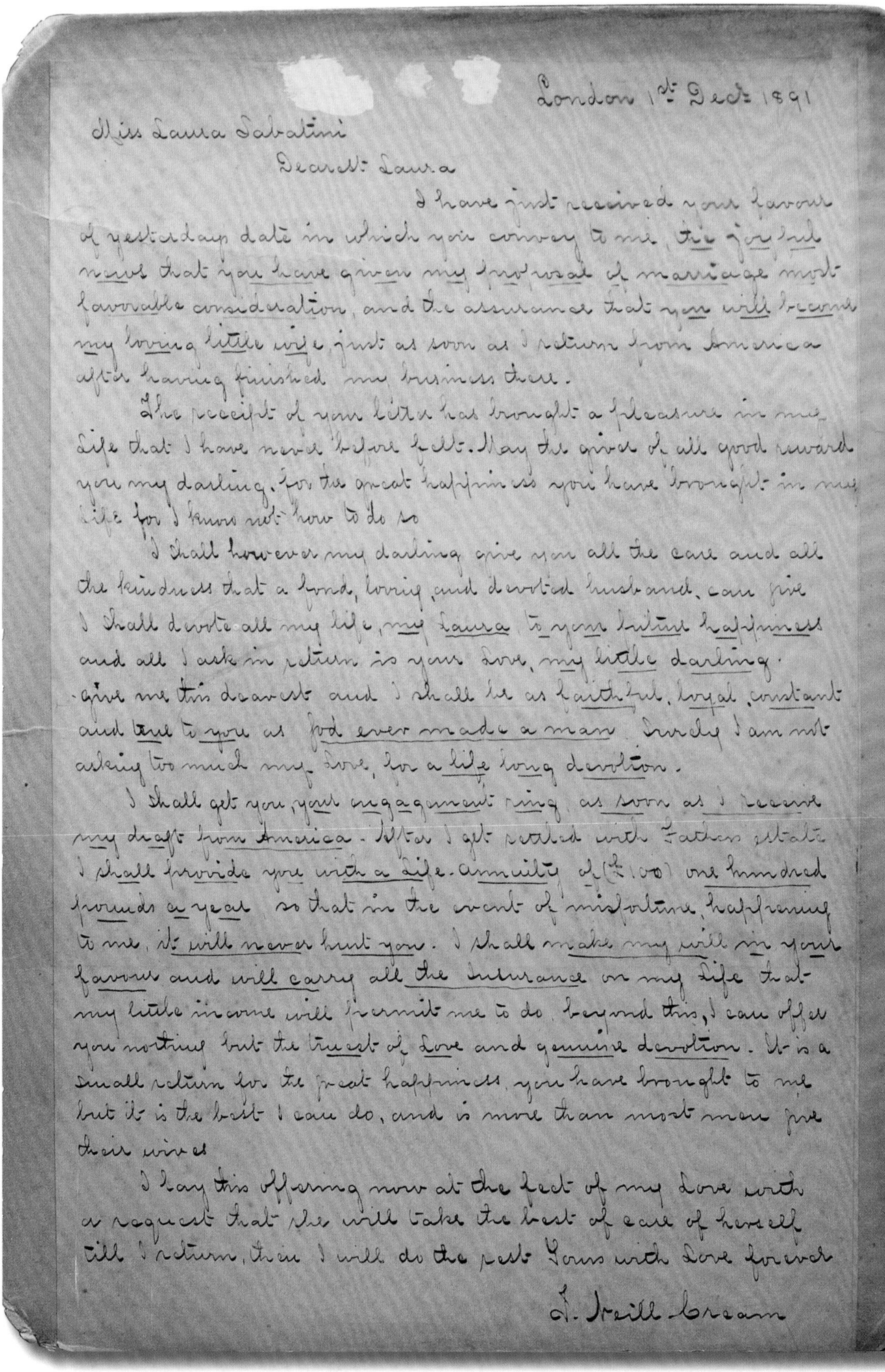

London 1st Decr 1891

Miss Laura Sabatini

Dearest Laura

I have just received your favour of yesterdays date in which you convey to me, the joyful news that you have given my proposal of marriage most favorable consideration, and the assurance that you will become my loving little wife, just as soon as I return from America after having finished my business there.

The receipt of your letter has brought a pleasure in my life that I have never before felt. May the giver of all good reward you my darling, for the great happiness you have brought in my life for I know not how to do so

I shall however my darling give you all the care and all the kindness that a fond, loving, and devoted husband, can give I shall devote all my life, my Laura to your future happiness and all I ask in return is your Love, my little darling. give me this dearest and I shall be as faithful, loyal, constant and true to you as God ever made a man. Surely I am not asking too much my Love, for a life long devotion.

I shall get you, your engagement ring as soon as I receive my draft from America. After I get settled with Fathers estate I shall provide you with a Life-annuity of (£100) one hundred pounds a year so that in the event of misfortune, happening to me, it will never hurt you. I shall make my will in your favour and will carry all the Insurance on my Life that my little income will permit me to do, beyond this, I can offer you nothing but the truest of Love and genuine devotion. It is a small return for the great happiness, you have brought to me but it is the best I can do, and is more than most men give their wives

I lay this offering now at the feet of my Love with a request that she will take the best of care of herself till I return, then I will do the rest Yours with Love forever

T. Neill Cream

Letter dated 1 December 1891 written by suspect Dr Thomas Neill Cream to his fiancée Laura Sabatini. (Photograph courtesy of Richard Whittington-Egan) present included Colonel Smith, Assistant Commissioner of the City Police force. Cream was stated to be calm and composed and he thanked all the officials for their kindness to him while he had been in their charge. A drop of 5 feet was given by hangman Billington and a cheer went up from the crowd outside the prison when the black flag was hoisted to show that the sentence had been carried out. However, a strange story about the execution subsequently began to be circulated, allegedly from the lips of Billington himself. The story ran that as the executioner put his hand on the lever Cream started to say 'I am Jack —', but was cut off as the trapdoors opened and he fell to his death.

In 1903 another serial poisoner of women, Severin Klosowski (alias George Chapman), was found guilty of disposing of three women, all of whom were living with him at the time of their murders. Tales about Klosowski being a likely 'Jack the Ripper' were given some force when they were endorsed by Inspector Abberline, who was then living in retirement in Bournemouth. At least Klosowski had been living in the East End at the time of the murders, although his candidacy is doubtful. However, Cream and the Billington story received a mention during a newspaper interview with Abberline in the *Pall Mall Gazette* of Tuesday 31 March 1903:

> "But what about Dr. Neil Cream? A circumstantial story is told of how he confessed on the scaffold – at least, he is said to have got as far as 'I am Jack —' when the rope cut short his remarks."
>
> "That is also another idle story," replied Mr. Abberline. "Neil Cream was not even in the country when the Whitechapel murders took place. No; the identity of the diabolical individual has yet to be established, notwithstanding the people who have produced these rumours and who pretend to know the state of the official mind."

The Cream theory was the basis for an article '"Jack the Ripper" – The Final Solution', by Donald Bell in *The Criminologist* of summer 1974. The Editor of the magazine, Nigel Morland, wrote a footnote to this story:

> The Editor of this journal well remembers a letter in the possession of an uncle, a retired prison doctor, from James Billington, the executioner of Cream, written four years before Billington's death in 1901. In answer to a direct question, Billington wrote that 'I heard the condemned man cry "I am Jack the —" just as the trap fell.'

This letter is not known to have survived and the story is hearsay at best. Indeed, there is every reason to doubt the veracity of this oft-repeated tale as one of the witnesses at the execution was the great raconteur Henry Smith of the City Police and he never mentioned such an incident. Bell's theory involved countering the 'fatal flaw' of the idea that Cream might have been the 'Ripper' – his incarceration in the USA at the time of the Whitechapel murders. Bell developed a complicated argument that Cream had bribed his way out of prison, or had even escaped, and that the prison authorities had hushed up his disappearance.

Bell's article in *The Criminologist* is followed by '"Jack the Ripper" – The Handwriting Analysis' by Derek Davies, MScG, MInst, MSM who was then forty-one and had been studying handwriting since the age of sixteen. He started practice as a handwriting examiner in forensic disputes in 1965. Unfortunately this was the sort of article that could lead an expert into contentious areas where he was way out of his depth, for he then examined this 'latest suspect', the subject of the Bell article. In fairness to Dr Davies he was approached to do the analysis of the handwriting and he did admit that he 'had not studied the case in any depth before'. One can see the Editor, Nigel Morland, at work here, for he had a long-standing interest in the 'Ripper' and knew many forensic experts, Dr. Davies was given samples of Cream's handwriting in the shape of a letter used by the police for checking against blackmail letters in the Cream case, and a letter Cream had written to Miss Sabbatini. But what documents did Davies have to compare Cream's handwriting with in order to ascertain that he was 'Jack the Ripper'? He was given a copy of the famous Lusk 'From hell' letter, which he stated 'has generally been accepted as an authentic specimen, whilst the letter signed "Jack the Ripper" was assumed a hoax'. The 'Jack the Ripper' letter referred to was not the original 'Dear Boss' missive, but the one sent to Dr Openshaw on 29 October 1888 and reproduced in Professor Francis Camps' article on the correspondence. Davies' examination took into account 'many hundreds of factors' and reached a conclusion 'that the "Lusk" and "Ripper" letters were of common authorship with an intentional disguise to the handwriting'. Incredibly, Dr Davies then decided that Cream had written both the 'Lusk' letter and the Openshaw 'Ripper' letter, 'using as much disguise as possible on each occasion'.

We include a sample of Cream's handwriting, his letter to Miss Sabbatini, now in the collection of Richard Whittington-Egan (*see* page 210).

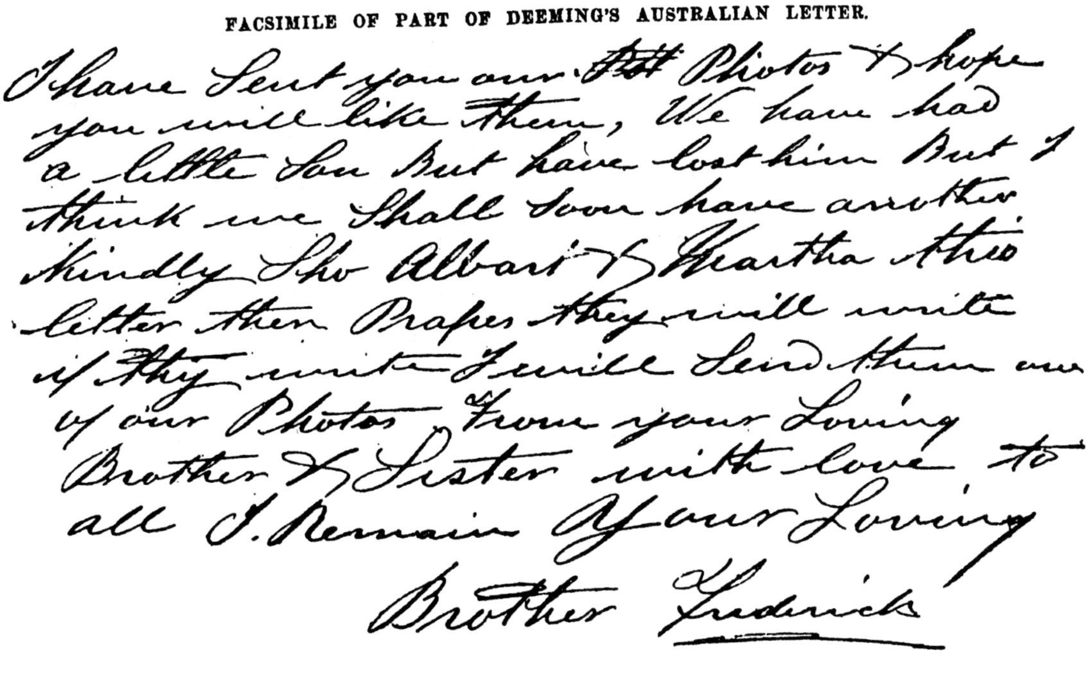
FACSIMILE OF PART OF DEEMING'S AUSTRALIAN LETTER.

I have Sent you our ~~Pot~~ Photos & hope
you will like them, We have had
a little Son But have lost him But I
think we Shall Soon have another.
Kindly Sho Albart & Martha this
letter then Prapes they will write
if they write I will Send them one
of our Photos, From your Loving
Brother & Sister with love, to
all I Remain Your Loving
Brother Frederick

Sample of suspect Frederick Bailey Deeming's handwriting.

Suspect Frederick Bailey Deeming just before his execution in Melbourne, Australia, May 1892. He had murdered his wife and there were rumours that he was 'Jack the Ripper'.

Frederick Bailey Deeming

Aged forty-six in 1888, Deeming murdered his wife and four children in Rainhill, Liverpool, in 1891, and killed his second wife the following year in Melbourne, Australia. It is possible he also had other victims. He was hanged on 23 May 1892 in Melbourne. Despite there being no real reason for suspecting Deeming of complicity in the Whitechapel murders, his name is often associated with 'Jack the Ripper'. This association can be dated as far back as Deeming's detention in Australia. A report in the *Pall Mall Gazette* of 8 April 1892 stated that 'scores upon scores' of letters had been received at Scotland Yard since Deeming's arrest. These were written by 'more or less imaginative persons in the East End of London' anxious to prove that Deeming was prowling around Whitechapel at the time of the murders. The police attached no credit to this theory whatsoever. However, the tales persisted and it was said that Deeming himself had claimed responsibility for the Whitechapel murders while he was in prison. Nevertheless, it would appear that in late 1888 he was in South Africa. A death mask taken of Deeming after his execution was sent to Scotland Yard and can still be seen in the Crime Museum. According to a recent curator, Bill Waddell, this death mask had been pointed out by some of his predecessors as being that of 'Jack the Ripper'. A sample of Deeming's handwriting has been included for comparative purposes.

Part Two

The Letters

'Jack the Ripper' Correspondence Held in the Public Record Office and the City of London Record Office

THESE letters have been transcribed using, mainly, a hard copy from the microfilmed records, and in most cases with reference to the originals. Because of the poor quality of some of the prints, and the often poor handwriting, the task of transcription has been problematical. Another difficulty was encountered when it was found that the original letters and the police backing sheets, carrying postmark, date and location details, had apparently been mixed up before placement in the protective folders by the archive section. Thus the letters do not run chronologically in their preserved state. The sequential folio (f) numbers are most important to research as they are required to order a specific copy from the Public Record Office. However, for the reason stated, these folio numbers do not run chronologically. This listing is as accurate as possible, given the stated caveats, and represents the only existing, chronological record of the 'Jack the Ripper' letters. All the PRO folio numbers relate to file MEPO 3/142, unless otherwise stated, and the City letters are indicated by their CLRO reference number.

NB . . . indicates text unreadable [ ] indicates authors' notes / indicates the end of a page in the original

Date/Source	**Addressee**	**Text, Sender and Remarks**
24 September 1888 London S.E.	Sir Charles Warren Commissioner of Police Scotland Yard	Sep 24 1888 Dear sir I do wish to give myself up I am in misery with nightmare I am the man who committed all these murders in the last six months my name is so [silhouette of coffin] and so I am a horse slauterer and work at Name [blocked out] address [blocked out] I have found the woman I wanted that is chapman and I done what I called slautered her but if any one comes I will surrender but I am not going to walk to the station by myself so I am yours truly [silhouette of coffin]/ – keep the Boro road clear or I might take a trip up there photo [silhouette of knife] of knife this is the knife that I done these murders with it is a small handle with a large long blade sharpe both sides [Black ink, docket no. 244, ff. 4–5]
27 September 1888 London E.C.	Dear Boss Central News Office London City	25 Sept. 1888. Dear Boss, I keep on hearing the police have caught me but they won't fix me just yet. I have laughed when they look so clever and talk about being on the right track. That joke about Leather apron gave me real fits. I am down on whores and I shant quit ripping them till I do get buckled. Grand work the last job was, I gave the lady no time to squeal How can they catch me now, I love my work and want to start again. you will soon hear of me with my funny little games. I saved some of the proper red stuff in a ginger beer bottle over the last job to write with but it went thick like glue and I cant use it. Red ink is fit enough I hope ha. ha. The next job I do I shall clip the lady s ears off and send to the/ police officers just for jolly wouldnt you. Keep this letter back till I do a bit more work then give it out straight. My knife's so nice and sharp I want to get to work right away if I get a chance, good luck . yours truly Jack the Ripper Dont mind me giving the trade name [Written at right angles to the above part of second page] wasnt good enough to post this before I got all the red ink

Date/Source	Addressee	Text, Sender and Remarks
		off my hands curse it. No luck yet. They say I'm a doctor now <u>ha ha</u> [Red ink, letter measures 7.1 × 8.9 inches, envelope measures 4.75 × 3.7 inches, see text and illustration. Facsimile of the original 'Jack the Ripper' letter, ff. 2–3. NB The original 'Dear Boss' 'Jack the Ripper' letter, together with the covering letter from the Central News Agency, is held at MEPO 3/3153, ff. 1–4]
1 October 1888	Editor Daily News Office City	London E. Monday. I am so pleased to see another chance of ripping up a dear creature. I shall be in Buck's Row or very close to between 12 & 2 in morning on Wednesday I have got/ the girl set & as I have been offered dooble money for her woomb and lower part of body mean to have them at any price I do like to find them nice parts. I do pity Leather Apron. I've got some/ one to write this for me. yours truly Boss Ripper [Written in black ink. CLRO Pol. Box 3.23 No. 396 with two envelopes and *Daily News* letter to Col. Fraser.]
2 October 1888 London E.C.		2 October Dear Boss Since last splendid success . two more & never a squeal. oh I am master of the art. I am going to be heavy on the guilded whores now, we are . some dutchess will cut up nicely & the lace will show nicely. You wonder how ! oh we are masters no education like a butchers no animal like a nice woman . the fat are best On to Brighton for a holiday but we shant idle splendid high class women there my mouth waters . Good luck there . If not you will hear from me in West End . My pal will keep on at the east a while yet . When I get a nobility womb I will send it on to C. Warren or perhaps to you for a keepsake O it <u>is</u> jolly . George of the high Rip Gang [drawing of knife] red ink still but

Date/Source	Addressee	Text, Sender and Remarks
		a drop of the real in it [Red ink, measures 9 × 7 inches. 5, CO 4 10/88 No. 2, ff. 344–5]
3 October 1888 London E.C.	Sir James Fraser City Police London E.C	I will write to you again soon / Just a card to let you know that I shall (if possible) do some more of my business in the West part of London & I hope to be able to send you my victims ears. I was not able to last time. My bloody ink is now running out so I must get some more. It amuses me that you think I am mad you will see when I am caught but it is death to the first man who touches me. It will be most probaly the end of October or it may be before all depends Jack the Ripper [Postcard, black ink, CLRO Pol. Box 3.22 No. 381]
4 October 1888 Found in front area of 6 Vincent Sq. Westminster.	Vine Street Station [drawing of crossed daggers] I [illeg.] this as I was passing	October 4th 1888 Spring Heel Jack The Whitechapel Murderer I am an american I have been in london the last ten months and have murdered no less than six women I mean to make a dozen of it now while I am about it I think I may as well have six men in blue to make the number as I see there is a few too many knocking about the East End looking for me but I am close upon their heel every day and will be for some time yet and I was in the crowd at Berners Street watching the blue boys wash the blood marks away sorry to give you so much trouble but what I have sworne to do I will at the cost of my own life at nights I have been sleeping in Bow cemetary one thing I have to tell you know is the policemen who has found the women it is those/ I mean settleing as they will not g[et] the chance of giving evidence against me I shall shortly have to shift or short my quarters from Bow cemetary as I have enlightened you a bit about I have written this on the Embankment near Waterloo. Jack the Ripper I will rip a few maore So help my God I Will [drawing of two daggers] [Measures 9.5 × 12.25 inches. Two pages, written in pencil, 262, Docket No. 666, ff. 195–7]

Date/Source	Addressee	Text, Sender and Remarks
4 October 1888 London S.E.	R. Voss, 115A Blackfriars, London	Prepare for thy doom. For I mean to settle you You villain you've lived long enough Yours Truly Jack the Ripper' [Pencil, 263, Docket No. 556, ff. 201–2]
4 October 1888 London W.	Superintendent Scotland Yard White Hall	I beg to inform the police I am the Whitechapel murder I intend to commit two murders in the Haymarket tonight take a note of this Whitechape is to warm for one now my knife has not/ been found yet for I still have the knife I intend to keep it untill I finish 20 then try & find me [Two pages, 'DSS Say he is the murderer' in top left corner. Black ink, Docket No. 484, ff. 198–200]
4 October 1888 Bolton		Bolton Oct 4th 1888 Dear Gentlemen. I have got to Bolton, and I have got a scent of another Girl. of mine that has been at London and I shall do it for her. i have one to do in Bolton – and one to finish in Burnley Lancashire before Oct 14th and I will give myself up at Manchester this part of country is slow and innocent I am getting sick so I will not be long before I have finished my work Yours Jack the ripper/ I have written this in a hurry I have not got a stamp, its to late but I shall stay at Bolton until I accomplish my work and then go to Burnley Jack the Ripper I shall give myself up on Oct 14th [Two pages, pencil, 17, 5 10/88 No. 7, ff. 283–4]
4 October 1888 London S.W.	C. Warren <u>Murder</u> Scotland yard London XFROM YACK RIPPERX On back of	Dear Boss <u>excuse</u> <u>slang</u> I hearby wish to give you notice that on october 7th 1888 I Jack the Ripper will rid the world of a dark & fair whore the ears & noses shall be cut off & sent as a reward to the [illegible] first nabs me I come down to Brixton for a walk to day business I mean.

Date/Source	Addressee	Text, Sender and Remarks
	envelope – XBLOODX X.	old Charles Warren shall die– Jack Ripper [Note on back of envelope – 'This letter was collected from the Pillar Box opposite 304 Brixton Road at 8.30 a/m on the 4th inst. J.G. S.W.D.O. 4 Octr. 88'. Black ink, W. 4 10/88 No. 8, ff. 300–3]
5 October 1888	Sir Chas Warren Head Police Officer	Dr Boss You have not found me yet I have done another one and thrown it in the river and I mean doing another one before the weeks out. You can put as many bloodhounds a you like but you will never catch me Yours Truly Jack Ripper [Postcard, black ink, f. 463]
5 October 1888 London	Hackney Standard Clapton Road E	[Drawing of knife & X bones] 55, Flower & Dean street Whitechapel Get your type ready my boys I'll give you a job for your paper I'm going to vissit Hackney on Saturday night Ill have a corpse in the Churchyard for parson Sundy morning Glorious fun. 14 more to make the twenty. Good luckk Jack the Ripper [Postcard, red ink, Docket No. 554, f. 180]
5 October 1888 London	Bryant & Mays Fairfield Road Bow	Friday Oct 5 88/. I hereby notefy that I am going to pay your Girls a visit I here that they a bragging what they will [ ] do with me I am going to see what a few of them have in their Bellies and I will take it out of them so that they will never have any more of it on the quite Dear Boss RIPPER [Written down left side of page – "I am in Poplar today"] [Black ink, blue-lined, red cash-ruled paper, 264, Docket No. 558, ff. 204–6]

Date/Source	Addressee	Text, Sender and Remarks
5 October 1888 Bradford, Yorks.		Boss Have arrived safe Here after a pleasant journey I murdered a woman last night and have cut off her womb I shall sent it by parcels post. I like the work some more blood the last letter was not from me I remain Jack the cunquerer Amen He[illeg.] [Red ink, 23, ff. 224–5]
5 October 1888 Eastern District Post Office	TO{Chas Warren Head of Police Central News Office TO{Chas Warren Head of Police Central News Office (2)	Dear Boss if you are willing enough to catch me I am now in City Road lodging but the number you will have to find out and I mean to do another murder tonight in Whitechapel Yours Jack The Ripper [Two Post Office Telegraphs forms, note on back of second form – 'Received at 9.35 pm 5.10/88 A. Hare. Inspr.'. Pencil, ff. 296–9 Pencil, f. 298 is a TELEGRAM NO CHARGE FOR DELIVERY 'Important Sir Charles Warren Head of Police Central News Office – To be delivered to the Chief Superintendent on duty at Scotland Yard'.]
5 October 1888 London	Central News Agency [To Chief Constable A.F. Williamson, Scotland Yard]	THE CENTRAL NEWS LIMITED. 5 New Bridge Street, London E.C. Oct 5 1888 Dear Mr Williamson At 5 minutes to 9 oclock tonight we received the following letter the envelope of which I enclose by which you will see it is in the same hand writing as the previous communications "5 Oct 1888 Dear Friend In the name of God hear me I swear I did not kill the female whose body was found at Whitehall. If she was an honest woman I will hunt down and destroy/ Her murderer. If she was a whore God will bless the hand that slew her, for the women of of Moab and Midian shall die and their blood shall mingle with the dust. I never harm any others or the Divine power that protects and helps me in my grand work would quit for ever. Do as I do and the light of glory shall shine upon you. I must get to

Date/Source	Addressee	Text, Sender and Remarks
		work tomorrow treble event this time yes yes three must be ripped . will send you a bit of face by post I promise this dear old Boss . The police/ now reckon my work a pr<u>actic</u>al joke, well well Jacky's a very practical joker ha ha ha Keep this back till three are wiped out and you can show the cold meat" Yours truly Jack the Ripper" Yours truly <u>T.Jbulling</u> A F Williamson Esqr [Three pages, black ink, ff. 491–2]
6 October 1888 Found between Princess Rd & Selhurst Rly. Stn.	The Inspector Police St: Gipsy Hill	Friday Oct 5/10/8 A WARNING At midnight – A woman will be murdered at the High Level St. Be on you guard Leather – Apron [Measures 7 × 4.25 inches. Red ink, 267, Docket No. 586, ff. 136–8]
6 October 1888		Dear Sir I don't think I do enough murders so shall not only do them in Whitechapel but in Brixton, Battersea & Clapham. If I cant get enough women to do I shall cut up men, boys & girls. Just to keep my hand in practice. Ha! ha! You will never find me in Whitechapel. By the discription in the papers 5 ft 7 inches is all wrong. Ha! Ha. I expect to rip up a woman or to on the Common at Clapham Junction one day turn/ next week. Ha.ha.ha. I will send you the heart by parcels post. Ha! Ha! By By Dear Sir Yours when Caught <u>The Whore Killer</u> Sir Charles Warren .B. Great Scotland Yard W.C.'

Date/Source	Addressee	Text, Sender and Remarks
		[Initialled top left corner 'DSS claiming to be murderer'. Black ink, ff. 243–4]
7 October 1888 London S.E.	Mr C Warren Metropolitan Office 4 Whitehall Place Whitehall	Oct 7 1888 Dear Boss Just a few lines to tell you I shall begin my knife operations again on or near Blackfriars Bridge this time I shall/ Do for three ['of' deleted] more women I shall keep on till ten more is out of the way then I shall give myself up I am now lodging in a lodging/ house and my name & address you will have to find out. Yours truly Jack The Ripper [Police note top left corner of first page 'DSS murderer Telegram to L.Div.'. Pencil, ff. 146–8]
7 October 1888 London E.C.	Scotland Yard Trafalgar Square Parliament Street Westminster	Saturday 7/8/8/8 Dear Old Boss You see I have some Black blood instead of Red [ ] know I did not have a chance to do what I intended on Saturday night Else there would have been another horrible murder in the East End I will give my self up 8 o'clock @ Peckham Station/ Monday I am wearing a light/s'uit With love to all {Leather Apron} {Jack the Ripper} [Across top left corner – '?Hoax'. Two pages, black ink, 28, ff. 292–5]
8 October 1888 London N.W.		6 Oct 1888 You though your-self very clever I reckon when you informed the police But you made a mistake, if you though I dident see you now I know you know me and I see your little game, and I mean to finish you and send your ears to your wife if you show this to the police or help them if you do I will finish you. It no use your trying to get out of my way Because I have you when you don't expect it and I keep my word as you soon see and rip you

Date/Source	Addressee	Text, Sender and Remarks
		up Yours truly Jack the Ripper [vertically down left side] You see I know your address [Measures 4.5 × 7 inches. Black ink, 268, Docket No. 575, f. 139]
8 October 1888 Found pinned to the passage wall at 22 Scott St, Brady St. Bethnal Green		Berner Street E. Oct. 9th. '88. To Sir C. Warren, Another dreadful murder will be committed by me tomorrow morning. Jack the Ripper [Red ink, 269, Docket No. 802, ff. 143–4]
8 October 1888 Innerleithen		8/10/88 Galayshiels Dear Boss, I have to thank you and my Brother in trade, Jack the Ripper for your kindness in letting me away out of Whitechapel I am on my road to the tweed Factories I will let the Innerleithen Constable or Police men know when I am about to start my nice Little games. I have got my knife Replenished so it will answer both for Ladies and Gents Other 5 Tweed ones and I have one my wager/ I am Yours Truly The Ripper [Black ink, 271, Docket No. 784, ff. 149–50]
8 October 1888 Lille	Monsieur le Chef de la Police Angle[terre] Londres Angleterre	Lille, le 9 8he [missing] Monsieur le Chef [missing] Pendant que vous vous [missing] rechercher a Londres l'auteur [missing] sinats de femmes, l'assas[missing] est es ce moment a Lille [missing] il s'acurpe de l'analyse [missing] de as femmes. C'est lui [missing] vous ecrit, et n'vous osez, venez [missing] chercher ici, Je reviendrai dan[s] moi recommencer dans un antil que [missing]

Date/Source	Addressee	Text, Sender and Remarks
		Corit a vous mes salutations Isidore Vasyvair [Measures 8 × 5 inches. Black ink, Docket No. 763, ff. 154–6]
8 October 1888 Birmingham	Detective Offices Scotland Yard London	[Red ink smudge, drawings of crossed daggers, skull and crossbones with halo, coffin and skeleton in black ink] I am as you see by this note amongst the slogging town of Brum and mean to play my part well & vigorously amongst its inhabitants I have already spotted from its number 3 girls and before one week is passed after receiving this 3 Families will be thrown into a state of delightful mourning. Ha. Ha. My Bloody whim must have its way do not be surprised 15 murders must be completed then I kill myself to cheat the scaffold. For I know you cannot catch me & may I be even present in your dreams Jack the Ripper [Measures 7.7 × 5 inches. Written in red ink, ff. 160–2]
8 October 1888 London E.C.		Dear Boss I am now in the Kentish Town district and you will here of me on friday with my funey little games. Now if you think you can catch me by the writing in the first letter I wrote. You cant, because I can write two or three hands of writing Yours Truly Jack the ripper. Trade [Black ink, No. 14, f. 173]
8 October 1888 Dublin	Commercial Street police Station London	Charles Warren Sir I have pleasure in telling you that I am the man that has committed the disturbance in London by killing everybody I mean to committ two more to-night and then I will try the police i am living in Calcutta Yours Jack the Ripper [Black ink (browned), 34, H 9 10/88 No. 15, ff. 188–9]

Date/Source	Addressee	Text, Sender and Remarks
8 October 1888 Whitechapel		Whitechapel 8 October 1888 Dear Boss Although you have not yet succeeded in catching me I presume you 'live in ope' I have not yet settled my account with whores & mean to do the dozen I originally stated – Yours with love Jack the Ripper C. Warren Esq [Black ink, ff. 290–1]
9 October 1888 London N.W.		Oct. 10/10 Dear Boss You will be surprised to heare that you had little Jacky In your Pub the other night, What fun to think the Police were Wating for me/ at the East End Which I was Injoying my Little Self good by you Bet I will see you beffor long I am Your Truly Jack the Ripper [Black ink, CO 9 10/88 No. 16, ff. 177–8]
9 October 1888 London E.	To the Commissioner of the Police Leman St Station	No Street Whitechapel Dear boss I am going to do another job right under the very nose of the damed old Charley Warren You have had me once but like fools let me go Jack the Ripper [Black ink, 38, ff. 207–9]
9 October 1888 London E.		Oct. 9th Brick Lane Dear Boss, Very quiet lately, been sharpen-ing my knife, you will hear of me next Saturday night with my funny

Date/Source	Addressee	Text, Sender and Remarks
		game's again at Silvertown or very likely before, no doubt on Friday night, I mean to Rip up two girls that work at Silver's, I have watched them this last week, curse the ink its/ Fell over it has gone pale. You have not caught me yet. I have been in Whitechapel all the while. You can offer all the reward you like but you wont catch me next two girls I will fetch their Hearts to the Police Station and lay them on the step of Leman Street Station. No doubt you/ have been on the watch for me No more at present Jack the Ripper [Written in pencil with red ink blot and smudges on first page, ff. 357–9]
9 October 1888 Plymouth		To the Central Police Authorities London Dear Boss I am sure you find me if you look for me as I have been hiding my self in a quarry I am going to the 6 bares to a tree in a country place & there rip them up Yours truly Jack the Ripper [Black ink, f. 365]
10 October 1888 London W.		Baye [?] 2–9 R Basin [?] dear Sir, I drop a line to say hav sniped enother and send . . . so I'll do me job furst he gon on catle bote or with muckers Yours truly J.R. Rite gain in a weak . . . [Police note, top left (torn): 'Pu[t with] other [lette]rs (?)'. Two pages, difficult to read, black ink, Docket No. 791, ff. 63–4]
10 October 1888 South Lambeth, S.W.		Jack the Sir Ripper you had better be carefull How you send those Bloodhounds about the streets because of the single females wearing stained napkins – women smell very

Date/Source	Addressee	Text, Sender and Remarks
		strong when they are unwell [Black ink, ff. 152–3]
10 October 1888 London S.E.	To the Head Boss Metropolis Police Scotland Yard London	Old Boss The Ripper will soon be on the trak agin, nose and ears he wants next as present for Boss. Wen he gets em will be able to unite in blood, aha aha, blood blood blood, Yours Bill the Boweler. [Purple ink, postcard, f. 233]
10 October 1888		HAVE YOU SEEN THE "DEVIL" [Cutting] If not Hampstead Oct 10/10/88

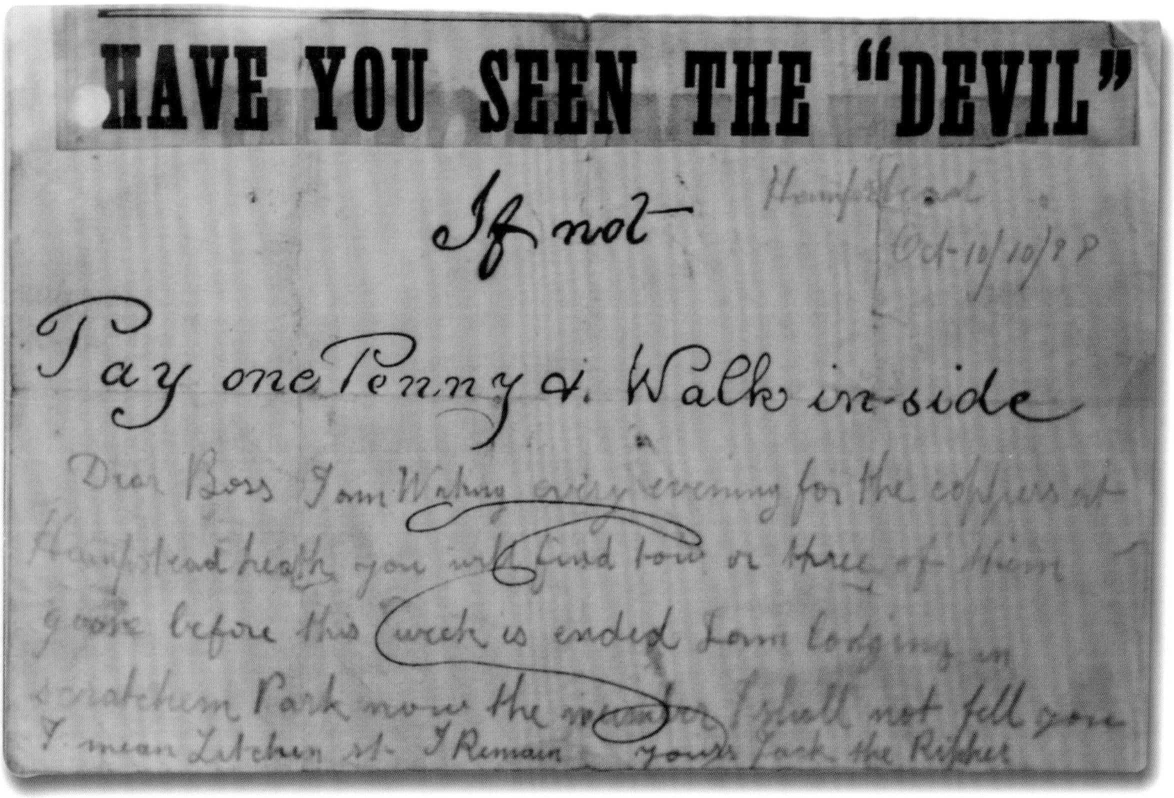
HAVE YOU SEEN THE "DEVIL"
If not
Hampstead
Oct 10/10/88
Pay one Penny & Walk in-side
Dear Boss I am Waking every evening for the coppers at Hampstead heath you will find tow or three of them gone before this week is ended I am lodging in Scratchem Park now the weather I shall not fell gone I mean Litchen st- I Remain Yours Jack the Ripper

Letter of 10 October 1888 including a newspaper cutting.

Date/Source	Addressee	Text, Sender and Remarks
		Pay one Penny & Walk in-side Dear Boss I am Waiting every evening for the coppers at Hampstead heath you will find tow or three of them goone before this week is ended I am lodging in Scratchem Park now the number I shall not tell you I mean Litchin st I Remain yours Jack the Ripper/ Hampstead Oct 10/10/88 Dear Boss I am waiting [Type in bold and written in black ink, rest in pencil, f. 282]
10 October 1888 Leicester	Sir C. Warren Chief Commissioner of Police Scotland Yard London	Dear Boss (you are the biggest fool in London I am in Lester now for a holiday What a dance I am leading all those fools about London why I am Passing them by dozens against Scotland yard way & don't I laugh & say Damd fools you work them too hard Poor fellows but I say good joke about those things being a Hoax ha!ha!ha! please look out for me in London again between now & next wednesday Jack the Ripper [Postcard, red ink, ff. 363–4]
10 October 1888 London S.W.	The Inspector Scotland yard London	Oct 9. double event to night will give up Kings X met 12 o'clock on Oct 10 Jack the ripper [Postcard, pencil, ff. 366–7]
10 October 1888 Edinburgh	Sir Charles Warren Scotland Yard London.	Edinburgh 10/10/88. Dear Boss You will be wondering why I have been so quiet. Fact is I was nearly caught. over the last job Will start again next week mean to be hard on the Fairies. Jack the Ripper [Postcard, black ink, ff. 378–9]

Date/Source	Addressee	Text, Sender and Remarks
12 October 1888 London E.C.	O.H.M.S. Gt Scotland Yard [On reverse of envelope – 'TRADE [drawing of knife] MARK']	Friday 88 Dr Boss I hear you have bloodhounds for me now But I will deceive them & you dogs too & I am sertain that I shall do one to night In C.R which you will have to find out/ [drawing of knife] what that means I remain Yours J the R [Large drawing of knife] [Initialled top left corner 'DSS'. Two pages, pencil, ff. 245–6]
13 October 1888 Colchester	Scotland Yard S.W.	Sirs, I am sorry that such a letter should be sent to you, viz, the one signed Jack the Ripper . . . I can assure you it is nothing to do with us whatever . . . I caution persons playing such tricks . . . to beware of their Bodies for 'it's' no joke . . . I am yours truly. Mr Englishman Colchester Oct. 13. 1888. 1213. Shall not return to the E. end trust Sir C. Warren to make such a fuss . . . . [Written in purple ink, f. 490]
13 October 1888 Nottingham	Charley Warren Scotland Yard Westminster London	Narrow marsh Nottingham [I] is at Nottingham now if you wants me shall begin business on Monday Jack the Ripper but one who did Wightechapel [Postcard, pencil, ff. 59–60]
13 October 1888 New Cross S.O.		59– Place Whitechapel Jack Porns. This is to give you notice that I intend to rip your little fat belly up next week. A man so infernally conceited, and such a liar as you are deserves no mercy at

Date/Source	Addressee	Text, Sender and Remarks
		the hands of JACK THE RIPPER [Small pencil drawing of skull and crossbones over a coffin] [63, W 15 10/88, red ink, ff. 408–10]
14 October 1888 Woolwich	To the Woolwich People	13th of Oct Sirs Do you think that you can catch me and my pals if so say it at once and when you have said what you have to say why then we can lofe about, had to jump up just now, thought you had, next time I do any thing it will be at the town in which I write this letter I remain yours murderyfied J.J. Thompson alias J. the Rippers Nephewx PS Excuse bad writing J.J.T. [Red ink, two pages, ff. 65–7]
15 October 1888 Leeds		Leeds Oct 15th Gents yes I have made six successful attempts I shall make the next in Leeds in the Leylands to night I shall protect all honest women & all the fat ones I shall meet the first I shall send to you From JR P.S. my pal shall be in the west end to night at your place. [Black ink, f. 472]
15 October 1888 Bristol		–Hotel. Bristol Old Pal I am one of Jacks foremen. I am in Bristol at present and mark me if there is not 3 murders done in Bristol within a week from now then I'll betray the whole gang. Until then Good Bye, A.R.M. [68, ff. 476–7]

Date/Source	**Addressee**	**Text, Sender and Remarks**
15 October 1888 London W.C.		Sunday Oct. 14, 1888 Mr, Smith,/ A few line to you to let you know that you will soon meet your death, I have been watching you lately and I know you must have money by you, therefore, I Jack the Ripper will come and/ serve you the same as I did the other whores in Whitechapel I shall come quite unexpecet, and I shant give you time to sqeal for my knife is nice and sharp yours truly Jack the Ripper [drawing of knife 'the knife' on handle] [Black ink, two pages, Docket No. 986, ff. 102–4]
15 October 1888 London N.W.		Lodging London Dear Boss I was passing the Houses of Parliament the other day & every po-lice-man I did come across look at me expeccially number 1.a I was going to do another murder at York street Lambeth Friday I am going up to Palmerston Rd to do 3 murders I am going to take my/ Knife with me it is nice & sharp & it will kill 10 more mid-ages women & 8 children the oldest shall be 18 I have not told you at what number I am going to committe those 9 murders but it is near the Baths because I can throw them in the water Jack Ripper PS Excuse bad writing because bad wood [Noted 'DSS' in top left corner of first page. Black ink, 67, ff. 460–2]
15 October 1888	Sir Chas Warren Head Police Officer	Dr Boss You have not found me yet I have done another one and thrown it in the river and I mean doing another one before the weeks out. You can put as many bloodhounds as you like but you will never catch me Yours Truly Jack Ripper [Postcard, black ink, ff. 463–4]

Date/Source	**Addressee**	**Text, Sender and Remarks**
16 October 1888 Portsmouth	Mr Warren Head Police Station London	Memo from. What they tell me the <u>true</u> Jack the Ripper 16/10/88 Sir To show you what a lot of idiots you London Policemen are. I will murder several Rich women in Clerkenwell from 6 days of This date. Yours respectfully. H.L. (over) Sir I don't know if you are married if so you had better look after your wife. HTB[?] [Black ink, initialled '<u>DSS</u>', 71, ff. 473–5]
16 October 1888 London S.E.	The Supt. Vine St Police Station W	Oct 18th 1888 Albany Road Sir, Look out to night for me in the neighbourhood of London Road they are some hot ones there if these fogs continue What a chance I shall have I am getting tired of my rest and I want to get to work again I shall not write any-more. Yours truly J the R [Date on letter '16' changed to '18'. Black ink, C 16 10/88 No. 19, ff. 52–3]
17 October 1888 London N.W.		P S– If you have not gone . . . you soon will [illegible] You old [?] Funker [?]/ Yours Truly Jack the Ripper I will do you Next' [Pencil, Docket No. 992, ff. 101–2]
17 October 1888 Croydon		Dear Parkin, Having not seen you for a long time I'm coming to see you, getting tired of Whitechapel I thought it best to give this town a turn and I think you will suit my purpose a treat meet me at Thornton Heath Friday night at 8 oclock

Date/Source	Addressee	Text, Sender and Remarks
		if you fail you will be a dead un. Beware Yours Truly Jack the Ripper [reverse, stain] This is blood from the woman I done in Mitre Square I might have some of yours [Black ink, W 17 10/88 No. 30, ff. 116–18]
18 October 1888 Bethnal Green, S.O.	O.H.M.S Sir ChasWarren Scotland Yd WC	[On Post Office Telegraphs form] To City Dedective. from the old Jewry – to day was wasting his time at Johnsons' Gracechurch St looking at articles for today sale silks particular & under garments – we do not pay our rate for the kind of thing – tall – fine – tall hat with band up – dark hair & Countenance also one in the fact & I may add he parts his hair behind also – Jack the Ripper [Black ink, 78, ff. 240–2]
19 October 1888 Dublin	Messrs. Bensdorp & Co. London E.C.	Please send 1 Bottell Whiskey I intend to murder one in Dublin to night Grand job I made of the last. Don't forget to meet me in Patrick st. J the R Yours truly Jack the Ripper [Pencil, forwarded to the Superintendent of the City Police by Messrs. Bensdorp. CLRO Pol. Box 3.18 No. 225]
19 October 1888 London	Inspector Detective Dept 26 Old Jewry City E.C. [Penny lilac stamp]	19th Oct 1888 Sir, The crime committed In Mitre Square City and those in the district of Whitechapel were perpetrated by an Ex Police Constable of the Metropolitan Police who/ was dismissed the force through certain connection with a prostitute The motive for the crimes is hatred and spite against the authorities at Scotland Yard one of whom is marked as a victim after which the crimes will cease Yours truly An Accessory [Third page annotated 'Copy sent to Scot. Yard'] [Black ink, CLRO Police Box 3.22 No. 359 a–b]

Date/Source	Addressee	Text, Sender and Remarks
19 October 1888 Found in letter-box at 37 West Ham Lane	To the Occupier [drawing of postage stamp]	From Hell I am <u>somewhere</u> 19/10/88 [drawing of crossbones] <u>To the finder</u> <u>Dear Sir or Madam</u> I hope you are pretty well Dear old <u>Boss</u> I shall visit you shortly in about 3 or 4 weeks time I can write 5 hand writings if anybody recognises the writing I shall kill the first female I see in this house or if there is no females I shall be down on the boss. I mean to have Charlie Warren yet even if I get him asleep poor old begger P.T.O./ yours Jack the Ripper./ From Hell/ P.S. The call me a "Fiend" Hah Hah, Hah Dear old Boss I wonder how Mr Lusk liked the half of a kidne I sent Him Last Monday. [Pencil, Docket No. 1036, ff. 95–6]
19 October 1888 London S.E.		Ripper as you have written to the . . . not to be answered be fore this by some and I am . . . capable but you will see I do tho I shall be . . . with Especially/ as I am such a sinner & cant wate . . . you are expert scholar . . . I want your answer E i will/ . . ./ I have written to the other Newspapers [Largely illegible, four pages. Very shaky handwriting. Pencil, Docket No. 1035, ff. 98–9]
19 October 1888 London W.C.		Central news office I was very glad to hear that you have go the Kidney and the next thing i send it will be the knife and the next murder I do I will cut the womens pratt . . . Right out . . . send/ to you and Charles Warren will send the Bloodhounds out and then they wont cat[ch ?] Jack the Ripper me [Blue crayon, two pages. Report No. 20, ff. 248–50]

Date/Source	Addressee	Text, Sender and Remarks
19 October 1888 Brierley Hill.	Sir Charles Warren Chief Commisioner Of Police Scotland Yard London	Wouster Oct. 19) 1888 Dear boss iff you are the boss you have not got the right man 100 miles off scent bloodhounds no use will not catch me have been in Wouster a week have spotted 3 out will visit them again shortley dont know much about this part off too Brum to-day/ Post this on me way, hope I shall have luck there The Atmosphere was to hot at Whitechapel had to clear off smelt a rat saw last victim burried I felt rather down hearted over my knife which I lost comming here must get one to night. I shall kill 15 at Brum call and settle 3 I have spotted at Wouster Ishall then finish/ up at Hull before going to Poland. Silly looking in low lodging houses for me do not vissit them description posted at Ploice stations nothing like me look out for Octer. 27th at Brum will give them ripper. Jack a poland Jew

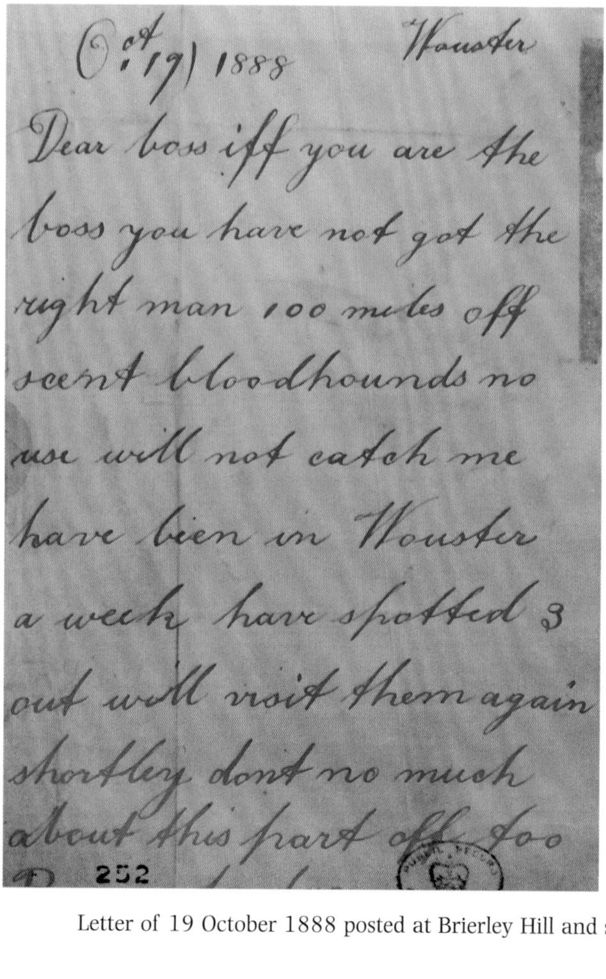
Oct 19) 1888 Wouster
Dear boss iff you are the
boss you have not got the
right man 100 miles off
scent bloodhounds no
use will not catch me
have been in Wouster
a week have spotted 3
out will visit them again
shortley dont no much
about this part off too
252

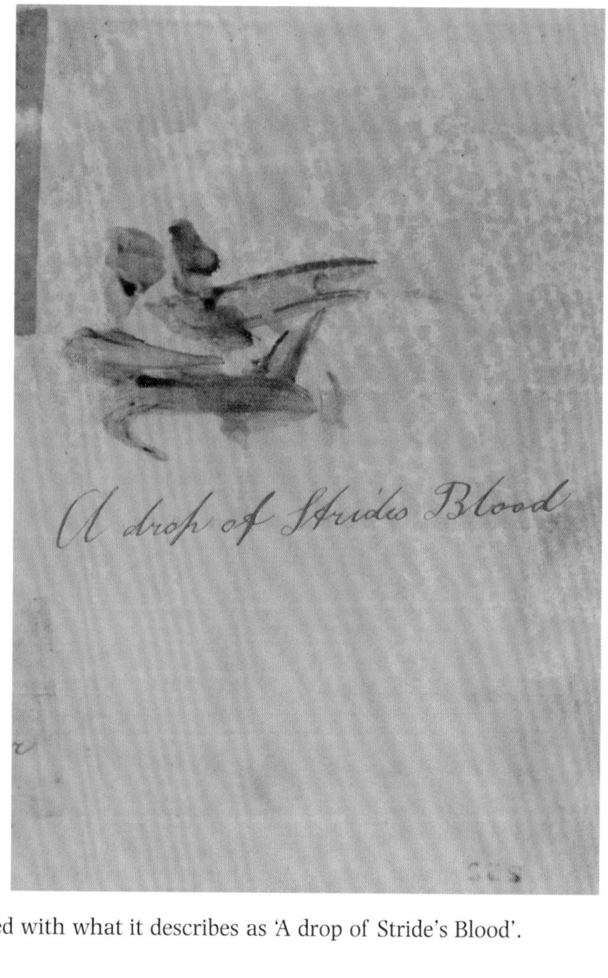

Letter of 19 October 1888 posted at Brierley Hill and smeared with what it describes as 'A drop of Stride's Blood'.

Date/Source	Addressee	Text, Sender and Remarks
		Better known as Jack the ripper [On fourth page are brown smears, possibly blood – 'A drop of Strides Blood'] [Envelope black ink, red blot. Letter red ink, four pages, ff. 252–4]
20 October 1888 London N.W.	Cheif Inspector Scotland Yd London	Hampstead Rd Dear Boss You have not caught me Just yet, but just to give you a little clue I am living in Hampstead Road. Yours truly Jack the Ripper [Down left side – 'Two more murders on Oct 27 What a lark'] [Postcard, black ink, ff. 256–7]
20 October 1888 Walthamstow	to Postman to be Deliver to the nearest Ploiceman [illeg.] in this town	Please let all the people know I am in Waltham – I was going to do two women if they were not to Saucy I nearly had one in the Victoria Road the other night had it not a been for a girl being with her just the Length I want I wish she had,: not a fine to high up . excuse this note as my right hand is very bad got bye I am ready when she comes . . . her self her face is to [illegible] I send [illeg.] & lock of her hair to her husband I saw her/ my knife is sharp blood more blood ha ha ha Good bye Jack Ripper Let Mr Lusk have a note to night as I cant Write with my hand no red ink now all gone right [?] . . . [illegible] [Down right side of page – 'this morning the pretty women I am not to good as in [illegible] keep this quiret till I have done one'] [Black ink, N 20 10/88 No. 27, ff. 258–60]
20 October 1888 Brentford Found tacked to a tree at Ealing Road		Dear Boss Since last no success [ ] am going to have a try in the slums of Brentford Yours truly

Date/Source	Addressee	Text, Sender and Remarks
		Jack the Ripper [Large brown blot and smear, possibly blood (?)] [Purple pencil, T 20 10/88 No. 26, ff. 261–2]
20 October 1888 London E.C.	Mr. Toby Baskett 13 Newman Street Whitechapel	Dear Old Baskett Yer only tried ter get yer name in the papers when yer thought you had me in the Three Tuns Hotel I'd like to punch yer bleeding nose Jack the Riper [Postcard, undated, red ink, smudged, sent to Albert Bachert of the Whitechapel Vigilance Committee, f. 265]
22 October 1888		22/10/88 Dear Sir Take my advice and trouble yourself no more about me. Talk about having caught a "Jack the Ripper" at Bradford, why I'm all safe and sound its all bosh. If I was in your place I'd/ let my men search the different houses and alleys where if they looked they would find two more women which I killed & cut up before a bobby's nose. he was rather drunk. If I ketch any of your bloodhounds I'll kill and eat them, wont you come and help me to kill a few women, it's a jolly nice lark. Yours Jack the Ripper I have disguised my writting a bit because you were almost on me [Red ink, two pages, f. 251]
22 October 1888 London S.W.		One of the two women I told you about is a Chelsea girl and the other a Battersea girl. I had to over come great difficulties in bringing the bodies where I hid them. I am now in Battersea. Good bye ta ta.

Date/Source	Addressee	Text, Sender and Remarks
		[Red ink, 93, H 24 10/88 No. 21, ff. 276–7. Below this letter is a card, f. 278, 'Jack the Ripper M.D.' in red ink]
23 October 1888 Found in Bird Cage Walk	TO{ Mr Thurston 17 Shor[missing] TO{Fat headed snukig[?] Tiddley boyar	[missing]n long skinny gi[missing] [missing]ow Good bye big[missing] Jack the ripper sent these [2] Strong Mrs [missing] Jack the ripper sent this fat Mrs Thurston [Telegrams, two pages, black ink, ff. 92–3]
23 October 1888 London S.W.		23/10/88 Dear Sirs I Jack the Ripper thanks you for your trouble in trying to catch me, but it wont do. I suppose you would like to know why I am killing so many women, the answer is simply this. "When I was at San Francisco in July, 1888, I lent three women from London about £100 sterling to pay some debts. they had got into, promising to pay me back in a months time, and seeing that they had a ladylike look I lent the money. Well when the month passed by I asked for my money but I found that they had sneaked off to London/ so I swore that I would have my revenge, the revenge was this. that I would go to London and kill as many women as possible. I've killed 9 as yet. you've not found all the corpses yet. Ha. Ha. I've told Sir C. Warren that in a letter of the 22nd inst. In the last women I killed I cut out the kidneys and eat them. you'ill find the body in one of the sewers in the East End. The ['(corpse)' – deleted] leg you found at Whitehall does not belong to the trunk you found there. The police alias po-lice, think themselves devilish clever I suppose they'ill never catch me at this rate you donkeys, you double-faced asses, you had better take the blood-hounds away or I will kill them. I am on the/ scent of those women that swindled me so basely, living like well to do ladies on the money they sneaked from me, never mind, that, I'll have em yet, afore I'm done, damn em, To tell you the truth you ought to be obliged to me for killing such a deuced lot of vermin, why they are ten times

Date/Source	Addressee	Text, Sender and Remarks
		worse than men. I remain. etc. Jack the Ripper Alias H.I.O. Battersea. [Three pages, red ink, blue-lined paper with red margin lines, 94, H 24 10/88 No. 21, ff. 304–6]
24 October 1888 Lisbon	Charles Warren Director da Police News, Central Office Londres	Care Boss Cheguei agora mesmo no-Elbe-e Guando receber esta carta es tarei . . ./ Receba o meu amigo e a prespicar policia Tugk za as filicilacoes do [illegible] Jack, o estripador [Red ink, two pages, Docket No. 1075, ff. 86–9]
24 October 1888 Victoria Docks. E		Dear Boss I am going to do Jack the ripper in this town to day I will visit Eagle Street and will cut some ladies ther I will warn them to look out I will do for as many as I can they say they have got a clue of me but they have not, I will keep on my work till I do get buttled [Drawing of crossbones (?), coffin, crossed clubs] Jack the Ripper [Reverse noted 'Found in the Barking Rd collection OC' and noted bottom left corner of same page – 'Circulated &ent O.B. 24.10.88 J.B.' Black ink, ff. 270–1]
? October 1888 Philadelphia U.S.A.		Honorably Sir I take great pleasure in giving you my present whereabouts for the benefit of the Scotland Yard Boys. I am very sorry that I did not have time to finish my work with the London whores and regret to state that I must leave them alone for a short while I am now safe in New York and will travel over to Philadelphia and when I have the lay of the locality I might take a notion to do a little ripping there. Good bye "dear friend" I will let you here from me before long with a little more Culling and Ripping I said 20 and I fancy I will make it 40 on account of the slight delay in operations

Date/Source | **Addressee** | **Text, Sender and Remarks**

Yours lovingly
"Jack"
the ripper

[Black ink, 986, Docket No. 1157, ff. 90–1]

---

26 October 1888

Dear Boss
If you are Willing enough to catch me I am now in Goswell Road by Carter P. office 12 o'clock I am the man from texas, the mysterious murders in Whitechapel caused [?] i give myself up to night/
My height is 5ft 7½ inch Dark complexion age 38 years
Yours
Truly
Jack the
Ripper

[Black ink, two pages, ff. 263–4]

---

27 October 1888
London S.E.

SIR CHARLES
WARREN
SCOTLAND
YARD
S.W.

MANSELL STREET
ALDGATE
HONd. SIR
YEW HAVE'NT CAUGHT ME YIT, ALTHOUGH YOU ARE SO BIG BEWARE. FOR I START AGAIN

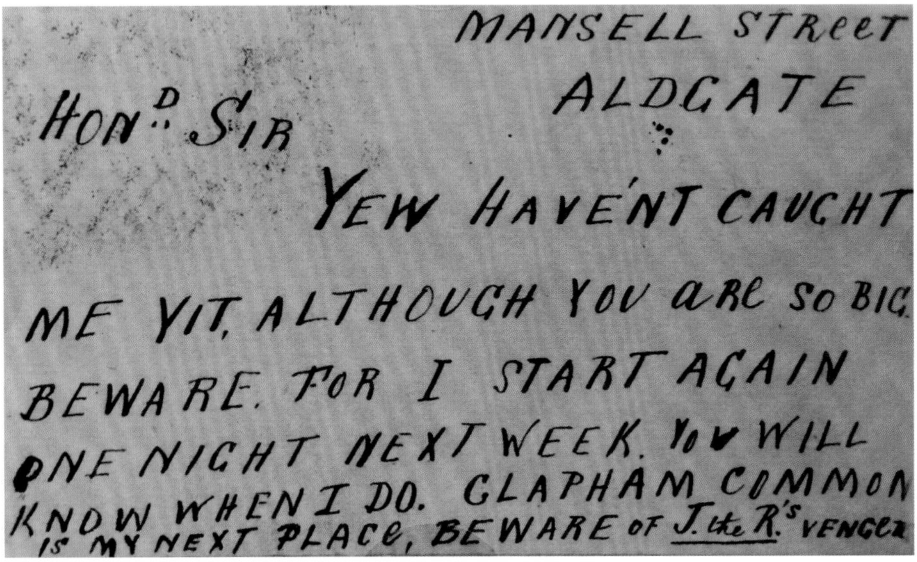
MANSELL STREET
ALDGATE
HOND. SIR
YEW HAVE'NT CAUGHT ME YIT, ALTHOUGH YOU ARE SO BIG BEWARE. FOR I START AGAIN ONE NIGHT NEXT WEEK. YOU WILL KNOW WHEN I DO. CLAPHAM COMMON IS MY NEXT PLACE, BEWARE OF J. the R.'s VENGER

Postcard of 27 October 1888 — 'Yew haven't caught me yit . . .'

Date/Source	Addressee	Text, Sender and Remarks
		ONE NIGHT NEXT WEEK. YOU WILL KNOW WHEN I DO. CLAPHAM COMMON IS MY NEXT PLACE, BEWARE OF J. the R.'s VENGENCE [Postcard, black ink, ff. 311–12]
30 October 1888 From G.P.O.		Dear Boss I hope you are q[missing] well as I am going to [missing] another woman and I have picked out the [missing] think will suit and [missing] sent the hearts in a [missing] parcel Post Yours truly Jack the Ripper [missing] knives are still sha[rp] Ah Ah The Boss Central n[missing] [missing] [Pencil, No. 83., f. 15]
31 October 1888 London W.C.	Old Street Police Station Goslew Rd	Dear Boss, I am living in 129 C Rd..,. and I mean to do another murder in PEN Rd to night Yours truly Jack the ripper [Black ink, 109, No. 35, ff. 508–11]
31 October 1888 London S.W.	Henry Matthews Home Office Whitehall	Dear Old Boss, I daresay you are in a bit of a fix not being able to catch me, shall take a rest for some time yet and then commence work again, it is no good your'e tryin to catch me because it wont do – Jack the Ripper [Postcard, 108, No. 34, black ink, f. 499]

Date/Source	Addressee	Text, Sender and Remarks
31 October 1888 Upper Holloway	Sir charles warren Scotland yard London	C / h / h / h/ Sir, You had mind yourself for I am going to ripe another holy womern again two night and I take joly [illegible] yer wont catch me for I think you have had a gud fist now I willnt say where yer no I have got another one wo not me so catch me if you can I'm Jack the riper as yer call me I make yer swear don't forget [Drawing of knife after signature] [No stamp, black ink, 107, ff. 487–9]
2 November 1888 London E.C.		Important Sir Chas Warren Sir Charles Warren I must have some more Blood tomorrow night – Lookout Ripper [Black ink, 'Blood' underlined in red ink, ff. 496–8]
3 November 1888 Belfast		at a meeting of the council of midnight wanderers of Belfast the following resolution was unanimously passed.

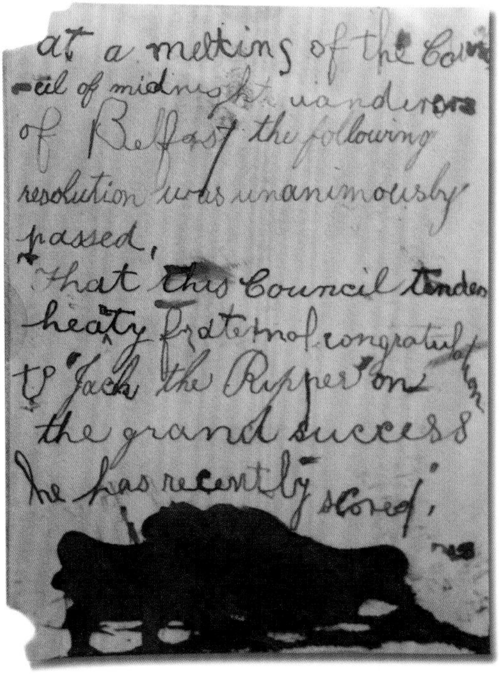
at a metking of the Coun-
-ceil of midnight uanderers
of Belfast the following
resolution was unanimously
passed,
'that this Council tenders
heaty fraternal congratulations
to Jack the Ripper on
the grand success
he has recently scored'

Letter of 3 November 1888 posted in Belfast.

Date/Source	Addressee	Text, Sender and Remarks
		That this Council tenders hearty fraternal congratulation to 'Jack the Ripper' on the grand success he has recently scored. [Large red blot across bottom of page] [Red ink, 111, ff. 493–4]
3 November 1888 London	Chief Police Scotland Yard <u>London</u> <u>Ingland</u>	Asleep hitalion Lunon Dockes cattelmain SS Gorn [?] wil send mi Yours Obligeing adress fur reciord RHB mate to mu[missing] arristed hime Whitechapel [Postcard, black ink, ff. 503–4]
4 November 1888 Neath		['October 27.' Deleted] Nov. 3rd 1888 To Mr Charles warren head Police Scotland yard detectivs. I. hame pleased to year that I was caught at neath on saturday night at the falcon hotel old market st but you have not had the pleasure of catching me yet by the time you have had this one or two more will feel my knife I have been helpin the police in the seaorch with blood – hounds and rejoices in hearing them say they were on the right track J. T. Ripper Ah! ah. over/ next one I copp I'll send the toes and earoles to you for supper J. T. Ripper [Drawing of hand holding knife] [Black ink, 113, ff. 501–2]
5 November 1888 London E.C.	POLICE STATION LEMAN STREET EC	Keep a extra look out in Whitechapel tonight Jack the Ripper P.S. THERE IS ONE OLD WHORE WHO I HAVE GOT MY EYE ON SO LOOK OUT J.T.R. [ff. 164–5]

Date/Source	Addressee	Text, Sender and Remarks
7 November 1888		7 . 11 . 88 Dear Boss I am writing you this while I am in bed with a sore throat but as soon as it is better I will set to work again. on the 13th of this month . and I think that my next Job will be to polish you off and as I am a member of the force I can soon settle accounts with you I will tear your liver out before you are dead and show it to you/ and I will have your kidneys out also and frie them with pepper and salt and send them to lord Sablisbrury as it is Just the sort of thing that will suit that old Jew and I will cut of your toes and slick of your behind and make macaroni soup of them and I will hide your body in the houses of parliament so you grey headed old pig say your prayers before I am ready/ [Written at right angles down third page] & I cannot say any more at present boss yours truly Jack the Ripper [crude drawing of profile of man with buttons down front of jacket] – this is yourportrait. [Police note at top left of first page, 'DSS No Envelope'. Black ink, three pages, ff. 515–16]
8 November 1888 London E.	To Kingslands Road Police Station	Your friend Jack the Ripper I am very please to send you this little as I am your friend I have been having a nice rest but now my rest is over I am going to make a fresh start again. Now first of all I am going to settle 4 of Barratts girls at woodgreen next month/ and then after I have done this I am going to slay 2 boys and 3 girls between 14 and 15 years of age and after this I and going to France and start my work there. I often laugh to myself when I hear that the men have calling out Cleaver capture of Jack the Ripper [Black ink, two pages, top initialled 'DSS', ff. 82–3]
8 November 1888 London E.C.	Sir Charles Warren Scotland Yard Whitehall W.	Whitechapel 8/11/88 Dear Boss I am still knocking about Down Whitechapel I mean to put to Death all the dirty old ores because I have cought the pox and cannot piss I have not done any murders lately

Date/Source	**Addressee**	**Text, Sender and Remarks**
		but you will find one done before long. I shall send you the kidney and cunt so that you can see where my prick has been up I am in one of the lodging houses in Osborn street but you will have a job to catch me I shoudent advise any coppers to catch hold of me because I shall do the same to him as I have done others./ Old packer the man I bought the grapes off saw me the other night but was to frighten to say anything to the police. he must have been a fool when there is such a reward offered never mind the reward will not be given. You will hear from me a little later on that I have done another murder. But not just yet. Dear Boss if I see you about I shall cut your throat. The Old Queen is none other but one of those old ores I have Been up her arse and shot sponk up her I remain Dear Old Boss Jack the Ripper [Black ink, two pages, 121, ff. 512–14]
9 November 1888 London E.C.	On her majysters service To the Comessisun Of. Police Scotland Yard London	Dear Boss Be good enough to send a fiew of your clever policmen down here the time is nearley up for another job so look out, the knife is in good condishion and so am I Boss, the police pass me close every day, and I shall pass one going to post this, now then Boss just keep this letter a bit quiert till you here of me again I tell you that I don't like to be made/ so publick Greenwich is a nice place and I am not far off South Street Black Heath Hills Good buy old Boss Jack the Ripper and the Beester [drawing of knife] Novr 9th P.S. Ecxcuse red ink [Black ink, Docket No. 1190, ff. 132–4]
10 November 1888 London E.C.	On Her Majesty's Service The Inspector Leman St Police	10/11/88 WELL YOU SEE I'VE KEPT MY WORD, AND DONE FOR THE ONE I SAID I WOULD. I SUPPOSE YOU TOOK NO NOTICE OF WHAT I SAID. THOSE OTHER

Date/Source	Addressee	Text, Sender and Remarks
	Station E	LETTERS WERE NOT WRITTEN BY ME AT ALL AND HAS SOME ONE HAS BEEN KIND ENOUGH TO GIVE ME THE NAME OF "JACK THE RIPPER" I'LL ACCEPT IT AND ACT UP TO IT. LOOK OUT FOR THE NEXT P.S. YOU CAN'T TRACE ME BY THIS WRITING SO ITS NO USE ON THE POLICE STATIONS [Black ink, 290, Docket No. 1241, ff. 129–30]
10 November 1888 London N.	Sir Charles Warren Scotland Yard London	Hell Dear Bofs Just a line a I feel certain amount of sympathy for you Placed in the Circumstances you are and I am also surprised at the so called Public that upraid you of what you cane not quit [?] and call it quibbing [?] I hope you will not lose your Billett through not being efficent enough to catch me as I can assure you it will take a [?] man than you are [?] to decite me [?] the gent Bying walnuts it . . . I have as 4 more to slaughter then I . . . of all other . . . and the last will be the Bloody old queen the last did not so much as struggle becase . . . as I have Proved to be at an engagement in the Mille End Rd I . . . advise you to see . . ./ We can only be busy for one as . . . and we will have it . . . Haste I am Sory to hear . . . Jack [illegible scribble] [Three pages, very bad handwriting in thick blue crayon, largely illegible, 126, ff. 525–8]
10 November 1888 Rotherhithe S.E.	For the Boss Scotland Yard Detective Office	Fair Three this time – . . . newspaper yet . . . Say Boss this time . . . in a mighty powerful . . . Dropped a letter in Kennington telling you what I was going to do . . . [Further writing sideways in middle of above text – 'Yours one who aint such a fool to sign his name . . .']

Date/Source	Addressee	Text, Sender and Remarks
		[Postcard, brown ink (possibly blood?), very hard to read, 125, ff. 529–30]
11 November 1888 Folkestone	Mrs McCarthy No 28 Dorset St London East End	From Jack ['sheridan' deleted] The ripper Folkestone. Nov 11 1888 Dear Boss I am getting on the move Lively baint i made a good Job Last time getting better Each time a good Joke i played on them three Laides one ['death' smudged out] Died two frighened Next time a woman and her Daughter tata Dear Boss [Drawing of stick man with knife standing over fallen victim, 'P' and man with knife, ?] [Postcard, black ink, f. 182]
11 November 1888 Hull	[Press Association]	Nov. 11th [Crude drawing of skull and crossbones] Sirs – this time I am not afraid of letting you know the whereabouts I am I can't help but laugh at idea of Sir C. Warren & his blood hounds It is of no use the police to be so reticent in the matter next time head clean off I have my eye on the next on the list there is plenty in Hull all good blood/ I have lost the real stuff. Take warning next time I carrie the head away with me in my bag the blood wont [illegible]? I take good care of the uterus. I will give next one gip [?] no mersey. Jack the R– [Police note in top left corner – 'DSS Rec'd from Press Afsociation 13/11'. Two pages, black ink, 127, ff. 522–4]
12 November 1888 London W.C.		This is my Photo of Jack the Ripper [Drawing of head and shoulders of unshaven man] 10 more and up goes the Sponge Sig Jack the Ripper' [Black ink, 135, ff. 175–6]

Date/Source	Addressee	Text, Sender and Remarks
12 November 1888 Paddington W.	On Her Majesty's Service	Inspector on Duty Scotland Yard Reason for Supposing Jack the ripper. a tailor from his letter. first (Ripper) is a tailors word. (Buckle) a tailors word. they wont (fix) fix buttons (proper red stuff) = army cloth or suits (real fits) tailors words – good fits men generally . uses expressions borrowed from this trade Yours truly Mathematician [134, ff. 517–19]
12 November 1888 London N.	Cheif Inspector Kings X Police Station Kings X Rd WC	To . . . Kings X Police Station 11/11/1888 Sir, Being an accomplice of "Jack the ripper" I am able to tell you that he will sail for "New York" from Liverpool on Thursday next "^^" Yours truly M Baynard [Line blotted out with black ink at top of page, and section blotted out under date] [Postcard, black ink, 130, ff. 520–1]
12 November 1888 London	To the Leman St Police Station London E	November 9.1888 Dear Boss You see I have done Another good thing for Whitchaple Yours in luck Jack the ripper J.F.W. [Black ink, smudged, ff. 531–3]

Date/Source	Addressee	Text, Sender and Remarks
12 November 1888 London E.C.	Dear Boss Lemen St Police Station	Dear Boss Guess what make me fits & keep on laghing at the Detectives I shall make them Busy next Thursday A woman Jane Batemore in at place I may not explain as I may be prevented I mean to kill Packer the fruiter in Berner St he knows me to well they can offer A hundred Free Pardons they will not catch me I mean to do 12 more I will do them How can they catch me Poor old Sir C Warren he is getting trouble if he likes I can put away wish me by murdering him I am A Patentee of murdering/ The prositues I promised Kelly it 2/6 for to have A [smudged word] Fuck & she gave a Little scream but I act quickly by putting a chop in neck the Dear old knife who committed these murders is down the thames If Government will give me A Free Pardon I shall give myself up [previous in black ink, following in pencil] no, after doing twenty I tried to do one last week but was prevented Good old Boss Yourstruly Jack the Ripper [Written on a torn piece of lined notepaper, two sides, ff. 534–6]
12 November 1888 London E.C.		Nov 12 18/88 Dear Boss just A line to Let you know that i got over my job all right i shall Do a another job about 2 or 300 yards from the same spot within 3 or 4 day. Singed Jack the Ripper [Purple ink, 139, No. 44, ff. 537–9]
13 November 1888 London	The Inspecter Detective Scotlandyard London	Dear Sir As you see I am still knocking about Ha. Ha. what chances there are to be sure I think I will give the East End a rest now & have a look round the suburbs have just met two nice girls in Norwood just the bit I like its no use you Slops trying to get me till I have got my number 6 then you may do what you like with me What for the [remainder is cross-written over preceding and difficult to read] bobbies arecan't get a man like me Why I speak to

Date/Source	**Addressee**	**Text, Sender and Remarks**
		about 6 a day & then they don't know me. Norwood seems a very quiet place I think I will cause a little excitement I cant say no more now will say more later on am in a hurry now yrs with love, Jack Ripper [Postcard, black ink, ff. 542–3. NB – 'slops' is an abbreviation of 'ecilops', back-slang for police.]
13 November 1888 London E.C.	O.H.M.S. [Drawing of stamp] Got no money to post it The Boss Leman Street Whitechapel	Dear Boss Have no money to send it by post I reside in one of the City Road lodgeing houses if you want me. I am going to try and do another murder in clapton on Saturday night Hoping this will find you well I remain Jack the Ripper [reverse] this got screw up last time Description of me Green & Black velvet coat and speckle trousers with 50[?]buttons down it & I carry a black bag [Full page drawing of a pearly king wearing a bowler and smoking an upside-down pipe. Written across at right-angles either side of drawing]

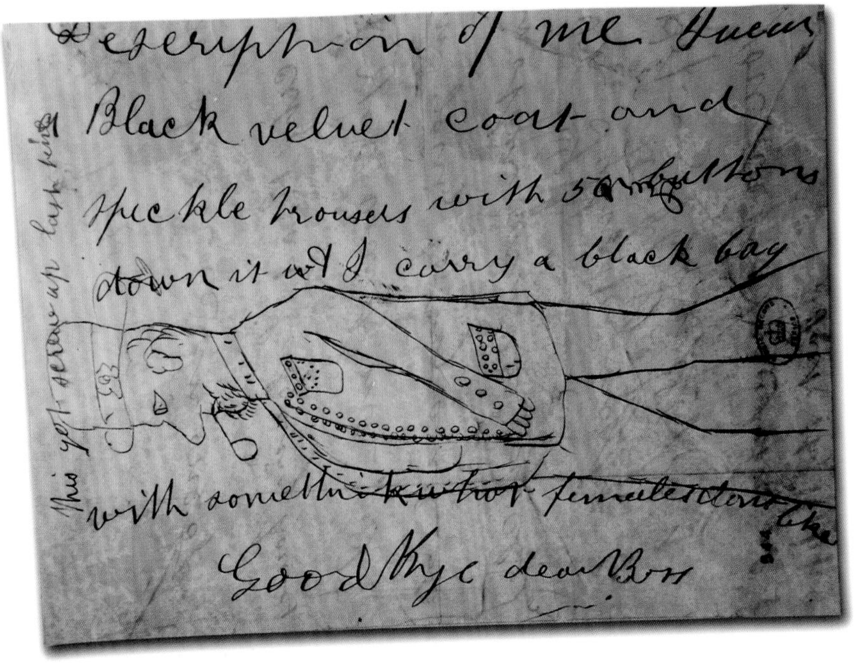
Description of me Green
Black velvet coat and
speckle trousers with 50 buttons
down it & I carry a black bag
with somethin [illegible]
Good bye dear Boss
This got screw up last time

Letter of 13 November 1888 with a drawing of a pearly king. This is the second page.

Date/Source	Addressee	Text, Sender and Remarks
		with somethink in that females don't like GoodBye dearBoss [Black ink, 140, No. 44, ff. 544–6]
14 November 1888 Found at Cage Lane Plumstead		November 14/18/88 Dear Boss I heard last week that you had caught me but you will find I am not yet you will hear of me and my works [?] again I am going to commit 3 more 2 girls and a boy about 7 years old this time I like ripping very much especialy women because they dont make a lot of noise Yours Jack the Witechapel Ripper hopping that you Will soon hear of my works <u>Again</u> [?] [146, f. 307]
14 November 1888 London W.C.		Dear Boss, I am going in next for A lady in [?] Operation. Shall leave off first time i miss a whore Jack [Difficult to read, ff. 540–1]
15 November 1888 Hackney E.	Inspector Leman St Police Court Wh<u>itechap</u>el	15/11/88. Dear Boss, I always address my letters to Boss my dear old cousin I mean to do another murder in Whitechapel on Wednesday. Mind you look out for me. I will cut her hears off nose off and pull her gutts out. I am yours Truly <u>Jack the Ripper</u> [Black ink, blue-lined paper, 23, ff. 226–7]

Date/Source	Addressee	Text, Sender and Remarks
15 November 1888 Ulverston		Dear Boss I made a good job last time. I intend doing another murder in the Furness district a week next Sunday night and dont forget to look out for me next Tuesday night Yours Jack the ripper [Black ink, 162, ff. 318–19]
15 November 1888 London E.C		excuse paper cannot afford to Buy any dear Boss i shall Be at my work in City Road on Monday Jack the Ripper Dont be Frightened [Black ink, 156, No. 53, ff. 469–70]
15 November 1888 Tottenham N.		Dear Boss you shall have a Nice parcel like the Boss lusk Wen I due Job I have 13 booked for blood and will Given my self VR my cousin is one of the ripper . We got tow parcel to send one to you and one to the landlord McCarthy Good By Dear Boss We will Ripper up Cox Next Jack the Ripper [Brown smudge at bottom of page and heavy brown smudging of reverse of page, possibly blood. Red ink, 159, No. 56, ff. 480–1]
15 November 1888 London S.E.	Inspector of Police Kings Cross Road Police Station	Dear Boss I wish to Inform you that I will in a few hours perform Business in this locality Kings Cross &c Yours Jack the Ripper [Postcard, black ink, f. 485]

Date/Source	Addressee	Text, Sender and Remarks
15 November 1888 London E.	The Boss Leman St. Police Station Whitechapel E. LONDON	14/11/1888 5-20 P.M. Dear Boss I gave you warning that I would clip the lady's ears off, grand work it was, Had plenty of time. finished her straight off. Shall not keep you waiting long. Will try & clear, 3 woman next time. I shall snap the fingers & toes off next time. My knife is a treat. But where are the Bloodhounds? Curse the Red Stuff it clogs so thick on me good bye till you hear from me again I'm 35 Jack the Ripper & Still Alive? [Black ink, ff. 505–7]
16 November 1888 London N.W.		16/11/88 [brown paper wrapper among reports] To the Supt, I know you are looking for me everywhere but you will never find me. I am chiefly in Hampstead Rd &

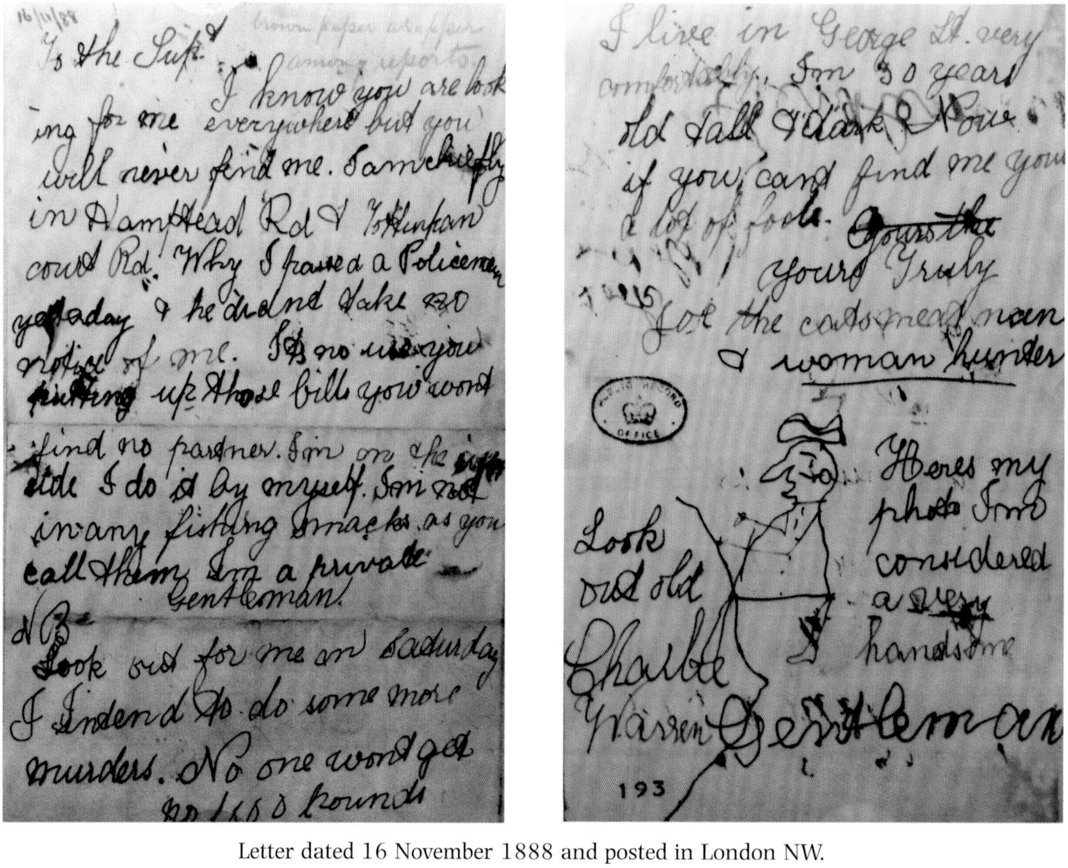
16/11/88
To the Supt
I know you are looking for me everywhere but you will never find me. I am chiefly in Hampstead Rd & Tottenham court Rd. Why I passed a Policeman yesterday & he did not take no notice of me. It's no use you putting up those bills you won't find no partner. I'm on the safe side I do it by myself. I'm not in any fishing smacks as you call them I'm a private Gentleman.
N.B.
Look out for me on Saturday I intend to do some more murders. No one won't get no £150 pounds
I live in George St. very comfortably. I'm 30 years old tall & dark & Novice if you can't find me you a lot of fools. Yours truly
Jack the cats meat man & woman hunter
Heres my photo I'm considered a very handsome Gentleman
Look out old Charlie Warren
193

Letter dated 16 November 1888 and posted in London NW.

Date/Source	Addressee	Text, Sender and Remarks
		Tottinham court Rd. Why I passed a Policeman yesterday & he didnt take no notice of me. Its no use you putting up those bills you wont find no partner. I'm on the right side I do it by myself. Im not in any fishing smacks as you call them Im a private Gentleman. Look out for me on Saturday I Intend to do some more murders. No one wont get no 1000 pounds./ I live in George St. very comfortable. Im 30 years old tall & dark [ ] if you cant find me your a lot of fools. Yours Truly Joe the cats meat man & woman hunter [Crude side view drawing of a man] Look out old Charlie Warren. Heres my photo Im considered a very handsome Gentleman [Two pages, black ink, 160, No. 58, ff. 193–4]
17 November 1888 Bow E.	Leman Street Police Station Whitechapel	Sat: Nov: 17th 1888 Dear Old Boss I am going to do another murder as soon a I see the chance I will do the next one worse than the last. I shall take her heart left kidny cassues and brains. Dear Old Boss you think your going to catch me now/ my mean cousin has been and gave the discription of me but you will find it the mistake out [two pages largely illegible because of heavy staining with blood (?)] going/ to murder my cousin the first time I see him . . . Jack the Ripper/ dear Boss I have ornamented the paper well so you can see I have got the proper stuff this time [Four pages in brown ink (?), 167, No. 59, ff. 184–6]
17 November 1888 Chiswick	To the officer of the White chaple Police Station E	18 Miller's Court Whitechapel Dear Boss You have not caught me yet or are you likely to. No. 8 I have only got settle 12 more in less than 4 weeks. The Dectives seem to such lot [?] as for Sir Charles Warren Puppeys they are not good at all From your Friend Jack the

Date/Source	Addressee	Text, Sender and Remarks
		Ripper [Note at bottom in pencil – 'There is no 18 Miller's Court 19.11.88 . . .'] [Black ink,168, No. 60, ff. 315–17]
18 November 1888 Plymouth		Plymouth Dear Boss How is it you cant find me I am at Plymouth at Present and I think I will do a little business down here with the whores as they are quite as bad as they are in the old place. Keep the bloodhound ready as I shall be back again by Christmas. Yours truly Jack the Ripper [Black ink, 169, ff. 313–14]
19 November 1888 London S.E.		18. November 1888. Dear Boss The police officers 'ave not caught me yet How can they when I am used to police work. I shall [k]eep on ripping whores till [I] do get buckled. I want to get to work right away if I get a chance and will do another one indoors. The last job was a grand one/ It took me a long time to do. My knifes so nice and sharp I shall take the next ladys scalp. You will hear of my funny little games again on Friday night Good luck Yours truly Jack the Ripper [Police note across top left corner of first page – 'Inspector Abberline' initials illegible] [Black ink, f. 320]
19 November 1888 Ipswich	To the Leman Street Police Station Whitechapel	Jacky the Ripper Dear Boss/ being near Ipswich I must not leave that delicious town for these lovely young women there is a friend of mine belong to this town tells me this Polly

Date/Source	Addressee	Text, Sender and Remarks
	London East End	Wright living not far away from The Church at opposite mark with barracks Luisa Whitning may be her colour of near my short blade . . . most likely you wont know the murder I have just committed F. for the Handicap fixed for next week I must see race & I hear you are a racing chap . . . Ink Pen & Paper are all very poor they won't let me have them semely about whitechapel Look out the St Clements district including Welcome Sailor Gardner's Arms & etc. [Two pages. Also a High Court of Justice Life Assurance form with message 'near Gardner's Arms or in Myrtle Road St Clements <u>Ipswich</u> I hear there was on Saturday after noon a murder Committed / <u>Bramford</u> / but Ill good bye Yours Dear Boss Jack.Ripper . . .'. Black ink, ff. 47–50]
19 November 1888 London E.		Poplar– I am very much amused at the description of myself in the paper. If you want a full description and a truthfull one, find the Good woman that took me across Hackney Common and through the Parks/ a fortnight ago. I had made up my mind to work that day on the first I met, we were in a dark place for it was foggy. But if I am the Devil I could not/ touch her. she is the only good woman I have met in England I told her I was Jack the Ripper and I took my hat off and she is the only one/ that has seen my face. I am the man you will have a hard job to find her, she was going to work and had got her girl with her. I could have done mother & daughter easy, she was to good. Jack the Ripper [Pencil, four pages, ff. 68–9]
19 November 1888	The Boss Police Station Calton Bridge	Dr Boss I am still in the third Avenue here and I am still amusing myself with the most <u>important</u> arrest of your men which are being made daily Well my friend I have done another last night of which this is the blood I mean to leave it a little longer before I tell you where I have done the/ four not yet found [illegible] May. This blood [illegible] your bloodhounds at their work I shall stay here until further notice. Yours Dr Boss

Date/Source	Addressee	Text, Sender and Remarks
		Jack the Ripper P.S. Take care of my cousin who bought the [illegible] Ha! Ha! [Pencil, two pages, splashed and smeared with brown stains, possibly blood. Envelope addressed in black ink. ff. 70–2]
19 November 1888 Glasgow	Metropolitan Police Office London	THE WHITECHAPEL ATROCITIES ALL ON THE WRONG SALVAGE! I AM IN A FIRST-CLASS AT GOVAN WANTED young lady the 24th instant B GOD I SHALL CLEAR GLASGOW AND GOVAN AND POLLOCSHIELDS OF 16 ENGLISH WHORE LADIES AND GENTLEMEN THE LORD WILL DO HIS GUARANTEED Work BY SCUTCHER. 300 Pieces REQUIRED NO CLUE. [Postcard with address and message made up of press cuttings, ff. 74–5]
19 November 1888 Stratford E.	please send this to Scotland yard The Headquarters of the police	I am Jack the Ripper Catch me if you can/ shall have one in Woolwhich This week Look out for me at Woolwhich' [Black ink, drawing of back of man wearing astrakhan trimmed coat on first page.] [Black ink, ff. 76–7]
19 November 1888 Weston-Super-Mare		Royal Hotel Weston-S-M. 11/17/88 Dear Old Boss. I am now going to make my way to Paris and try my little games on them as you aint sharp enough for me here I have done eleven murders so you aint found them out after al. Two gone down suers. God bless you. Good by I'm of to Paris. Believe me ever Yours affectionatly [Black ink, ff. 80–1]

Date/Source	Addressee	Text, Sender and Remarks
20 November 1888 Birmingham		From Jack the RipperaliasLeather Apron Dear Boss I think I will give myself up because I makes me wretched but I wanted to get rid of these old tales & I hope you will forgive me when I have murdered you Yours Truly Jack the Ripper Bham [Pencil, ff. 42–3]
20 November 1888 Paddington	To The commercial street plice station Whitechapal	Dear Boss 2[?]4/11/1888 I hope you are quite well as It leaves me at present for I am going to commited another murder on Wenesnday just as bad as the other. look out for me for I am going to her head off and her legs off. In fashion street I will be there of all day long. Plese will you pass this to sir Charlie dear Charlie. Yours truly Jack the Ripper I was round the euston when the law [?] took a man on suspion. Don't forget I wrote when very quick becaus I had to catch the trian for queens park [Black ink, No. 64, ff. 44–6]
21 November 1888 London E.C.	Inspector Abberline Scotland Yard	Jack the Ripper wishes to give himself up will Abberline communicate with him at number 39 Cutler Street Houndsditch with this end in view Jack the Ripper This is written with the '<u>Blood of Kelly</u>' all Long Liz's blood is used up [Measures 5.25 × 8.25 inches. Telegram, red ink, No. 73, ff. 23–4]
21 November 1888 Crawley	Mr. MacKean 6 [illegible] Hilldrop Crescent Regents Park London	<u>Notice</u> I.Jack.the.Riper Will Pay Shortly a visit to your Residence or your City shop Truly yours Jack Riper" [Pencil, reverse of envelope states 'not known at 6 Hilldrop Cres Holloway', ff. 31–4]

Date/Source	Addressee	Text, Sender and Remarks
21 November 1888 London N		Near the Spot Nov 21/88. Dear Boss/ Being still at large –thanks to the energetic efforts of the Police to effect my capture. I take the liberty of writing to you to say that it is my intention of committing one or two outrages & murders in or near your locality-perhaps on the steps of your office. I am not living far away from Cavendish Street, near your office. The reason of my writing this in ink instead of human blood is that I was not fool enough to keep any from last jobs in Whitechapel. Yours Jack the Ripper [Two pages, black ink, No. 67, ff. 37–8]
21 November 1888 Hornsey, N.		To Dear old Boss from <u>Jack the Ripper</u> [With appended cutting 'F.F.G. – In England and Wales there is one policeman to every seven hundred and seventy-five people.' [Black ink, ff. 40–1]
22 November 1888 Manchester		Manchester Nov. 22nd 88 Dear Boss I am staying in Manchester at present but dressed as a poor man a navvie. saw the paper and you have had a letter from someone signed J. Ripper from Portsmouth soon after I did the last job (Kelly) i have been in Manchester since. Had nothing to do since kelly but seen Jervis's girls [?] every day will visit London about Sunday ready to be in time again on Monday. when i will do another i will tell you all when i get copped. Good Bye old fellow till i return. Yours Truly Jack the Ripper. [Black ink, No. 72, ff. 25–6]

Date/Source	Addressee	Text, Sender and Remarks
22 November 1888 London N	Stoke Newington Police station N.	Dear Boss Catch me I you can, you will soon hear of me again, Yours Respectfully "Jack the Ripper" [Postcard, black ink, No. 70, f. 27]
22 November 1888 Liverpool		hear I am again Dear Boss I was nr coming a cropper on a nice gal patrige to slice into in Ashton Street and was just going to make a bargain when all of a sudden a nurse or someat like one comes out of a hospital close by and spoils my little game she was a perky one mind you to for she stood in the road to watch me til i wated carles like away but by Jove if she comes in my way again ille make her feel something sharp in her dainty carcass ille try Ashton Street again there is nice cosy little draw rooms where i can do it comfortteley they ill find/ lots of red raddle spilt some day they ill find nice little partriges breasts some day in there cuburds i met a young woman in Scotland Road the night I smiled at her and she calls out Jack the ripper She dident know how right she was i am goin up tonight ther to shop in Liverpool but I'll try again soon Jack the Ripper wont be better meet me at Euston same place did you see that 1818 stone partrige She ill cut up well Boss [Two pages, black ink, No. 69, f. 29]
22 November 1888 London		22 Nov. 1888 Dear Boss I do larf when I hears you have cort me I shall do for two more next Saturday so look sharp and catch me if you can I will send their ears and bloody guts to you good by Boss Jack the Ripper You see I am not far off [Black ink, No. 73, ff. 141–2]

Date/Source	Addressee	Text, Sender and Remarks
23 November 1888 Birmingham		Rea St Lodging House Birmingham Dear Sir, I beg to inform you that I have read about that bungling affair yesterday morning in Whitechapel, this is to say that I have had no hand in it, but I think it must be one of my apprentices who has been practising, while I have been away, I am pleased to say that I arrived safe in B'ham last friday, where I have been since, I come to record my vote last saturday in/ support of the Bible candidate, for the school board election I am taking a holiday for a week I will again give you a standby visit, but I am going to try my luck here, before I come over, as I can see good chances for my practise, regretting you have been compelled to retire, wishing you better luck from the Old Original Jack the Ripper PS Kindly let the public know how disgusted I am with that offer, but I will make out next time [Red ink, ff. 20–1]
23 November 1888 London E.C.	London News Agency London	E.C. dear Boss Next week we polish of another maiden Yours truly, Jack <u>the Ripper</u> [Red ink, Docket 1610, ff. 58–60]
25 November 1888 Gloucester		Dear Boss, Just a few lines to you to tell I am stopping near Glos'ter for a few days I intend waiting here till the last affair is blown over and then may return on another visit to to Whitechapel dont you think I'm having a good Grinn abbout the man with the black moustache; ha ; ha ;/ Dear Boss: tell the Glostorins not to be to much alarmed as I dont feel up to having a game with them at present; I remain yours faithfuly Jack the <u>Ripper</u> [Black ink, two pages, 206, ff. 478–9]

Date/Source	Addressee	Text, Sender and Remarks
26 November 1888 London W.		Dear Boss / I Send a Line to say that I shall be at Work again on next Thursday morning / Yours / Truly / Jack the Ripper [Red ink, No. 78, f. 13]
26 November 1888 London N.W.		Dear Boss Just a line to tell you that I shall do another murder on some young youth such as printing lads who work in the City I did write you once before but I don't think you had it I shall do them worse than the women I shall take their hearts/ and rip them up the same way I shall be up the City some time next week so I will atack on them when they are going home as I want to do some more as I like the job very much I shall kill 20 or 30 before you can kitch me any Youth I see I will kill but you will never kitch me put that in your pipe and smoke it how about the bloodhounds Good bye Dear Boss Your truly Jack Ripper I am all over Whitechapel and City Also see your brave worrors police I see them and they cant see me [Pencil, 209, Docket 1639, ff. 309–10]
27 November 1888 London S.E.	Private Whitechapel Police Whitechapel Road London	.E. 17 Whitechapel Road .E. Dear Boss / I hope when you get home you will find your mother murdered for that is what you deserve Yours truly Jack the Ripper [Black ink, ff. 9–11]
27 November 1888 Richmond		Hell 26/11/88 Dear Boss/ Was not that jolly at scare about that woman

Date/Source	Addressee	Text, Sender and Remarks
		who thought that Jack the Ripper. They think they have got hold of my description I laughed myself into fits over that I have got a jolly lot of false whiskers & moustachios in my black bag. The last job was nice & clean. I carried away a part of her. (Conundrum Try & find what part). I am going to do another on Friday. & I shall give the police enough running about on Christmas. Jack the Ripper [Black ink, f. 167]
28 November 1888 Kilburn		[This letter is written on the inside of an opened up envelope] [Top flap] kilburn lodging house Gentlemen this is the first note you have had from the real man. but that dont matter for i am not yet my number is sixteen in this country six i have done and the rest i mean to do if it is to hot in the east i will come to the west i went in the hide park the other night and found some nice little dears but it was to light from the moon to do business but you will hear [left flap] of one there praps before you get this they have had me and i will have them [right flap] Yours [?] the black brunswick boy [Black ink, ff. 547–8]
3 December 1888 London E.	Sir Charles Warren Scotland Yard London	Dear Boss, You have not caught me yet and you are not likely to. I shall keep on at my work for I love it, and I will send

Date/Source	Addressee	Text, Sender and Remarks
		you something for a christmas box. Yours Jack the Ripper [Postcard, black ink, 235, f. 114]
4 December 1888 Taunton	TimES office London Private Editor	Dear Boss [largely illegible] Jack THE Skipper [Black ink, 292, Docket No. 1035, ff. 126–8]
4 December 1888 London E.C.	–Saunders Esqr. Police Magistrates London	England Dear Boss Look out for 7th inst. Am trying my hand at disjointing and if can manage it will send you a finger Saunders Esqr Yours Police magistrate Jack the Ripper [Envelope purple ink, written over at bottom in black ink – 'Thames Police Court E'. Letter measures 6 × 7.25 inches and is written on a cutting from a newspaper, purple ink, 237, No. 90, ff. 552–3]
6 December 1888 London	Mrs. Shirley 3 Annerley Road Junction Road Upper Holloway N.	(1) London Dec 6th 1888 To Mrs. Shirley Madam, you are not aware of the way in which your husband carries on when he is out of your sight, but I can tell you he must look out for himself, as an outraged temper is determined to have revenge. For you, you saucy cat, it will not be your cheeks that will be/ Slapped, but your heart-strings will be pulled before long. We are on your husbands track the carrotty looking cur, the sooner, and better he carts himself and you out of this neighbourhood he will enjoy more his personal safety, for I tell you that either myself or some other member of my family, are waiting to take revenge. You can substantiate this,/

Date/Source	Addressee	Text, Sender and Remarks
		That if he is clever at nothing else, he is a pretty good hand at getting children. Your eyes are closed long enough, but I tell you they will be opened before long, it would perhaps pay you to watch the ginger looking swine a little closer, but, the poor devil. I pity you. no name [Black ink, (308), Y. 21. 12. 88., ff. 454–7]
8 December 1888 Chatham		Chatham/Saturday/December 8th/1888 Dear Boss I am still at liberty the last job was not bad in (Whitechapel) but I guess the next will be a (dam) sight worse the police about here are fine looking fellows I had the pleasure of drinking with one this morning and/ asked him what he thought about my glorious work I guess I will make a double shuffle of it this time me and my pal (you bet) I have got one or two set and soon shall have more (Ha_Ha_Ha) I can see better specimens in garrison town look out in a day or two yours (not yet) jack the Ripper (Ha,Ha) [Black ink, f. 8]
19 December 1888 Liverpool	Editor of the Times newspaper Printing House Square London	Dear Boss I have left London because it was too hot for me. Monroe made it too hot for me. I have come to Liverpool & you will soon hear of me Yours [red ink blot] Jack the ripper PS some of the real stuff but I have to be verry sparing of it [Black ink, 293, Docket No. 1035, ff. 124–5]
21 December 1888 Y	[Mrs Shirley]	London 21 (3) I Have wanted to be your friend with mi letter i did not want to met you it wos to appear yours by a my the Bastard Riiper . . . one hart [largely illegible] . . . i will

Date/Source	Addressee	Text, Sender and Remarks
		Rip you up the first time meet ought to punish the Bastard JACK THE Ripper [Measures 9 × 7 inches. Very thick block-lettered writing. Black ink, ff. 554–5]
23 December 1888 Limerick	The Head Postmaster London	England Limerick Ireland Dear Boss I am on leave now I will be all till after Xmass don't trouble London for me I want my holidays. I must travel all Ireland and Scotland the Police here are not of much use I have been happy to say I have been traveling with some of your Dectives which I met on the 15 in hollihead we was together as far as dublin when we parted on Sunday morning of the 16th Jack the Ripper [Black ink, 294, No. 97, ff. 119–22]
8 January 1889		Dear Boss I write these few lines to you just to inform you that I shall soon be on the job again very shortly near blackheath., I have my eye on a few gay women. You have thought you have had me but I have laughed ha ha ha I Remain Yours very truly Jim the Cutter [Letter marked with brown finger smudges, probably blood] [Black ink, 298, 3/52983 / 1852, ff. 222–3]
15 January 1889 C Division		Dear Boss I will [illegible] rip another woman on [illegible] in Whitechapel last I chucked some old wo[missing] in the thames because [missing] began to sqeal but I . . .

Date/Source	Addressee	Text, Sender and Remarks
		[illegible] . . . I riped up little boy in Bradford [missing] in Slough. Dear Boss you will hear [missing] me soon. yours truly Jack Bane [?] Alias Jack the Ripper[?] [Red ink (?), No. 299 / No. P52983/1845. ff. 17–18]
16 January 1889		Alma Rd N Jany 16 88 [*sic*] Dr Boss As to the Tunis scare I am still in London After my trip to Bradford. I shall remain still for a 2 time I am preparing a draught, that will kill & leave no marks those I shall give it to will fall in various places, either being runover or die from its effect 3 for the future I am Scarlet Runner should you wish for particulars of the Bradford mystery give me a corner in the echo (to Scarlet Runner 4 I fear not your detectives as my disguises are as numerous as theirs. I know I shall be caught one day, as I often rush against a boby in my haste. Scarlet Runner Further particulars When I note corner [Four pages, black ink, ff. 267–8]
4 February 1889 London S.E.	Mr Monro City Superintendant of Police Authoritys	Dear Boss Be on the look out . as I am coming to visit Mile-end and do for the rest to number 15 then I give myself up to the Police Yours- Jack the Ripper

Date/Source	Addressee	Text, Sender and Remarks
		returned from America [Postcard, pencil, CLRO Police Box 3.22, No. 383]
18 February 1889 London E	O.H.M.S. Chas. Warren Esqre. Home Office SW	'Perhaps you don't know who I am My name is Jack the Ripp[er] From the police I'm a gr[eat] Slipper My real name is Raffa[ ] And I am to be found in Whitechapel Augustus Robertson Raf[ ] formerly of 24 Goulso[n?] Whitechapel now of Vanbrugh Park Blackhea[th]' [Envelope in red ink; 'Home' deleted in black ink and 'Police Scotland Yard' added. Letter measures 10.4 × 7 inches, approx. 1 inch strip torn from down right side of page. Red ink, 3/52983 1952 No. 313, ff. 482–4]
31 March 1889	Commissioner of police Scotland Yard	March 31st Dear Boss Just a line to say I think its time to commence my little games again so keep your boss eye open the first week in April/ Yrs, truly Jack the Ripper [Black ink, two pages, No. 3/52983/ 1999, ff. 285–8]
18 July 1889 Leicester	Central Police Station London	July 18th 1889 Races Leicester Dear Boss I write you a few lines hoping you are geting on nicely they call me an American butcher now. never mind I have started ['operaiton' – deleted] killing again its grand work I dont like give it up just now. I had not time to finish the

Date/Source	Addressee	Text, Sender and Remarks
		last one. I shall be in London again to night. Do they think they got a clue they perhaps would like to have. they is another one I have got my eye on her I will close this letter to Dear Boss I Remain Jack the Ripper [Black ink, No. 3 52983/2072, ff. 322–4]
19 July 1889 London S.W.	Mister Monro Head of police Scotland Yard S.W. From "Jack the rip"	Say now boss no "narrow escape" your officers are lying free. I had heaps of time . guess I am coming west now for I am a moral man and am determined to put down wholesale whoredom I am going for "lady prostitutes" now and there are millions. then too some well known card sharper, and other sports will be attended to I have located one a scorcher not far from portman square who will be found properly carved and his tool ears tongue and ears I shall cut off and send you leaving his guts on the side walk this wont be mean anyway I am a new god to reform abuses and advantage players, must be stopped going around – no more crimping at poker , and the sucker shall have a look in no more ringing in a cold deck no more reflectors for that boss I guess he may chuck his bugs and/ [missing]lds out for I am – to his vile [ ] right away , he euchred a male of mine and so I am going to stick him and others, pig sticking I call it shall be around Scotland yard soon I am "a foreign butcher" am I you cannot locate me I guess but you see I am an instrument of god for good and when I divide neatly some killed bosses wife a lady lord I guess you will be mad and feel a bit mean and there is no one to squeal for I do it all myself . . . a word of warning beware and protect your low immoral pot bellied prince god has marked him for destruction and "mutilation" , keep your men about pimlico and belgravia – soon there will be two more stiff on the side walks and ladies now [drawing of knife with finger pointing at it 'his tool'] Jack the ripper" n.b. other letters nd gen[missing] [Black ink, two pages, small neat hand, envelope has large blot of red ink under seal, No. 3/52983/ 207, ff. 106–7]
19 July 1889 London E.	Commercial [ ] Police Station	E. July 19, 1889

Date/Source	Addressee	Text, Sender and Remarks
		Dear Boss Will be Saturday 20. And Sunday 21. Night in 3. Princess street Spitalfields the Club and see what can do Watch and catch me if you can Jack the Ripper [Red ink, 26A, No. 96R, ff. 229–32]
19 July 1889 London S.W.	The head one of the policemen Scotland Yard London	I will cut out There Abdomen I dare say you Know what That means Whitechapel Three women done me wrong in Whitechapel So I will kill every women there. 20 because of Them I am Jack the Ripper. I am going to have another women in two more days time in Whitechapel near castle alley I am a mark on the women The police ant artfull enough for me. I do it when I get a chance not when I see police coming I will do it one of those times when a copper looking and the I'll do the same to him. [This paragraph in pencil] I live in Whitechapel Yours Truly I have been Jack the Ripper [signature in pencil] over in america all the summer I am in [illegible & torn]/ They searched all them barrows and carts Near the castle alley But they didn't search the one I was in I was looking at the police all the Time. [Black ink, 15A, No. 3/52983 , ff. 346–8]
19 July 1889 London	J. Monroe Esq C.B. Commissioner Office 4 Whitehall Place SW	Dear Sir I accomplished my eighth victim without interruption I shall now wait quietly till 27th when two shall fell the knife to celebrate the Royal wedding so to make more news for papers for this work I am paid by a

Date/Source	Addressee	Text, Sender and Remarks
		society abroad whose name wille not be mentioned I intend finishing my work late in August when I shall sail for abroad Believe me sir The Worlds surprise Jack the Ripper [Black ink, ff. 354–5]
22 July 1889 London E.C.		Angust Hotel Nr B Street City July 22nd 1889 Dear Boss I am about to do another murder tomorrow night or Wednesday night I cant keep from my work long for I love it to much, catch me if you can. this is the last one this side of the water, the next Im/ going to give the other side a turn, I had a bit of a job with the last one. I had to leave it before I could finish signed Jack the Ripper [Purple crayon, 11A, No. 3/52983 2083, ff. 337–8]
22 July 1889 London W.		London W. Dear Boss Back again & up to the old tricks. Would you like to catch me? I guess you would well look here – I leave my diggings – close to Conduit St to night at about 10.30 watch Conduit St & close round there – Ha – Har I dare you 4 more lives four more cunts to add to my little collection &/ I shall rest content Do what you will you will never trap Jack the Ripper Watch P.C. 60.C. light moustache Shaven clean rather stout he can tell you almost as much as I can – G.F.S. [? deleted] F Place. R. St. W/ [drawing of a knife blade] not a very big blade

Date/Source	Addressee	Text, Sender and Remarks
		but o sharp [Police note top left corner, first page – 'Yes/DSS' (Chief Inspector Donald Sutherland Swanson). Black ink, three pages, 10A, No. 3/52983 2082, ff. 339–41]
24 July 1889 London E.		24/7/89 Sir, I will commence again on the 5th August Yours very truly Jack the Ripper [Police note top right-hand corner – 'Yes/DSS'. Black ink, 7A, No. 3/52983 / 2086, ff. 332–3]
25 July 1889 London N.W.		London W. Dear Boss You have not caught me yet you see, with all your cunning, with all your "tecs" with all your blue bottles. I have made two narrow squeaks this week, but still thogh disturbed I got clear before I could get to work – I will give the foreigners a run now I think – for a change – Germans especially if I can – I was conversing with two or three of your men last night – their eyes <u>of course were shut</u> & thus they/ Did not see my bag. Ask any of your men who were on duty last night in Piccadilly (Circus End) last night if they saw a gentleman put 2 dragoon guard sergeants into a hansom. I was close by & heard him talk about shedding blood in Egypt. I will soon shed more in England. I hope you read mark & learn all that you can if you do so you may & may not catch Jack the Ripper/ If you want to know where Jack the Ripper is Ask a policeman So long old boys au revoir somday I shall meet you again ha ha ha Your old friend (the enemy) Jack [Police note top left-hand corner – 'Yes/DSS'. Black ink (bronzed), 8A, No. 3/52983/2086, ff. 328–30]

Date/Source	Addressee	Text, Sender and Remarks
26 July 1889 London N.W.	W.M. Commissioner of Police Scotland Yard	July 26th 1889 Somers Town DEAR BOSS, I am very sorry I have given you all the trouble I have, but my thirst for blood must be satisfied, when I have slaughtered 6 more I shall give myself up to your dogs, before this month is gone you will hear of me again, this time it shall be Kings Cross where a few of the whores want thinning. Boss your dogs are too hot for me at Whitechapel or I should have done the rest there, the man who catches me will be a clever one, and will have to fight very hard for the reward offered. I am now living/ in Somers Town, but I must not tell you my address. I remain Dear Boss Your truly "Jack the Ripper" P.S. please excuse the writing, you shall hear from me again/ [Somerstown was the geographical district of St Pancras. Note top left corner – 'Yes/'. Blue paper, lined, black ink, 24A, No. 3/52983 2087, ff. 349–50]
30 July 1889 London	The Commr. of Police Old Jewry E.C.	SURELY THE LORD IS IN THIS HOUSE [Red printed message, CLRO Police Box 3.22, No. 385 a–b]
7 August 1889 Victoria Docks		7/8/89 To the Evening & Post/ Boss/ I now write these Horrible line to you to let the people of Canning Town know I am hunting about I was with a good looking winter [?] last night at the church I thought I would let her live a day or so, over/ so as I could sharpen my tools ready for her Hold me tight you cunning lot of coppers the next time you catch me I am Jack the Ripper catch me if you can I do shake writing these lines [Black ink, No. 3/52983/2092, ff. 109–10]

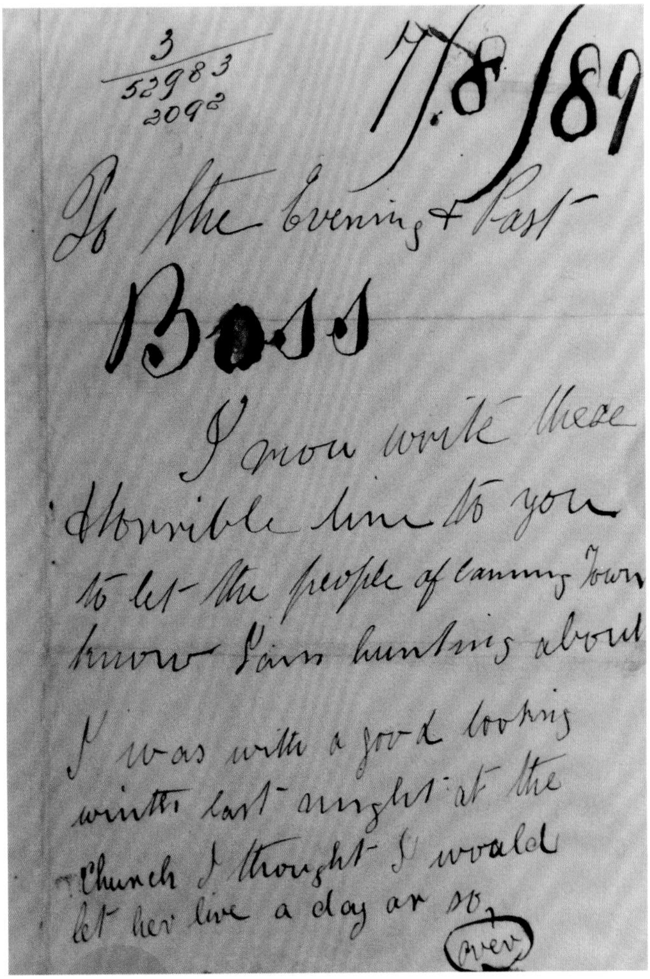
3
52983
2092
7/8/89
To the Evening Post
Boss
I now write these horrible line to you to let the people of Canning Town know I am hunting about I was with a good looking wench last night at the Church I thought I would let her live a day or so.
over

Letter of 7 August 1889 — 'I am Jack the Ripper catch me if you can . . .'

Date/Source	Addressee	Text, Sender and Remarks
21 August 1889 South Lambeth	The Standard Studios 35 Buckingham Palace Belgravia	thinks old Pal but I don't want any taken this week I saw my Photo a short time ago in the Police News you know Johnny Rippers will give you a call in a day or t[ ]/ as you have a lot in your district wants a look up yet. Mr one ready say Friday next about 12.45 am where in Bird Cage Walk one of the old girls of Westminster yours Jack Rippers of nobles [Black ink, written on back of two 'Standard Photographic Studio 35, Buckingham Palace Road, Belgravia' special offer tickets, 32A, ff. 169–71]
AU (?) 28 1889 London W.C.	Mrs Crawford 1. Queens Rd Battersea	I Jack the Ripper will committ a murder in Queens Road on Friday, Yours &c. Jack the RIPPER [Black ink, 33A, 146/R, ff. 219–21]

Date/Source	Addressee	Text, Sender and Remarks
2 September 1889 Found in a bottle washed ashore between Sandwich & Deal.		Sep. 2nd/89 S.S. Northumbria Castle Left ship- am on trail yours Jack the Ripper [Measures 2 × 6.25 inches. Pencil, ff. 458–9]
4 September 1889 London S.W.		4 Sept '89 Dear Boss I will do [illegible] my work again this time in York Street I have got/ My eyes out to do nice quite young women Yours Jack Ripper [illegible] [Written in thick scrawl, black ink, 34A, 52983/2100, ff. 352–3]
10 September 1889 London W.C.		I can write a great many hands this is one far from detection From Jack the Ripper Wednesday 10/1889 Dear Bos Just a few lines before-hand I warn you to be on your guard. I mean to begin again and with more determination. Oh how I crack my sides with laughing when I read of dear Old Jack and to think the Shiny button are baffled. I must say you/ are clever in finding out things you are quite perfect. I am a Student and I have been employed at one of the largest Hospitals in London. I am a French man by birth but through reduce circumstances and partly by English Woman I have been brought to poverty and oblige to take refuge in Whitechaple revenge/ is sweet so the Englishman say and I mean to have it I mean to do 20 and then I mean to give myself up. That last one was a devilish tuff one the knife had to be sharpened up a great many times you are quite right I did do it in a house were she lived and took me home I gave one of her ears to a passing dog so if you find the other parts you will not find the Ear the Poor old Sailor you mention in the

Date/Source	Addressee	Text, Sender and Remarks
		Paper gave a grunt while I was/ devilish P.S. I am leaving the [illegible] of Whitechapel excuse blunder I scarcely know what I am doing Jack depositing the bag that nearly made me Jump out of my boots poor Old chap how sad to be taken for Jack the Ripper I glory in it keep your spirits up dear Bos and be on your guard all though this as been written with a beating heart and a Shakey hand its from Dear Old Jack who wish you luck. [Black ink, four pages, 58895/16, ff. 375–7]
10 September 1889 London E.	The Evening News and Post Whitefraires St London	Whitechapel Sept. 10 Dear Boss The Ripper scare this morning is an infernal scandal on me you know. I never do my ripping in that fashion but give them a chance to catch me ha ha I'd show you again soon wont be long but this will delay my opperations untill it bloodhounds [?] Jack the Ripper [Postcard, pencil, 39A, 57885/186, ff. 402–3]
11 September 1889 Stockton		Stockton Sep. 11 /89 Dear Sir Please will you oblige me by Putting this into your Paper to let the People of England now that I ham [?] still living and running at larg as yet & intends to [illegible] I thought I would Have a new House at the north to see what there was going on there/ the People in London . . . [illegible, damaged] . . . way out off it I moved into Stockton last night from Kings Cross theres a few . . . Stockton I should like th[illegible] cut up Wisly . . . [illegible] . . . fast I ham leaving for newcastle to [illegible] you will soo Hear of me in Whitechapple again/ I have 2 more in London & then it might be Stockton or Newcastle soon I put well Paid for it so you see I ham

Date/Source	Addressee	Text, Sender and Remarks
		getting on well I shall leave Newcastle tomorrow for London again the last ones cut up well so I have to close from yours. Jack the Ripper so Long [Black ink, three pages, ff. 372–4]
11 September 1889 London S.W.		Whitechapel. E. 11th Sep[t 1]889. Sir. To clear up this matter re the whitechapel murders. no doubt you think [ ]vious that [I]am not cought. but I must confess I was as nere cought this morning as possible. PC passed me while i was carring my deadly parcel to the arch off cable st or nere their. I must one I am fortunate to eskape the law so/ long but I have sworn to kill fifteen wimmans in Whitechapel and bye Gods help so I will. I can tell you I am miserable as one can be and shall be glad when my bloody worke is over as I find it is reccherd at nite to sleep I have some dredfull dreames I do not care if i am cought or no. now I am in london I will remain till I finished/ my work. I bought a paper this morning red the news and wished I was ded. Yours JMS Clarke Not Jack the ripper [Police note at top left corner of first page – 'Yes/DSS/'. Black ink, three pages, 58895/H, ff. 380–2]
12 September 1889 London N.	Mr. Monro Chief Commissioner of Police Scotland yard	Jack the rippers hole Whitechapel Dear Boss I shall certainly have you wife or Daughter of theirs leg Before another month she will be mutilated in a cruel manner But I can't help that Signed [illegible] [On reverse of envelope, 'shall write the next letter in Blood implements of torture.' (drawings of gun, razor and knives). Letter black ink, ff. 368–70]

Date/Source	Addressee	Text, Sender and Remarks
12 September 1889 London W.C.	J. Munro, Esq 4 Whitehall Place Scotland Yard S.W.	London 12/9/89 Sir, . . . excuse me [missing] writing to you [missing] boldly, but [missing] intended to settle 4 more 2 in the east end, & 1 at Islington & 1, at West end near Regent St- some time next week/ for I have not got the right cow yet, I have sworn to catch the right one that as Injured me, I did not settle that one under arch way, but I know who did, I am not Jack the riper, as it is put about, I am Brumigan Bill the Slaughterman/ for they are all Brumigan Women, that I have settled for they have ruined many a honest man in their own native town, and have come to Injure honest men here but I intend to stop there little game I am Sir your's Brumigan Bill the Slaughterman Not Jack the riper [Black ink, three pages, 44A, 57885/207, ff. 440–2]
13 September 1889 London E.C.	Mep. Saunders Magestrait Harbour Square Police Court	Beware of my fire Arms From Eleven Jack Ripper I mean to start my work Again in a new slum in royal mint . st by the help of the devil next week but where I shall not mention I shall take the eyes nose only open the lower part of Victim an leave, I mean to start work the-/ new st [?] [illegible] during the week [middle portion of page largely illegible, torn with pieces missing] . . . Black gloves with smart walk Yours Jack the Ripper/ Bucks Row George Yard Browns Lane Doster St Berner St Mitre Square Castle Alley Back Ch lane You must give me a chance to do two more [Pencil, three pages, ff. 387–8]

Date/Source	**Addressee**	**Text, Sender and Remarks**
16 September 1889 London	Mr. Monr[missing] Chief Commissioner of Police Scotland Yard SW	Vauxhall any body . this time Sir I beg leave to inform you of my change in residence I have removed to the above where I intend to commence business as soon as possible I thought it best to tell you so as you should not waste your time over East Look out for tomorrow night I remain your I.N. alias Jack the ripper [Black ink, ff. 444–7]
18 September 1889 London	To the Maid care of Mr [missing] top flo[missing] 12 [missing]	You to are the next I shall require . Beware – my next visit is Camberwell 'Ah Ah = slip me if you can

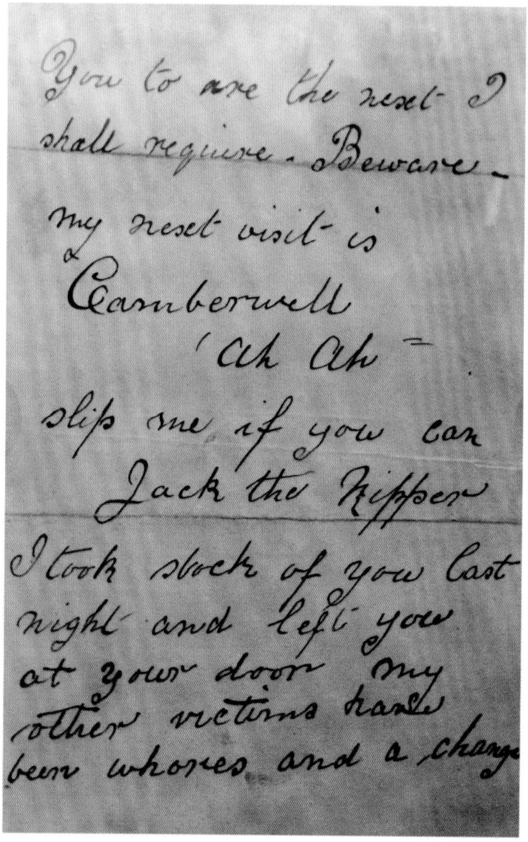
You to are the next I
shall require . Beware –
my next visit is
Camberwell
'Ah Ah =
slip me if you can
Jack the Ripper
I took stock of you last
night and left you
at your door my
other victims have
been whores and a chang

Letter of 18 September 1889 posted in London — 'You to are the next . . .'

Date/Source	Addressee	Text, Sender and Remarks
		Jack the Ripper I took stock of you last night and left you at your door my other victims have been whores and a change/ will [missing] tful it is not money but blood blood blood I crave for [Whole in black ink except for last two lines which are in red ink, followed by red ink blots. Two pages, 242/R 51A, ff. 396–7]
19 September 1889 Kingston on Thames	To the Editer of Surrey Comet Clearince Street Kingston on Thames Important	Wensday. Dear Boss I thought I would let you now jest to se if you could be clever enouft to stop me as I [me]an to give you a turn I mean to comense busenis before the weak is out I have spotted one or two near kingston station as I was down there last night minppouse [?] the slops have got [missing] in there eyes some has/ They have up the old spo[missing] but if they intefier with [m]e look out I got plenty of amineton & my long sticker is bleeding sharp I se by the papers you have yet 2 nice old strewbury nose top on the bench what price last one up the smock so good your old pal Jack the Ripper or look out to night [Two pages, black ink, 225/R, ff. 383–5]
23 September 1889 London S.W.	To the Inspector of Police Scotland Yard	Dear Boss I write these few lines to you hoping you are quite well as it . . . me at present the bloke that thinks that he is on my track is right off scent and now I have got my eye on four or five young girls from ponton road . . . Lane Vauxhall 2 of which I must have this week commencing . . . [sections illegible]/ . . . others later or . . . & good bye for the present From the Ripper and the dodger In the time that you receive this note I shall have my knife well sharpened and on my way there. You will hear . . . [sections illegible] [Two pages, 3/52983, ff. 393–5]

Date/Source	**Addressee**	**Text, Sender and Remarks**
27 September 1889 London N.W.	To the Chief Inspector of Commercial Street Police Station Shoreditch	The next turn out will be in a turning out of Commercial Road. Close to Gardner's Shop. Now I shall tell you what I am. Clerk in holy orders . few years ago at St Pancras Church. Good morning Amen Refr J. Ripper &c September 24.89 This letter was posted at Gray's new Road [Blue ink, 55A, 269/R, ff. 404–7]
28 September 1889 London	Press Association 7 Wine Office Court E.C.	E 28. Sep. Dear Editor I hope to resume operations about next Tuesday or Wenesday night. Don't let the coppers know. Jack The Ripper [Black ink, name underlined in red ink, square note, 54A, 3/52983 2113, ff. 390–2]
30 September 1889 N. Division	To The Metropolitan Police	I am Jack the Ripper I am at present living At the Neighbourhood of Islington I have got my eyes on the beauties I guess I will make Islington ring before I ave done do you think I am mad What of mistake you make So Prepare for Another Mutilation Case before this day week [Drawings of knife-point, dagger . . .] [Black ink, large writing, ff. 399–401]
30 September 1889 London N.	G Munroe Esqre Head Conisoner of Police Gt. Scotland Yard	Beware I am near Jack the Ripper The police are bust looking for me I'm like a monkey up a tree not to be found as you will see While there is work for rippers three This is the ninth murder we have done Yet it seems we have not begun But now the Evenings are getting dark With the loose Girls we'll rip up

Date/Source	Addressee	Text, Sender and Remarks
		Not time for more Too Busy for more now – [Black ink, 57A, 3/52983 2114, ff. 415–17]
1 October 1889 London	The Sergeant Police Office Leman Street E	Look out Im acomin Jack the Ripper [Black ink, postcard, ff. 413–14]
7 October 1889 London W.	To the Police Commissioner Munro Scotland Yard	Dear Boss I shall do another murder shortly and shall outwit you all Yours truly Jack the Ripper [Black ink, postcard, ff. 411–12]
7 October 1889 Leith	SUPERINTENDEN T SCOTLAND YARD <u>LONDON</u>.	[Drawings of a pistol, coffin, poison jar, dagger and knife through a heart] These.are.for.you Doubly . dyed villain. THIS IS NO JOKE I AM IN EDINBURGH FOR A SHORT SEASON WILL COMMENCE WORK SHORTLY IN LONDON.

Postcard of 7 October 1889 from Leith – 'I am in Edinburgh for a short season . . . Jack the Ripper'.

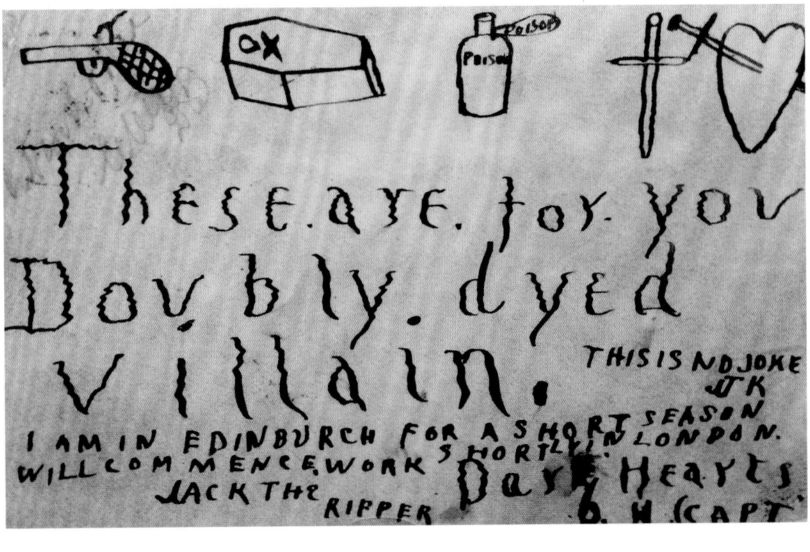

Date/Source	**Addressee**	**Text, Sender and Remarks**
		JACK THE RIPPER Dark Hearts 6.H. (CAPT) [Black ink, postcard, ff. 427–8]
8 October 1889 London S.E.	Chief of Scotland Yard	To the chief of Scotland Yd. I might say that none of the police are on or have been on my track. I will D.V. commit another murder on the 9 instant. The last murder was not done by me but by some one else. Jack the Ripper I do not wish to waste a stamp to such useless Dogs as you detectives [Black ink, very small writing, 3/52983/2123, 65A, f. 112]
16 October 1889	the Supreindtendent	I hope you can read what I have written, and will put it all in the paper, not leave Hall out. If you can not see the letters let me know and and I will write them biger.

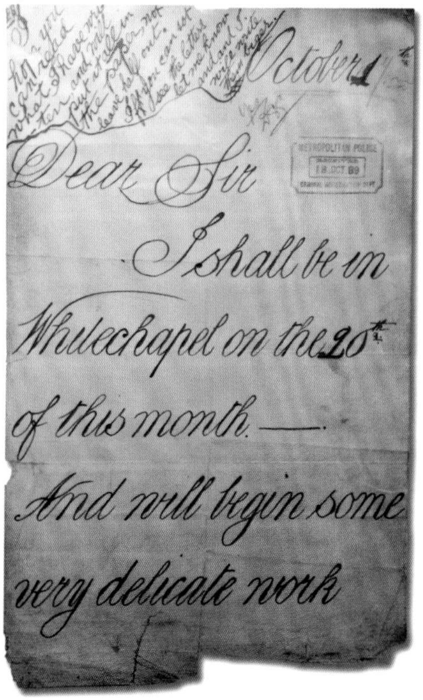
October 17

Dear Sir

I shall be in Whitechapel on the 20th of this month.—

And will begin some very delicate work

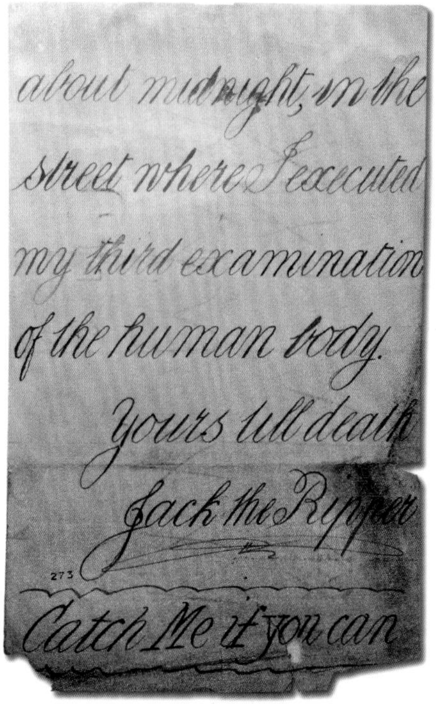
about midnight, in the street where I executed my third examination of the human body.

Yours till death

Jack the Ripper

Catch Me if you can

Letter dated 17 October 1889 — 'I shall be in Whitechapel on the 20th of this month . . .'

Date/Source	Addressee	Text, Sender and Remarks
	of Scotland yard Scotland yard London	October 17th Dear Sir I shall be in Whitechapel on the 20th of this month— And will begin some very delicate work/ "HA"!!!/ about midnight, in the street where I executed my third examination of the human body. Yours till death Jack the Ripper (Catch Me if you can)/ kisses XXXXXXXXX XXXXXXXX [Police note in pencil under date – 'Yes DSS'. Measures 12.25 × 8 inches. Four pages (two sheets written on both sides), red ink, ff. 272–4]
23 October 1889 London	Scotland Yard Police Force London	Oct 22 1886 [sic] Bloodworm Keep your candles open ['on' – deleted] The East End of or about the 9th of November Yours Truly Jack the Ripper [Crude drawing of a body on ground with man standing over it waving a dagger] [Police note – 'Put with other letters DSS' bottom right of page. Black ink, ff. 429–32]
30 October 1889 London S.W.	Private To the Editor Clapham Observer Manor Street Clapham	"Jack the Ripper" I am coming over to Clapham on the 8 or 9 November when I intend to have a turn at some of your Jews [?] J the R The Editor Clapham Observer Please insert this in your Paper [Black ink, 68A 309/R W Division, ff. 418–20]
30 October 1889 Boston Mass.	Editor of the Lo . . . Londonengland	Editor of the London Times. As I was obliged to go to America that murder which was promised within a week

Date/Source	Addressee	Text, Sender and Remarks
		failed to be performed. There's plenty of time yet in which to complete the fifteen. Some of your police regulations are so absurd that I have to laugh at them. Here the officers are armed and allowed to use their discretion. There the whole system is stupid. I did not see it so much till I came here where such a series would not be possible. However I hope you won't wake up until I am through. I will follow this one week later. Then look out—— Jack the Ripper [Black ink, 66A, 3/52983 2124, ff. 421–3]
8 November 1889 London S.W.	To Superintendent of Great Scotland Yard London	Dear Boss 30 Bangor St Novr. 8/89 My finest shot to justify myself I now fire, You will see by this that I am not a liar; Funk stupid Fool, believes, me to be insane; His next shotlog will be that 'I'm tame, In the papers you sometimes see – Letters written by him, but none by me, He declares an accomplice is concerned, That he has to prove and learn – He describes my complexion, dark with good looks; Tells the public he has my boots, Togs 8 suits, many of hats I wear, And people at me often stare Those shots are bully clogs and not fair, The true shots I pack'd 2 pails in High St, To pay rents, buy food (no gin) but meats. The togs have I 2 suits both dark and blue over Coats, Hard felt hat and blue ruff on my throat, Long hair, no beard and none on chin Do neither smoke, swill, or touch gin. . . . At Finsbury, St Paul's hard near, I never dost the rents are too dear, Whitechapel High St hard near my home – I always do my work alone, Some months hard gone near Finsbury Sqre; An eccentric man lived with an unmarried pair – Mad on Vivisection (the cutting up of animals) He gave me a threat, He would get hold of a dog or cat for a joke, With one cut of the knife sever its throat, He was very dark, teeth (if new) pocked mark'd, disease on nose) did him meet

Date/Source	Addressee	Text, Sender and Remarks

The tale is false there never was a lad,
Who wrote essays on women bad,
I'm not a flash away Belgavian swell,
Altho, self taught I can write and spell,
The Miller's Court murder a disgusting affair
Done by a Polish Knacker rather fair
The morn (of the murder) I went to the place –
Had a shine but left in haste,
I spoke to a policeman who saw the sight,
And informed me it was done by a Knocker in the night. . . .
I told the man you should try and catch him;
Say another word old Chap I'll run you in,
Flunk, old Donkey, say he can me catch;
He would soon find in me his match,
The detectives of London, are all Hind;
They know they cannot me search and find.
Flunk you should a spark make –
He would soon be tired and try to escape –
Operations you'll begin this month again,
Despatch the police and good strong men –
Whitechapel alone is the place,
The man is keen; quick, and leaves no trace –
My blood boils and with indignation rages,
To perpetuate more bloody outrages –,
Prostitution against which I desperately fight;
[To] destroy the filthy hideous whores of the night;
[D]ejected, lost, cast down, ragged, [ ] and thin,
Frequenters of Theatres, Music Halls and drinkers of Hellish gin.
My knives are sharp and very keen,
Determined I swear what [ ] mean. . . .
The swellish flashaway Tecks I very often see-
Treating whores and asking them for tea.
One night hard gone I did a policeman meet –
Treated and walked with him down High St,
The letter addressed to 22 Hammersmith Road –
Was written by some vulgar lying toad,
Old Funk, thinks me a flashaway swell –
A first rate man, and in a fine house I dwell.
A fourpenny doss I have at a Common East End Doss House
And do not dine on aristocratic grouse,
When I by luck some browns and bobs do make –
Sometime early, but at others very late,
He thinks a very large fortune I have got,
And loves to ridicule and me knock,

Date/Source	**Addressee**	**Text, Sender and Remarks**
		He well knows the reason why I kill, The whorish women and them thin, Money (of which) Sir, I have none; But I detest ridicule of my sarcastic plans and fun. J. Ripper I will write more in a few days. [Four pages of rhyme. Black ink, postscript in red ink, ff. 212–15]
		22 November 1889
Clapham S.W. [Pun]ch		& Judy St Halifax Dear Boss I am writing to let you know although I have not done what I intended to do on the 9th could not get a chance as the people in Clapham are too wideawake as yet but I mean to carry out my threat sooner or later I am in Clapham now as you will see but what hart you will have to find out if the people here only new/ who I was they would shiver in their shoes I now come to a close with this old Snuff Yours in Haste Jack the Ripper Ha Ha [Black ink, two pages, 81a, 52983/2159, ff. 424–6]
29 November 1889 London N.	Head Officer Scotland Yard London England	Dear Boss Beware Jack the Ripper is going to commit another murder on the 1st December 1889 Farewell Jack the Ripper [Pencil, 82a, ff. 437–9]
25 January 1890	TO{ The Commisioner of Police	Look out for another murder in or near Bakers Row. It will be a woman about 60. I am going to chop her legs & arms off but not kill her. Most likely next Saturday night.

Date/Source	Addressee	Text, Sender and Remarks
		(1/2/90) Yours truly, FROM{ Jack the Ripper/ I am going to do 2 more & then go abroad. This game pays well J.T. Ripper [signature in red ink] [Post Office Telegraphs form, black ink, f. 433]
28 January 1890 South Lambeth	S.W. Sir James Munro Commissioner of the Police Scotland Yard Parliament Street	Dear Sir I shall commit another murder in Whitechapel on Wednesday 29th and you will not find it out very easily for I have a secret place and a fixed victim. I had not a penny to buy a stamp but I gave it to you to pay 2d. Yours Truly Jack the Ripper Good bye Boss [Brown (black?) ink, 88a, 52983/2166, ff. 448–50]
2 April 1890 London W.C.	Mr. Munro Commissioner of Police Scotland Yard London	Beware. Whitechapel again, beginning of next week. Have done 10 5 more to finish Jack the Ripper [Black ink, postcard, ff. 465–6]
10 April 1890		Mr Matthews beware on or before May 14/90 beware . beware . beware J the R [Enclosed in heavy blotted lines of red ink or paint. Letter written in black ink, ff. 467–8]
16 April 1890	[Sent to Home Office]	April 16 Clifton Mr Matthews

Date/Source	Addressee	Text, Sender and Remarks
		Sir Do you think yourself a man for if you do I dont in stead of young davis been hung you ought to have been hung instead let me ever put/ my eyes on you I will blow your brains out hav sure heard your name is what it is you are a bad caule fellow and no mistake about it I shall be close after your heals if I am hung/ You [rest of line missing] thing you done Justice if you do I dont it shant pass of how easy how you think so look out till I come back Jack the Ripper So look out [Three pages, black ink, letter marked 'A51374/286–', ff. 451–3]
6 December 1890 London	<u>On her Majestys Service</u> The Controller of General Savings Bank Department Queen Victoria St. London E.C.	I shall commence again very soon in Mile End (not Whitechapel) for thats rather too hot for me now. This will be my last but one. The victim lives in Frimley St Mile End. Signed Dear boss <u>Jack the Ripper</u> J.R./ It was not that . . . [illegible] Mrs Hoggs not Pearcey. <u>JR</u> This is some of Mrs Hoggs Blood [Blot on page] Jack the Ripper [Reverse] Not to be opened by anyone except The <u>Controller. Himself</u> [Black ink, 7, ff. 334–5]
3 March 1891 London	The Commissioner of the Metropolis Police 4 Whitehall Place Scotland Yard London S W 1	You see I am about again another one for you to Get on the Job with I ll wake up your babies about here for you they are going to sleep and the next one I do will be right in front of you and then you wont catch me you dont know the way I Know Scotland Yard well as you and the leaden steps in 77 Jack the Ripper [Black ink, ff. 237–9]

Date/Source	Addressee	Text, Sender and Remarks
27 April 1891 London E.C.	The Chief Scotland Yard London E.C.	Dear Boss I hope that by now that you find I am to witty for you <u>things</u> I.N. Constables uniform I will show my Contem pt by doing a Job where you little think IM.A [?] [Black ink, ff. 325–7]
14 October 1896		Dear Boss You will be surprised to find that this comes from yours as of old Jack-the-Ripper. Ha. Ha If my old friend Mr Warren is dead you can read it. you might remember me if you try and think a little Ha Ha. The last job was a bad one and no mistake nearly buckled, and meant it to be best of the lot curse it, Ha Ha Im alive yet and you'll soon find it out. I mean to go on again when I get the chance wont it be nice dear old Boss to have the good old times once again. you never caught me and you never will. Ha Ha/ You police are a smart lot, the lot of you could nt catch one man Where have I been Dear Boss you d like to know. Abroad, if you would like to know, and just come back. ready to go on with my work and stop when you catch me. Well good bye Boss wish me luck. Winters coming "The Jewes are people that are blamed for nothing" Ha Ha have you heard this before Yours truly Jack the Ripper [Red ink, subject of report by Chief Inspector Moore and Superintendent Swanson, ff. 234–5]
No date		Jack the Ripper / I am on your track you are/my next victim. The one who I/am going to murder next will/live in City Road. I will do/the murder in a empty house/down one of the Back turnings/I live in the City road the number/his from 50 to 60. I will/give her beans she shall have/worst the others I will/take away her liver / Yours truly, / Jack the Ripper [Pencil, f. 17]

Date/Source	Addressee	Text, Sender and Remarks
No date		Johney/ ripper/ Whitechapel/ London/ Road/ I shall kill seven more wommon be the 23 of march next and shall kill 7 plocemen in may and for soldiers gone so be on the watch/ [printed crown and 'Regd. 26 89 31495'] and cut of their tools eat the bugger/ so remember me to all the old plocemen I have treated four in edgeway road in last December Tseventh/ O good by old pil I might have luck enough to see you soon I hope and I shall give my self in the month of july beware./ jack ripper and son with best love good bye old chums. [Black ink, four sides, ff. 35–6]
No date		To THE Occupier of THIS House/ Fool? Ass? Duffer??/ Woman???/ Beware? the Avenger is on your track, and you had better make tracks for America if you want to save your bacon. Shall pay you a visit soon so beware.??? Jack THE Ripper X [drawing of coffin] your fate Amen./ Jack the Invinceble So ketch me if you can Amen?/ Be ye therefore ready to meet thy Doom Woman??? Amen. [Red crayon, ff. 55–7]
No date		Genl Booth dear sir Just a few lines to tell you when I am about to commit this murder . . . chance to . . . and now Im about to do this I hear you are . . ./ I'm about to commit this murder on the 16 of this . . . but bare in mind you and your wife will be dead before the 17 of this month I am yours very affectionate John the ripper amen [Partially illegible, pencil, two pages, 3/52983/ 2122,64A, f. 191]

Date/Source	Addressee	Text, Sender and Remarks
No date London E.	Leman St. Police Station Whitechapel E.C.	From Jack the Ripper [drawing of knife] In Angel Alley Whitechapel Boss Beware for Sunday morning next I have planned out another since the one in all I want is to show you I am not the one in Algiers Puzzle for the next "Find the head" [crude drawing of a large head on small body with mole on left side of face] Photo of the next victim [?] the mole . . . her face to night . . . ave her. I am yours Jack the Ripper [Written down left side of page 'catch me if you can Beware! Beware!'] [Two red blots (ink?) on envelope. Black ink, 38, ff. 216–18]
No date		Dear Boss I am sorry to say that I am not going to rip any more up in Whitechapel but one and that is one who was kicking up a row outside a public House in Commercial Road/ a few night ago I am going to Poplar and Bromley & Plaistow. Five nice fat en I got I will give em trossicks [?]. I live in a dust yards my name is (He. Yes still ripping) (em up) You will hear of me to morrow a good en because it is my birthday [Red ink, f. 269]
No date	Mrs Somebody edwards lane Church st.	Mrs I do not know your name but you may expect Jack any minit as I warn you because you are a respectable person. If you want to know how many there are there are three of us there is Bill the Cutthroat Jack the Ripper and the grandson of Wainwright. I am up stamfor A hill signed D B J A [Pencil, 98, ff. 279–80]

Date/Source	Addressee	Text, Sender and Remarks
No date		Jack the Ripper is in town JR Written on back of a ticket to 'SONG SERVICE BY FULLERTON & SMITH'] [Pencil, 13A, ff. 342–3]
No date		. . . . another murder and told you . . . . To catch me I passed through Commercial Rd last night @ 25 m . . . to 7. & posted a letter contain the way to catch me, and I should do another Yours Jack the Ripper [Damaged and barely decipherable, with envelope, black ink, eight red spots on note, ff. 360–2]
No date (possibly November 1888)		every body no's me TRADE MARK [drawings of bottle, body, knife and crossed knives] P S. I give you a good chance to cach me, so have a try, Signed Catch me who can. or Jack Sharpe/ have there livers & heart this time, dont be late in catching in me. you will no me by me looks, you have all seen me Good old Darling Yours. Catch me Jack the Ripper TRADE MARK [drawing of knife and man wearing hat] [Red ink, f. 495]
No date	Dear Boss Scotland Yard	Grovenor Hotel Dear Boss I must tell you that I am still looking out for the

Date/Source	Addressee	Text, Sender and Remarks
		young girls of Commercial Road. I am giving you a rest for a few months and will go from the Hotel on Saturday morning and I am going to my house in the East India Docks Road the number I will not inform you But I have my eye on one or two more if all goes well I must ask you to inform the police that I will run their fat lean for them, I keep my . . . instrument pretty sharp My Bang Bangs are always Loaded redey fore the first Insulter. I remain a true and faithfull servant John or Jack the Ripper London good night Grovenor Hotel [Written down left side of page – I shall be obliged to give myself up when I am once tackled goodnight] [Police note top left corner – 'Put with others'. Black ink, written on blue-lined paper, 307, ff. 549–50]
No date	To inspector Reilly Bromley Police Station	Sir I received your letter beware you are doomed Delaney will make it hot for you United U.F. Brotherhood/ If you will give me £1 0 0 sd I will inform you where the whitechapel Murderer Is hiding But if you dont chose then he will start work on some of the hores of Bromley Jack the Ripper [Black ink, No. 315, 3/52983, ff. 557–8]
No date	Mr. Boss Desford Industrial School Near Liecester	Dear . Boss I write these few lines to you That the ripper is coming over on the 9th Novr don't? . ,forget Mr Boss Desford Industrial School Near Liecester [Black ink, CLRO Police Box 3.22, No. 375 a–b]

Date/Source	Addressee	Text, Sender and Remarks
No date	Mr. James Fraser. City of London Police office 26 old jewery E.C.	[missing] Fraser [drawing of heart] hart [drawing of face] poor annie [drawing of rings] rings I have those in my Possession good luck You may trouble as long as you like for I mean doing my work I mean pollishing 10 more off before I stop the game. So I dont care a dam for you or any body else. I mean doing it. I aint a maniac as you say I am to dam clever for you Written from who you would like to know [drawing of knife] my knife [Black ink, postcard, CLRO Police Box 3.18, No. 224]
No date		Dear Boss The police will not Get me, they think they Will, I hope they do I am sure that they will not I will ripp some more up soon, I am taken them away Jack the RIPPER/ It is nice to go home with a woman it is only 2/4 sometimes they charge more But Farwell Yours Jack the RIPPER and Gang PS. We are paying a visit all over th count. ry [Black ink, CLRO Police Box 3.23, No. 394]
No date		Whitechapel [Large red ink blot] I come from Boston You spanking ass. Glad you prented my last letter. Having no more of the right sort I wright with red ink You'll hear of another murder before the month is out. Yes, you'll hear of Saucy Jacky very soon Will send next ears I clip to Charly Warren Nice work isnt it. Ye damned fool are the ['perlise' – deleted] Police. Jack the Ripper [Red ink, CLRO Police Box 3.23, No. 395]

Bibliography

Acland, Theodore Dyke, *A Collection of the Published Writings of William Withey Gull, Bart., M.D., F.R.S. &c. Memoir and Addresses*, London, The New Sydenham Society, 1896
Anderson, Sir Robert, KCB, *The Lighter Side of My Official Life*, London, Hodder & Stoughton, 1910
Begg, Paul, Fido, Martin and Skinner, Keith, *The Jack the Ripper A–Z*, London, Headline, 1996 (revised paperback)
Bell, Donald, '"Jack the Ripper" – The Final Solution', *The Criminologist*, Vol. 9 No. 33, summer 1974
Berry, James, *My Experiences as an Executioner*, London, Percy Lund, nd (1895)
Camps, Professor F.E., 'More About "Jack the Ripper"' (includes 'THE LETTERS OF JACK THE RIPPER'), *The Criminologist*, No. 7, February 1968 (reprinted from *The London Hospital Gazette*, April 1966)
Clarkson, C.T., and Richardson, J.H., *Police*, London, Simpkin, Marshall, 1889
Cullen, Tom, *Autumn of Terror: Jack the Ripper, his Crimes & Times*, London, The Bodley Head, 1965
Davis, Derek, MScG, '"Jack the Ripper" – The Handwriting Analysis', *The Criminologist*, Vol. 9 No. 33, summer 1974
Dickens, Charles, *Dickens's Dictionary of London 1888*, Moretonhampstead, Old House Books (reprint)
Dorsenne, Jean, *Jack L'Eventreur* (English translation), Great Malvern, Cappella Archive, 1999 (original publication in French, Les Editions de France, 1935)
Ellen, David, *The Scientific Examination of Documents*, London, Taylor & Francis, 1997
Evans, Stewart P., and Skinner, Keith, *The Ultimate Jack the Ripper Sourcebook*, London, Constable & Robinson, 2000
Feldman, Paul H., *Jack the Ripper: The Final Chapter*, London, Virgin, 1997
Gordon, W.J., *How London Lives*, London, The Religious Tract Society, nd (*c.* 1890)
Harris, Melvin, *Jack the Ripper The Bloody Truth*, London, Columbus Books, 1987
Hopkins, R. Thurston, *Life and Death at the Old Bailey*, London, Herbert Jenkins, 1935
Howells, Martin, and Skinner, Keith, *The Ripper Legacy*, London, Sidgwick & Jackson, 1987
Hunt, Robert, 'Duffy and the Devil', in *Popular Romances of the West of England; or, The Drolls, Traditions, and Superstitions of Old Cornwall*, pp. 239–47, London, John Camden Hotten, 1871
Knight, Stephen, *Jack the Ripper: The Final Solution*, London, Harrap, 1976
Kwok, Godfrey, *The Royal Ripper!*, privately published, 1972
McCormick, Donald, *The Identity of Jack the Ripper*, London, Jarrolds, 1959, and London, John Long, (revised) 1970
MacLeod, C.M., 'A "Ripper" Handwriting Analysis', *The Criminologist*, No. 9, August 1968
Macnaghten, Sir Melville L., CB, *Days of My Years*, London, Edward Arnold, 1914
Mann, Thomas J., 'The Ripper and the Poet: A Comparison of Handwritings', *The WADE Journal*, Vol. 2 No.1, June 1975
Marjoribanks, Edward, MP, *The Life of Sir Edward Marshall Hall*, London, Victor Gollancz, 1929
Marshall, C.F. Dendy, *The British Post Office From Its Beginnings to the End of 1925*, London, Humphrey Milford, Oxford University Press, 1926
Matters, Leonard, *The Mystery of Jack the Ripper*, London, Hutchinson, 1929
Odell, Robin, *Jack the Ripper in Fact & Fiction*, London, Harrap, 1965

Richardson, J. Hall, *From the City to Fleet Street*, London, Stanley Paul, 1927

Rumbelow, Donald, *The Complete Jack the Ripper*, London, Penguin, 1988 (revised paperback)

Simonis, H., *The Street of Ink*, London, Cassell, 1917

Sims, George R., *Living London*, 3 vols, London, Cassell & Co., 1901

Smith, Lt-Col Sir Henry, KCB, *From Constable to Commissioner*, London, Chatto & Windus, 1910

Sugden, Philip, *The Complete History of Jack the Ripper*, London, Robinson, 1995 (revised paperback)

Waddell, Bill, *The Black Museum*, London, Little, Brown, 1993

Whittington-Egan, Molly, *Doctor Forbes Winslow, Defender of the Insane*, Great Malvern, Cappella Archive, 2000

Wilson, Colin, *A Casebook for Murder*, London, Leslie Frewin, 1969

Winslow, L. Forbes, MB, DCL, LLD, *Recollections of Forty Years*, London, John Ouseley, 1910

Newspapers, Journals and Internet Site

Blackwood's Magazine
Borough of Hackney Standard
Bradford Citizen
Bradford Daily Telegraph
Cardiff Times
Casebook: Jack the Ripper (Internet site): www.casebook.org
Cassell's Saturday Journal
Daily Express
Daily News
Daily Telegraph
Dundee Advertiser
East Anglian Daily Times
East London Advertiser
East London Observer
Eastern Post and City Chronicles
Empire News
Evening News
Evening Post
Glasgow Herald
Glasgow Weekly Herald
Hemel Hempstead Gazette
Illustrated Police News
Liverpool Daily Post
Lloyd's Weekly News
Manchester Daily Mirror
Manchester Evening News
Monmouthshire Merlin and South Wales Advertiser
New York Herald
New York Times
Pall Mall Gazette
Punch
Referee
Reynolds News
Ripperana
Ripper Notes
Ripperologist
Star
Star of the East
Sun
Sunday Chronicle
Sunday Times, The
Times, The
Weekly Budget

Acknowledgements

The invaluable help of the staff at the Public Record Office, Kew, the Corporation of London Record Office, the Guildhall Library, the Archive and Museum Departments of the Metropolitan Police, the Metropolitan Police Library, The Royal London Hospital Archives and Museum, City of London Police Museum, British Library Newspaper Library, West Sussex Record Office, Post Office Archives, and the National Archives of Scotland, is gratefully acknowledged. Acknowledgement is also made to the Controller of Her Majesty's Stationery Office, via the above offices.

Both authors would like to thank the following individuals for their support and generosity in the compilation of this work: Andy Aliffe, Coral Atkins, Paul Begg, Maggie Bird, Andrew Brown, Stephen Butt, Galla Cassettari, Martin Childs, Richard J. Childs, Alex Chisholm, Nick Connell, Roy Deeley, Kumari Dharmeratnam, Christopher-Michael DiGrazia, R. Dixon Smith, Heather Edwards, Jonathan Evans, Paul Feldman, Martin Fido, Seren Fisher, A. Dylan Gable, Christopher T. George, Melvin Harris, Rosemarie Howell, Albert and Allen Hughes, Sue Iremonger, Timothy J. McCann, Jessica Newton, Adrian Phypers, Julian Rixer, Donald Rumbelow, Stephen P. Ryder, Jim Sewell, Richard ('Supreme Being') Sharp, Robert Smith, Phil Sugden, Jim Swanson, Christine Thomas, Julia Todd, Tom Wescott, Molly Whittington-Egan, Richard Whittington-Egan, and Jane Crompton and Sarah Moore of Sutton Publishing for their wise counsel and invaluable guidance.

And our thanks to Bruce Robinson for his special contribution to, and interest in, this work.

Main Index

Numbers in *italics* denote facsimiles of letters.

Index of Signatories

Note: Page numbers in *italics* indicate facsimiles of letters; postcodes/dates are shown within brackets; locations indicated on correspondence itself precede brackets.

Letters:

Postcards:

Telegrams: